MARRIAGE, HEALTH, AND THE PROFESSIONS

RELIGION, MARRIAGE, AND FAMILY

Series Editors

Don S. Browning
John Wall

MARRIAGE, HEALTH, *and the* PROFESSIONS

*If Marriage Is Good for You,
What Does This Mean for
Law,
Medicine,
Ministry,
Therapy, and
Business?*

Edited by

John Wall, Don Browning,
William J. Doherty *&* Stephen Post

WILLIAM B. EERDMANS PUBLISHING COMPANY
GRAND RAPIDS, MICHIGAN / CAMBRIDGE, U.K.

© 2002 Wm. B. Eerdmans Publishing Co.
All rights reserved

Wm. B. Eerdmans Publishing Co.
255 Jefferson Ave. S.E., Grand Rapids, Michigan 49503 /
P.O. Box 163, Cambridge CB3 9PU U.K.

Printed in the United States of America

07 06 05 04 03 02   7 6 5 4 3 2 1

Library of Congress Cataloging-in-Publication Data

Marriage, health, and the professions: if marriage is good for you,
what does this mean for law, medicine, ministry, therapy, and business? /
edited by John Wall . . . [et al.].
p.   cm.
Includes bibliographical references.
ISBN 0-8028-4392-1 (pbk.: alk. paper)
1. Marriage — United States.   2. Marriage — Health aspects.
3. Married people — Services for — United States.
4. Family services — United States.
5. Professional ethics — United States.   I. Wall, John, 1965-

HQ536.M325   2002
306.81′0973 — dc21

2001059214

www.eerdmans.com

Contents

Introduction   1
John Wall and Don S. Browning

PART I: MARRIAGE AND HEALTH

1. The Health Benefits of Marriage   13
   Linda J. Waite

2. The Personal and Social Costs of Divorce   33
   David Popenoe and Barbara Dafoe Whitehead

PART II: MARRIAGE, HEALTH, AND THE PROFESSIONS

Law

3. The Goods and Goals of Marriage:
   The Health Paradigm in Historical Perspective   49
   John Witte, Jr.

4. Is the Genie out of the Bottle?   90
   Muller Davis

Medicine

    5. Health, Marriage, and the Ethics of Medicine   108
        Stephen G. Post

    6. The Family as a Clinical Entity   130
        Edmund D. Pellegrino, M.D.

Ministry

    7. Whose Marriage? Whose Health?
       A Christian Feminist Ethical Response   145
        Christine Firer Hinze and Mary Stewart Van Leeuwen

    8. Health, Marriage, and the Practice of Ministry   167
        Richard A. Hunt

Therapy and Counseling

    9. Health, Christian Marriage Traditions,
       and the Ethics of Marital Therapy   186
        John Wall and Bonnie Miller-McLemore

   10. Health and the Ethics of Marital Therapy and Education   208
        William J. Doherty and Jason S. Carroll

Business

   11. Familial, Social, and Professional Integrity
       in Relationship to Business   233
        Max L. Stackhouse

   12. Reconstructing Home: Business Responsibility for the Family   254
        Shirley J. Roels

PART III: WIDENING THE DISCUSSION

   13. Do Religion and Spirituality Contribute
       to Marital and Individual Health?   283
        David B. Larson and James P. Swyers

14. Marriage, Family, and Health in Selected World Religions:
    Different Perspectives in an Increasingly Pluralist America   305
    Paul D. Numrich

    Contributors   324

Introduction

John Wall and Don S. Browning

The purpose of this book is to investigate how the professions should approach marriage in today's world of high divorce, cohabitation, and nonmarital births. Specifically, the book is a response to and analysis of recent social scientific evidence that marriage is on the whole good for the partners involved, their children, and society. This evidence contradicts widely held assumptions, growing out of previous but now disputed social scientific studies, that marriage is generally good for only men and not women, and that marital dissolution does not harm children or have negative effects on society. In fact, it turns out that being married is, on average, a positive factor in the psychological well-being, physical health, and even longevity of both men and women. Having married parents is, again on average, better for the emotional, physical, and economic health of children. And finally, marriages appear to have positive effects on the community at large, contributing to greater community cohesion, lower rates of crime, and increased worker productivity.

What has not been studied, however, are the implications this new social scientific understanding of marriage might have for the professions. Professionals of various kinds deal with and have responsibilities toward marriages in their day-to-day practice. Family lawyers, for example, have a significant impact on the way marriages are dissolved. Physicians' treatment of their patients often profoundly involves and affects patients' marriage partners. Clergy and rabbis not only marry people but also influence the way marriages are formed and how they are handled when they dissolve. Therapists change the way people view their marriages both directly in family counseling and indirectly in therapy with individuals. And business leaders make demands upon employees' married lives and pay the consequences in worker productivity when marriages are disrupted.

Unfortunately, issues around marriage receive little attention in the professions. Marriage tends to be viewed as a strictly private and personal affair. Professionals on the whole prefer to leave marital issues for partners to deal with on their own, and consider supporting marriages to lie outside their professional responsibilities. This view is, however, relatively recent in professional culture. It grows out of a late-twentieth-century Western culture of individualism, which draws sharp distinctions between the public and private spheres of life and places near unconditional value on personal freedom. Despite the great advantages of this high respect for the individual, one result has been widespread cultural and professional confusion about how to support and handle valuable *social institutions,* such as marriages, families, and communities. The result has been at once a growing deterioration of social institutions along with a weakening capacity of professions and society to understand how to relate to them.

Progressive Familism

This book addresses how professionals should understand their responsibilities toward marriages from the perspective of what one commentator has called "progressive familism." Progressive familism — or, alternatively, critical familism — affirms the value of marriage and family as social institutions but accepts the need to modify their form and meaning in response to contemporary feminist and liberal critiques. It stakes out a middle and in our view more constructive ground in the polarized contemporary debate between a conservative "noncritical familism," which seeks to return our understandings of marriage and family to earlier and reputedly better forms, and a hyper-liberal "inclusive familism," which simply embraces the trends of modernity and claims that all family forms are equally valuable and good for their members. The presupposition of this book is that the institution of marriage as such does indeed have a unique value for partners and their children, a value which is not as readily available (although still possible) in cohabitation, single parenting, and divorce; but at the same time, marriage itself needs to be understood in an egalitarian and flexible way, so that men and women are equally involved in *both* the private household and public working realms of family life. Even though a couple essays in this book indirectly address whether this model should be applied to gay and lesbian partners as well, the focus of this book is on heterosexual marriage and its relation to individual and social health, leaving for future discussions whether the marital institution should be extended to same-sex relationships.

On this basis, the essays in this book take up the implications of the health benefits of marriage both appreciatively and also reflexively and critically. On the one hand, if marriage is on average good for those involved, barring situations like abuse and neglect, this news may support a reaffirmation of the social institution of marriage and a rededication of marriage-related professionals to its maintenance and support. On the other hand, however, does the idea that marriage is "good for you" grasp the full dimensions of the marital bond? Can the language of the "health benefits" of marriage include other marital values like commitment, mutuality, love, sacrifice, and obligation? Do marriage's personal health effects somehow depend upon partners' commitment and dedication to their marriage as a public and social institution? Finally, can professionals reenvisage their roles and responsibilities with regard to marriage on the basis of its health benefits alone, or do they need to support the kinds of marital commitment and mutuality upon which its health benefits may depend?

In order to help professionals better understand how they might approach marriage today, this book brings recent social scientific evidence in support of the positive health effects of marriage into mutually critical dialogue with more traditional understandings of marriage. In fact, as some of the essays in this volume show, it is only recently that legal, medical, religious, therapeutic, and business professionals have come to view marriage as a predominantly private and individualized relationship. And it is more recently still that professionals have started to adopt the language of marriage's benefits to health. Many of these professions have rich histories of how to understand their role with respect to marriage as in part also a public and social institution involving mutual commitments and responsibilities. However, these cultural, moral, and religious understandings of marriage in the professions have today been largely forgotten or misunderstood. Without engaging these deeper professional marriage traditions, the language of health is likely eventually to take over the field of professional marriage ethics entirely. Before this happens, it is worth examining what such a health paradigm of marriage implies for professional thought and practice, and what alternatives this paradigm should be brought into conversation with.

Plan of the Book

This book is intended for use by the practitioners of the five professions it addresses (law, medicine, ministry, therapy, and business), by students in graduate and undergraduate programs in these fields, and by scholars of both marriage and the professions. The essays are written by leading scholars in these fields and are addressed to both theoretical and practical concerns. Although the professions discussed here are diverse, it is our contention — and the essays in this volume bear witness to this — that they are significantly more dependent upon one another around family issues than at first may be apparent. Lawyers and therapists, physicians and clergy, business leaders and counselors are all addressing similar underlying professional issues and can deal with them effectively only through greater common understanding and coordination. It is hoped therefore that practitioners and scholars of each profession can also learn about the problems and possibilities of interprofessional cooperation, and that this will stimulate a richer overall interprofessional marriage culture.

Part I of this book, titled "Marriage and Health," lays out the case for the health benefits of marriage and the health costs of divorce. The two chapters in this part lay the groundwork for the subsequent discussions of each particular profession. The first chapter summarizes the groundbreaking research of noted University of Chicago sociologist Linda Waite and argues that marriage has benefits for partners and children in various areas of physical and mental health, longevity, financial health, and life satisfaction. The second chapter, by sociologists David Popenoe and Barbara Dafoe Whitehead, examines evidence that points to the overall personal and social costs of divorce. Taken together, these two chapters lay out the social scientific evidence for linking marriage, in general, to personal and social health.

Part II, "Marriage, Health, and the Professions," is then a response to this data from the perspective of each of five major professions: law, medicine, ministry, therapy, and business. Each profession is the subject of two chapters. An initial chapter, in each case written by a leading scholar of that profession, examines the broader philosophical, religious, and ethical question of how the profession should position health language with respect to its overall responsibilities and commitments toward marriage. A second chapter, written by a scholar who is also a practitioner in the field, subsequently investigates the practical question of what a renewed marriage ethic for that profession might look like, a marriage ethic informed by health language but not overwhelmed by it. These two chapters for each profession collectively help us understand how the professions can adopt the language of the health benefits of marriage while also supporting elements of marital equality, commitment, responsibility, and concern for children and the social good.

Part III, "Widening the Discussion," concludes the book with two essays on the relation of marital health to religion and spirituality. The first essay looks at social scientific evidence that indicates broad benefits of religion and spirituality for both individual and marital health, and asks whether religion should therefore be a factor in professionals' understanding of their approaches to marriage. The second examines traditional approaches to marriage in three world religions — Buddhism, Hinduism, and Islam — and asks how professionals should understand the impact of these religions on North American marriage culture today. These two chapters are both directly and indirectly addressed by the authors of the chapters on individual professions in part II. They widen the discussion by providing greater understanding of the factors which contribute to marital health and the non-Western philosophical and religious perspectives on marriage that are increasingly part of North American society. These chapters together point toward promising new directions for further developing a more robust interprofessional marriage culture.

Emerging Themes

In order to provide some initial guidance into the rich mosaic of discussions you are about to enter, we would like to point out three major themes which emerge from the following essays. These themes are by no means exhaustive of the various conversations these chapters enter into, and the authors were not provided advance direction on the themes they should discuss. However, pointing out some of the recurring and important insights should provide the reader some initial signposts into this book, as well as a taste of the kinds of theses he or she will be able to feast upon in the chapters ahead. These three themes are, briefly, (1) what it means, both today and from the point of view of our historical marriage traditions, to say that marriage should be viewed as a *good;* (2) what it could mean to say that marriage should be supported as not just an interpersonal relation but also a social *institution;* and (3) the ethical, religious, and theological premises upon which marriage as a healthy and good institution may rest.

First, then, it is worth noting that there are diverse ways in which the *goodness* or *health benefits* of marriage can be understood today and have been understood in the past. As John Witte remarks in his essay in this volume, "the health paradigm of marriage is both very new and very old." In its "new" manifestations, the goodness of marriage can be spoken of on a variety of levels. With respect to the marriage partners themselves, Linda Waite's essay makes the strong sociological assertion that marriage is not only correlated with better health for the couple, but in fact can be shown to *cause* better health. On the basis of the findings of her recent best-selling book, *The*

Case for Marriage, coauthored with Maggie Gallagher, Waite argues that this is because marriage performs certain relatively unique functions. Among other things, it tends to provide each partner with a live-in, trusted confidant, and this generally reduces persons' levels of stress; it usually furnishes men in particular with a higher level of "social monitoring," causing them to engage in fewer risky behaviors like drinking and not eating well; and it generally gives women in particular greater economic and social resources than our culture would otherwise afford them.

On a different level, marriage improves the health not only of the couple but also of their children, and moreover, has still broader *social* goods. David Popenoe and Barbara Dafoe Whitehead point out that children either born out of wedlock or living at home during their parents' divorce are on average less healthy, experience more delinquency, and grow up to enter into worse marriages themselves (further deepening the cycle of ill health for themselves and their own children). What is more, marital breakdown leads to broad secondary costs to society like young people being afraid to enter marriage and women in their late twenties being unable to find men who will join them in a committed relationship and child rearing. In still a different way, Muller Davis, a lawyer, argues in his essay for a need to attend to the "good" of the *innocent* parties to divorce, namely, the spouse wanting to keep the marriage together (if there is one) and any children who may be involved. Current legal practice, he claims, has shifted the balance of power in marital dissolution away from protecting those who may be hurt and toward protecting the interests primarily of the one seeking to get out.

But these "new" understandings of the health benefits of marriage should be understood against the background of an almost unanimous Western moral and theological tradition of viewing marriage as a "good." Witte's essay documents the historical development of understandings of the benefits and intrinsic worth of marriage from the ancient Greeks and Romans up through medieval Catholicism, the Reformation, American Protestantism, and contemporary Catholic and Protestant marriage theologies. As classically formulated by Augustine, for example, marriage has three chief goods (or *fines* or *bona*): "the ordained means of procreation *(proles)*, the guarantee of chastity *(fides)*, and the bond of permanent union *(sacramentum)*." This classic formulation has received different emphases at different points in the Western tradition. For example, Catholics have tended to emphasize that marriage is *inherently* a good, being a sacramental expression of Christ's love for his church, whereas Protestants have tended to emphasize marriage's *instrumental* goodness, producing various benefits for the couple, children, and society at large.

These reflections on the goodness of marriage, which appear in different forms throughout the essays in this volume, have various kinds of significance for the professions. For the legal community they point, among other things, to a need to reevaluate the contemporary litigious nature of divorce law, and to examine again the legal dimensions of not only marriage's exit but also its formation and entry, as for example is being done in new "covenant marriage" laws in Louisiana and Arizona. The medical community, as Edmund Pellegrino suggests in his essay, should reexamine how much individual patient health is dependent upon the health of one's marital and family life. Ministers and therapists could embrace marriage as a good to be generally fostered (although not of course in all circumstances), as for example in new efforts at marriage education. And business leaders should be more aware of how work practices which strain marriages might rebound on both the workplace itself and the structures of civil society upon which workplaces depend.

A second general theme that emerges in these essays is the notion that the goods of marriage come about in large part from the fact that marriage is an *institution*. Waite claims that the health benefits of marriage are absent in noninstitutionalized sexual relationships like nonmarital cohabitation (cohabitation not explicitly intending marriage). Larson and Swyers likewise suggest that the health benefits of marriage may be related, like the better-known health benefits of religious participation, to persons having made a commitment to a social institution larger than themselves. Married couples' increased health may not be a result of each partner exploiting the *instrumental utility* of being married, so much as a *secondary effect* of the partners' prior commitment to the marital institution itself.

The institutional nature of marriage raises, further, the issue of whether the health effects of marriage rest on a certain kind of marital *commitment*. William Doherty and Jason Carroll's essay develops what they call a critical promarriage ethic for the therapies. They argue that marriage counselors and therapists have unfortunately tended to undermine precisely this commitment dimension of marriage. Ironically, this means they have contributed to married persons' *decreased* psychological and physical health by uncritically playing into a culture of marital dissolution. Instead, marital therapists should recognize the value of marriage commitments to the person's individual health, and in most cases — absent abuse or psychological destruction — gently help couples understand and explore, among other things, the nature of their commitments and responsibilities toward each other.

Other essays point to the need for support for partners' commitments to the marital institution from other professionals as well. Mary Stewart Van

Leeuwen and Christine Firer Hinze, bringing together both Protestant and Roman Catholic insights, urge ministers and religious leaders to support a "reinstitutionalization of marriage," but without the gendered "separate spheres" that emerged out of the industrialization of the early nineteenth century. Instead, religious and other professionals should help promote a new "social partnership" model of marriage in which men and women are equal contributors toward a lasting lifelong bond. Shirley Roels likewise argues that business leaders should embrace a more robust "stakeholder" model of corporate responsibilities which includes greater support for the families of employees on whom corporations so much depend.

A third and final theme that emerges in these essays is the nature of the deeper moral, religious, and theological grounds upon which marriage as a health-promoting institution should rest. This moral and religious dimension can be viewed from a variety of angles. John Wall and Bonnie Miller-McLemore argue that the therapeutic and marriage education professions should reexamine Western theological traditions which help us understand marriages as not just private interpersonal relations but also public and social covenants. They point in particular to different dimensions of the institutional nature of marriage found in Catholic subsidiarity theory, Protestant covenant theology, and the more recent liberationist political theology.

In a similar vein, Max Stackhouse urges the business community to develop new modes of "covenanted integration" between work and family life. Religious perspectives are needed to strengthen and build the kinds of "networks of trust" that can prevent families from becoming victims of the new global economy. Richard Hunt likewise calls for ministers and other religious professionals to embrace strengthening marriage as a fundamental and urgent task of religious communities, including developing marriage education ministries, couples-mentoring programs, and broad-based community marriage policies.

It may be, furthermore, that religious perspectives support the institution of marriage because they tend to offer a worldview which decenters the self, promotes a certain amount of other-regard, and draws individuals up into larger communities of meaning. Stephen Post, for example, argues that the medical community needs to recognize more clearly the value of religion and spirituality in helping patients and their families deal with "limit situations" like terminal illnesses. Religious traditions help patients gain a broader perspective on medical crises in their lives, and in addition situate the patient within indispensable marital, familial, and communal "covenants of care." Likewise, Paul Numrich points out that Buddhist, Hindu, and Muslim traditions — the largest "new" religions in North America — tend to view marriage as first and foremost the joining of two extended families, and only secondarily as a union of two individuals. This suggests that professionals dealing with married couples from these traditions should recognize and value the profound degree to which such partners' marriages are embedded in larger religio-communal networks of support and care which are vital to individuals' senses of personal well-being.

The above themes are just a sampling of the rich and varied themes that emerge in this fascinating array of essays. We expect that this book will raise more questions than it answers. But that precisely is the point. Our collective professional culture has neglected the issue of marriage for so long that the first task is to expand our own imaginations so that marriage can once again become an important professional concern. The fact that marriage appears to be a strong factor in persons' individual health and well-being should stir professionals of all kinds to reconsider its significance to their work. But more than that, we hope this volume excites new debate about the various professions' responsibilities and obligations toward marriage as such, given that we live in a time when marriage as an institution is in a state of profound vulnerability and crisis.

How to Read This Book

This is not a book which has to be read from cover to cover. We suggest that readers first familiarize themselves with the arguments about marriage and health made in the two chapters that constitute part I. These are the basis for all the discussions that follow. After that readers might skip to the chapters in part II that deal with the profession of most direct interest or concern to them. We hope readers will be subsequently led to explore the connections that will naturally arise to other professions. The authors of this volume met to discuss the common questions they would pursue and to explore areas of overlap between their essays, and these discussions are reflected in frequent cross-references throughout the book to discussions in other chapters. Many readers may want to delve eventually, although perhaps not initially, into Witte's long and important chapter entitled "The Goods and Goals of Marriage," which although dealing primarily with the profession of law, provides an in-depth discussion of marital "health" or "goods" in a broad historical perspective. We suggest, finally, that somewhere along the way the reader look into the two chapters that make up part III, so that the conversation may be enriched by a better understanding of marriage's multiple and complex religious and spiritual dimensions. Through this process, we hope the reader finds greater insight into the challenges, possibilities, and promise of a renewed professional and interprofessional marriage culture.

This Volume's Relevance

The essays in this volume are highly relevant to emerging conversations in our society. We can point to concrete social movements and experiments that demand a new discussion between the professions about the good of marriage. There is a new marriage movement developing in the United States. This has been sparked by recent evidence, of the kind summarized in this volume, on the importance of marriage for the well-being of both adults and children. This new movement takes several forms. We mention only two expressions that are particularly vigorous in demanding interprofessional conversation and cooperation.

One of the most important examples is the Greater Grand Rapids Michigan Community Marriage Policy — a community-wide program that brings together social workers, clergy, judges, medical doctors, marriage counselors and educators, and the business community to lower rates of divorce and nonmarital births and to prepare young people and engaged couples through marriage education for better communication skills and more satisfying marriages. Another example can be found in the initiatives of the state of Oklahoma. Studies showing that high rates of divorce and out-of-wedlock births were harming Oklahoma's economic development convinced Governor Frank Keating that marriage needed to be an object of public policy in that state. He started a movement among ministers and other professionals to elevate the importance of marriage in the public consciousness and to deepen marriage preparation for couples forming partnerships. This has required a new level of cooperation between the various professions and a deeper need to clarify their respective roles in encouraging and enabling marriage.

We could point to many more examples. Movements of this kind are bound to spring up around the country in the coming years. Such grassroots movements will require a new kind of education and preparation for all the professions. This book is designed to assist in this new form of introductory and continuing education for American professions.

PART I

MARRIAGE AND HEALTH

CHAPTER 1

The Health Benefits of Marriage

Linda J. Waite

Introduction

Married men and women — especially men — are likely to live longer than those who are not married. Researchers have known this for a long time. This is the case regardless of whether the single people have never married, whether they have ended a marriage, or whether their spouse has died. Casual observation confirms this pattern. Married people also report better physical and emotional health than the single. Husbands and wives are more likely to recover from serious illnesses than unmarried men and women.

What is it about marriage that improves the health of husbands and wives? Why do married men and women live longer than those who never marry and those whose marriage has ended? Perhaps healthy men and women are attractive partners, and those with health problems have trouble finding mates. Perhaps spouses are more likely to divorce if one becomes ill than if they both stay healthy. If this is so, those who are healthy may be more likely to marry than those who are not, so that health determines who will marry. This selection of the healthy into marriage and the unhealthy into singlehood might entirely explain the better health of married men and women. But I don't think so.

I argue that marriage as a social institution orders the lives of individuals in ways that *improve* their health and lengthen their lives. I argue that those same husbands and wives would live shorter, less healthy lives if they were not married. I think that being married *causes* improvements in health and lengthens life.

I am not suggesting that *all* of the better health and longer life that we observe for the married results from their legally married state. Rather, marriage as an institution *improves* the situation, whatever it may be, so that those who were healthy before they married retain and improve their health and those who were unhealthy experience slower declines in health, perhaps, than they would have if they stayed single.

Marriage seems to improve the physical and psychological health of both men and women, but the magnitude of the effect depends on which sex we are discussing. And the *mechanisms* though which marriage influences health depend on whether we are talking about physical health or psychological health, and whether we are talking about husbands or wives. Let's begin by looking at physical health.

Physical Health

People in good physical health feel fit and energetic, without pain, disability, or symptoms of disease. Good health means more than just the absence of disease or its symptoms; it means feeling robust and strong. Those in poor health may suffer from an ongoing "condition," like a bad back, poor eyesight, or a trick knee. Or they may have a disease, like AIDS or multiple sclerosis or hepatitis, that affects the way they feel and function. The most unfortunate have both.

If one of the hallmarks of good health is energy, one of the primary characteristics of poor health is its opposite; those in poor health are often tired, run-down, fatigued, without energy, and unable to accomplish the basic physical tasks of living, like walking from their car to the store, lifting groceries or the vacuum, bending to tie shoes or pick up a glove they dropped, or even getting out of bed and getting dressed (Waldron 1988). Poor health may limit what people can do while leaving them able to function fairly well within those limits, so that a person with a bad back might be just fine if he does his exercises and is careful about lifting. And someone with diabetes might be just fine if she is strict about her diet, monitors her levels of blood insulin carefully, and administers appropriate medication to herself. Poor physical health can interfere with employment, causing people to miss work or get less done at work, or limiting the hours they can work or the types of work they can do. And those in the poorest health may be unable to hold a job at all.

Physicians monitor the health of individuals by giving them lab tests and physical exams. Social scientists generally ask people to rate their health, to report on their symptoms, to recall the number of days they missed work or couldn't perform their usual activities because of illness. In fact, individuals seem to know quite a lot about their own physical well-being. The answers to a simple question like "How would you rate your health? excellent, good, fair, poor" tell us more about the future health — and even death — of individuals than a list of diseases and conditions, suggesting that people have a deep, perhaps intuitive, understanding of the workings of their body.

Good health is a resource. It gives people access to activities and achievements that they value. And most people badly want to be free from pain, fatigue, and symptoms of disease. But men and women who are married are more likely to get the "benefits" of good physical health than are the unmarried.

The Wild Lives of Single Men

Men who are not married frequently live lives that put them in harm's way. For men, being single often includes a fair amount of drinking. Evenings at the bar with buddies, a six-pack or two in front of the ball game on TV, even drinking alone all seem to be more common for men who aren't married. One out of four young single men reported in a recent national survey that he drinks enough to cause him problems at work or problems with aggression. Young married men the same age — who were also similar in level of education and race — showed substantially fewer problems with alcohol. Single men probably see more problems from drinking because they drink more — almost twice as much as married men. One out of four married men drinks so little that he qualifies as an "abstainer"; only one out of six or seven single men drinks this little (Miller-Tutzauer, Leonard, and Windle 1991). Divorced and widowed men also show substantially more problems with alcohol than married men (Umberson 1987).

It isn't very surprising, perhaps, that single men find that drinking fits into their lives and lifestyles better than it does for married men. Some men are single *because* they drink. But single men who are heading toward marriage *reduce* their drinking up to a year before the ceremony, so that although they start with the same heavy drinking patterns as their friends who stay single, by the time they marry they drink much less than they did a year earlier. At the same time, the alcohol consumption of young men who stay single remains high, and they continue to experience problems from drinking. Apparently young men's values change as they move from bachelors to husbands, with the change taking place gradually as they develop a closer relationship with the women they will marry. Young men who were light drinkers, moderate drinkers, and heavy drinkers prior to marrying, *all* drink less after they marry than they did before (Bachman et al. 1997; Miller-Tutzauer, Leonard, and Windle 1991). This evidence says to me that marriage *causes* these changes in men's behavior. Getting married moves men away from destructive and unhealthy drinking behavior and toward moderation or abstinence. Of course, those hard-drinking young men who are unable or unwilling to moderate their habits probably have a difficult time finding someone to marry.

Single men don't just drink more than married men. They also are more likely to drink and drive, get into fights, and take risks that increase the chances of accidents and injuries (Ross, Mirowsky, and Goldsteen 1990; Umberson 1987). Alcohol plays a role in many of these behaviors. People drink and drive when they need to get home after an evening of drinking somewhere else. And excessive drinking can precipitate fights, arguments, and accidents. Some people drink to deal with depression, anxiety, or other emotional problems; heavy drinking reduces depression in the short run but increases it in the long run (Parker, Parker, Harford, and Farmer 1987).

Alcohol and its party partners are not the only specter facing single men. Jerald Bachman and his colleagues use a large national study of high school seniors to trace patterns of smoking, drinking, and drug use in young adulthood; the study follows them into their thirties and compares cigarette consumption, marijuana and cocaine use, and drinking during the senior year of high school with these activities later (Bachman et al. 1997). Young adults acquire more freedom and more responsibility as they leave high school and move into the wide variety of activities that come later. During this period, both men and women tend to begin smoking or, if they already smoked, increase their consumption. Alcohol use and heavy drinking become much more common. Use of cocaine increases dramatically. Only marijuana use tends to fall soon after the end of high school.

Marriage dramatically alters this picture. Getting married slows or eliminates this general drift toward unhealthy and abusing behavior for both sexes. In the year before marriage both men and women moderate their smoking, drinking, and use of cocaine. Marijuana use, which tends to drop off after high school, drops two to three times more rapidly among those who marry. At the same time that their classmates are increasing their use of cocaine and experiencing more bouts of heavy drinking, those who get married dramatically reduce their levels of both these problem behaviors.

Heavy drinking, alcohol dependency, and drinking that causes problems at work or problems with aggression are all signs of poor health now and indicators of larger problems to come. Drug use is at least as serious a concern. Marriage seems to reduce men's exposure to these unhealthy patterns, perhaps because the social lives — and sex lives — of married men require much less lubrication from alcohol and drugs than those of single men. Married men don't need to spend their evenings at singles bars to find a sex partner or just someone to talk to. Married men spend less time with their single male friends — who often arrive with alcohol — and more time with their wives. And these wives seem to put a damper on their husbands' drinking and drug use, often deliberately.

Of course, men wouldn't give up drinking and drug use when they married unless they got something they valued more in the bargain. What they get is an ordered home life, a regular sex life, companionship, and a good deal of housework. They also get someone who cares very much about their health and well-being and works hard to see that they stay healthy. And they get someone for whom they care, and for whom they want to stay healthy.

Wives seem to improve their husbands' health by discouraging smoking, drug use, or heavy drinking in the house (Ross, Mirowsky, and Goldsteen 1990). They cook low-cholesterol meals and keep fattening foods out of the house. They schedule checkups and monitor medication. And they negotiate with medical bureaucracies like hospitals, doctors' offices, pharmacies, and insurance companies on behalf of the family, making appointments, finding and contacting specialists (Litwak and Messeri 1989).

But married men and women are disadvantaged — or at least not as healthy — as the single on one dimension. Married men and women are more likely to be overweight and less likely to exercise than the unmarried, perhaps because being married decreases the incentives to appear physically attractive to the opposite sex (Ross, Mirowsky, and Goldsteen 1990).

What about Women?

What about women? Does marriage improve their health too? The answer seems to be "yes and no." Married women are healthier than single women, but the difference is smaller than the one between married and single men. For one thing, at least at older ages, single women *already* lead lives that are relatively stable and well ordered so that marriage has little scope for improvement. Women drink much less than men under any circumstances; both single and married women report very low levels of alcohol consumption. Excessive drinking seems to be a particularly male pattern of social pathology that women generally manage to avoid (Horwitz and White 1991; Robbins and Martin 1993).

Marriage also seems to benefit women during the young adult years, when they are most likely to smoke, drink heavily, and use drugs. Although young women drink less often or less heavily than young men, and less often use cocaine or marijuana, those who marry reduce these negative behaviors dramatically compared to those who stay single (Bachman et al. 1997).

So women don't seem to need quite the same push that marriage gives men to improve their health habits, to drink less, smoke less, give up recreational drug use, eat healthier meals, and eat and sleep adequate amounts on a regular schedule. But marriage gives women a health advantage that men don't need — more money. Women have much lower incomes than men on average, primarily because they earn much less, even if they work full-time. Because married women share their husbands' earnings, they have access to much greater levels of resources than single women. Single women with young children are especially disadvantaged economically (Peterson 1996; Hahn 1993). Married women have higher incomes than women who are not married, even when we take into account the number of people who share that income. Marriage is the only way an average woman can get access to substantially more income than she earns (except for government transfers like Aid to Families with Dependent Children or Social Security, and even the latter depends on a woman's previous earnings or those of her husband). Although a wife doesn't get *all* the husband's earnings, she does get the material benefits of this income and a sense of security from sharing the responsibility for supporting the family with another person. Higher income brings access to better housing and better neighborhoods — married women are more likely to own their own homes than are unmarried women. Owning a home is both a mark of adulthood and an indicator of financial security (Rindfuss and VandenHeuvel 1990). It connotes the success and stability of the family, and its lack can take a toll in anxiety and stress for families headed by unmarried women (Hahn 1993). Women with income in excess of their own rated their health as better than did women without these financial resources.

Marriage also gives women access to private health insurance, an increasingly precious commodity in the contemporary United States. A recent study by Beth Hahn showed that just over half of divorced, widowed, and never-married women had private health insurance, compared to 83 percent of married women. Women with private health insurance rate their health significantly higher than women without it. Insurance coverage improves health directly, by giving women access to health care services, and it improves psychological health by giving people a sense of security about their health care (Hahn 1993).

No one is surprised that people who own their own homes, those with more money, and those with private health insurance are healthier than people without these advantages. But the study by Hahn showed that even after they take these economic advantages into account — and other factors like age, weight, and health habits — divorced, separated, widowed, and never-married women reported worse health than married women. So marriage brings economic benefits to women, but other important benefits as well, benefits that improve married women's health.

All marriages are not equal. The quality of the relationship between the spouses makes a difference. Couples whose marriages improve over time also see improvements in the physical health of husband and wife, primarily through the improvements in psychological well-being that accompany better marriage quality (Wickrama et al. 1997).

Cohabiting

If marriage is just a piece of paper, then cohabiting couples who live in "marriagelike" relationships, sharing a place and a bed, should behave about the same way as those who are married. But this is not the case. People who choose the piece of paper, with its public, legally enforceable, and long-term commitment, are different people than those who avoid the entanglements and obligations of marriage. And cohabitation is a different institution than marriage. For both these reasons, those who live with someone of the opposite sex do not exhibit the same healthy behaviors as husbands and wives.

Patterns of alcohol use and drug use show this dramatically. *Monitoring the Future*, a survey that followed high school seniors through the next decades of their lives, indicates quite clearly that young men and young women who later cohabit were different even while still in high school (Bachman et al. 1997). Cohabitors drank more as high school seniors than those who made different choices later; they also were much more likely than other seniors to use marijuana and cocaine. Clearly, young men and women who decide to live with someone later were already different from their classmates by their senior year.

Cohabitors also follow a different, less healthy path through the transition to adulthood. Cohabitors were more likely to begin smoking after leaving high school if they hadn't already started. Those who married, in contrast, tended to cut down or quit smoking, with the greatest changes occurring in the year or two surrounding marriage. Cohabiting men and women reduce their drinking from fairly high levels during high school to more moderate levels later, while those who marry dramatically reduce heavy drinking, and those who live in dorms, alone, or in other situations dramatically *increase* heavy alcohol use. Perhaps most alarming, cohabitors seem to increase marijuana use slightly and cocaine use substantially in the years after high school. So, during their twenties, young men and women living with someone in a sexual relationship showed very high and increasing rates of health-destroying and dangerous behaviors. Those who married started out with moderate levels of smoking, drinking, and drug use during high school but improved on all fronts, often dramatically, to end up with the healthiest behaviors of all their classmates for everything but smoking, on which they fell in the middle. Only from heavy alcohol use does cohabitation seem to provide some protection, but even here, much less than does marriage.

What accounts for the higher-risk behaviors of cohabiting men and women? They seem to be different people than those who get married — less conventional in their behaviors and more likely to take risks of various kinds. The same forces that impel young men and women to choose to cohabit may also drive their choices about drinking and drug use. Alternatively — or in addition — the experience of living with someone and the relationship formed may help cohabitors clean up their act. The relationship that is formed with a live-in boyfriend or girlfriend may encourage young adults to improve their behavior. Although cohabitation does not protect young adults as much as marriage, on the important dimension of alcohol use it does seem to improve the situation.

All cohabiting relationships are not equal; those on their way to the altar look and act like already-married couples in most ways, and those with no plans to marry look and act very different. For engaged cohabiting couples, living together is a step on the path toward marriage, not a different road altogether. Three-quarters of cohabitors in some studies say they plan to marry their partner (Brown and Booth 1996).

These engaged cohabitors seem to get all the emotional benefits of marriage (at least if this is the first such relationship for both partners and neither one has children), express levels of commitment to their relationship that are as high as those of married couples, are less likely than uncommitted cohabiting couples to be violent, and are not distinguishable from married couples in frequency of disagreements, happiness, conflict management, and levels of interaction (Brown and Booth 1996; Stanley and Markman 1997; Waite and Gallagher 2000). Where we can, it is important to distinguish cohabitors who have the hall rented and the ring bought from those who see their relationship in different, less permanent terms.

Psychological Health

Emotional well-being consists of feeling hopeful, happy, and good about oneself. Those in good emotional health feel energetic, eager to get going, and connected to others. Psychological distress may come in the form of depression, with symptoms of sadness, loneliness, and hopelessness. People suffering from depression feel demoralized and worthless, may wish they were dead, have trouble concentrating, have trouble sleeping, may not feel like eating, cry at things that wouldn't ordinarily bother them, and feel run-down and unable to get going. Psychological distress may also appear as anxiety, with symptoms of tenseness or restlessness. People who are anxious feel worried, afraid, or irritable, with the acid stomach, sweaty palms, and cold sweats associated with the "fight or flight" response. Anxiety can produce shortness of breath and hard, rapid beating of the heart in the absence of exercise. Depression and anxiety constitute the two biggest threats to emotional well-being. And as the descriptions of it make clear, emotional distress may produce physical symptoms, linking psychological to physical health. Anxiety and depression often appear together in the same unfortunate individual and afflict everyone occasionally. Depressed and anxious individuals are also more likely than others to drink heavily, and to suffer from other affective problems such as anger and from cognitive problems such as paranoia (Mirowsky and Ross 1989).

Mental and emotional well-being are important components of health and necessary ingredients to a happy life. And these advantages seem to accrue more often to the married than to the single. Married men and married women report less depression, less anxiety, and lower levels of other types of psychological distress than those who are single, divorced, or widowed (Mirowsky and Ross 1989). When social observers first noted this pattern, they wondered whether simply living with another person — which almost all married persons do — was the source of the psychological health of the married. Perhaps living alone causes distress, and those unmarried men and women living with others get the psychological benefits of marriage. Gove and Hughes tested this idea by comparing married and unmarried adults who lived alone with those who lived with someone else. They were surprised to find that living with someone did not provide the same boost in psychological well-being as being married. Single adults were more depressed than married adults, and living with others didn't solve the problem (Gove and Hughes 1979).

Most married couples would have no trouble understanding this finding. Almost by definition, married people share their lives with their spouses to a much greater extent than do single adults with the people they live with. Roommates, parents, adult children all have their own separate lives to a much greater extent than spouses do. Even parents and children are supposed to be relatively more independent of each other emotionally and financially — at least once they are all adults — than we expect husbands and wives to be. So in marriages that are working reasonably well, husbands and wives have a built-in confidant to offer them support to an extent not generally available to those who are single. Good marriages provide the partners with a sense of being cared for, esteemed, loved, and valued as a person. And no matter what else is going on in life, these feelings make problems easier to bear.

But the psychological benefits of marriage come only from *good* marriages — those rated by the individual as "very happy." A bad marriage — one rated as not too happy or not at all happy — actually makes things worse. Not surprisingly, men and women in the relatively small number of unhappy marriages show *more* psychological distress than the single. People who say that their relationships are unhappy, that they would like to change many aspects of their relationship, and that they often consider leaving their spouse or partner have higher distress levels than people without partners at all (Ross 1995). If a good marriage is a source of support and intimacy, an unhappy marriage is the source of pain and self-doubt.

Cohabitation and Emotional Health

If being married improves emotional health, do people who are living with someone in a marriagelike relationship get the same benefits? Researchers know relatively little about the impact of cohabitation on mental health, perhaps because most couples live together for relatively brief periods before they either marry or go their separate ways. As we noted earlier, just living with someone else does not produce the psychological rewards associated with marriage. But live-in lovers share emotional bonds that roommates usually lack, leading perhaps to psychological well-being.

Both adults who have never been married and those who have separated or divorced may use living with someone in an intimate relationship as a stepping-stone to marriage. These couples may try out the relationship before deciding to make it legal. But those who decide they will live with someone rather than marry directly, often do so because they think they are poor marriage material. Cohabitors are more likely than those who marry to report that they or their partners have personality problems that make them difficult to get along with, are unable to handle money, or have been in trouble with the law (Booth and Johnson 1988). While still in high school, those who will cohabit later are more likely than their classmates to smoke, drink heavily, and use marijuana and cocaine. An informal relationship may fit the needs of these people better than marriage, at least in the short run.

Those who have been married before seem to find cohabitation especially attractive. The experience of divorce may make people wary of entering another marriage. But having lived in a sexual relationship while married seems to break down inhibitions about living with someone again in an informal sexual arrangement. The majority of people who remarry following a divorce live with their new spouse before they marry him or her (Bumpass, Sweet, and Cherlin 1991). And for these people — those who have recently divorced — living with someone seems to substantially improve emotional well-being, especially in the first three years following the end of the first marriage (Mastekaasa 1994). So finding and living with a new love seems to help those whose marriage failed to return to emotional well-being. But in the long run, living with someone stops helping divorced people who do not remarry their partner; their emotional well-being three years after the divorce is no better than that of the divorced who are living alone. Both report lower levels of well-being than those who remain married.

The Strain of Divorce and Widowhood

One reason unmarried men and women lead less healthy lives than the married is that the *end* of a marriage causes tremendous strain. Losing a spouse to death is a wrenching experience, with profound emotional consequences. Widowhood, although extremely difficult, is the expected end point of successful marriage, embodied in the promise "till death us do part." Widows and widowers receive both social and financial support not available to the divorced; for example, those with dependent children receive Social Security for those children until they are eighteen. Life insurance, pension benefits, and inheritance of shared assets, especially the house, all cushion the blow for many of the widowed but none of the divorced. As we will see later, widows and widowers have substantially greater assets than divorced or separated people of the same age. Men and women whose spouse has died also receive emotional support from their children and families, and from the community generally, to a much greater extent than divorcing people do.

Losing a marriage to divorce carries much of the same emotional freight as widowhood, but may also bring hostility and aggressive behavior between former spouses and a sense of guilt or disappointment over the failure of the marriage. In addition, divorce is often costly, consuming assets in the legal process and leaving each former spouse with less. The need to support two separate households on the same income that formerly supported one — with the loss of the economies of scale of marriage — means that each of the exes lives less well after the divorce than before.

It should come as no surprise that men and women sustain different losses with divorce. Women suffer a substantial decline in income following divorce, on average between 25 and 33 percent, even when we take into account the fact that their household includes one less adult. Men's income rises by about 10 percent on average after divorce, given the number of people in their household (Peterson 1996). This happens because children tend to remain with their mothers following divorce, so the mother's needs remain high. Responsibility for children limits women's hours of work, the types of jobs they can take, and their earnings. Men tend to earn substantially more than women even before they have children, and parenthood widens the divide; men generally take their higher earning power with them when the family dissolves. Child-support awards and payments do not equalize the financial situation of men and women following divorce, at least on average (Beller and Graham 1993).

Husbands do better financially than their wives and children following divorce — although everyone is worse off — but lose as parents. Many divorced men lose contact with their children within a few years, and most do not manage to rebuild close relationships when their children are adults (Lye et al. 1995). Men also lose the social and emotional supports that marriage provides. Often both spouses have to move as a result of the end of the marriage.

The acrimony and emotional strain of the breakdown of the marriage and the divorce process, the need to give up one lifestyle and rebuild, and the financial devastation of divorce all cause stress. Some people deal with this stress by drinking, driving too fast, taking risks, and getting into fights. Men who divorce or separate smoke and drink more than they did when they were married. The end of a marriage lowers body weight for both men and women who were underweight to start with, and reduces hours of sleep for women (Umberson 1992). Loss of income for women and loss of emotional support for men lead to psychological distress for the separated and divorced (Gerstel, Reissman, and Rosenfield 1985). As we saw earlier, psychological distress often leads to poor health behaviors and to declines in physical health.

Many of the same forces assault the physical and emotional health of widows and widowers, with many of the same results. Widowed women often experience a decline in their financial resources, and widowed men lose the intimacy, health monitoring, and household management that their wives often provided (Holden and Smock 1991). During bereavement, the newly widowed face dramatically increased chances of dying themselves from everything from heart disease to suicide and auto accidents. Death of a spouse poses a danger to both widows and widowers, but the danger is greater for men (Kaprio, Koskenvuo, and Rita 1987). The financial losses that often accompany widowhood apparently are not as problematic for women as the loss of intimacy, health monitoring, and household management is for men.

Husbands and Wives Live Longer Lives

Married men and women are less likely than unmarried to engage in behaviors that endanger their health. They report better mental and emotional health. Perhaps as a result, married men and women tend to live longer than those who have never married or whose previous marriage has ended. Widowed and divorced men seem especially vulnerable. The small number of men who become widowers while young face very high chances of dying themselves, particularly at their own hand (Smith, Mercy, and Conn 1988).

In my own research, with Lee Lillard, I have examined the effect of being married on chances of dying for men and women (Lillard and Waite 1995). This research uses a large national study that began in 1968 with about six thousand families. The men and women in this study have been followed as they got married, divorced, lost their spouse, and sometimes died. We tracked men and women into and out of marriages, into remarriages, periods of separation, and divorce. During each of these periods, we noted the other changes in their lives, like moving in with others, changes in income, and children added to or taken from the household. We took into account differences between people that might change their life chances, like their age and the level of education they had completed, whether they were black or white, and the year of their lives in which they married for the first time or became divorced. We also considered how long they had been married or unmarried.

What we found startled me, and started me on my exploration of the benefits of marriage for individuals. Our results showed very clearly that married men and married women were much less likely to die than those who were not married. To illustrate the size of the advantage enjoyed by married people, we carried out a thought experiment to make our results, obtained with statistical techniques, easy to understand. If we could begin with a group of men and women all of whom were forty-eight years old, who were exactly alike in all the other important ways we can measure, how many would live to age sixty-five? How many married men of forty-eight would reach sixty-five? What about divorced men? Separated men? Those men who had never married? We assigned some people in our thought experiment to be married at age forty-eight, and some to have never married. What if some of the married men and women in our thought experiment became widowed or divorced at age fifty-two? What if some remained married? What if those who had never been married by age forty-eight remained unmarried? Then we performed the same exercise for women. We found that of 100 married men alive at age forty-eight, almost 9 in 10 — about 88 percent — were alive at age sixty-five. Separated men were the worst off; just over 6 in 10 lived to retirement age. Divorced and widowed men did almost as badly. Two aspects of these results struck me. First, I was amazed at the survival advantage enjoyed by married men. Second, I was struck by the huge disadvantage faced by all unmarried men, regardless of how they ended up alone; having *been* married seemed to offer no protection to men once they lost that protected status.

The picture for women was similar, at least in outline. Of 100 married women alive at age forty-eight, more than 9 in 10 — about 92 percent — reached age sixty-five, compared to 82 and 83 percent of never-married and divorced women, respectively. But widowhood did not seem to put women at risk of dying early, although it certainly did so for men.

Both men and women seem to live longer if they are married than if they are not. If you look closely at the figures above, however, it becomes clear that marriage raises men's chances of living until sixty-five from about two in three to almost nine in ten. For women, marriage brings an increase from over eight in ten to over nine in ten. Men's gain clearly outweighs women's, primarily because being unmarried is so much more dangerous for men than for women. If we compare the situation of married men and married women, we see that more wives than husbands in our thought experiment live to retirement age, so that marriage is better — at least in that sense — for women than men. But being unmarried is less bad for women, so being married buys them less.

Marriage buys people longer lives, not just in the United States but in every society that scientists have examined. Demographers Yuanreng Hu and Noreen Goldman looked at death rates in a large number of developed countries. Their findings contradict conventional wisdom that holds that marriage rates have fallen in many industrialized countries because marriage has become less relevant or less useful (McLanahan and Casper 1995). Hu and Goldman (1990) found that the advantages of marriage for lengthening life have actually *increased* over the last two or three decades. In all the countries they studied they found that divorced people, but particularly divorced men, are especially likely to die. The end of a marriage seems to be especially dangerous for young adults; divorced and widowed men and women in their twenties and thirties face greatly increased chances of dying compared to those the same age who are married. And the more unusual it is to be unmarried, the more disadvantaged the single in length of life.

How Does Marriage Improve Health?

How does marriage improve health? For one thing, marriage provides individuals — especially men — with someone who monitors their health and keeps track of things like their diet, smoking, and exercise and encourages them to take care of themselves (Ross 1995; Umberson 1987, 1992). As part of the marriage bargain, spouses give each other some say over how they live their lives together. They also give each other some power over the parts of their lives that take place outside the marriage, for example, their work lives. A wife can remind a husband to order the low-fat entree at dinner. A husband can urge his wife to see a doctor about that bump on her leg. Spouses can beg, nag, cajole, or threaten each other to encourage good health practices like healthy eating, or to discourage bad health practices like smoking. Married people tend to eat most meals together, which generally improves both the quality and nutritional value of the meals that men eat. The social lives of married people generally revolve around alcohol to a much smaller extent than do the social lives of single men. And married people tend to sleep and eat on a more regular schedule than the single, in part because they coordinate these activities with another person. Nutritious and regular meals, regular sleep, and moderate amounts of alcohol are all important components of a healthy lifestyle (Berkman and Breslow 1983).

Neither sex has a monopoly on healthy nagging. Both husbands and wives can encourage and support the healthy lifestyle choices of their partners. In reality, though, wives provide this marriage benefit for their husbands more often than they receive it. Sociologist Debra Umberson found that married men are much more likely than single men to report that someone monitors their health; that person is almost always their wife (although sometimes it is their mother). Married women don't report any more health monitoring than single women. Eight out of ten married men say their wife tells them or reminds them to do something to protect their health, which Umberson calls "social control of health behavior." Six out of ten married women say their husband does this for them. For wives, their parents and children often substitute for husbands as advocates for healthier living. As a result, marriage provides less social control of health practices for women than for men.

The task of keeping an eye on their husbands' health seems to fall to wives because, according to Umberson, women generally know more about health-related issues, are more likely to monitor their own health, and are less likely to engage in risky health behaviors than men are. Wives tend to be responsible for shopping for and preparing food and for keeping track of health supplies and prescriptions. Traditionally, wives have also seen to the emotional health of family members, providing nurturing and caring. Nursing sick family members was, historically, an essential function of families performed almost exclusively by women (Bullough and Bullough 1978). Traditional female roles emphasize this caring, emotionally supportive aspect of women's behavior, giving women license to concern themselves with their husbands' health, and giving men license to cede authority over these behaviors to their wives.

For the husbands and wives who get health advice and even nagging, the effects are important. Umberson identified spouses who said someone tells them or reminds them to do something to protect their health and compared their health behaviors three years later with married people who didn't have this support. The supported and monitored husbands and wives reduced their cigarette smoking, and the supported and monitored wives increased their average hours of sleep and their physical activity (Umberson 1992).

Marriage — and the parenthood that often accompanies it — also seems to provide individuals with a sense of meaning in their lives. Husbands and wives in good marriages realize that their partners' well-being depends on them. They recognize how devastated their family would be by their illness, injury, or death, and this realization makes them more cautious and careful. The obligation that married people feel to their partner inhibits them from driving dangerously, drinking excessively, or failing to take their medication. It gives them the incentive to take care of their health, so that they can meet their obligations to those who are counting on them (Gove 1973; Umberson 1987). Married people seem to monitor their *own* health more closely because of their sense of responsibility for others. And they allow their partner to monitor their health on their behalf. A husband may respond more positively to his wife's urgings to take care of himself because he knows that she — and their children — depend upon him, and because he knows that she is concerned for his welfare.

A good marriage also gives people someone they can count on for help, moral support, advice, and a shoulder to cry on. This social support helps individuals deal with stress, bolstering both physical and emotional health. Support can take the form of help in a crisis. A wife might help her husband in a job search by making phone calls and contacting friends and relatives who might know of work. A husband might help his wife restore computer files that she accidentally destroyed as a major project deadline approached. Support can also take the form of encouragement and sympathy, as when a husband listens to his wife's complaints about her boss. Both kinds of support make things better.

Marriage improves health by giving people access to an intimate relationship. Although lots of people get support from friends, parents, lovers, roommates, or even their lawyer or therapist, married men and women generally have much more supportive intimate relationships than single people (Kessler and Essex 1982), because *every* married person has a spouse, and what spouses provide is unique and uniquely valuable. Intimate relationships give people the feeling that they are not facing problems alone, that someone important to them cares and will help. Intimacy fosters feelings of self-esteem and mastery (see Pearlin and Johnson 1977). In a study of depression, sociologists Ron Kessler and Marilyn Essex found that the intimacy of relationships with spouses and other important confidants is such an important resource that in its absence almost nothing else helps and in its presence almost nothing else hurts. The resource of intimacy is one of the most important benefits of marriage.

Feeling that one is loved and cared for improves emotional well-being, decreasing depression and anxiety and increasing psychological resources such as self-esteem, mastery, and confidence. The intimacy and emotional support that are part and parcel of a good marriage, then, lead to better emotional health in husbands and wives. They also seem to lead to better physical health. Emotional health and resources may affect how physically healthy people *feel* by improving the way their bodies function; emotional health seems to help in maintaining proper neuroendocrine reactivity. It also improves immune function, especially cellular immunity. People with strong networks of social support are less likely to get colds after exposure than people with less support (Cohen et al. 1997; Herbert and Cohen 1993). Emotional health gives people the resources and support to undertake and continue with a healthy lifestyle, which directly improves their physical health (Duncan and McAuley 1993).

BIBLIOGRAPHY

Bachman, Jerald G., Katherine N. Wadsworth, Patrick M. O'Malley, Lloyd D. Johnson, and John E. Schulenberg. *Smoking, Drinking, and Drug Use in Young Adulthood.* Mahwah, N.J.: Lawrence Erlbaum, 1997.

Beller, Andrea H., and John W. Graham. *Small Change: The Economics of Child Support.* New Haven: Yale University Press, 1993.

Berkman, Lisa, and L. Breslow. *Health and Ways of Living.* New York: Oxford University Press, 1983.

Booth, Alan, and David Johnson. "Premarital Cohabitation and Marital Success." *Journal of Family Issues* 9, no. 2 (1988): 255-72.

Brown, Susan L., and Alan Booth. "Cohabitation versus Marriage: A Comparison of Relationship Quality." *Journal of Marriage and the Family* 58 (1996): 668-78.

Bullough, Vern, and Bonnie Bullough. *The Care of the Sick: The Emergence of Modern Nursing.* New York: Prodist, 1978.

Bumpass, Larry, James A. Sweet, and Andrew Cherlin. "The Role of Cohabitation in Declining Rates of Marriage." *Journal of Marriage and the Family* 53, no. 4 (1991): 913-27.

Cohen, Sheldon, William J. Doyle, David P. Skoner, Bruce S. Rabin, and Jack M. Gwaltney, Jr. "Social Ties and Susceptibility to the Common Cold." *Journal of the American Medical Association* 277 (1997): 1940-44.

Duncan, Terry E., and Edward McAuley. "Social Support and Efficacy Cognitions in Exercise Adherence: A Latent Growth Curve Analysis." *Journal of Behavioral Medicine* 16, no. 2 (1993): 199-218.

Gerstel, Naomi, Catherine Kohler Reissman, and Sarah Rosenfield. "Explaining the Symptomatology of Separated and Divorced Women and Men: The Role of Material Conditions and Social Networks." *Social Forces* 64, no. 1 (1985): 84-101.

Gove, Walter R. "Sex, Marital Status, and Mortality." *American Journal of Sociology* 79 (1973): 45-67.

Gove, Walter R., and Michael Hughes. "Possible Causes of the Apparent Sex Differences in Physical Health: An Empirical Investigation." *American Sociological Review* 44 (1979): 126-46.

Hahn, Beth A. "Marital Status and Women's Health: The Effect of Economic Marital Acquisitions." *Journal of Marriage and the Family* 55 (1993): 495-504.

Herbert, Tracy B., and Sheldon Cohen. "Depression and Immunity: A Meta-analytic Review." *Psychological Bulletin* 113 (1993): 472-86.

Holden, Karen C., and Pamela J. Smock. "The Economic Costs of Marital Dissolution: Why Do Women Bear a Disproportionate Cost?" *Annual Review of Sociology* 17 (1991): 51-78.

Horwitz, Allan V., and Helene Raskin White. "Becoming Married, Depression, and Alcohol Problems among Young Adults." *Journal of Health and Social Behavior* 32 (September 1991): 221-37.

Hu, Yuanreng, and Noreen Goldman. "Mortality Differentials by Marital Status: An International Comparison." *Demography* 27, no. 2 (1990): 233-50.

Kaprio, Jaakko, Markku Koskenvuo, and Heli Rita. "Mortality after Bereavement: A Prospective Study of 95,647 Widowed Persons." *American Journal of Public Health* 77, no. 3 (1987): 283-87.

Kessler, Ronald C., and Marilyn Essex. "Marital Status and Depression: The Importance of Coping Resources." *Social Forces* 61, no. 2 (1982): 484-507.

Lillard, Lee A., and Linda J. Waite. "Til Death Do Us Part: Marital Disruption and Mortality." *American Journal of Sociology* 100 (1995): 1131-56.

Litwak, Eugene, and Peter Messeri, in collaboration with Samuel Wolfe, Sheila Gorman, Merril Silverstein, and Miguel Guilarte. "Organizational Theory, Social Supports, and Mortality Rates: A Theoretical Convergence." *American Sociological Review* 54 (1989): 49-66.

Lye, Diane N., Daniel H. Klepinger, Patricia Davis Hyle, and Anjanette Nelson. "Childhood Living Arrangements and Adult Children's Relations with Their Parents." *Demography* 32 (1995): 261-80.

Mastekaasa, Arne. "The Subjective Well-Being of the Previously Married: The Importance of Unmarried Cohabitation and Time Since Widowhood or Divorce." *Social Forces* 73 (1994): 665-92.

McLanahan, Sara, and Lynne Casper. "Growing Diversity and Inequality in the American Family." In *State of the Union: America in the 1990s*, vol. 2, *Social Trends*, edited by Reynolds Farley, pp. 1-46. New York: Russell Sage, 1995.

Miller-Tutzauer, Carol, Kenneth E. Leonard, and Michael Windle. "Marriage and Alcohol Use: A Longitudinal Study of 'Maturing Out.'" *Journal of Studies on Alcohol* 52 (1991): 434-40.

Mirowsky, John, and Catherine E. Ross. *Social Causes of Psychological Distress*. New York: Aldine de Gruyter, 1989.

Parker, Douglas A., Elizabeth S. Parker, Thomas C. Harford, and Gail C. Farmer. "Alcohol Use and Depression Symptoms among Employed Men and Women." *American Journal of Public Health* 77 (1987): 704-7.

Pearlin, Leonard I., and Joyce S. Johnson. "Marital Status, Life Strains and Depression." *American Sociological Review* 42 (October 1977): 704-15.

Peterson, Richard R. "A Re-evaluation of the Economic Consequences of Divorce." *American Sociological Review* 61, no. 3 (1996): 528-36.

Rindfuss, Ronald R., and Audrey VandenHeuvel. "Cohabitation: Precursor to Marriage or Alternative to Being Single?" *Population and Development Review* 16 (1990): 703-26.

Robbins, Cynthia A., and Steven S. Martin. "Gender, Styles of Deviance, and Drinking Problems." *Journal of Health and Social Behavior* 34 (December 1993): 302-21.

Ross, Catherine E. "Reconceptualizing Marital Status as a Continuum of Social Attachment." *Journal of Marriage and the Family* 57 (1995): 129-40.

Ross, Catherine E., John Mirowsky, and Karen Goldsteen. "The Impact of the Family on Health: Decade in Review." *Journal of Marriage and the Family* 52 (1990): 1059-78.

Smith, Jack C., James A. Mercy, and Judith M. Conn. "Marital Status and Risk of Suicide." *American Journal of Public Health* 78, no. 1 (1988): 78-80.

Stanley, Scott M., and Howard J. Markman. *Marriage in the Nineties: A Nationwide Random Phone Survey.* Denver: PREP, 1997.

Umberson, Debra. "Family Status and Health Behaviors: Social Control as a Dimension of Social Integration." *Journal of Health and Social Behavior* 28 (1987): 306-19.

Umberson, Debra. "Gender, Marital Status and the Social Control of Health Behavior." *Social Science and Medicine* 34, no. 8 (1992): 907-17.

Waite, Linda J., and Maggie Gallagher. *The Case for Marriage: Why Married People Are Happier, Healthier, and Better Off Financially.* New York: Doubleday, 2000.

Waldron, Ingrid. "Gender and Health-Related Behavior." In *Health Behavior: Emerging Research Perspectives,* edited by D. Gochman, pp. 193-208. New York: Plenum, 1988.

Wickrama, K. A. S., Frederick O. Lorenz, Rand D. Conger, and Glen H. Elder, Jr. "Marital Quality and Physical Illness: A Latent Growth Curve Analysis." *Journal of Marriage and the Family* 59, no. 1 (1997): 143-55.

CHAPTER 2

The Personal and Social Costs of Divorce

David Popenoe and Barbara Dafoe Whitehead

It is a surprising fact that an unprecedented number of Americans become wealthier by the year, yet become no happier or mentally healthier. Indeed, happiness and positive mental health among children and youth may be on the decrease, as measured by trends in drug abuse, behavioral and eating disorders, delinquency, depression, and suicide.[1] One of the central reasons for the lack of any psychological improvement coming from increased wealth is that much of our happiness and sense of well-being come not from material things but from having close personal relationships. The most important relationships are those found in family life, and as family relationships weaken — a trend strongly linked to affluence — happiness and personal well-being drop.[2]

Perhaps nothing in recent years has affected family life, and therefore happiness and personal well-being, more negatively than divorce. This article summarizes the major findings of social science research in recent decades about the impact of divorce, as measured by the personal costs to those involved and the social costs to communities and societies.

---

1. See, for example, a recent study in the June 2000 issue of the journal *Pediatrics*, by Kelly Kelleher and others, which reports that problems such as attention deficit/hyperactivity disorders, depression, and learning disabilities more than doubled from 1979 to 1996. The authors state that differences in doctor training in identifying such problems did not account for the increases, and suggest that much of the change may be due to the increase in poor and single-parent households. Reported in the *(Trenton, N.J.) Times*, 6 June 2000, p. A-15.

2. See David G. Myers, *The American Paradox: Spiritual Hunger in an Age of Plenty* (New Haven: Yale University Press, 2000) and *The Pursuit of Happiness* (New York: Avon, 1993); Robert Fogel, *The Fourth Great Awakening and the Future of Egalitarianism* (Chicago: University of Chicago Press, 2000).

Whereas the proportion of U.S. marriages ending in divorce in the 1930s through the 1950s was about 25 percent, it climbed to a high point of around 55 to 60 percent in the early 1980s and stands today at between 45 and 50 percent.[3] Divorce gradually had been increasing in America almost from the beginning of the Republic, but the recent increase has been so sudden, and so steep, that it has been labeled a "divorce revolution."[4] We have largely replaced a pattern of lifelong monogamy with what might be termed sequential polygamy based on divorce. An estimated one out of six adults today is expected to have two or more divorces over the course of life.[5]

Although a majority of divorced persons eventually remarry, the growth of divorce has led to a sharp increase in the percentage of adults who are currently divorced. This percentage was only 1.8 for males and 2.6 for females in 1960. By 1998 these percentages had more than quadrupled, climbing to 8.2 percent for males and 10.3 percent for females.[6] The percentage of divorced is higher for females than for males primarily because divorced men are more likely to remarry than divorced women. Also, among those who do remarry, men generally do so sooner than women.

The presence of children used to be a key inhibitor of divorce, but no longer. Married parents are almost as likely to divorce as married couples without children.[7] Today parental divorce has become a common childhood experience. Over a million children each year experience marital dissolution, a number that has remained relatively steady since the mid-1970s.[8]

Fifty years ago social scientists knew little about the negative effects of divorce. Indeed, when the divorce revolution first began, some social scien-

---

3. Andrew J. Cherlin, *Marriage, Divorce, Remarriage* (Cambridge: Harvard University Press, 1992); in the middle of the nineteenth century, when statistics on divorce first became available, only about 5 percent of marriages ended in divorce or permanent separation. S. H. Preston and J. McDonald, "The Incidence of Divorce within Cohorts of American Marriages Contracted Since the Civil War," *Demography* 16 (1979): 1-26; on the leveling of the divorce rate since reaching a peak in the early 1980s, see Joshua R. Goldstein, "The Leveling of Divorce in the United States," *Demography* 36, no. 3 (1999): 409-14.

4. Barbara Dafoe Whitehead, *The Divorce Culture* (New York: Alfred A. Knopf, 1997).

5. Cherlin, *Marriage, Divorce, Remarriage*.

6. Data summarized in *The State of Our Unions: 2000: The Social Health of Marriage in America* (New Brunswick, N.J.: National Marriage Project, June 2000).

7. Tim B. Heaton, "Marital Stability throughout the Child-Rearing Years," *Demography* 27, no. 1 (1990): 55-63; Philip Morgan, Diane Lye, and Gretchen Condran, "Sons, Daughters, and the Risk of Marital Disruption," *American Journal of Sociology* 94, no. 1 (1988): 110-29; Linda Waite and Lee A. Lillard, "Children and Marital Disruption," *American Journal of Sociology* 96, no. 4 (1991): 930-53.

8. Data from *The State of Our Unions: 2000*.

tists were quite sanguine about its effects. Divorce must be good for at least one of the adults involved, the thinking went; otherwise why would one or both individuals seek it? Divorce must be beneficial for women who had been economically dependent on marriage in the past and had been forced to "stick it out," no matter how painful or destructive the marriage. It must be good for society because it permitted bad marriages to dissolve and thus preserved social confidence in the institution of marriage. What's more, it gave adults a second chance at finding happiness with a new partner, or as a single. As for children, their happiness depended on the happiness of their parents. Consequently, the reasoning went, if divorce is good for parents, it cannot be all that bad for children. What keeps parents happy should keep children happy too.

However, the social science evidence from studies conducted in recent decades provides little support for such an optimistic appraisal. Though divorce is sometimes the only solution to a troubled marriage, the widespread breakdown of marriage comes at a high cost. We now have compelling evidence that the personal and social costs of divorce are substantial and consequential.

The opinions of some mid-twentieth-century social scientists notwithstanding, divorce has always come at a high cost, both personal and social. Historically, women and children typically were left in financial and psychological distress following divorce. Indeed, in order to minimize the costs, divorce has long been surrounded by a variety of strong legal, religious, and social controls.

The negative impact of each divorce today may actually have increased in certain respects, despite our more egalitarian and welfare-oriented society. Postmodern societies and economies depend on highly autonomous and competent individuals who are also able to act as responsible members of communities and families. This increasingly demanding standard in contemporary life requires a sense of purpose, an ability to resist hedonism, and especially secure connections to others. With smaller families, weaker neighborhoods and communities, and a more unstructured and loose-knit society, the nuclear family — held together by marriage — has become more important than ever as the primary source of enduring connections. In the absence of intact families people are cast adrift, psychologically and socially, perhaps more than ever before.

The Negative Effects of Divorce on Children, Adolescents, and Young Adults

The most serious negative effects of divorce are undoubtedly borne by the children and youth who are directly involved. At one time many social scientists believed that the discord and conflict in the marriage leading up to the divorce was far more negative than the divorce itself. Divorce merely freed children from an otherwise intolerable situation. To this day it has proven difficult to separate the negative effects on children of the divorce itself from the consequences of marital strife that occurred prior to the divorce. Yet most scholars now believe that the divorce itself compounds problems for many children.

Virtually all scholars now agree that the children in a family typically experience many problems around the time of divorce. According to a 1994 report issued by the American Academy of Pediatrics, studies indicate that up to half of children manifest a clear and serious symptomatic response during the first year after the parents' divorce. The risks of divorce for children and youth include the following:

> Children under the age of 3 years may reflect their caretaker's preoccupation, grieving and distress; they may respond with irritability, crying, fearfulness, separation anxiety, sleep problems, aggressive behavior, or regression in development skills and it may show up in depression, anxiety, lower academic achievement, and premature sexual activity and other behavior problems.
>
> Children at 4 to 5 years of age often blame themselves for the absence or unhappiness of parents and are highly vulnerable concerning their own self-worth. School-age children may be moody, preoccupied, daydream, have tantrums, or be overly aggressive.
>
> Adolescents may develop a premature degree of emotional autonomy as a way of dealing with feelings about the divorce.... Angry feelings may emerge as aggression, antisocial behavior, or substance abuse.
>
> At all ages, psychosomatic complaints may be an unconscious solution to feelings of anger or loss.[9]

The divorce itself usually triggers a series of events that have a further impact on children. The family home may have to be sold, with the children moving to a new community and school system and giving up their friends.

---

9. American Academy of Pediatrics, "The Pediatrician's Role in Helping Children and Families Deal with Separation and Divorce," *Pediatrics* 94, no. 1 (July 1994): 119.

One parent may drop out of the children's lives while the other parent begins work or works longer hours, and one or both parents may experience substantial emotional disturbance that hampers their ability to parent. There may be losses of secondary relatives such as aunts and uncles and grandparents. And the children may be forced to live on a much lower income.

The children of divorce are far more likely to live in poverty than the children of intact families. By the best recent estimates, the income of the household in which the child remains following a divorce instantly declines by about 21 percent per capita on average, a loss that remains stable at least through the first year.[10] Expenses go up and, over time, the economic situation for the child often deteriorates further. In 1994, a year when 22 percent of U.S. children lived below the poverty line, 38 percent of the children living with a divorced mother were in poverty.[11]

The divorce revolution is associated with an overall increase in child poverty during the late 1970s, the 1980s, and the early 1990s. Child poverty climbed from 14 percent of all children under the age of eighteen in 1973 to 22 percent in 1994.[12] One study concluded that between 1960 and 1988, the growth of single-parent households was responsible for about one-third of the rise in child poverty.[13]

A group of experts from developmental and clinical psychology, sociology, social welfare, and law met in 1994, under the sponsorship of the U.S. National Institute of Child Health and Human Development, to review "existing knowledge regarding the ways in which children are affected by divorce." In general agreement with the statement from the American Academy of Pediatrics noted above, this group concluded that

> Overall, most children of divorce experience dramatic declines in their economic circumstances, abandonment (or fear of abandonment) by one or both of their parents, the diminished capacity of both parents to attend meaningfully and constructively to their children's needs (because they are preoccupied with their own psychological, social, and economic distress as well as stresses related to the legal divorce), and diminished

---

10. Judith Seltzer, "Consequences of Marital Dissolution for Children," *Annual Review of Sociology* 20 (1994): 235-66.

11. U.S. Census Bureau, "Marital Status and Living Arrangements, March, 1994," in *Current Population Reports (P20-484)* (Washington, D.C.: Government Printing Office, 1996).

12. U.S. Census Bureau, *Statistical Abstract of the United States* (Washington, D.C.: Government Printing Office, 1996).

13. D. J. Eggebeen and D. Lichter, "Family Structure and Changing Poverty among American Children," *American Sociological Review* 56 (1991): 801-17.

contact with many familiar or potential sources of psychosocial support (friends, neighbors, teachers, schoolmates, etc.), as well as familiar living settings. As a consequence, the experience of divorce is a psychosocial stressor and a significant life transition for most children, with long-term repercussions for many.[14]

Although scholars are now in agreement about the short-run effects of divorce, some controversies remain about the long-lasting nature of these effects. Studies conducted early in the divorce revolution tended to show that, while divorce may cause short-term difficulties for children, these are eventually resolved and children are left no worse off than before.[15] Also, whatever long-term problems remain, it was thought, probably stem much more from predivorce marital conflict than from the divorce itself. But the early studies of divorce and resulting single-parent families did not follow their subjects over time. Some studies, rather than independently measuring children's conditions, relied on parents' characterizations of the effects of the divorce, naively assuming the parents to be unbiased observers of the situation.

Thanks to major longitudinal studies that were begun several decades ago, the much more complete and reliable information we have today suggests that the long-term effects on children can be substantial, and they are not just due to marital discord that predated the divorce. Two recent studies are illustrative of this. The first is a British study drawing on a larger investigation that has been following — and interviewing periodically — all children born in Britain in the first week of March 1958. The most recent interview, reported in 1998, took place when the 11,759 subjects reached age thirty-three. The study found that a substantial amount of emotional turmoil stemmed from the divorce and its aftermath, not merely from parental conflict during the marriage. And the negative effects for the children continued into adulthood, even after they had left home.[16]

The second study, in America, began with telephone interviews of a

---

14. Michael E. Lamb, Kathleen J. Sternberg, and Ross A. Thompson, "The Effects of Divorce and Custody Arrangements on Children's Behavior, Development, and Adjustment," *Family and Conciliation Courts Review* 35, no. 4 (October 1997): 393-404.

15. For example, Elizabeth Herzog and Cecelia E. Sudia, "Children in Fatherless Families," chap. 3 in B. Caldwell and H. Ricciuti, eds., *Review of Child Development Research* 3 (1973).

16. Andrew J. Cherlin, P. Lindsay Chase-Lansdale, and Christine McRae, "Effects of Parental Divorce on Mental Health throughout the Life Course," *American Sociological Review* 63, no. 2 (April 1998): 239-49.

national random sample of 2,033 married individuals in 1980. Further interviews with this sample were conducted periodically in subsequent years; many of the couples subsequently divorced. In 1995, 430 offspring who had been living with these couples in 1980 were interviewed. Like the British study, this one found that divorce had substantial, long-term negative emotional consequences for the young. With regard to predivorce conflict, this study found that if such conflict was very high, divorce may be best for the mental health of the offspring. Where marital conflict was not so high, however, divorce made things considerably worse. In a surprising finding, the study determined that nearly 70 percent of the marriages ending in divorce were of the low-conflict variety. Concerning these marriages, not fraught with serious conflict or abuse, the authors state: "future generations would be well served if parents remained together until the children are grown."[17]

In general, the authors conclude: "Parental divorce is associated with more problematic parent-child relationships (less affection, less consensus, less contact, and less perceived support); an increased probability of divorce among married offspring; and lower socioeconomic attainment (lower education, lower occupational status, and greater economic adversity). Furthermore, these associations are independent of predivorce conflict between parents. In other words, for these outcomes, low parental marital quality lowers offspring well-being and parental divorce lowers it still further."[18]

The number of studies that reach similar conclusions about the effects of divorce on young people as they reach adulthood, many of them large scale and longitudinal, is now substantial. One methodologically sophisticated study, for example, was conducted in Sweden. It followed into the teenage years all children born in Stockholm in 1953 (and still living there in 1963) — some 7,719 males and 7,398 females. Focusing on psychiatric disturbances, the investigation found that "the experience of family disruption involving parental separation or divorce has negative effects on later mental health whenever it occurs and regardless of the socioeconomic status of the household or of later changes in family structure."[19] Another study, using data from a national sample of 9,643 American respondents collected through the 1987-1988 National Survey of Families and Households, yielded this conclu-

---

17. Paul R. Amato and Alan Booth, *A Generation at Risk: Growing Up in an Era of Family Upheaval* (Cambridge: Harvard University Press, 1997), p. 238.

18. Amato and Booth, p. 219.

19. Duncan W. G. Timms, *Family Structure in Childhood and Mental Health in Adolescence*. Research Report, Project Metropolitan (Stockholm, Sweden: Department of Sociology, 1991), p. 93.

sion: "Family disruption during childhood has long-term consequences for the subjective well-being of both women and men."[20]

Most studies have determined that only a minority of children, probably no more than 25 percent, are negatively affected by divorce in a serious way over the long run. The good news, therefore, is that perhaps 75 percent of the offspring of divorce may be resilient enough to overcome the divorce effects and go through adulthood without major difficulties.[21] It should be pointed out, however, that we don't yet know how the effects of divorce will play out over the full course of life. Some findings, although still tentative, suggest that the long-term effects could be much greater than we now realize.[22]

The 25 percent of children who are seriously affected looms as a huge percentage when stacked up against the children from intact, nondivorced homes. Many studies have compared the outcomes of children growing up in single-parent families with those growing up in intact families; in general, it can be said that they have two to three times the risk of having many of life's more serious problems. This is a risk differential of very substantial magnitude.

One extensive review, based on data from five nationally representative, large-scale social surveys, concluded that the children of single-parent families are 3.0 times more likely to have a child out of wedlock, 2.5 times more likely to become teen mothers, 2.0 times more likely to drop out of high school, and 1.4 times more likely to be idle (out of school and out of work). The conclusions were reached, it is important to add, after adjusting for such income-related variables as race, sex, mother's education, number of siblings, and place of residence. In other words, the lower economic level of the children from single-parent families cannot account for their differential risks.[23]

In conclusion, divorce affects a very large number of children, more than one million each year. Many children of divorce are able to move on to adulthood with seemingly few problems, in some cases fewer than children growing up with parents in very troubled marriages. The long-term effects, however, have not yet been fully studied. A large minority of children have serious and lasting problems. Especially due to its extensiveness, one prominent

---

20. Paul R. Amato, "Parental Absence during Childhood and Depression in Later Life," *Sociological Quarterly* 32, no. 4 (1991): 543-56.

21. See E. Mavis Hetherington, ed., *Coping with Divorce, Single Parenting, and Remarriage: A Risk and Resiliency Perspective* (Mahwah, N.J.: Lawrence Erlbaum Associates, 1999).

22. Judith S. Wallerstein and Sandra Blakeslee, *The Unexpected Legacy of Divorce* (New York: Hyperion, 2000).

23. Sara McLanahan and Gary Sandefur, *Growing Up with a Single Parent* (Cambridge: Harvard University Press, 1994).

scholar has concluded: "divorce may be responsible for a mean decline in the well-being of future generations that is equivalent to that of more damaging but less commonly encountered stresses (such as neglect or abuse)."[24]

The Negative Effects on Adults

Although divorce may benefit some adults who otherwise would remain in troubled and conflict-ridden marriages, there are many negative consequences as well. A large number of these are the result of not being married and are covered in the companion article on marriage by Linda Waite. But some are the direct result of the divorce itself.

Just as divorce has led to an increase of children living in poverty, so has it generated increased economic insecurity for women. Although the earned-income gap between men and women has narrowed in recent decades, there has actually been a net decline in women's standard of living relative to men's. This is in large part due to the high rate of divorce.[25] As one scholar has concluded, "divorce is shifting large numbers of mothers into the ranks of the poor, thus undermining the movement toward gender equality."[26]

Good relations with family members and relatives over the life course have been found to be very important for health and well-being.[27] Yet studies have found that contact between adult offspring and their parents has declined in recent decades.[28] It is reasonable to suppose that the high rate of divorce is a major factor in this decline, and that the decline may grow steeper in the years to come.

Among the divorced, the fabric of intergenerational relations is often torn asunder. The relationships between divorced parents and their children tend to be much more problematic than those found in intact families, and the problems can extend throughout life. Following marital breakup custodial mothers often have strained relations with their children, not all of which is due to predivorce issues. More strained by far, however, are the postdivorce

---

24. Paul R. Amato, "Children of Divorced Parents as Young Adults," in *Coping with Divorce, Single Parenting, and Remarriage*, p. 160.

25. D. Spain and S. M. Bianchi, *Balancing Act: Motherhood, Marriage, and Employment among American Women* (New York: Russell Sage Foundation, 1996).

26. Paul R. Amato, "The Postdivorce Society," in *The Postdivorce Family*, ed. R. A. Thompson and P. R. Amato (Thousand Oaks, Calif.: Sage, 1999), p. 176.

27. See Alice S. Rossi and Peter H. Rossi, *Of Human Bonding: Parent-Child Relations across the Life Course* (New York: Aldine de Gruyter, 1990).

28. L. L. Bumpass, "What's Happening to the Family?" *Demography* 27 (1990): 483-98.

relationships with fathers, most of whom are noncustodial. Over time, in fact, many divorced fathers lose touch with their children.[29]

A recent study found that, especially when the divorce took place at a young age, adolescents have significantly lower feelings of attachment to their parents and more negative perceptions of the maternal and paternal care and protection provided to them during childhood.[30] Adult children of divorced parents continue to feel less affection for their parents, see them less often, and exchange assistance less frequently. This is particularly true concerning divorced fathers.[31] This could pose a serious health care issue in the future as the many divorced fathers who have not remarried reach old age with few family relationships to count on for both emotional and financial assistance.

The loss of family relationships undoubtedly plays a major role in why the divorced tend to fare poorly in measures of health and well-being. An early study by the National Institutes of Mental Health found marital disruption to be "the single most powerful predictor of stress-related physical as well as emotional illness."[32] Divorced adults, especially men, have a much higher risk of both psychiatric illness and physical disease and are more likely to engage in risky behavior. A seventy-year prospective study of longevity, for example, found that the divorced had a 40 percent greater risk of premature death than those steadily married. Men who remained single following divorce fared much worse, with a 120 percent greater risk of dying sooner. Women remaining single after divorce increased their risk by 80 percent. All told, the effect of divorce on longevity was similar to smoking two packs of cigarettes a day![33]

---

29. The research is reviewed in David Popenoe, *Life without Father* (Cambridge: Harvard University Press, 1999).

30. L. Woodward, D. M. Furgusson, and J. Belsky, "Timing of Parental Separation and Attachment to Parents in Adolescence: Results of a Prospective Study from Birth to Age Sixteen," *Journal of Marriage and the Family* 62 (2000): 162-74.

31. P. R. Amato, S. J. Rezac, and A. Booth, "Helping between Parents and Young Adult Offspring," *Journal of Marriage and the Family* 57 (1995): 363-74; W. S. Aquilino, "Impact of Childhood Family Disruption on Young Adults' Relationships with Parents," *Journal of Marriage and the Family* 56 (1994): 295-313; T. M. Cooney, "Young Adults' Relations with Parents: The Influence of Recent Parental Divorce," *Journal of Marriage and the Family* 56 (1994): 45-56; F. F. Furstenberg, Jr., S. D. Hoffman, and L. Shrestha, "The Effect of Divorce on Intergenerational Transfers: New Evidence," *Demography* 32 (1995): 319-33.

32. B. M. Rosen, H. F. Goldsmith, and R. W. Rednick, *Demographic and Social Indicators from the U.S. Census of Population and Housing: Uses for Mental Health Planning in Small Areas* (Rockville, Md.: National Institutes of Mental Health, 1977).

33. H. S. Friedman, J. S. Tucker, J. E. Schwartz, C. Thomlinson-Keasey, L. R. Martin, D. L. Wingard, and M. H. Criqui, "Psychosocial and Behavioral Predictors of Longevity," *American Psychologist* 50, no. 2 (1995): 69-78.

Divorce is also one of the factors most strongly linked to suicide. The divorced have a suicide rate that is about three times that of married people.[34] A similar differential risk has been found in such areas as alcohol and drug abuse and stress-related diseases.[35]

The Broader Social Costs

Beyond the negative consequences for the physical and mental health of the people involved, today's high divorce rate seriously affects the broader social health of our nation. Divorce is not merely a personal event but, when extensive, can influence the character and tone of an entire culture.

The Dating and Mating Culture

The ability to form trusting and long-lasting interpersonal relationships is essential to physical as well as mental health. Yet young people today seem to be finding this ability more elusive than ever, and they are growing more cynical about the possibility of forming such relationships. Part of the reason may be our high-divorce society. It is likely that where marital instability is high, people's approach to close relationships will be affected. A recent study of college undergraduates found, for example, that "current undergraduates worry a great deal about divorce . . . they are desperate to have only one marriage and they want it to be happy. They don't know whether this is possible anymore."[36]

In a study conducted by the National Marriage Project, the high rate of divorce has shown up as an important influence on the mating and dating culture of today's young adults. The study found that people still look forward to marriage as much as ever, but due in part to the high divorce rate they are acting in ways that, while seemingly rational, tend to go against their abil-

---

34. J. Smith, J. Mercy, and J. Conn, "Marital Status and the Risk of Suicide," *American Journal of Public Health* 78, no. 1 (1988): 78-80; S. Stack, "Marriage, Family, Religion and Suicide," in *Assessment and Prediction of Suicide*, ed. R. Marris (New York: Guilford Press, 1992), pp. 540-52.

35. For a complete review of the literature, see David B. Larson, James P. Swyers, and Susan S. Larson, *The Costly Consequences of Divorce* (Rockville, Md.: National Institute for Healthcare Research, n.d.).

36. Arthur Levine and Jeanette S. Cureton, *When Hope and Fear Collide: A Portrait of Today's College Student* (San Francisco: Jossey-Bass, 1995).

ity to have successful marriages.[37] Wary of relationships that end with breakup or divorce, young people are increasingly taking precautionary and seemingly preventive measures. These include the establishment of a historically new system of "trial marriages," or nonmarital cohabitation, in which people have marriagelike relationships without marriagelike commitments or personal responsibilities.[38] The relationships are easy in, easy out, designed often to ease one's way into marriage and at the same time, in the words of the young people, "to be sure this is absolutely the right one for me." The offspring of divorced families are particularly susceptible to the lure of cohabitation.[39]

While young adults view nonmarital cohabitation as precautionary and preventive, there is no evidence that it leads to stronger marriages and some evidence that it actually increases the risk of eventual divorce. The higher risks for divorce may stem from the fact that low-commitment attitudes toward relationships become the norm, especially among those who serially cohabit with many partners, and such attitudes are precisely the opposite of what one needs in a long-term marriage.[40] In other words, the prevalence of divorce not only generates nonmarital cohabitation, but such cohabitation, in its own right, generates still further marital instability. Certainly, cohabitation does not seem to be the answer to insuring permanent unions.[41]

It is often claimed, with substantial empirical support, that the movement of women into the labor force in recent decades has been a potent generator of divorce. Women don't need to accept marriage on men's terms, as they once did, and can leave marriages more easily without serious economic consequences. Yet there is also a reverse causality: the problem of divorce causes women to put ever more emphasis on their own careers and economic well-being.[42] We find that today's women have become little different from

37. B. D. Whitehead and D. Popenoe, "Sex without Strings, Relationships without Rings," in *The State of Our Unions: 2000.*

38. Pamela J. Smock, "Cohabitation in the United States," *Annual Review of Sociology* 26 (2000).

39. E. O. Laumann, J. H. Gagnon, R. T. Michael, and S. Michaels, *The Social Organization of Sexuality* (Chicago: University of Chicago Press, 1994).

40. W. G. Axinn and J. S. Barber, "Living Arrangements and Family Formation Attitudes in Early Adulthood," *Journal of Marriage and the Family* 59 (1997): 595-611.

41. D. Popenoe and B. D. Whitehead, *Should We Live Together? What Young Adults Need to Know about Cohabitation before Marriage* (New Brunswick, N.J.: National Marriage Project, 1999).

42. S. J. Rogers, "Women's Income and Marital Quality: Are There Reciprocal Effects?" (unpublished manuscript, Department of Sociology, University of Nebraska, Lincoln, Neb., 1997).

men in their desire for economic independence, and one of the main reasons is that, because of widespread divorce, women can't rely on male economic support over the long run. This pressure, in turn, causes them to delay marriage for longer periods to acquire adequate educational credentials and job security. Yet the longer they wait, the lower become their marital chances.[43]

Men, on the other hand, are spending ever-longer periods in a dating culture in which sexual opportunity and not marriage is the goal. Men can — and do — wait longer for marriage than women. They are increasingly in no hurry to wed, and make up a male singles culture that is not necessarily in their own best interests or those of society. Indeed, many of our most serious forms of deviance stem from the subculture of young single males.[44]

Marital Happiness

It is an interesting fact that as the divorce revolution has advanced, marital happiness has dropped slightly.[45] Thus divorce is associated with less marital happiness rather than more. This is surprising, because one would have thought that removing distressed marriages from the pool of married couples would leave the remaining marriages on average happier.

A plausible explanation for why the widespread prevalence of divorce might generate less marital happiness is that, due to the high risk and growing tolerance of divorce, couples are ultimately less willing to make the kinds of sacrifices and investments in marriage that lead to happiness in the long term. The greater ease and acceptability of divorce have caused people to look at their marriages in the highly individualistic terms of short-term happiness. In other words, in the face of marital impermanence it makes sense in a way for people to put their own needs first.

There is some empirical support for this explanation. One longitudinal study found, unsurprisingly, that those persons who over time became more accepting of divorce and less committed to the norm of lifelong marriages experienced decreases in marital happiness and increases in marital conflict.[46]

---

43. Popenoe and Whitehead, "Sex without Strings, Relationships without Rings."

44. David T. Courtwright, *Violent Land: Single Men and Social Disorder from the Frontier to the Inner City* (Cambridge: Harvard University Press, 1996).

45. N. D. Glenn, "Values, Attitudes, and the State of American Marriage," in *Promises to Keep: Decline and Renewal of Marriage in America*, ed. D. Popenoe, J. B. Elshtain, and D. Blankenhorn (Landham, Md.: Rowman and Littlefield, 1996), pp. 15-34.

46. P. R. Amato and S. J. Rogers, "Do Attitudes toward Divorce Affect Marital Quality?" (paper, American Sociological Association, Toronto, 1997).

Another study found that married people who have a weak commitment to the norm of lifelong marriage are more likely to divorce.[47]

Conclusion

It is clear that children are hurt by divorce, often seriously and much more than many adults seem to believe. And high rates of divorce create a social climate in which the kinds of intact families most likely to help children thrive are in ever-shorter supply. Through its gradual corruption of a strong culture of marriage, childbearing, and child rearing, divorce may have negative consequences for society far greater than we now realize.

The widespread prevalence of divorce probably has been a major contributor to the continuing decline of child-centeredness in modern times. The percentage of households that contain children has decreased in just four decades from about half of all households to only 34 percent. Children increasingly have been pushed from center stage. It is fair to say that a society that disregards its children is surely disregarding its future.

---

47. P. R. Amato, "Explaining the Intergenerational Transmission of Divorce," *Journal of Marriage and the Family* 58 (1996): 628-41.

PART II

MARRIAGE, HEALTH, AND THE PROFESSIONS

Law

CHAPTER 3

The Goods and Goals of Marriage: The Health Paradigm in Historical Perspective

John Witte, Jr.

The New Health Paradigm

The central thesis of the new health paradigm of marriage is that, on the whole, it is healthier: (1) to be married or remarried than to remain single, widowed, or divorced; (2) to have two parents raising a child rather than one or none; and (3) to have marital cohabitation rather than nonmarital cohabitation for couples who are planning to be together for the long term. On average, a number of recent studies show, married parties are less likely to abuse alcohol, drugs, and other addictive substances. Married parties take fewer mortal and moral risks, even fewer when they have children. They live longer by several years. They are less likely to attempt or to commit suicide. They enjoy more regular, safe, and satisfying sex. They amass and transmit greater per capita wealth. They receive better personal health care and hygiene. They provide and receive more effective coinsurance and sharing of labor. They are more efficient in discharging essential domestic tasks. They enjoy greater overall satisfaction with life, measured in a variety of ways. Men, on average, enjoy more of these health benefits of marriage than women. The presence of children in the household decreases the short-term benefits but increases the long-term benefits of marriage for both spouses. Most children reared in

---

I would like to express my thanks to Don Browning, Patrick Brennan, Michael Broyde, and Mark Jordan for their insightful critique of an earlier draft of this article, and to Penelope Brady, Jeffrey Hammond, and Jimmy Rock for their able and ample research assistance.

two-parent households perform better in their socialization, education, and development than their peers reared in single- or no-parent homes.[1]

These general data on the health benefits of marriage do not pretend to describe all particular cases. There are plenty of happy singles. Sometimes widow(er)s and divorced persons thrive after surviving or escaping miserable marriages. There are plenty of successful single parents. Sometimes their children thrive in the absence of perennial parental abuse or conflict and/or upon negotiation of a suitable joint custody or visitation arrangement. There are plenty of committed couples that transfer smoothly from nonmarital to marital cohabitation. Sometimes such experiments convince couples to forgo marriage and to spare themselves and their prospective children the painful costs of divorce. But the recent social science data suggest strongly that these exceptions, though ample and diverse in number, do not overcome the basic presumptions about the superior utility and healthiness of monogamous marital unions and intact two-parent families.[2]

I read these new social science data on the health benefits of marriage as a historian. In my view, these data help to corroborate and to elaborate a number of ancient and enduring teachings on the goods and goals of marriage that have undergirded the classic professions of the West — especially the professions of law and theology. The aim of this chapter is: (1) to compare these new social science data with some of the traditional Western legal and theological formulations of the goods and goals of marriage, and (2) to explore the role of law in defining and defending these marital goods and goals.

---

1. See sources and discussion in the chapters herein by Linda Waite, Stephen G. Post, and Barbara Dafoe Whitehead and David Popenoe. See also Linda J. Waite and Maggie Gallagher, *The Case for Marriage* (New York: Doubleday, 2000); Linda J. Waite, "Does Marriage Matter?" *Demography* 32, no. 4 (1995): 483; Barbara Dafoe Whitehead, "Dan Quayle Was Right," *Atlantic Monthly* 271, no. 4 (April 1993): 47-84; Barbara Dafoe Whitehead, "The Failure of Sexual Education," *Atlantic Monthly* 272, no. 10 (October 1994): 55-80; David Popenoe and Barbara Dafoe Whitehead, *The State of Our Unions, 1999* (Rutgers, N.J.: National Marriage Project, 1999); David Popenoe and Barbara Dafoe Whitehead, *The State of Our Unions, 2000* (Rutgers, N.J.: National Marriage Project, 2000); Stephen G. Post, *More Lasting Unions: Christianity, the Family, and Society* (Grand Rapids: Eerdmans, 2000), pp. 5-42.

2. What has apparently not yet been closely studied by social scientists are the comparative health benefits of (1) monogamous versus polygamous unions, (2) committed married lives versus committed monastic lives, or (3) committed heterosexual versus committed homosexual unions.

The Goods and Goals of Marriage: Classical Formulations

It has long been common in the Western Christian tradition to speak of the end *(finis)* of marriage. The Latin term *finis* is a term both of ontology and of teleology. It describes both the *goods* of marriage (its virtue, its reason for being, its intrinsic worth) and the *goals* of marriage (its purposes, its expected consequences, its instrumental value). To signal this distinction, early Catholic canonists and moralists sometimes spoke of the purpose *(causa)* and effect *(effectus)* of marriage, or its inherent goods *(fines operis)* and its actualized goals *(fines operantis)*.³ Early Protestant jurists and theologians repeated these distinctions but also spoke of the reason *(ratio)* and use *(usus)* of marriage. Most Western Christian writers — Patristic, Catholic, and Protestant alike — spoke to both the goods and the goals, the intrinsic and the instrumental values, of marital institutions and activities. But Catholics have tended to emphasize the intrinsic goods of marriage, its ontology.⁴ Protestants have tended to emphasize the instrumental goals of marriage, its teleology.⁵

The Western Christian tradition inherited this idea of marital goods and goals from classical Greece and Rome.⁶ A number of Greek and Roman writers regarded marriage as a natural institution that served the couple, the children, and the community at once. In a suggestive passage in the *Republic*, for example, Plato (ca. 428–ca. 347 B.C.) said it was "obvious" that a "just republic" "must arrange [for] marriages, sacramental so far as may be. And the most sacred marriages would be those that were the most beneficial."⁷ In his *Laws,* when advising young men on how to choose a wife, Plato

---

3. See sources and discussion in Francis W. Carney, *The Purposes of Christian Marriage* (Washington, D.C.: Catholic University of America Press, 1950); Theodor Mackin, *What Is Marriage?* (New York: Paulist Press, 1982); Alain Mattheeuws, *Union et procréation: Développements de la doctrine des fins du mariage* (Paris: Cerfs, 1989); Dietrich von Hildebrand, *Marriage* (New York: Longmans Green, 1942).

4. See, e.g., Germain Grisez, *The Way of the Lord Jesus: Living a Christian Life,* 2 vols. (Quincy, Ill.: Franciscan Press, 1993), vol. 2, pp. 556-59; Robert P. George and Gerard V. Bradley, "Marriage and the Liberal Imagination," *Georgetown Law Journal* 84 (1995): 301-20, at 305ff. For medieval prototypes, see James A. Brundage, *Law, Sex, and Christian Society in Medieval Europe* (Chicago: University of Chicago Press, 1987).

5. See sources and discussion in my *From Sacrament to Contract: Marriage, Religion, and Law in the Western Tradition* (Louisville: Westminster John Knox, 1997), chaps. 2–4.

6. I have not addressed the use of Judaic sources in the early church, ably and amply discussed in Leo G. Perdue et al., *Families in Ancient Israel* (Louisville: Westminster John Knox, 1997), and Carolyn L. Osiek and David Balch, eds., *Families in the New Testament World: Households and House Churches* (Louisville: Westminster John Knox, 1997).

7. *Republic* 5.458e, in *The Collected Dialogues of Plato, Including the Letters,* ed. Edith Hamilton and Huntington Cairns (Princeton: Princeton University Press, 1961).

wrote: "A man should 'court the tie' that is for the city's good, not that which most takes his own fancy."[8] Once married, the man should restrict "procreative intercourse to its natural function," for such "moderation" will bring "untold good. It is dictated, to begin with, by nature's own voice, leads to the suppression of the mad frenzy of sex, as well as marriage breaches of all kinds, and all manner of excess in meats and drinks, and wins men to affection of their wedded wives. There are also numerous other blessings which will follow. . . ."[9]

Aristotle (384-322 B.C.) viewed marriage as the foundation of the republic and the prototype of friendship. "[M]an is a political animal" who forms states and other associations "for the purpose of attaining some good," Aristotle wrote famously in his *Politics*. "[E]very state is composed of households." Every household, in turn, is composed of "a union or pairing of those who cannot exist without one another. A man and woman must unite for the reproduction of the species — not from deliberate intention, but from the natural impulse . . . to leave behind something of the same nature as themselves."[10]

Aristotle extended this insight in his *Ethics*, now emphasizing goods of marriage beyond its political and social expediency:

> The love between husband and wife is evidently a natural feeling, for Nature has made man even more of a pairing than a political animal in so far as the family is an older and more fundamental thing than the state, and the instinct to form communities is less widespread among animals than the habit of procreation. Among the generality of animals male and female come together for this sole purpose [of procreation]. But human beings cohabit not only to get children but also to provide whatever is necessary to a fully lived life. From the outset, the partners perform distinct duties, the man having one set, the woman another. So by pooling their individual contributions [into a common stock] they help each other out. Accordingly there is general agreement that marital affection combines the useful and the pleasant. But it may also embody a moral ideal, when husband and wife are virtuous persons. For man and woman have each their own special excellence, and this may be a source of pleasure to most. Children, too, it is agreed, are a bond between the parents — which ex-

---

8. *Laws* 6.773b in *Collected Dialogues*. Cf. Gen. 6:2 (complaining that "the sons of men saw that the daughters of men were fair and took to wife such as them as they chose" — RSV).

9. *Laws* 8.839a-b in *Collected Dialogues*.

10. *The Politics of Aristotle*, trans. Ernest Barker (New York: Oxford University Press, 1962), 1.1.1; 1.2.2; 1.2.9; 1.3.1.

plains why childless unions are more likely to be dissolved. The children do not belong to one parent more than to another, and it is the joint ownership of something valuable that keeps people from separating.[11]

To ensure that marital couples would remain bonded together for the sake of their children, Aristotle (emulating some of Plato's teachings) prescribed a whole series of laws on the ideal ages, qualities, and duties of husband and wife to each other and to their children.[12]

The Roman Stoics repeated and glossed these classical Greek views about marriage, even while many of them celebrated celibacy as the higher ideal. Cicero (106-43 B.C.), for example, the leading jurist and moralist of his day, called marriage a "natural sharing" of the person and property of husband and wife that served for the procreation of children, for companionship, and ultimately for the broader cultivation of "dutifulness, goodness, liberality, kindness, courtesy, and similar virtues."[13] Musonius Rufus (b. ca. A.D. 30), an influential moralist, described marriage in robust companionate terms, anticipating by many centuries the familiar language of the Christian marriage liturgy:

> The husband and wife . . . should come together for the purpose of making a life in common and of procreating children, and furthermore of regarding all things in common between them, and nothing peculiar or private to one or the other, not even their own bodies. The birth of a human being which results from such a union is to be sure something marvelous, but it is not yet enough for the relation of husband and wife, inasmuch as, quite apart from marriage, it could result from any other sexual union, just as in the case of animals. But in marriage there must be above all perfect companionship and mutual love of husband and wife, both in health and in sickness and under all conditions, since it was with desire for this as well as for having children that both entered upon marriage.[14]

---

11. *The Ethics of Aristotle*, trans. J. A. K. Thomson, reprint ed. (Baltimore: Penguin Books, 1965), 8.12. (The interpolation "into a common stock" is an alternative translation that appears in several other editions of the *Ethics*.)

12. *Politics* 7.16-17; *Ethics* 8.10-12; see also Plato, *Republic* 5.457d, 459-461; *Laws* 772d-e; 774a-b. See further sources and discussion in Sarah Pomeroy, *Families in Classical and Hellenistic Greece: Representations and Realities* (Oxford: Oxford University Press, 1997), and the discussions of comparable sentiments in Xenophon in Sarah Pomeroy, *Xenophon Oeconomicus: A Social and Historical Commentary* (Oxford: Oxford University Press, 1994).

13. Cicero, *De finibus* 3.20; 3.23; 5.65; *De republica* 1.43; 4.5; 5.5; *De officiis* 1.17.54.

14. Musonius Rufus, frag. 13A, "What Is the Chief End of Marriage?" reprinted and translated in Cora E. Lutz, ed., *Musonius Rufus: The Roman Socrates* (New Haven: Yale Univer-

Musonius further insisted that sexual intercourse was "justified only when it occurs in marriage and is indulged in for the purpose of begetting children," and he praised those lawgivers who "consider the increase of the homes of the citizens [through procreation] the most fortunate thing for the cities and the decrease of them [through infanticide] the most shameful thing."[15] Indeed, he wrote, "whoever destroys human marriage destroys the home, the city, and the whole human race."[16]

Musonius's student, Hierocles, argued more strongly than his teacher that it was incumbent upon all men, even philosophers seeking quiet contemplation, to marry and to maintain a household. For "marriage is the basis of the household, and the household is essential to civilization."[17] While procreation remained the ultimate ideal of marriage, in Hierocles' view the consistent companionship and mutual care of husband and wife were no less important, even in the absence of children: "[T]he beauty of the household consists in the yoking together of a husband and wife who are united together by fate, are consecrated by the gods who preside over weddings, births and houses, agree with each other and have all things in common, including their bodies, or rather their souls, and who exercise appropriate rule over their household and servants, take care in rearing their children, and pay an attention to the necessities of life which is neither intense nor slack, but moderate and fitting."[18]

The great Roman historian and moralist Plutarch (A.D. 46-120), though a critic of Stoicism on many points, wrote much like a Stoic on the pleasures of love, intimacy, and friendship within the marital household. The ideal marriage, he wrote, is "a union for life between a man and a woman for the

---

sity Press, 1997), p. 88. Musonius was aware that this is an ideal of marriage, which is not always realized: "Where, then, this care for each other is perfect, and the two share it completely, each striving to outdo the other, this marriage is, therefore, proper and is worthy of envy, for such an association is beautiful. But where each looks only to one's own interests and neglects the other, or, by God, when one holds the other thus, and lives in the same house but fixes one's attention outside, not willing to tend toward one's yoke fellow or to achieve unity, then of necessity the association is destroyed and their common interests fare badly, and either they are separated entirely or they hold their staying together as worse than solitude" (frag. 13A, in *Musonius Rufus*, p. 89).

15. Frag. 12, "On Aphrodisia," and frag. 15, "Should Every Child That Is Born Be Raised?" in *Musonius Rufus*, pp. 86, 96. See further Roy B. Ward, "Musonius and Paul on Marriage," *New Testament Studies* 36 (1990): 281-89.

16. Frag. 14, "Is Marriage a Handicap to the Pursuit of Philosophy?" in *Musonius Rufus*, p. 92.

17. Judith Evans Grubb, *Law and Family in Late Antiquity: The Emperor Constantine's Marriage Legislation* (Oxford: Clarendon Press, 1995), p. 59.

18. Quoted in Grubb, p. 60, from Andrew Malherbe, *Moral Exhortation: A Greco-Roman Sourcebook* (Philadelphia: Westminster, 1986), p. 102.

delights of love and the getting of children." "In the case of lawful wives, physical union is the beginning of friendship, a sharing as it were, in great mysteries. The pleasure [of sexual intercourse] is short, but the respect and kindness and mutual affection and loyalty that daily spring from it . . . [render] such a [marital] union a 'friendship.'"[19] And again: "No mutual pleasures are greater, no mutual services more constant, no form of affection is more enviable and estimable for its sheer beauty than 'when man and wife in harmony of mind keep house together.'"[20]

The ideal marital household, Plutarch continued in his *Advice to the Bride and Groom*, is a sharing of the person, property, and pursuits of its members, under the gentle leadership of the paterfamilias. Plutarch piled metaphor upon metaphor to drive home his point:

> When two notes are struck together, the melody belongs to the lower note. Similarly, every action performed in a good household is done by the agreement of the partners, but displays the leadership and decision of the husband. . . .
>
> Plato says that the happy and blessed city is one in which the words "mine" and "not mine" are least to be heard, because the citizens treat everything of importance, so far as possible, as their common property. Even more firmly should these words be banished from a marriage. Doctors tell us that an injury on the left side refers the sensation to the right. Similarly, it is good for a wife to share her husband's feelings, and a husband his wife's, so that, just as ropes gain strength from the twisting of the strands, so their communion may be the better preserved by their joint effort, through mutual exchanges of goodwill. Nature joins you together in your bodies, so that she may take a part of each, and mixing them together gives you a child that belongs to you both, such that neither of you can say what is his or her own, and what the other's. Community of resources also is particularly appropriate for the married; they should pour

---

19. Plutarch, *Life of Solon* 20.4; *Erotikos* 769. See John Finnis, "Law, Morality, and Sexual Orientation," *Notre Dame Law Review* 69, no. 5 (1994): 1049-76, at 1063-64; John Finnis, "Is Natural Law Theory Compatible with Limited Government?" in *Natural Law, Liberalism, and Morality*, ed. Robert P. George (Oxford: Clarendon Press, 1996), pp. 1-26, at 12-17.

20. Plutarch, *Erotikos* 770a, quoting in part Homer, *Odyssey* 6.183ff. See Lisette Goessler, "Advice to the Bride and the Groom: Plutarch Gives a Detailed Account of His Views of Marriage," in *Plutarch's Advice to the Bride and Groom and A Consolation to His Wife*, ed. Sarah B. Pomeroy (New York and Oxford: Oxford University Press, 1999), pp. 97-115, at 112-14. See also *Erotikos* 769e ("In marriage, it is more important to love than to be loved. It helps us to rid ourselves of so many mistakes — indeed from all the errors that corrupt and destroy marriages").

everything into one fund, mix it all together, and not think of one part as belonging to one and another to the other, but of the whole as their own, and none of it anyone else's.[21]

Plutarch also wrote at length on the natural affinity and affection of parents, especially mothers, to their children. Among the "the first mothers and fathers, there was no law ordering them to have families, no expectation of advantages or return to be got out of them." "But the love of one's offspring implanted by nature, moves and influences" parents even then to have and nurture children, much as it moves many other animals. "[T]here is no power or advantage to be got from children, but that the love of them, alike in mankind as among the animals, proceeds entirely from nature."[22] Nature also teaches that mothers should nurse and nurture their own infant children, and that both mother and father should cooperate in the upbringing, discipline, and education of their children.[23]

Some of these views about marriage entered classical Roman law well before the conversion to Christianity of the Roman emperor and empire in the fourth century. For example, two mid-third-century legal texts define marriage thus: "Marriage is a union of a man and a woman, and a sharing for the whole of their life [or a sharing for their whole life] *(consortium omnis vitae)*, in accordance with divine and human law." And again: "Marriage, or matrimony, is a union of a man and a woman that involves a continuous or undivided sharing of life."[24] Other second- and third-century Roman law texts emphasized that marriage was a "sacred and enduring" union, voluntarily contracted for the sake of "marital affection" and the propagation of offspring.[25]

Such were some of the sentiments about marriage among pre-Christian

---

21. Plutarch, *Advice to the Bride and Groom*, precepts 11, 20, reprinted and translated in *Plutarch's Advice*, pp. 6, 8. See also precept 34, in *Plutarch's Advice*, p. 10, and *Erotikos*, chap. 21, 767de, quoted in *Plutarch's Advice*, pp. 112-13.

22. Plutarch, *Affection for One's Offspring*, in *The Complete Works of Plutarch* (New York: Kelmscott Society, 1909), 5:21-27, at 25, 27.

23. Plutarch, *The Training of Children*, in *The Complete Works of Plutarch*, 5:1-20.

24. *Digest* 23.2.1, quoting Modestinus (ca. 224) ("Nuptiae sunt coniunctio maris et feminae et consortium omnis vitae, divini et humani iuris communicatio"); Justinian, *Institutes* 1.9.1, quoting Ulpian (d. ca. 228) ("Nuptiae autem sive matrimonium est viri et mulieris coniunctio, individuam consuetudinem vitae continens").

25. See Gaius, *Institutes* 1.56ff.; *Digest* 24.1.32; 35.1.15; 25.1.3; Justinian, *Institutes* 1.10.pref. For a full study of Roman law texts before and after Christianization, see Susan Treggiari, *Roman Marriage: "Iusti Conjuges" from the Time of Cicero to the Time of Ulpian* (Oxford: Clarendon Press, 1991), esp. pp. 1-13, 183-319; Grubb, *Law and Family in Late Antiquity*; Jane F. Gardner, *Family and "Familia" in Roman Law and Life* (Oxford: Clarendon Press, 1998).

writers. These classical sources illustrate that the West has long recognized that marriage has natural goods and benefits for the couple, their children, and the broader community. Particularly perceptive were Aristotle's insights that marriage is a natural institution fundamental and foundational to any republic; that marriage is at once "useful," "pleasant," and "moral" in its own right; that it provides efficient pooling and division of specialized labor and resources within the household; and that it serves both for the fulfillment and happiness of spouses and for the procreation and nurture of children. Also influential was the Stoic and Roman natural law idea that marriage is a "sacred and enduring union" that entailed a complete sharing of the persons, properties, and pursuits of husband and wife in service of marital affection and friendship, mutual caring and protection, and mutual procreation and education of children.

These classical sources also illustrate that the Christian tradition, from the beginning, had at its disposal an ample natural logic and language about the goods and goals of marriage. To be sure, when compared to the modern social science data about the health benefits of marriage, these classical reflections were more avuncular than statistical, more anecdotal than inductive, more prudential than scientific. And, to be sure, they were only very small fragments within a vast Greco-Roman literature that also condoned sexual norms and habits that the Christian tradition would later condemn — prostitution, concubinage, pedophilia, homosexuality, polygamy, mixed bathing, communal propagation, anonymous parentage, casual consortium with slaves, and more.[26] But in these vast classical sources, the Christian tradition could pluck out a number of touchstones about the natural goods and goals of marriage that would prove helpful to its broader theological formulations about marriage. Natural arguments about marriage could not provide the Christian tradition with a complete theology of marriage. But a theology of marriage could not be complete, or cogent, without some natural foundation and corroboration.

Early Christian Formulations

Thus the Western Christian tradition has always included a natural perspective in its theology of marriage. To be sure, marriage is more than a natural

---

26. See Philip L. Reynolds, *Marriage in the Western Church: The Christianization of Marriage during the Patristic and Early Modern Periods* (Leiden: E. J. Brill, 1994), pp. 38-40, 156-72; Brundage, pp. 10-123.

institution. The Christian tradition has also understood it as a spiritual, social, economic, and contractual association — subject to the church, state, community, and couple at once. But at its foundation marriage is also a natural institution, subject to the laws of nature communicated in Scripture, reason, and conscience and reflected in tradition, custom, and experience.

Patristic, Catholic, and Protestant writers alike taught that marriage was created and ordered by God. Already in Paradise, God had brought the first man and the first woman together and commanded them to "be fruitful and multiply." God had created them as social creatures, naturally inclined and attracted to each other. God had given them the physical capacity to join together and to beget children. God had commanded them to love, help, and nurture each other and to inculcate in each other and in their children the love of God, neighbor, and self. These duties and qualities of marriage, the Christian tradition has long taught, continued after the fall into sin. After the fall, however, marriages also became a remedy for lust, a balm to incontinence. Rather than allowing sinful persons to burn with lust, God provided the remedy of marriage, in order for parties to direct their natural drives and passions to the service and love of the spouse, the child, and the broader community.

On this common foundation about the created origin and natural order of marriage, Christian writers over the centuries devised various formulas to define the goods and goals of marriage. The most famous and enduring formulation came from Saint Augustine, the bishop of Hippo (354-430). Like his classical predecessors, Augustine called marriage a "true and loyal partnership," the "seedbed of the city," the "first step in the organization of men."[27] He also quoted his Greek contemporary, Saint John Chrysostom (ca. 347-407), about the political and social utility of marriage: "The love of husband and wife is the force that welds society together. Because when harmony prevails, the children are raised well, the household is kept in order, and neighbors and relatives praise the result. Great benefits, both for families and states, are thus produced."[28]

In its essence, however, Augustine wrote, marriage has three goods *(bona)*. Marriage "is the ordained means of procreation *(proles)*, the guarantee of chastity *(fides)*, and the bond of permanent union *(sacramentum)*."[29]

---

27. Augustine, *City of God* 14.10, 21, 22; 15.16; 19.7, 14.

28. John Chrysostom, "Homily 20 on Ephesians 5:22-33," in *St. John Chrysostom on Marriage and Family Life* (Crestwood, N.J.: St. Vladimir's Press, 1986), pp. 43-44.

29. Augustine, *On Original Sin*, chap. 39, in Philip Schaff and Henry Wace, eds., *A Second Library of Nicene and Post-Nicene Fathers of the Christian Church*, 2nd ser., reprint ed. (Grand Rapids: Eerdmans, 1952), 5:251; hereafter *Fathers Library*.

As a created, natural means of procreation, Christian marriage rendered sexual intercourse licit. As a contract of fidelity, marriage gave husband and wife an equal power over the other's body, an equal right to demand that the other spouse avoid adultery, and an equal claim to the "service, in a certain measure, of sustaining each other's weakness, for the avoidance of illicit intercourse."[30] As a "certain sacramental bond," marriage was a source and symbol of permanent union between Christians.[31] "[M]arriage bears a kind of sacred bond," Augustine wrote; "it can be dissolved in no way except by the death of one of the parties. The bond of marriage remains, even if offspring for which the marriage was entered upon, should not follow because of a clear case of sterility, so that it is not lawful for married people who know they will not have any children to separate and to unite with others even for the sake of having children."[32]

Procreation, fidelity, and sacrament: these were the three goods of marriage, in Augustine's view. They were the reason the institution of marriage was good. They were why participation in marriage was good. They were the goods and goals that a person could hope and expect to realize upon marrying. Augustine usually listed the goods of marriage in this order, giving first place to procreation. At least twice he underscored this priority by writing that "the institution of marriage exists for the sake of procreation; for this reason did our forebears enter into the union of marriage and lawfully take to themselves their wives, *only* because of the duty to beget children."[33]

Augustine, however, did not call procreation the primary good of marriage and the others secondary. He sometimes changed the order of his list of marital goods to "fidelity, procreation, and sacrament" — passages that inspired later canonists and theologians to develop theories of "marital affection" as the primary marital good.[34] Even when he listed procreation as the first marital good, Augustine made clear that spousal fidelity and sacramental stability were essential for a marriage to be good — and sufficient when mar-

---

30. Augustine, *De bona conjugali,* chaps. 4–7, in R. J. Deferrari, ed., *St. Augustine: Treatises on Marriage and Other Subjects* (New York: Fathers of the Church, 1955).

31. Augustine, *On Marriage and Concupiscence,* chaps. 11, 19, in *Fathers Library,* 5:261, 271.

32. Augustine, *De bona conjugali,* chap. 15.

33. Augustine, *De incompetentibus nuptiis* 2.12, in Deferrari, p. 116 (emphasis added). See also Augustine, *Contra Faustum Manichaeum,* chap. 19, n. 26.

34. Augustine, *Commentary on the Literal Meaning of Genesis,* bk. 2, chap. 7, n. 12. See later medieval theories in John T. Noonan, Jr., "Marital Affection among the Canonists," *Studia Gratiana* 14 (1967): 489; Jean Leclercq, *Monks on Marriage: A Twelfth Century View* (New York: Seabury Press, 1982), pp. 11-39, 71-81.

ried couples were childless or their children had left the household. In doing so he followed the classic authors in highlighting some of the benefits of marriage to the couple themselves:

> [Marriage] does not seem to me to be a good solely because of the procreation of children, but also because of the natural companionship *(societas)* between the two sexes. Otherwise, we could not speak of marriage in the case of old people, especially if they had lost their children or had begotten none at all. But, in a good marriage, although one of many years, even if the ardor of youth has cooled between man and woman, the order of chastity still flourishes between husband and wife. . . . there is observed that promise of respect and of services due to each other by either sex, even though both members weaken in health and become moribund, the chastity of souls rightly joined together continues the purer, the more it has been proved, the more secure, the more it has been calmed.[35]

Augustine's account of the goods of marriage was more positive than most early Christian formulations. Many other Church Fathers, before and after him, not only treated marriage as less virtuous than chastity and celibacy, but also spoke of marriage and of sexual intercourse even within marriage in increasingly deprecatory and discouraging terms. Augustine's views ultimately proved more enduring in the Western tradition. Both Catholic and Protestant writers took him as their touchstone, and his formulation of the goods of marriage was subject to endless repetition and elaboration.

Roman Catholic Formulations

One of the most important transmissions and elaborations of Saint Augustine's views of marital goods came during the Papal Revolution of circa 1075-1300. This was the era when the Catholic clergy, led by Pope Gregory VII (1073-85), threw off their royal and civil rulers and established the Roman Catholic Church as an autonomous legal and political corporation within Western Christendom. The church's revolutionary rise to power triggered an enormous transformation of Western society, politics, and culture. The first modern Western universities were established in Italy, France, and England, with their core faculties of law, theology, and medicine devoted to the study

---

35. Augustine, *De bona conjugali,* chap. 3. See further John J. Hugo, *St. Augustine on Nature, Sex, and Marriage* (Chicago: Scepter, 1969), pp. 126ff.; Augustine Regan, "The Perennial Value of Augustine's Theology of the Goods of Marriage," *Studia Moralia* 21 (1983): 351-78.

of the rediscovered ancient texts of Greek philosophy, Roman law, and Patristic theology.[36]

It was in this revolutionary context that the Roman Catholic Church developed a systematic theology and law of marriage. From the twelfth century forward, the church's doctrine of marriage was categorized, systematized, and refined, notably in Hugh of Saint Victor's *On the Sacraments of the Christian Faith* (ca. 1143), Peter Lombard's *Book of Sentences* (1150), and Thomas Aquinas's *Summa theologica* (ca. 1265-73) — and the scores of thick glosses and commentaries on these texts published in subsequent centuries. From the twelfth century forward, the church's canon law of marriage was also systematized, first in Gratian's *Decretum* (ca. 1140), then in a welter of later legal commentaries and new papal and conciliar laws that eventually would form the *Corpus iuris canonici*. These core theological and legal texts of medieval Catholicism repeated Saint Augustine's formulation of the marital goods of procreation, faith, and sacrament. Each of them gave Augustine's formulations a new accent and application — medieval canonists and civilians often adducing Roman law texts in so doing, medieval theologians and philosophers often adducing Aristotle and the Stoics.

Thomas Aquinas's formulations of the three marital goods, which systematized more than a century of high medieval legal and theological thought, provide a good illustration of emerging Roman Catholic teaching. Thomas wrote at great length on the theology and law of marriage. Especially important were his commentaries on Peter Lombard and Aristotle.[37] He included in the former commentary a long discussion of marital goods, in the latter a number of glosses on Aristotle's notions of marriage as an institution of nature and a prototype of friendship. These latter themes came in for further comments in his *Summa contra Gentiles*.[38]

Thomas first dealt with objections that Augustine's list of faith, chil-

---

36. See Harold J. Berman, *Law and Revolution: The Formation of the Western Legal Tradition* (Cambridge: Harvard University Press, 1983).

37. *Scriptum super Libros Sententiarum Petri Lombardiensis*, in *Opera Omnia Sancti Thomae Aquinatis Doctoris Angelici* (Rome, 1882-), vol. 7.2; hereafter *Comm. Sent*. This commentary recurs almost verbatim in Thomas Aquinas, *Summa Theologica*, trans. Fathers of the English Dominican Province (Allen, TX: Christian Classics, 1981), vol. 5, Supplement (hereafter *ST SUPP*, q. 49. Thomas's commentaries on Aristotle's *Ethics* and *Politics* appear in his *Opera Omnia*, vols. 47 and 48, but the commentary on the *Ethics* (hereafter *Comm. Eth.*) breaks off at chapter 6, just before Aristotle's crucial passage on marital love quoted above (n. 11). See discussion in Mackin, pp. 176-91; John Finnis, *Aquinas: Moral, Political, and Legal Theory* (Oxford: Oxford University Press, 1998), pp. 143-54.

38. Aquinas, *Summa contra Gentiles*, trans. and ed. Vernon Bourke (Notre Dame: University of Notre Dame Press, 1975), bk. III, pt. II, chaps. 122-26; hereafter *SCG*.

dren, and sacramentality *(fides, proles, et sacramentum)*[39] might be "insufficiently enumerated." After all, critics of the day argued, Augustine had not taken into sufficient account Aristotle's insights that marriage is not only for procreation but also for spouses to enjoy a common life, a common stock, and companionship. Maybe love, charity, and sacrifice between spouses would be a better understanding of a "marital good" than *fides*. Maybe *proles* should be considered a derivative good, since children are not essential to marriage and many married parties do not have them. Maybe *sacramentum* is not really a marital good at all, since Augustine is referring to the indissolubility of marriage, and indissolubility does not seem to be an essential feature of a sacrament. Maybe marriage should also have a good of justice, since it involves the discharge of marital rights and conjugal debts. Maybe the goods of marriage would be better if they were listed as those qualities of marriage that are "useful" rather than "virtuous."[40]

Thomas defended Augustine's three goods as a sufficient and complete account: "The goods which justify marriage belong to the nature of marriage, which consequently needs them, not as extrinsic causes of its rectitude, but as causing in it that rectitude which belongs to it by nature." "From the very fact that marriage is intended as an office or as a remedy [from sexual sin] it has the aspect of something useful and right; nevertheless both aspects belong to it from the fact that it has these goods by which it fulfills the office and affords a remedy to concupiscence."[41] "Matrimony is instituted both as an office of nature and as a sacrament of the church. As an office of nature it is directed by two things, like every other virtuous act. One of these is required on the part of the agent and is the intention of the due end, and thus the offspring *(proles)* is accounted a good of marriage; the other is required on the part of the act, which is good generically through being about a due matter; and thus we have faith *(fides)*, where a man has intercourse with his wife and with no other woman. Besides this it has a certain goodness as a sacrament, and this is signified by the word sacrament *(sacramentum)*."[42]

Thomas elaborated these three Augustinian goods of marriage, however, in a way that both integrated them more fully than Augustine had done and resolved more clearly the question of their priority. While his views were not fully developed, he argued effectively that marriage is a three-dimensional institution and that each of the marital goods anchors one of these three dimensions.

39. Thomas generally renders the list in this order. See *Comm. Sent.* IV, Dist. 31, q. 1; *ST SUPP*, q. 49, art. 2.
40. *Comm. Sent.* IV, Dist. 31, art. 2, q. 1; *ST SUPP*, q. 49, art. 2, obj. 1-7.
41. *ST SUPP*, q. 49, art. 1; *Comm. Sent.* IV, Dist. 26, art. 1, 2.
42. *ST SUPP*, q. 49, art. 2.

If marriage is viewed as a natural institution, Aquinas argued, procreation *(proles)* is the primary good. Building on both Augustine and Aristotle, Aquinas argued that man and woman are naturally inclined to come together for the sake of having children, and that nature teaches that the licit means of doing so is through a voluntary act of marriage.[43] Procreation, however, means more than just conceiving children. It also means rearing and educating them for spiritual and temporal living — a common Stoic sentiment. The good of procreation cannot be achieved in this fuller sense simply through the licit union of husband and wife in sexual intercourse. It also requires maintenance of a faithful, stable, and permanent union of husband and wife, so that both mother and father may participate in the education and rearing of their children. In this natural sense the primary good of marriage is procreation; the secondary goods are faith and sacramental stability.[44]

If marriage is viewed as a contractual association, faith *(fides)* is the primary good. Marital faith is not a spiritual faith but a faith of justice, Aquinas argued. It means keeping faith, being faithful, holding faithfully to one's promises made in the contract of marriage. Marital faith requires, as Augustine had said, forgoing sexual intercourse with another and honoring the connubial debt (that is, yielding to the reasonable sexual advances of one's spouse). But marital faith also involves, as Aristotle and the Stoics had said, the commitment to be indissolubly united with one's spouse in body and mind, to be the "greatest of friends," to be willing to share fully and equally in the person, property, lineage, and reputation — indeed, in the "whole life" — of one's spouse. It is to be and bear with each other in youth and in old age, in sickness and in health, in prosperity and adversity. Marital faith, in this richer understanding, is a good in itself, Aquinas insisted. It need not necessarily be expected or intended for the procreation of children; indeed, a marriage promise need not even be consummated to be valid and binding. If it is consummated

---

43. *Comm. Sent.* IV, Dist. 26, q. 1; Dist. 33, q. 1; *Comm. Eth.,* par. 1719, 1720, 1723. See Mackin, pp. 182-83; Grisez, *The Way,* pp. 558-60.

44. *Comm. Sent.* IV, Dist. 26, q. 1; *ST SUPP,* q. 49, art. 2-3, 5; *SCG* 3.2.123.1-10; 124.3. In *ST SUPP,* q. 49, art. 3, Thomas writes: "[F]aith and offspring may be considered as in their principles so that offspring denote the intention of having children and faith the duty of remaining faithful, and there can be no matrimony without these also, since they are caused in matrimony by the marriage compact itself, so that if anything contrary to these were expressed in the consent which makes a marriage, the marriage would be invalid. Taking faith and offspring in this sense, it is clear that offspring is the most essential thing in marriage, secondly faith, and thirdly sacrament; even as to man it is more essential to be in nature than to be in grace, although it is more excellent to be in grace." See further Don S. Browning et al., *From Culture Wars to Common Ground: Religion and the American Family Debate* (Louisville: Westminster John Knox, 1997), pp. 113-24; Don S. Browning, "Altruism and Christian Love," *Zygon* 27, no. 4 (1992): 421-36.

faithfully, sexual intercourse is a good act in itself, even if procreation is a natural impossibility.[45] In this contractual sense the primary good of marriage is faith *(fides)*; the secondary goods are sacrament and procreation.[46]

If marriage is viewed as a spiritual institution, *sacramentum* is the primary good. Marriage between baptized Christians is a sacrament of grace, Aquinas argued, citing Lombard — much like the sacraments of baptism, eucharist, penance, and others. The temporal union of body, soul, and mind within the marital estate at once symbolizes the eternal union between Christ and the church and confers sanctifying grace upon the couple, their children, and the community. Viewed as a spiritual institution, Aquinas wrote, "sacrament is in every way the most important of the three marriage goods, since it belongs to marriage considered as a sacrament of grace; while the other two belong to it as an office of nature; and a perfection of grace is more excellent than a perfection of nature."[47]

A sacramental marriage, once properly contracted between Christians in accordance with the laws of nature and of the church, is an indissoluble union, Aquinas insisted, a permanently open channel of grace. For marriage partakes of the quality that it symbolizes, namely, the indissoluble bond between Christ and the church:

> [S]ince the sacraments effect what they figure, it is to be believed that grace is conferred through this sacrament on the spouses, whereby they might belong to the union of Christ and the Church. And this is very nec-

---

45. *Comm. Sent.* IV, Dist. 26, q. 2; Dist. 27, q. 1; Dist. 31, q. 1; Dist. 33, q. 1; Dist. 41, q. 1; *ST SUPP*, qq. 42, 47, 49; *SCG* 3.2.123.3, 4, 8; 124.4-5; 125.6; 126.1-6. See Finnis, *Aquinas*, pp. 143-48.

46. While Thomas spoke explicitly of ways in which *proles* and *sacramentum* could be viewed as primary and the other goods as secondary, he never, so far as I have found, spoke explicitly of *fides* as the primary end. But this is a natural implication of his argument about the faith of the marriage contract and the friendship of the marital institution. Thomas comes close to saying this in his argument that the marriage of Mary and Joseph was "perfect" even though not consummated: "Marriage or wedlock is said to be true by reason of its attaining its perfection. Now perfection of anything is two-fold. The perfection of a thing consists in its very form from which it receives its species; while the second perfection of a thing consists in its operation, by which in some way a thing attains its end. Now the form of matrimony consists in a certain inseparable union of souls, by which husband and wife are pledged by a bond of mutual affection that cannot be sundered. And the end of marriage is the begetting and upbringing of children, the first of which is attained by conjugal intercourse; the second by the other duties of husband and wife, by which they help one another in rearing their offspring. Thus we may say, as to the first perfection, that the marriage of the Virgin Mother of God and Joseph was absolutely true, because both consented to the nuptial bond but not to the bond of flesh" (*ST SUPP*, q. 29, art. 2).

47. *Comm. Sent.* IV, Dist. 31, q. 2; *ST SUPP*, q. 49, art. 3.

essary to them so that as they concern themselves with carnal and earthly matters, they do not become detached from Christ and the Church. Now since the union of husband and wife designates the union of Christ and the Church, the figure must correspond with that which it signifies. Now the union of Christ and the Church is a union of one to another, and it is to last in perpetuity. For there is only one Church, . . . and Christ will never be separated from His Church. As He Himself says in the last chapter of Matthew, "Behold I am with you even unto the end of the world. . . ." It follows necessarily then that a marriage, in so far as it is a sacrament of the Church, must be one holding to another indivisibly.[48]

Aquinas's understanding of the good of *sacramentum* went well beyond the formulations of Augustine. Augustine called marriage a sacrament to demonstrate its symbolic stability. Aquinas called marriage a sacrament to demonstrate its spiritual efficacy. Augustine said that marriage as a perennial symbol of Christ's bond to the church should not be dissolved. Aquinas said that marriage as a permanent channel of sacramental grace could not be dissolved. Augustine called marriage a sacrament because it was indissoluble. Aquinas called marriage indissoluble because it was a sacrament.

This understanding of the good of *sacramentum* also elevated and integrated the goods of procreation and faith. On the one hand, the sacramental quality of Christian marriage helped to elevate the natural acts of marriage to spiritual significance. At minimum, it helped to remove the stigma of sin in sexual intercourse and to elevate the procreation and nurture of children into an act useful for the church. More fully conceived, the sacramental quality effectively placed the natural institution of marriage into the hierarchy of church orders as something of an institution and instrument of grace — though one clearly subordinate to the celibate clerical and monastic orders. On the other hand, the sacramental quality of Christian marriage helped to elevate the marriage contract into more than just a bargained-for exchange between two parties. At minimum, it rendered marriage an "adhesion contract" that was indissoluble: the terms of the marital bargain were already set by nature, and as a symbol of Christ's bond with the church the marital bond was perforce indissoluble. More fully conceived, the exchange of consent between the couple also signified an exchange of consent of the couple with God and the church. In essence, the parties consented to bind themselves to each other and to God and the church and thus to accept God's sacramental grace and the church's spiritual nurture for their marriage.

48. *SCG* 4.78.

Thomas Aquinas's elegant integration of the three goods of marriage found a growing team of champions in the fourteenth through sixteenth centuries. The fresh rise and extension of Thomism among such sixteenth-century Iberian luminaries as Francisco de Vitoria, Francisco Suárez, and Thomas Sánchez eventually helped to transmit Aquinas's understanding of marriage and its goods very widely, not only in Catholic and Protestant Europe but also among the many new Latin American colonies.[49]

These views also entered the canon law and catechism of the Catholic Church. The great Council of Trent (1545-63) took Thomas's and related medieval views of marriage as dispositive, and reflected them in a series of canons under the decree *Tametsi* of 1563.[50] The catechism, commissioned by the council and issued in 1566, spoke directly to the goods of marriage.[51] Citing the "general opinion of the theologians," it defined marriage, much as Aquinas had done, "as a natural union, since it was not invented by man but instituted by nature," and "as a Sacrament, the efficacy of which transcends the order of nature." As a natural union, created by God in Paradise, marriage has "three reasons" *(causae)* for its existence — (1) the "companionship of husband and wife," (2) "an antidote to avoid sins of lust," and (3) "the desire of family, not so much, however, with a view to leave after us heirs to inherit our property and fortune, as to bring up children in the true faith and service of God." As a sacramental union, marriage "is far superior . . . and aims at an incomparably higher end." "For as marriage, as a natural union, was instituted from the beginning to propagate the human race; so was the sacramental dignity subsequently conferred upon it in order that a people might be begotten and brought up for the service and worship of the true God and of Christ our Savior."

Marriage brings "three goods" *(bona)* to the couple, the 1566 catechism states: (1) "offspring, if it is the Lord's will"; (2) faith, which is "a special, holy, and pure love"; and (3) "sacrament," now used in the Augustinian sense of stability and permanence. God confers those blessings where couples abide by his duties for marriage — set out in the natural law and elaborated in the Bible. "It is the duty of the husband to treat his wife generously and honorably," to be "constantly occupied in some honest pursuit with a view to provide

---

49. See especially Thomas Sánchez, *De sancto matrimonii sacramento* (Louvain, 1637). For other neo-Thomist writers of Spain and Portugal, see Brian Tierney, *The Idea of Natural Rights* (Atlanta: Scholars Press, 1997), pp. 255-315.

50. Reprinted in H. J. Schroeder, *Councils and Decrees of the Council of Trent* (St. Louis: B. Herder Book Co., 1941).

51. All quotes are from *Catechism of the Council of Trent for Parish Priests,* trans. John A. McHugh and Charles J. Callan (Rockford, Ill.: Tan Books and Publishers, 1982), pp. 338-55.

necessaries for his family and to avoid idleness, the root of almost every vice." Wives, in turn, must "never forget that next to God they are to love their husbands, to esteem them above all others, yielding to them in all things not inconsistent with Christian piety, a willing and ready obedience."

Both the nuance and the balance of these medieval and Tridentine formulations of marital goods were increasingly lost on the church after the sixteenth century. By the later nineteenth century, many of the church's doctrinal statements and legal texts treated procreation as the primary good, sometimes even the exclusive good, of marriage, and outlawed with increasing sternness contraception, abortion, and other actions that obstructed or compromised the good of procreation.[52] The good of marital faith, in the full sense that Thomas and others had described it, was reduced to a dispensable means to the end of procreation.[53] The good of the marital sacrament, in the rich, integrating sense in which medieval and Tridentine theology had defined it, was reduced to simple platitudes about grace and the church's jurisdiction over its instruments.

The 1917 *Code of Canon Law* sealed this shift in perspective, stating repeatedly the priority of the good of procreation: "The primary good or end [*finis*] of marriage is procreation and the nurture of children; its secondary end is mutual help and the remedying of concupiscence." "Marital consent is an act of the will by which each party gives and accepts a perpetual and exclusive right over the body for acts which are of themselves suitable for the generation of children." And again: "[M]arriage is a permanent society for the procreation of children."[54]

Pope Pius XI's encyclical letter *Casti connubi* (1930) underscored this shift in perspective: "Among the blessings of marriage, offspring holds the first place," Pius wrote, citing (selectively) from Augustine. "The conjugal act is of its very nature designed for the procreation of offspring," and any acts to the contrary are condemned.[55] Pius also confirmed a ruling of the Holy Office that condemned "certain modern writers" who gave priority to marital

---

52. See generally John T. Noonan, Jr., *Contraception: A History of Its Treatment by the Catholic Theologians and Canonists* (Cambridge: Harvard University Press, 1965); Mackin, pp. 192-224.

53. Grisez, *The Way*, 2:561, and more generally Germain Grisez, *Contraception and the Natural Law* (Milwaukee: Bruce Publishing, 1964).

54. Title VII, Canons 1013, 1081.2, 1082.1, reprinted in T. Lincoln Bouscaren et al., *Canon Law: A Text and Commentary*, 4th rev. ed. (Milwaukee: Bruce Publishing, 1966), pp. 466, 565-67.

55. *Papal Teachings: Marriage*, trans. M. J. Byrnes (Boston: Beacon Press, 1963), item 11 (pp. 224-25).

love and companionship in expression of new European personalist and phenomenological theories. Such views were considered anathema, for they "either deny that the primary end of marriage is the generation and education of children, or teach that the secondary ends are not essential to the primary end."[56] Marital love must be viewed as a means to the end (or good) of procreation, not as an end in itself.

At the end of *Casti connubi,* however, Pius XI offered several pastoral sentiments about marital love that would help to return the church to the more nuanced position of the Council of Trent, and indeed to go beyond it: "The action in the home is not confined to mutual help," Pius wrote; "it must have as its higher and indeed its chief objective that of shaping and perfecting the interior life of husband and wife. Their life partnership must help them to increase daily in the practice of virtue, and above all to grow in the true love of God and their neighbor...."[57] And then, more generously still: "This mutual interior formation of husband and wife, this persevering endeavor to bring each other to the state of perfection, may in a true sense be called, as the Roman Catechism calls it, the primary cause and reason of marriage, so long as marriage is considered not in the stricter sense as the institution designed for the creation and education of children, but in the wider sense as a complete and intimate life-partnership and association."[58]

Pius XI's pastoral aside eventually became a doctrinal priority. The Second Vatican Council (1962-65), after anguished and angry debate, returned to the fuller formulation of the goods of *fides, proles, et sacramentum* that had been adumbrated by Augustine and elaborated by Saint Thomas and the Tridentine reformers. In its pastoral constitution, *Gaudium et spes,* the council declared: "God himself is the author of matrimony, endowed as it is with various goods *(bona)* and ends *(fines).* All of these have a very decisive bearing on the continuation of the human race, on the personal development and eternal destiny of the individual members of a family, and on the dignity, stability, peace, and prosperity of the family itself and human society as a whole."[59]

---

56. Quoted and critically discussed in Lisa Sowle Cahill, "Marriage: Institution, Relationship, Sacrament," in *One Hundred Years of Catholic Social Thought,* ed. John A. Coleman (Maryknoll, N.Y.: Orbis Books, 1991), pp. 103-19, at 108. Cahill elaborates her reconstructive critique in *Sex, Gender, and Christian Ethics* (New York: Cambridge University Press, 1996). The most influential of these European writers, whose work was censored, was Herbert Doms, *Vom Sinn und Zweck der Ehe* (Breslau: Ostdeutsche Verlagsanstalt, 1935), translated (imprecisely) as *The Meaning of Marriage* (New York: Sheed and Ward, 1939).

57. *Papal Teachings: Marriage,* item 23 (p. 231).

58. *Papal Teachings: Marriage,* item 23 (p. 231). See also Mackin, pp. 215-18.

59. *Gaudium et spes,* par. 48, using the translation of Walter M. Abbott and Joseph

The Second Vatican Council amplified this latter concern for the role of the family within broader society, elaborating, as no church council before had done, the social and political goods of marriage. "The well being of . . . human and Christian society is intimately linked with the healthy condition of that community produced by marriage and family."[60] "The family is a kind of school of deeper humanity," holding out a model of love, charity, stewardship, authority, dignity, faithfulness, education, nurture, discipline, and care for each new generation of children to learn, and for other institutions to emulate. "Thus the family is the foundation of society. In it the various generations come together and help one another to grow wiser and to harmonize personal rights with the other requirements of social life. All those, therefore, who exercise influence over communities and social groups should work effectively for the welfare of marriage and the family. Public authority should regard it as a sacred duty to recognize, protect, and promote their authentic nature, to shield public morality, and to favor the prosperity of domestic life."[61] In *Lumen et gentium* the council pronounced famously: "The family is, so to speak, the domestic Church." The parents are "the first preachers" who nurture the faith not only of their children but of broader society as well.[62]

Gaudium et spes was even more expansive in its treatment of marital love and affection as indispensable to the "well being of the individual person."[63] In Vatican II's formulation, marital love was no longer simply a form and function of marital faith, as was traditional. It was the good that permeated and integrated all three of the classic goods of faith, children, and sacrament:

> The intimate partnership of married life and love has been established by the Creator and qualified by His laws. It is rooted in the marriage covenant of irrevocable personal consent. . . . [A] man and a woman, who by the marriage covenant of conjugal love "are no longer two but one flesh" (Mt. 19:6), render mutual help and service to each other through an intimate union of their persons and of their actions. Through this union they experience the meaning of their oneness and attain to it with growing perfection day by day. As a mutual gift of two persons, this intimate

---

Gallagher, eds., *The Documents of Vatican II* (Chicago: Follet Publishing, 1966), p. 250. The council cites, inter alia, the passages from Augustine, Aquinas, and *Casti connubi* quoted above. *Documents of Vatican II*, p. 250, n. 154. The translation renders the phrase *bona et fines* as "benefits and purposes"; I have rendered it "goods" and "ends."

60. *Gaudium et spes*, par. 47.
61. *Gaudium et spes*, par. 48, 49, 52.
62. *Lumen et gentium*, par. 11, in *Documents of Vatican II*, p. 29.
63. *Gaudium et spes*, par. 47.

union, as well as the good of children, imposes total fidelity on the spouses, and argues for an unbreakable oneness between them. Christ the Lord abundantly blessed this many-faceted love, welling up as it does from the fountain of divine love and structured as it is on the model of His union with the Church. For as God of old made himself present to His people through a covenant of love and fidelity, so now the Savior of men and the Spouse of the Church comes into the lives of married Christians through the sacrament of matrimony.[64]

Marital love involves "the good of the whole person," *Gaudium et spes* continued. It "ennobles" those "special ingredients and signs of the friendship distinctive of marriage." It impels spouses to make "a free and mutual gift of themselves, a gift proving itself by gentle affection and by deed." It expresses itself in sexual intercourse, which is "good," "noble and worthy," regardless of any procreative promise, intent, outcome. It is structured through the "equal personal dignity of husband and wife, a dignity acknowledged by mutual and total love." Marital love brings to the couple "the needed cultural, psychological, and social renewal" that they need daily to survive, flourish, and indeed to perfect themselves.[65]

In an appendix to *Gaudium et spes,* the council again underscored that marriage was "a covenant of love" formed voluntarily. "Marital consent of its essence intends the unity of this covenant, its indissolubility and the love that is devoted to the service of life. The stronger and purer the marital love, the more strongly and perseveringly will the spouses accept and realize marriage's specific traits and its essential goods.... No one is aware of how seriously necessary it is that love be fully present in the act of consent, and increase throughout the married life. For love will fulfill, and cause to be fulfilled what the consent has said and has promised."[66]

A number of subsequent doctrinal and canonical documents have repeated Vatican II's integrative theory of the three goods of the covenant of marriage.[67] But several recent church statements, particularly on abortion

---

64. *Gaudium et spes,* par. 48.
65. *Gaudium et spes,* par. 49.
66. Quoted in Mackin, p. 261.
67. See, e.g., *Code of Canon Law* (1983), Title VII, Canon 1055: "The matrimonial covenant, by which a man and a woman establish between themselves a partnership of the whole of life, is by its nature ordered toward the good of the spouses and the procreation and education of offspring; this covenant between baptized persons has been raised by Christ to the dignity of a sacrament." See also John Paul II, *Familiaris consortio, Acta Apostolicae Sedis* (AAS) 74 (1982): 92, *Oservatore Romano,* 21-28 December 1981, 3, and discussion in Michael J. Wrenn, ed., *Pope John Paul II and the Family* (Chicago: Franciscan Herald Press, 1983).

and contraception, have emphasized anew the marital good of procreation.[68] In his encyclical *Humanae vitae* (1968), for example, Pope Paul VI speaks favorably of "total, faithful, and exclusive" conjugal love and mutual self-giving and self-perfection in and through marriage.[69] But these familiar refrains from Vatican II seem almost drowned out in the robust new orchestrations on procreation. Marital union and procreation are "inseparable," *Humanae vitae* reads, and it "is necessary that each matrimonial function *(matrimonii usus)* remain ordained in itself to the procreating of human life." "[C]onjugal love requires that spouses be fully aware of their mission *(munus)* of responsible parenthood." Through marital union "the spouses perfect each other so that they might share with God the task of procreating and educating new living beings."[70] There follows a series of pronouncements against abortion, contraception, sterilization, and other interruptions of the natural "generative" and "procreative process." Critics have viewed *Humanae vitae* and its ample progeny as a retreat from the integrative theory of marital love developed by Vatican II. In particular, they see in these documents a tacit reassertion of an instrumentalist view of marriage and of the primacy of the good of procreation over that of marital faith and love — a trend underscored, in their view, by the church's many recent pronouncements against committed homosexual unions.[71] Defenders view this language as further confirmation of the church's new understanding of the covenant of marriage as a basic or intrinsic human good ordained by God for the mutual blessing of the couple, their children, and the broader communities of which they are a part.[72]

Protestant Formulations

The recent emphasis among Roman Catholics on love and companionship within the covenant of marriage and on the individual and social utility of

---

68. For various interpretations, see Janet E. Smith, *"Humanae Vitae": A Generation Later* (Washington, D.C.: Catholic University Press, 1991), pp. 267-95; Janet E. Smith, ed., *Why "Humanae Vitae" Was Right: A Reader* (San Francisco: Ignatius Press, 1993); Grisez, *The Way*, pp. 561-84; Germain Grisez et al., *The Teachings of "Humanae Vitae": A Defense* (San Francisco: Ignatius Press, 1988).

69. Paul VI, *Humanae Vitae*, 8, 9, AAS 60 (1968), 485-486, in the *Papal Encyclicals*, 5 vols. (Wilmington, NC: McGrath Publishing Co., 1981), vol. 5, p. 225.

70. Paul VI, *Humanae Vitae*, 8, 11, 12.

71. See, e.g., articles in Smith, *"Humanae Vitae,"* and Smith, *Why "Humanae Vitae" Was Right*; Mark D. Jordan, *The Silence of Sodom: Homosexuality in Modern Catholicism* (Chicago: University of Chicago Press, 2000).

72. See sources in notes 3, 4, 19, and 37.

marriage was a dominant theme of Protestant theology and law from the very beginning. The Protestant Reformation was inaugurated by Martin Luther of Wittenberg (1483-1546), in his famous posting of the Ninety-five Theses in 1517 and his burning of the canon law and confessional books in 1520. The Reformation, however, was the culmination of more than two centuries of dissent within the church against some of its sacramental theology, liturgical practice, canon law, and ecclesiastical administration. The Reformation ultimately erupted in various quarters of western Europe in the early sixteenth century, settling into Lutheran, Calvinist, Anglican, and Free Church branches.

The leading sixteenth-century Protestant reformers — Martin Luther and Philipp Melanchthon, John Calvin and Martin Bucer, Thomas Cranmer and Heinrich Bullinger — all wrote at length on marriage. In their view, God had created and ordered marriage to achieve three purposes *(causae)* or goals *(fines):* (1) the mutual love and support of husband and wife, (2) the mutual procreation and nurture of children, and (3) the mutual protection of both spouses from sexual sin — often put in that order of priority.[73]

This early Protestant formulation of the marital goods of love, procreation, and protection was no invention of the sixteenth century. This trilogy had already appeared more than a millennium before in Roman law and in Isidore of Seville's early seventh-century *Etymologies* (though Isidore made procreation the first good).[74] By the sixteenth century it had also become a standard formula among Catholic canonists and theologians to describe the purposes or reasons for marrying *(causae),* as opposed to the inherent goods *(bona)* of marriage itself. Most early Protestants rejected this medieval distinction between the purposes and goods of marriage. From God's point of view, they argued, marriage has built-in purposes that God wishes to see achieved among his creatures. From humanity's point of view, these are the created goods that we need to realize. To make fine distinctions between the goods and purposes, causes and effects, ends and means, motivations and measures of marriage, most early Protestants believed, is ultimately to engage in idle casuistry. For most Protestants, love, procreation, and protection was the essential formula.

---

73. See sources in my *From Sacrament to Contract,* pp. 96-108, 143-50. See also the interplay of the theology and practice of marital and familial love copiously documented in three books by Steven E. Ozment: *Ancestors: The Remaking of the Premodern European Family* (Cambridge: Harvard University Press, 2001); *Flesh and Spirit: Private Life in Early Modern Europe* (New York: Viking Press, 1999); and *When Fathers Ruled: Family Life in Reformation Europe* (Cambridge: Harvard University Press, 1983).

74. Isidore, *Etymologiae* 9.7.27. See discussion in Grisez, *The Way,* 2:558ff.

This formula overlapped with Augustine's formula of faith, children, and sacramentality, but amended it in critical ways. Like Augustine, Protestants emphasized the good of marital faithfulness *(fides)*. But they cast this good in increasingly overt terms of marital love, affection, friendship, and companionship, sometimes adducing Stoic and Roman sources in so doing.[75] Also, like Augustine, Protestants emphasized the good of procreating children *(proles)*. But they amended this good with the familiar medieval gloss that procreation included the Christian nurture and education of children. They underscored this amendment by insisting on the creation of schools for the religious and civic education of all children, and by producing a welter of catechisms, textbooks, and household manuals to assist in the same.[76]

Unlike Augustine, however, the early Protestant Reformers emphasized protection from sexual sin as a good in itself, not just a function of *fides*. Since the fall into sin, humankind has become totally depraved, the Reformers insisted. Lust has pervaded the conscience of every person. Participation in marriage has become an absolute necessity. For without marriage, the person's distorted sexuality becomes a force capable of overthrowing the most devout conscience. A person is enticed by nature to prostitution, masturbation, voyeurism, and other sexual sins. The "good gift" of marriage, Luther wrote, should thus be declined only by those who have received God's gift of continence. "Such persons are rare, not one in a thousand, for they are a special miracle of God." The apostle Paul has identified this group as the permanently impotent and the eunuchs; few others can claim such a unique gift.[77]

Also unlike Augustine, Protestants gave no place to the marital good of *sacramentum* — either in the Augustinian sense of symbolic stability or in the medieval Catholic sense of a permanent channel of sanctifying grace. For most early Protestants, marriage was neither a sacrament of the church on the order of baptism or the eucharist nor a permanent union dissolvable only upon the death of one of the parties. To be sure, Protestants, like Catholics, believed that marriages should be stable and presumptively indissoluble. But this presumption could be overcome if one of the other marital goods were frustrated. If there was a breach of marital love by one of the parties — by reason of adultery, desertion, or cruelty — the marriage was broken. The in-

---

75. See sources in my *From Sacrament to Contract*, pp. 96-108, 143-50.

76. See especially Luther's tracts on marriage in 1522 and 1530 in *Luther's Works* (Philadelphia, 1955-), 45:11-49; 46:259-320; hereafter *LW*. For sources and discussion of Lutheran and other Protestant views of public education as a form of communal procreation and nurture, see my "The Civic Seminary: Sources of Modern Public Education in the Lutheran Reformation of Germany," *Journal of Law and Religion* 12 (1996): 173-223.

77. *LW* 45:18-22; see also 28:9-12, 27-31.

nocent spouse who could not forgive this breach could sue for divorce and remarry. If there was a failure of procreation — by reason of sterility, incapacity, or disease discovered shortly after the wedding — the marriage was also broken. Those spouses who could not reconcile themselves to this condition could seek an annulment and at least the healthy spouse could marry another. And if there was a failure of protection from sin — by reason of frigidity, separation, or cruelty — the marriage was again broken. If the parties could not be reconciled to regular cohabitation and consortium, they could divorce and seek another marriage.

Most early Protestants, especially Lutherans and Calvinists, thus tended to view the goods of marriage in more teleological terms than their Catholic brethren. Marriage was a means to love, to children, and to protection. Where such goods failed, the marriage failed, and such goods should be sought in a second marriage. Martin Bucer, the Strasbourg Reformer who influenced Lutherans, Calvinists, and Anglicans alike, put the matter more flatly than most of his coreligionists. "A proper and useful" marriage, Bucer wrote, has "four necessary properties": "1. That the [couple] should live together. . . . 2. That they should love one another in the height of dearness. . . . 3. That the husband bear himself as the head and preserver of the wife instructing her to all godliness and integrity of life; that the wife also be to her husband a help, according to her place, especially furthering him in the true worship of God, and next in all the occasions of civil life. And 4. That they not defraud each other of conjugal benevolence." Marriages that exhibit these four properties must be maintained and celebrated. But even "where only one [property] be wanting in both or either party . . . it cannot then be said that the covenant of matrimony holds good between such." To perpetuate the formal structure of marriage after a necessary property is lost, Bucer argued, is not only a destructive custom, but an unbiblical practice. "[T]he Lord did not only permit, but also expressly and earnestly commanded his people, by whom he would that all holiness and faith of the marriage covenant be observed, that he could not induce his mind to love his wife with a true conjugal love, might dismiss her that she might marry to another" who is more meet and good.[78]

This more teleological view of marriage is also reflected in the tendency of early Protestants to introduce alternative formulations of the goods of marriage than those inherited from the tradition. Aquinas and other medieval writers had considered, but then rejected, the notion that marriage might have additional or alternative goods beyond the Augustinian goods of faith,

---

78. Martin Bucer, *De Regno Christi* (1550), bk. 2, chaps. 26, 38, 39, in Wilhelm Pauck, ed., *Melanchthon and Bucer* (Philadelphia: Westminster, 1969).

children, and sacramentality. The Protestant Reformers showed no such reticence. They held out all manner of personal, social, and political goods that marriage could offer — in part on the basis of a fresh reading of biblical and classical sources, in part in support of their relentless arguments against celibacy and monasticism.

One common Protestant formulation was that marriage had civil and spiritual "uses" in this life — a variant on the Protestant theory of the "uses of the moral law."[79] Both Luther and Calvin sometimes spoke in these terms. On the one hand, they argued, marriage has general *civil uses* for all persons, regardless of their faith. Marriage deters vice by furnishing preferred options to prostitution, promiscuity, pornography, and other forms of sexual pathos. Marriage cultivates virtue by offering love, care, and nurture to its members, and holding out a model of charity, education, and sacrifice to the broader community. Marriage enhances the life of a man and a woman by providing them with a community of caring and sharing, of stability and support, of nurture and welfare. Marriage enhances the life of the child by providing it with a chrysalis of nurture and love, with a highly individualized form of socialization and education. On the other hand, marriage has specific *spiritual uses* for believers — ways of sustaining and strengthening them in the Christian faith. The love of wife and husband is among the strongest symbols Christians can experience of Yahweh's love for the elect, of Christ's love for the church. The sacrifices one makes for spouse and child can be among the best expressions of Christian charity and *agapē*. For Christian believers, Calvin wrote, marriage can thus be "a sacred bond," "a holy fellowship," a "divine partnership," "a heavenly calling," "the fountainhead of life," "the holiest kind of company in all the world," "the principal and most sacred . . . of all the offices pertaining to human society." "God reigns in a little household, even one in dire poverty, when the husband and the wife dedicate themselves to their duties to each other. Here there is a holiness greater and nearer the kingdom of God than there is even in a cloister."[80]

Other Protestants emphasized not only the civil and spiritual uses of marriage, but also its social and political goods. Building especially on Aristotelian and Roman law antecedents, Lutheran, Calvinist, and Anglican writers alike treated marriage as the created, natural foundation of civil society and political authority.

---

79. See sources and discussion in my "The Three Uses of Law: A Protestant Source of the Purposes of Criminal Punishment?" *Journal of Law and Religion* 10 (1994): 433-65.

80. Calvin, *Comm. Gen.* 2:18, 21, 24; 6:2; *Serm. Deut.* 21:10-14; *Comm. Mal.* 2:14, 16; *Comm. Matt.* 19:11; *Comm. I Cor.* 7:14; 9:11; *Serm. 2 Tim.* 5.

For example, Philipp Melanchthon, Luther's eminent coworker in Wittenberg, opened a long discussion of political authority thus:

> The earthly life has orders *(Stände)* and works *(Werke)* which serve to keep the human race, and are ordained by God with certain limits and means. By this order we should know that this human nature is not created without the distinct counsel of God, and that God in this way lets his goodness shine on us to sustain and provide for us.
>
> Matrimony is first, for God does not want human nature simply to run its course as cattle do. Therefore God ordained marriage (Gen. 2; Matt. 19; I Cor. 7) as an eternal, inseparable fellowship of one husband and one wife.... [M]atrimony is a very lovely, beautiful fellowship and church of God, if two people in true faith and obedience toward God cheerfully live together, together invoke God, and rear children in the knowledge of God and virtue.[81]

Elsewhere Melanchthon, like Luther, emphasized that marriage was one of the three great estates *(drei Stände)*, along with the church and the state, that God had appointed for the governance of the earthly kingdom. The estate of marriage was to teach all persons, particularly children, Christian values, morals, and mores. It was to exemplify for a sinful society a community of love and cooperation, meditation and discussion, song and prayer. It was to hold out for the church and the state an example of firm but benign parental discipline, rule, and authority. It was to take in and care for wayfarers, widows, and destitute persons — a responsibility previously assumed largely by monasteries and cloisters. Marriage was thus as indispensable an agent in God's redemption plan as the church. It was as indispensable an agent of social order and communal cohesion as the state.[82]

Johannes Althusius (1557-1638), a distinguished Protestant jurist and political theorist, drew on sundry Christian and classical sources to construct a comprehensive covenantal theory of the state and society — again with marriage at its foundation.[83] "Politics is the art of associating men for the

---

81. Melanchthon, *Loci communes* (1555), chap. 36, translated in *Melanchthon on Christian Doctrine*, trans. Clyde Manschreck (New York: Oxford University Press, 1965), p. 323.

82. See sources in my *From Sacrament to Contract*, chap. 2. See Luther's exposition of the "three estates" theory in *LW* 41:3ff. See further on Melanchthon's views in Rolf B. Huschke, *Melanchthons Lehre vom ordo politicus* (Tübingen: G. Mohn, 1968).

83. Johannes Althusius, *Politica: Methodice digesta atque exemplis sacris et profanis illustrata*, 3rd rev. ed. (1614), reprint ed., Carl J. Friedrich, ed. (Cambridge: Harvard University Press, 1932), with partial translation by Frederick S. Carney (Indianapolis: Liberty Fund, 1995).

purpose of establishing, cultivating, and conserving social life among them," Althusius wrote, citing Aristotle. "The goal of political man is a holy, just, comfortable, and happy symbiosis, a life lacking nothing either necessary or useful."[84] All such political associations are formed by "individual men covenanting among themselves to communicate whatever is necessary and useful for organizing and living in private life."[85] At the base of every such association is marriage, which is a "natural, necessary, economic, and domestic society that is contracted permanently. . . . Therefore it is rightly called the most intense society, friendship, relationship, and union, the seedbed of every other symbiotic association."[86]

Althusius went on to elaborate the relations and functions of husband and wife, adducing scores of classical, biblical, and early Christian sources to support the early modern patriarchal ideal of a hierarchical household under the benign authority of the paterfamilias:

> Husband and wife, who are bound to each other, communicate the advantages and responsibilities of married life. The director and governor of the common affairs of the marital association is the husband. The wife and family are obedient, and do what he commands. The advantages and responsibilities are either proper to one of the spouses, or common to both. Proper advantages and duties are either those the husband communicates to his wife, or those the wife communicates to her husband. The husband communicates to his wife his name, family, reputation, station in life, and economic condition. He also provides her with guidance, legal protection, and defense against violence and injury [and] supplies her with all other necessities, such as management, solicitude, food, and clothing. . . . The wife extends to her husband obedience, subjection, trust, compliance, services, aid, honor, reverence, modesty, and respect. She brings forth children for him, and nurses and trains them. She joins and consoles him in misery and calamity. She accommodates herself to his customs, and without his counsel and consent she does nothing. And thus she renders to her husband an agreeable and peaceful life. There are common advantages and responsibilities that are provided and communicated by both spouses, such as kindness, use of the body for avoiding harlotry and for procreating children, mutual habitation except when absence may be necessary, intimate and familiar companionship, mutual love, fidelity, patience, mutual service, communication of all goods and

---

84. Althusius, *Politica* 1.1-3.
85. Althusius, *Politica* 2.2.
86. Althusius, *Politica* 2.14-15 (Althusius's citations omitted).

right . . . management of the family, administration of household duties, education of children in the true religion, protection against and liberation from perils, and mourning of the dead.[87]

Anglican and Anglo-Puritan writers argued even more expansively than Continental Protestants that marriage at once served and symbolized the commonwealth (literally the "common good") of the couple, the children, the church, and the state. William Perkins put it thus in 1590: "[M]arriage was made and appointed by God himself to be the foundation and seminary of all sorts and kinds of life in the commonwealth and the church. . . . [T]hose families wherein the service of God is performed are, as it were, little churches; yea, even a kind of paradise on earth."[88] Robert Cleaver opened his famous 1598 tract, *A Godly Forme of Householde Gouernment,* with an oft-repeated maxim: "A household is as it were a little commonwealth, by the good government whereof, God's glory may be advanced, the commonwealth which stands of several families, benefited, and all that live in that family, may receive much comfort and commodity."[89] William Gouge premised his massive eight-hundred-page *Domestic Duties* (1622) on the same belief that "the family is a seminary of the Church and the Commonwealth," and is indeed in its own right "a little church, and a little commonwealth, whereby a trial may be made of such as are fit for any place of authority, or subjection in Church or commonwealth."[90]

Like the political and ecclesiastical commonwealths, Anglican divines argued, the domestic commonwealth was created as a hierarchical structure. God had created Eve as "a helpmeet" for Adam. He had called Adam and Eve to mutual society among themselves and mutual procreation of children (Gen. 1:28; 2:18). After the fall he had commanded that Adam "shall rule over" Eve (Gen. 3:16). As heir of Adam, the modern husband was thus the head of his wife. As heir of Eve, the modern wife was his subject, his "helpmeet." Together husband and wife were the heads of their children and the rest of the household. Each of these offices in the family

---

87. Althusius, *Politica* 2.38-49 (Althusias's citations omitted).

88. William Perkins, *Christian Oeconomy or a Short Survey of the Right Manner of Erecting and Ordering a Family According to the Scriptures,* in *The Work of William Perkins,* ed. Ian Breward (Appleford: Sutton Courtney Press, 1970), 3:418-19. I have modernized the spelling and punctuation in this and the next five quotations from Anglican writers.

89. Robert Cleaver, *A Godly Forme of Householde Gouernment* (London: Thomas Creed, 1598), p. 1.

90. William Gouge, *Of Domesticall Duties: Eight Treatises* (London: J. Haviland, 1622), p. 27.

hierarchy was bound by a series of duties, rooted in the Bible and natural law, which dozens of thick household manuals and catechisms of the day elaborated.[91]

Faithful maintenance of domestic duties and offices, Anglican divines believed, was the best guarantee of individual flourishing and social order within the broader commonwealths of church and state. Cleaver put it thus: "[I]f masters of families do not practice catechizing and discipline in their houses and thereby join their helping hands to Magistrates, and Ministers, social order and stability will soon give way to chaos and anarchy."[92] "A conscionable performance of household duties . . . may be accounted a public work," Gouge echoed. For "good members of a family are likely to make good members of church and commonwealth."[93] Daniel Rogers concurred, arguing that a stable marriage and household served as "the right hand of providence, supporter of laws, states, orders, offices, gifts, and services, the glory of peace, . . . the foundation of Countries, Cities, Universities, . . . Crowns and Kingdoms."[94] Dozens of Anglican and Anglo-Puritan writers, from 1600 onward, expounded this "commonwealth model" of marriage.[95]

Early American Formulations

These classical and Christian formulations of the goods and goals of marriage did not remain confined to western Europe. They were also transmitted across the Atlantic to America during the great waves of colonization in the seventeenth and eighteenth centuries and of immigration in the nineteenth and early twentieth. Even a brief sampling of the vast American literature allows us to see how commonplace these traditional Western sentiments became in American theology and law.

Roman Catholic formulations of marriage and its goods, while not so prominent in early America, were present from the colonial beginnings not only in Lord Baltimore's Maryland, founded in 1649, but also and especially

91. See sources in my *From Sacrament to Contract*, chap. 4.
92. Cleaver, p. A4.
93. Gouge, pp. 17, 27.
94. Daniel Rogers, *Matrimoniall Honour* (London: Philip Nevil, 1642), p. 17.
95. See, e.g., G. J. Schochet, *Patriarchalism in Political Thought: The Authoritarian Family and Political Speculation and Attitudes Especially in Seventeenth Century England* (New York: Basic Books, 1975); Mary Shanley, "Marriage Contract and Social Contract in Seventeenth-Century English Political Thought," *Western Political Quarterly* 32 (1979): 79; Beatrice Gottlieb, *The Family in the Western World from the Black Death to the Industrial Age* (Oxford: Oxford University Press, 1993).

in the colonial South and Southwest.⁹⁶ Before the United States acquired the territories of Louisiana (1803), the Floridas (1819), Texas (1836), New Mexico (1848), and California (1848), these colonies were under the formal authority of Spain and the formal jurisdiction of Catholic bishops in San Domingo, Havana, and Mexico. The clergy taught the sacramental theology of marriage, particularly as set out in the Roman catechism of 1566. Both church and state authorities sought to enforce the church's canon laws of marriage, particularly the decree *Tametsi* of 1563 that required parental consent, two witnesses, civil registration, and church consecration for the formation of marriage and that prohibited clerical marriage, intermarriage with non-Catholics, and divorce and remarriage.⁹⁷

With the formal acquisition of these Spanish territories by the United States in the nineteenth century, jurisdiction over marriage shifted to the American Congress and, after statehood, to local state governments. These new civil governments at first rejected portions of the inherited Catholic tradition of marriage — sometimes introducing a persistent anti-Catholic bias in mainline American law and theology of marriage that lasted for more than a century. But the Catholic clergy in these vast former Spanish territories were generally left free to teach the doctrines and retain the canons of marriage for their own parishioners — a prerogative already extended to the growing numbers of American Catholic bishoprics along the Atlantic seaboard and in the Midwest.⁹⁸

In the nineteenth and early twentieth centuries, American Catholic bishops issued hundreds of sermons and pastoral letters that reflected traditional Catholic formulations on the goods of marriage.⁹⁹ They repeated and

---

96. See especially Hans W. Baade, "The Form of Marriage in Spanish North America," *Cornell Law Review* 61 (1975): 1-89.

97. This was not true of American Catholic communities, outside of Spanish territory, that came within the ecclesiastical provinces of Baltimore, Philadelphia, New York, and Boston and, later, ecclesiastical provinces in the West. The original settlers in these non-Spanish communities were mostly from Britain, Scotland, or other parts of northern Europe where *Tametsi* was not in effect. They thus continued to recognize the pre-Tridentine Catholic canon law that a secret marriage formed by mutual consent was valid, even without priestly consecration. This disparity continued among some American Catholics until the Tridentine legislation was written into the 1917 *Code of Canon Law*. Baade, pp. 19-24, 36-38; John T. Noonan Jr., *The Power to Dissolve: Lawyers and Marriages in the Courts of the Roman Curia* (Cambridge, Mass.: Belknap Press, 1972), pp. 255-56.

98. See sources and discussion in Noonan, *Power to Dissolve*, pp. 302-40; Brundage, pp. 608-17.

99. A number of these American pastoral letters were prompted by the promulgation of Pius IX's *Syllabus of Errors* (1864), which included a list of ten errors about marriage. See, e.g.,

glossed endlessly the traditional formula of *proles, fides, et sacramentum* — emphasizing, like their fellow European bishops, the goods of procreation and education, the ills of contraception and prostitution, and the mortal perils of intermarriage and divorce.[100]

More than a few American Catholic bishops, however, also emphasized the unique psychological, social, and political goods of marriage — anticipating by more than a century the formulations of Vatican II. An 1863 Lenten pastoral of Bishop Augustin Verot of Savannah, Georgia, provides a good example. Lamenting the breakdown of the family born of the budding urbanization, industrialization, and modernization of his day, newly exacerbated by the Civil War, Verot declared that the intact marital household "is at the bottom of all the good that can be done among men."

> The Family is a society instituted and appointed by God himself, for *nature* is but a borrowed name to express the Maker and Author of this universe, and of all the laws which govern it. It is God who instituted and blessed marriage, and from the laws of marriage husband, wife, and children form a perfect and close society, sacred on account of its author, and indissoluble by the very nature of the ties which unite the members of it together. Hence the domestic society, because it is directly and immediately the work of God, is or ought to be a mirror, reflecting the supreme law of heaven, order, peace, and holiness, more exquisitely and perfectly than civil or political societies, which are more or less of human origin.[101]

Verot then waxed at length about the social and political utility of the family — sounding very much like the Protestant reformers before him and the Vatican II reformers after him: "The Family is the first school where we learn good or evil. It is the source and fountainhead of morality or immorality, of a Christian or an infidel life, of virtue or vice, of good behavior or profligacy. . . . Oh! that this paramount importance of early impressions and of do-

---

Pastoral Letter of the Most Rev. Martin John Spalding (Baltimore: Kelly & Piet, 1865), pp. 1-43, esp. 41-42.

100. See, e.g., the collection in Hugh J. Nolan, ed., *Pastoral Letters of the American Hierarchy, 1792-1970* (Huntington, Ind.: Our Sunday Visitor, 1971). See discussion of shifting (American) Catholic views of marriage in Christine Firer Hinze, "Catholic: Family Unity and Diversity within the Body of Christ," in *Faith Traditions and the Family*, ed. Phyllis D. Airhart and Margaret Lambert Bendroth (Louisville: Westminster John Knox, 1996), pp. 53-72, and further the chapters by Hinze and Mary Stewart Van Leeuwen and John Wall and Bonnie Miller-McLemore herein.

101. *Lenten Pastoral of Right Rev. A. Verot, Bishop of Savannah and Administrator Apostolic of Florida for 1863* (Savannah, 1863), p. 4.

mestic training were well understood, felt, and acted upon. This would at once bring about the most salutary reformation in society, in church and state."[102] Properly viewed, Verot continued, marriage is "*a domestic church . . . a society bound by the ties of religion, faith, and virtue, yet more than by the bonds of a common origin and identity of blood.*"[103] The Christian family is "the first step in virtue, the foundation of solid merit, a school of morality and piety, a centre of union, love, and peace, an unfailing element of future usefulness and greatness, a terrestrial paradise, an image of the blessed City of God, where order and happiness prevail undisturbed and unalterable."[104]

Protestant formulations of marriage and its goods were more prominent in early American writings, and more influential in American law. By the turn of the nineteenth century, the Atlantic seaboard was a veritable checkerboard of Protestant pluralism — Anglican, Lutheran, Puritan, Presbyterian, Reformed, Huguenot, Baptist, Methodist, Moravian, and more. This Protestant pluralism only increased with the Second Great Awakening of 1800-1860.[105] These Protestant polities, though hardly uniform in their marital norms and habits, were largely united in their adherence to basic Protestant teachings about marriage inherited from western Europe.[106] While adhering to many of

---

102. *Lenten Pastoral*, pp. 4-5.

103. *Lenten Pastoral*, p. 9 (emphasis added).

104. *Lenten Pastoral*, p. 9. See comparable views in the pastoral letter of the Third Plenary Council of Baltimore (1884), in *Pastoral Letters of the American Hierarchy, 1792-1970*, pp. 175-76; *Pastoral Letter of the Right Rev. Michael Joseph O. Farrell, Bishop of Trenton on Christian Marriage* (New York: Benzinger Bros., 1883), esp. pp. 4-7; "Pastoral Letter Issued by the Roman Catholic Hierarchy of the United States" (1919), in *Pastoral Letters of the American Hierarchy, 1792-1970*, pp. 309-11. These views were elaborated in various Catholic household manuals and catechetical texts. See, e.g., Bernard O'Reilly, *The Mirror of True Womanhood* (New York: Peter F. Collier, 1878); this work is a 466-page spiritual "Dr. Spock" for women, premised on the assumption that the household is "a little Eden" (see p. 7).

105. For a detailed demographic study, see Edwin S. Gaustad, *Historical Atlas of Religion in America*, 2nd ed. (Oxford: Oxford University Press, 2000).

106. The most important difference among these colonies and early American states was over whether marriages could be contracted before a civil official only, as New England Puritans allowed, or required church consecration, as Anglican communities required. Among numerous recent studies, see sources and discussion in Peter W. Bardaglio, *Reconstructing the Household: Families, Sex, and the Law in the Nineteenth-Century South* (Chapel Hill and London: University of North Carolina Press, 1995); Richard Chused, *Private Acts in Public Places: A Social History of Divorce in the Formative Era of American Family Law* (Philadelphia: University of Pennsylvania Press, 1994); Stephen M. Frank, *Life with Father: Parenthood and Masculinity in the Nineteenth-Century American North* (Baltimore and London: Johns Hopkins University Press, 1998); Jan Lewis, *The Pursuit of Happiness: Family and Values in Jefferson's Virginia* (Cambridge: Cambridge University Press, 1983); Stephanie McMurray, *Masters of Small Worlds* (New

the same basic Christian norms of sex, marriage, and domestic life taught by Catholics, they rejected sacramental views of marriage and ecclesiastical jurisdiction over marital formation, maintenance, and dissolution. They encouraged ministers to be married. They permitted religious intermarriage. They truncated the law of impediments. They allowed for divorce on proof of fault. They encouraged remarriage of those divorced or widowed.

Protestant theologians, of various denominations, repeated the familiar Protestant trilogy of marital goods. Many Anglican and Methodist writers — following the Anglican *Book of Common Prayer* of 1662 and its Episcopalian revision of 1789 — rendered this trilogy as "procreation, love, and protection" and expressed ample reticence about the propriety of divorce and remarriage.[107] Most other Protestant writers — following Lutheran and Calvinist confessions and conventions — rendered this as "love, protection, and procreation" and countenanced divorce and remarriage if one or more of these goods of marriage were irreconcilably compromised by the fault of one of the parties.[108]

These variations on traditional formulations of marital goods did not prevent American Protestant theologians from underscoring the health benefits of marriage to the couple — particularly to the husband. John Bayley, for example, an influential Methodist preacher, wrote a lengthy volume in 1857 expounding the ideal nature, structure, and purpose of marriage. His central thesis was that "prudent marriages are favorable to health, long life, and prosperity."[109] He defended this proposition with twenty-odd pages of quotations from classical and Christian authors. Among his favorites was the Anglican divine Jeremy Taylor, who had rhapsodized: "If you are for pleasure, marry; if you prize rosy health, marry. A good wife is heaven's last best gift to man — his angel and minister of graces innumerable — his gem of many virtues — his casket of jewels."[110] Bayley then defended at length the conventional legal

---

York and Oxford: Oxford University Press, 1995); Daniel Blake Smith, *Inside the Great House: Planter Family Life in Eighteenth-Century Chesapeake Society* (Ithaca, N.Y., and London: Cornell University Press, 1980); Meril D. Smith, *Breaking the Bonds: Marital Discord in Pennsylvania, 1730-1830* (New York and London: New York University Press, 1991).

107. See, e.g., George Bourne, *Marriage Indissoluble and Divorce Unscriptural* (Harrisonburg, Va.: Davidson & Bourne, 1813), pp. 9-14, 23-35; Bufford W. Coe, *John Wesley and Marriage* (Bethlehem, Pa.: Lehigh Press; London: Associated University Presses, 1996), esp. pp. 52ff.

108. See, e.g., Howard Malcom, *The Christian's Rule of Marriage* (Boston: James Loring, 1834).

109. John Bayley, *Marriage as It Is, and as It Should Be* (New York: M. W. Dodd, 1857), p. 13. See pp. 9-29.

110. Quoted in Bayley, p. 26.

requirements of marital formation — formal betrothals, public banns, parental consent, two witnesses, civil registration, and church consecration — and set out the respective "duties of love" between husband and wife, parent and child.

George Bourne of Virginia, in his oft-reprinted tome, voiced comparable sentiments about the emotional and moral benefits of married life. God has created marriage to be "sacred and honorable, of high Distinction, and nearly combined with the dignity and fruition of human nature," Bourne wrote. When marriage is properly entered into, it provides "every blessing which man can enjoy during his abode in this pilgrimage state; it diminishes his pain, excites his sympathies, purifies his desires, invigorates his exertions, unfolds his usefulness, duplicates his enjoyments, counteracts his vicious propensities, exalts his character, animates his devotional principles for present rectitude and future bliss everlasting."[111] Scores of other theological tracts and sermons on marriage are at hand to document this common "Protestant temperament" about the individual goods and benefits of marriage.[112]

Ironically, it was the American jurists, more than the American Protestant theologians, who expounded the social and political goods of marriage and family — adducing Anglican moralists, Roman jurists, and Greek philosophers alike to drive home the legal priorities of marriage. For example, Chancellor James Kent, one of the great early systematizers of American law, wrote about the spiritual and social utility of marriage:

> The primary and most important of the domestic relations is that of husband and wife. It has its foundations in nature, and is the only lawful relation by which Providence has permitted the continuance of the human race. In every age it has had a propitious influence on the moral improvement and happiness of mankind. It is one of the chief foundations of social order. We may justly place to the credit of the institution of marriage a great share of the blessings which flow from the refinement of manners, the education of children, the sense of justice, and cultivation of the liberal arts.[113]

111. Bourne, pp. 9, 12, 113. See also p. 18 ("Early marriages combine advantages so numerous, personal sanctity, relative comfort, social utility, and national stability").

112. The phrase is from the landmark work of Philip Greven, *The Protestant Temperament: Patterns of Child-Rearing, Religious Experience, and the Self in Early America* (Chicago: University of Chicago Press, 1977). For a good sampling of American Protestant commonplaces about marriage from the turn of the twentieth century forward, see Airhart and Bendroth, *Faith Traditions and the Family*.

113. James Kent, *Commentaries on American Law,* 12th ed. by O. W. Holmes, Jr. (Boston: Little Brown, 1896), 2:76.

W. C. Rogers, a leading jurist at the end of the nineteenth century, opened his oft-reprinted treatise on the law of domestic relations with a veritable homily on marriage:

> In a sense it is a consummation of the Divine to "multiply and replenish the earth." It is the state of existence ordained by the Creator, who has fashioned man and woman expressly for the society and enjoyment incident to mutual companionship. This Divine plan is supported and promoted by natural instinct, as it were, on the part of both for the society of each other. It is the highest state of existence, ... the only stable substructure of our social, civil, and religious institutions. Religion, government, morals, progress, enlightened learning, and domestic happiness must all fall into most certain and inevitable decay when the married state ceases to be recognized or respected. Accordingly, we have in this state of man and woman the most essential foundation of religion, social purity, and domestic happiness.[114]

Other standard legal texts spoke of marriage as "the highest state of existence," "a public institution of universal concern," "the very basis of the whole fabric of civilized society," "a spiritual association ... transcendent in its importance both to individuals and to society."[115]

Likewise, the United States Supreme Court spoke repeatedly of marriage as "more than a mere contract," "a Godly ordinance," "a sacred obligation."[116] In *Murphy v. Ramsey* (1885), one of a series of Supreme Court cases upholding the constitutionality of antipolygamy laws, Justice Field declared for the Court: "For, certainly, no legislation can be supposed more wholesome and necessary in the founding of a free, self-governing commonwealth ... than that which seeks to establish it on the basis of the idea of the family, as consisting in and springing from the union for life of one man and one woman in the holy estate of matrimony; the sure foundation of all that is stable and noble in our civilization; the best guarantee of that reverent morality

---

114. W. C. Rogers, *A Treatise on the Law of Domestic Relations* (Chicago: T. H. Flood, 1891), sec. 2, p. 2.

115. James Shouler, *A Treatise on the Law of Marriage, Divorce, Separation, and Domestic Relations*, 6th ed. (Albany: Matthew Bender, 1921), 1:17-19; Joel Bishop, *New Commentaries on Marriage, Divorce, and Separation* (Chicago: T. H. Flood, 1891), 1:4-15; 2:217; Joseph Story, *Commentaries on the Conflict of Laws* (Boston: Hillard, Gray, and Co., 1834), sec. 109; Chester Vernier, *American Family Laws* (Stanford: Stanford University Press, 1931-38), 1:45.

116. *Maynard v. Hill*, 125 U.S. 190, 210-211 (1888); *Reynolds v. United States*, 98 U.S. 145, 165 (1879); *Murphy v. Ramsey*, 114 U.S. 15, 45 (1885); *Davis v. Beason*, 133 U.S. 333, 341-342 (1890).

which is the source of all beneficent progress in social and political improvement."[117]

The Supreme Court elaborated these sentiments in *Maynard v. Hill* (1888), in another opinion by Justice Field:

> [W]hilst marriage is often termed ... a civil contract — generally to indicate that it must be founded upon the agreement of the parties, and does not require any religious ceremony for its solemnization — it is something more than a mere contract. The consent of the parties is of course essential to its existence, but when the contract to marry is executed by marriage, a relation between the parties is created which they cannot change. Other contracts may be modified, restricted, or enlarged, or entirely released upon the consent of the parties. Not so with marriage. The relation once formed, the law steps in and holds the parties to various obligations and liabilities. It is an institution, in the maintenance of which in its purity the public is deeply interested, for it is the foundation of the family and society, without which there would be neither civilization nor progress.[118]

This famous passage has been quoted in 134 federal and state cases since its proclamation in 1888.

Summary and Conclusions

The health paradigm of marriage is both very new and very old. What is new is the wealth of recent statistical evidence demonstrating that, for most adult parties most of the time, married life is better than single life, marital cohabitation is better than nonmarital cohabitation, married parents do better than single parents in raising their children. According to several recent studies — ably and amply summarized in this volume — married folks on average live longer, happier, and safer lives. They are more satisfied, prosperous, and efficient. They receive better hygiene, health care, and coinsurance. Their children develop better emotional, social, and moral skills. These data on the health benefits of marriage are now emerging with increasing alacrity within a variety of modern professions. They have enormous implications for our professional responsibilities to couples and children, and to the institution of marriage itself.

117. *Murphy v. Ramsey*, p. 45.
118. *Maynard v. Hill*, pp. 210-11.

The health paradigm of marriage is also very old. It repeats and refines a number of ancient and enduring Western ideas about the goods and goals of marriage. Already in the centuries before Christ and before the Christianization of the West, classical Greek and Roman writers taught that marriage is a natural institution to which most men and women are naturally inclined; that marriage is a useful, pleasant, moral, and even sacred institution; that it provides an efficient pooling of property and division of labor and resources within the household; that it provides mutual care, protection, and compensation to couples; that it serves both for the fulfillment, companionship, and happiness of spouses and for the procreation, nurture, and education of children.

The Roman Catholic tradition, building on Augustine and Aquinas, wove these classical insights into the famous theory that marriage has three inherent goods: (1) *fides* — a faithfulness and friendship between husband and wife that goes beyond that demanded of any other temporal relationship; (2) *proles* — children, who are to be nurtured and educated to perpetuate the human species and to transmit and live out the proper norms and habits of spiritual and temporal life; and (3) *sacramentum* — an enduring expression of Christ's love for his church, an indissoluble channel of God's grace to sanctify the couple, their children, and the broader community. Particularly, since the Second Vatican Council (1962-65), the Catholic Church has emphasized the need to keep these three marital goods in balance and has held out the covenant of marital love as the new organizing idiom of the goods of marriage. The church has also recently emphasized that marriage serves for the physical, emotional, moral, and spiritual "perfection" of a man and a woman, and that the household is a "domestic church" and a model of love, charity, stewardship, authority, dignity, faithfulness, discipline, and care for each new generation of children to learn.

The Protestant tradition, from its sixteenth-century beginnings, placed emphasis not only on the intrinsic goods but also on the instrumental goals of the covenant or estate of marriage. Marriage was created by God to foster love, to deter sin, and to produce children. If one or more of these created marital goals were permanently frustrated, those parties who could not reconcile themselves to this condition could seek divorce and remarry. Particularly Luther and Calvin emphasized further that marriage has "uses" in life. Marriage deters vice by furnishing preferred options to prostitution, promiscuity, pornography, and other forms of sexual pathos. It cultivates virtue by offering love, care, and nurture to its members, and by holding out a model of charity, education, and sacrifice to the broader community. It enhances the life of a man and a woman by providing them with a community of caring and sharing, of stability and support, of nurture and welfare. It enhances the life of the child by providing it with a chrysalis of nurture and love, with a highly individualized form of socialization and education. Such views echoed loudly in the theological and legal literature of the American colonies and the early American republic.

For all its theological and philosophical diversity, therefore, the West has had a long and thick overlapping consensus that marriage is good, does good, and has goods both for the couple and for the children. Classical, Patristic, Catholic, and Protestant writers alike have all recognized the natural teleology and utility of marriage: (1) the natural drive on the part of most adults toward the institution of marriage because of the inherent goods of individual survival, flourishing, happiness, and even perfectibility that it provides; and (2) the natural capacity on the part of most adults to engage in the expected performance of marriage — the unique combination of sexual, physical, economical, emotional, charitable, moral, and spiritual performances that become marriage. Obviously, there are ample exceptions to this natural norm of marriage that the tradition has long recognized. Some are called to celibacy or to the single or widowed life. Some lack the physical capacity or emotional temperament to engage in marriage. Some who get married should not be, and need to be removed from the institution through annulment or divorce. But the general inclination and instruction of nature, of the human body, of the human psyche, of the human heart is for marriage, the Western tradition teaches.

The new social science data can thus be viewed as the start to a new chapter in a long and familiar Western story about the goods and goals of marriage. This new social science chapter supplements and supports somewhat the many more theologically explicit and expansive chapters that have been written and continue to be written. The new social science data present older prudential insights about marriage with more statistical precision. They present ancient avuncular observations about marital benefits with more inductive generalization. They reduce common Western observations about marital health into more precise and measurable categories. These new social science data thus offer something of a neutral apologetic for marriage. They provide a start to a useful bilingual vocabulary that allows us to move more easily between traditional and contemporary, theological and natural, spiritual and civil, confessional and professional terms and concepts of marriage.

What is still largely missing from this new social science chapter of marriage is a careful demonstration and documentation of the second core insight of the Western tradition — that marriage is good not only for the couple and their children, but also for the broader civic communities of which they are a part. The ancient Greeks and Roman Stoics called marriage "the foundation of republic," "the private font of public virtue." The Church Fathers called marital and familial love "the seedbed of the city," "the force that welds society together." Catholics called the family "a domestic church," "a kind of school of deeper humanity." Protestants called the household a "little church," a "little state," a "little seminary," a "little commonwealth." American jurists and theologians taught that marriage is both private and public, individual and social, temporal and transcendent in quality — a natural if not a spiritual estate, a useful if not an essential association, a pillar if not the foundation of civil society.

At the core of all these metaphors is a perennial Western ideal that stable marriages and families are essential to the survival, flourishing, and happiness of the greater commonwealths of church, state, and civil society. And a breakdown of marriage and the family will eventually have devastating consequences on these larger social institutions. To date, we have ample anecdotal evidence of the social pathos that sometimes follows the breakdown of the family, and ample political manipulation of the same, particularly in election years. But a careful measuring and mapping of the health benefits of marriage and the family for church, state, and civil society alike would be an apt conclusion to this latest chapter in the long Western story of the goods and goals of marriage.

Law

CHAPTER 4

Is the Genie out of the Bottle?

Muller Davis

Divorce is a disruption of the collective interests of the family by the self-interest of one or both of the spouses. Divorce is selfish. In thirty-three years of concentrating my practice in family law, I have seldom seen a spouse who obtained a divorce out of care for his partner or for the sake of his children.

Society has reacted to divorce in different ways. John Witte, Jr., writes about the historical formulations of marriage. After the Catholics had outlawed it, divorce was again introduced by the early Protestants in cases where one of the spouses committed an unforgiven breach of marital love, for example, by adultery, desertion, or cruelty.[1] Divorce law in America prior to the late 1960s in most instances also required the commission of a fault breach of the marriage, such as adultery, desertion, or cruelty, before a divorce could be granted. But, although the American divorce law was almost without exception restrictive in text, it permitted divorce in practice. Beginning in the late 1960s, movements emphasizing individual rights, and particularly the rights of women, began to sweep away the restrictive language of divorce statutes. Divorce proliferated. There were 479,000 divorces in 1965 and 1,036,000 divorces in 1975.[2] Currently almost 50 percent of those who marry, divorce. One million children per year lose a parent from their homes.[3] Young people have lost confidence in their ability to achieve lifetime marriages.[4]

---

1. See the article by John Witte, Jr., chap. 3 in this volume.

2. John W. Wright, ed., *The New York Times 2000 Almanac* (New York: Penguin Books, 1999), p. 295.

3. Barbara Dafoe Whitehead, "Dan Quayle Was Right," *Atlantic Monthly*, April 1993, p. 50.

4. David Popenoe and Barbara Dafoe Whitehead, *The State of Our Unions, 2000* (Rutgers, N.J.: National Marriage Project, 2000), p. 8.

Society treats marriage as a romantic ideal, but if the ideal does not work out for one of the partners, regardless of the desire of the other partner, society now endorses divorce. The process has been called "unilateral no fault divorce."[5] The bias is against marriage preservation.

A small but articulate reaction has emerged. The reaction says that the interests of those reluctant adults and children who do not believe that divorce is a solution to their problems are being sacrificed to the prerogatives of individuals to do what they want. One of the principal new arguments against divorce relies on analyses that attempt to demonstrate that spouses and children are better off when the family is intact.

The ripple of reaction is a beginning, but divorce has become entrenched in our society. To overcome the ethos of divorce will take a reformulation of societal values as fundamental as the one in the late 1960s and 1970s that changed society's disapproval of divorce to an acceptance of divorce. Even the root question: Do marriage and family have value that is worth defending against the challenge of alternative relationships and methods of child rearing? requires examination. Needless to say, the undertaking is a large one, and this chapter, which considers lawyers and the law, is only a small part of the pie.

Lawyers

What have practicing lawyers contributed to the support of marriage and the family, when the need for shoring up is so apparent? The answer has to be: not much. There are many reasons, beginning in the law schools, extending into the nature of practicing law, and reinforced with how and when fees are paid by clients to lawyers.

Most of the best law schools in the past have not given a high priority to family law. The emphasis was more on commercial practice. The family law courses that existed concentrated narrowly on the substantive law and the mechanics of getting people divorced. The lawyer's role in supporting marriage may not even have been considered relevant. The education for the most part was in the law and its processes, not in the emotional and psychological ramifications of divorce. Specialization has its benefits, but it seldom produces Renaissance men and women.

Law schools' attention to family law and its psychological ramifications

---

5. Lynn D. Wardle, "Divorce Reform at the Turn of the Millennium: Certainties and Possibilities," *Family Law Quarterly* 33, no. 3 (fall 1999): 783.

has improved,[6] but it is not yet apparent that the increased attention to psychology has carried over into the practice. Lawyers seldom address the human concerns that are at the core of marriage and divorce. Their focus remains on who gets what, be it income, property, or children.

Spouses in divorce are more frequently than not on different timetables. The spouse who has decided to divorce usually reaches his lawyer's office first. In the language of the psychologists, he has already gone through or is not interested in the process of mourning the loss of his existing marriage. His partner, on the other hand, may not want to give up her marriage or become a single mother to the parties' children. The spouse who seeks the divorce will have no difficulty finding a lawyer who speaks his language. The reluctant spouse, however, may interview many lawyers who will tell her what she can get out of the divorce, or how she can get even with her husband, before, if ever, she locates one lawyer who will listen to her desire to keep her marriage together and explain to her how to enlarge the possibilities of preserving her family. The aggressor male and reluctant female roles in the example are just as often reversed, with the same results.

Failure of attention to the spouse who wants to talk about keeping her marriage is not a necessary result. Lawyers can use their good and persuasive offices to support marriage. They can analyze what tools are available to the reluctant spouse to draw the aggressive spouse into conversations supervised by a mental health professional. For example, the aggressor spouse may be seeking his partner's cooperation in actually securing the divorce. Whenever someone wants something, it transfers to his counterpart a measure of negotiating strength. There can be a quid pro quo. The reluctant spouse can trade the possibility of her cooperation if counseling proves futile for an agreement from the aggressor spouse to enter counseling. Albeit the two spouses will have different agendas, the one to expedite his divorce, the other to reconcile her marriage, the door is open to a dialogue, the development of information, analysis, and there is no foregone conclusion.

This opportunity of course will never occur if the lawyer does not ask appropriate questions and listen, if he does not consider the support of marriage a part of his job description, if he takes the position that a client seeking to keep her marriage together is in the wrong office, if he believes that lawyers who encourage reconciliation appear weak, or if he tries to shunt the whole problem off to the mental health professionals.

Contributing to the failure of lawyers to support families is money. Lawyers are paid more for divorces than they are for reconciliations. The

---

6. Sanford N. Katz, "Prologue," *Family Law Quarterly* 33, no. 3 (fall 1999): 436, 441-42.

money incentive is therefore wrong, as it is in so much of divorce litigation. Fees tied to the number of hours expended, while giving the public some perception of precision, do not encourage brevity.

Fault Laws

If lawyers are not a strong influence in the preservation of the family, does the substantive law support marriage? The current law and the ideas for reform can best be judged against the past.

The laws in almost all states in America prior to 1969 were restrictive fault divorce laws. Marriage was loosely perceived as a contract between two parties that could be dissolved only if one of the spouses committed an act that was legally recognized as incompatible with the continuation of the marriage. The incompatible action was called a fault ground for divorce. Divorce was granted by courts only upon proof of a fault ground, such as adultery, extreme and repeated cruelty, desertion for the space of one year, and the like. At the granting of the divorce, there was an adjudication of a guilty party and an innocent party. The seemingly restrictive laws were satisfying to those people who for religious or other reasons believed that marriage was a union or a contract for life that could not be dissolved except in the most exceptional circumstances. But the fault laws also did not necessarily disappoint those more permissive thinkers who sought divorces, at least those who could afford the process.[7]

There were many avenues open to obtaining a divorce. The most common method was by agreement. But reaching the agreement almost invariably translated into money. If the spouse who sought the divorce was guilty of adultery, for example, he could not obtain a divorce in a fault state because he was guilty of a ground for divorce. He therefore had to financially satisfy the innocent spouse before the innocent spouse would agree to proceed against him to obtain the divorce. If the negotiations failed, a trial could result in denying the divorce, even under circumstances where each spouse proved the other guilty of a ground for divorce. Then the spouses, if they did not then come to an agreement, were consigned to continue their marriage after a prolonged, rancorous session in the courthouse.

A potential escape was a divorce in Nevada, and later a few offshore jurisdictions, which had more liberal divorce laws. But a Nevada divorce was

---

7. See Max Rheinstein, *Marriage Stability, Divorce, and the Law* (Chicago: University of Chicago Press, 1972).

expensive because it required a trip for out-of-staters, Nevada lawyers, and a stay in a Nevada hotel or other lodging for six weeks in order to establish the required residence. Afterwards, when the itinerant spouse returned to his home state, the Nevada divorce was often attacked with the argument that the Nevada residence was not bona fide and therefore the divorce should not be recognized in the home state.

This is an oversimplified summary of the tangle of fault divorce laws, but even it produces the inevitable conclusion that fault divorce laws did not readily produce equitable results and often favored the wealthy. Despite their inadequacies, a fair question is whether fault divorce laws, which at least on their face made obtaining a divorce more difficult, contributed to the preservation of marriages. Certainly they did not restrict the people who had the wherewithal to manipulate the system. There were, however, dramatically fewer divorces under the fault laws. A partial reason is that the less well-off had less access to the system. A more complete answer is that the restrictive divorce laws did not stand alone. They were a part of the cultural values of society that disapproved of divorce and favored the preservation of marriage. Marriage therefore had a framework of support in place, not only from the legal system, but also from families, churches, friends, children, schools, workplaces, media — from almost all of society. Marriages in need of repair had institutional resources from which to seek help. It was right to be married and wrong to be divorced.

No-Fault Laws

No-fault divorce laws were put in place quickly throughout America beginning in 1969.[8] The time periods and terms vary somewhat from state to state,[9] but every state now has no-fault grounds for divorce,[10] which permit a spouse who is dissatisfied with her marriage to obtain a divorce with proof of no more than her dissatisfaction.[11] The theory is that a marriage in which one or both spouses will no longer participate is irretrievably broken down.

Divorce has proliferated under the no-fault divorce laws in numbers never before seen in history.

8. Wardle, p. 783.
9. Linda D. Elrod and Robert G. Spector, "A Review of the Year in Family Law: Century Ends with Unresolved Issues," *Family Law Quarterly* 33, no. 4 (winter 2000): 907-19, chart 4.
10. Sandra Morgan Little, "Where We've Been and Where We're Headed," *Family Law Quarterly* 33, no. 3 (fall 1999): ix.
11. Wardle, p. 783.

Fault law and restricted divorce were a reflection of a more conservative society that did not approve of premarital cohabitation, adultery, or divorce. No-fault law and unrestricted divorce are part of a society whose concern for those norms has shifted from disapproval to acceptance. In terms of desirable goods, preservation of family units has given way to individual self-fulfillment.

Coincidentally, a body of research evolved that gave to easy divorce a respectable sociological and theoretical foundation. The research concludes that spouses in unhappy marriages are better off obtaining divorces and pursuing their own individual lives. Children are resilient and can recover from broken families. Psychological therapy and drugs can repair people under most circumstances, and therefore any damage that results from divorce can be fixed. The earlier concern for children of divorce and for the spouse who wanted to keep her marriage together was misplaced. The good outcome of the research also connects with the traditional emphasis in America on individual rights, and with the confidence of the women's movement that women can be independent and can make their own way.

One writer has described the change in society as follows:

[T]here has also been a . . . shift from a "moral" to a "psychological" view of personal affairs.

[A] central feature of the psychologic view is that it replaces moral discourse with medical discourse and moral thought with therapeutic thought. That shift may usefully be understood in terms of the role attributed to human happiness in social life. The old view held that men and women were obligated to lead a good life as that was defined by religious or social convention. Happiness was not the purpose of these conventions, but was expected to be a by-product of performing one's duties. If it did not come, however, one would be consoled by knowing one had led the right kind of life. The psychologic view, at least in its ideal type, denies that there are religious or social conventions that are independently valid. It holds that life's goal is the search for personal well-being, adjustment, and contentment — in short, for "health."

The doctrine finds its legal analogues in the law's tendency to see families in terms of their individual members and not as units and in the legal tendency to make it easier to leave a family. . . . These legal tendencies are sustained by psychologic man's pragmatic view of personal relations — the view that a relationship should be maintained only if it "works," that "options" should be kept numerous and open to "facilitate personal growth," and that living in a family is a matter of psychological adjustment, a technical matter of finding happiness, not a matter of moral relations. This view prefers temporary marriages, temporary nonmarital arrangements, and temporary children, and the law is coming to accommodate it.[12]

Rather than the psychologic view, Schneider might have called the change in society the solipsistic view.

It is not a surprise that a crumbling of the institutional support of marriage has accompanied society's change of attitude about the acceptance of divorce. For example, families, clergy, psychologists, and magazine columnists, who formerly supported lifetime marriage, now counsel on how to get through a divorce and live your life afterwards. The most pathetic example of the weakness of society's institutional support of marriage is found in our politicians who persist in giving voice to family values while committing public adultery with impunity in the highest seats of power.

William J. Doherty reports that over 60 percent of marriage and family therapists are "neutral" on the subject of marriage or divorce in therapy. It does not matter whether they facilitate a good marriage or a good divorce. The result is a substitution of values: marriage value is given up for individual self-interest value.[13]

An ironic application of society's exaggerated concern for individual prerogatives as opposed to the interests of the family unit occurs in individual therapy. If a person is unhappy despite his acknowledged freedom to pursue his own destiny, he seeks help from a counselor. The mental health professional works on the person's ego in isolation. For example, stated simply, if the patient has a weak ego and is depressed because he is insecure, the psychiatrist attempts to discover the causes of the weak ego and works to strengthen it, thereby improving the well-being quotient of the patient. But because this process occurs in the privacy of the psychiatrist's office, it does not take into account its effect on those around the patient outside the doctor's office.

Lawyers commonly see, but often do not recognize or know how to deal with, the phenomenon of the divorce that is caused by just one spouse undergoing therapy. The spouse in therapy is "cured." His weak ego is made strong, his anxiety is ameliorated, and he gains the measure of happiness that he is seeking. But at the same time, his solitary therapy shifts the balance in his marriage. The spouse not in therapy, without any preparation, is required to deal with a different person. The resulting marriage catastrophe, insofar as

---

12. Carl E. Schneider, "Moral Discourse and the Transformation of American Family Law," *Michigan Law Review* 83 (August 1985): 1845, 1847, 1855.

13. See article by William J. Doherty and Jason S. Carroll, chap. 10 in this volume.

the spouse not in therapy and the children are concerned, is compounded and made more inevitable by the rigid Freudian rules of therapeutic confidentiality. The treating doctor commonly refuses to speak to the spouse not in therapy. She is therefore completely cut off from any information concerning matters of critical importance to her own well-being, her marriage, and the parties' children.

The reason that this practice contributes to many divorces is that it ignores, as if they did not matter, the three entities of the marriage: husband, wife, and the marriage itself. Therapy, if it is to benefit the marriage, must involve all three entities. Therapy in fragile marriages that treats only one spouse will not strengthen the marriage. Marital therapy should involve both spouses and thereby be capable of reaching the marriage itself. If the spouses are being treated separately or one spouse is being treated alone, the two spouses should also meet with a joint therapist so that the marital entity is not left out, so that the strengthened ego, in our example, does not happen in isolation without the participation of the other spouse.

The Cost

There has been a recent reaction to the solipsistic view. The only question is whether it is a reaction of sufficient strength to dislodge the not surprising preoccupation with individual happiness in a society that emphasizes the rights of individuals in almost every context. Is the genie already out of the bottle?

The initial disquieting research, which may have first fueled the reaction, was published in 1985 and was conducted by Lenore J. Weitzman in California. She concluded that financially all was not as advertised in the divorce paradise. Contrary to expectations that were supported by the women's movement, women were not able to become financially independent after divorce at the same standards of living they had enjoyed during their marriages. Even worse, after a divorce men's economic circumstances dramatically increased, while the women's economic positions and those of their children living with them deteriorated.[14] Although some of her research methods and findings were later questioned, Weitzman's *The Divorce Revolution* caused the proponents of no-fault divorce and women's independence to relinquish one of their fundamental beliefs: that the majority of women could financially sustain themselves after a divorce without help. There followed in most states

---

14. Lenore J. Weitzman, *The Divorce Revolution* (New York: Free Press, 1985).

amendments to the spousal and children's support laws providing more and longer support for dependent women.

The next body of reaction to proliferating divorce has also been expressed in terms of cost, but it has broadened the concept beyond economic cost to women. Recent research emphasizes the costs of divorce to children. A child of divorce is commonly subjected to abrupt and traumatic changes: loss of father on a regular and consistent basis, live-in boyfriend or friends, stepfather, and so on.[15] Most divorces spawn an absent father. An absent father is likely to spend less money on his children for their schools, colleges, lessons, extracurricular activities, support, and the like than does a present, involved father. The absent father leaves his children less protected, more subject to abuse, and his daughters are more likely to become pregnant as teenagers. Stepfathers do not have the same tie to the children with whom they live as do the children's natural fathers. Stepfathers are seldom adequate substitutes for natural fathers. Children of divorce perform less well in school, are less likely to graduate, and are less likely to matriculate into college. The prevalence of delinquency in broken homes is 10 to 15 percent higher than in intact homes.[16]

Contrary to previous research, the findings are now that children may not recover from divorce and can suffer long-term negative effects. For example, significant numbers experience moderate to severe depression and difficulty in establishing love relationships.[17] Children of divorced parents are two to three times more likely to dissolve their own marriages than are children of intact marriages.[18]

The divorce process itself has a decidedly negative effect on children. From the beginning, no matter how bad the circumstances, almost no child wants his parents to divorce. A child whose parents are dissolving their marriage watches as the world on which he depends disintegrates. The situation can easily be exacerbated when the children are drawn into the process. Mindless parents use children as pawns against each other. For example, they threaten custody litigation for retribution or in order to coerce satisfactory financial arrangements. They employ a flawed syllogism to inflexibly insist on sole custody, which produces litigation: you were a bad husband, and therefore you cannot be a good father. Parents who cannot resolve their custody issues outside the courthouse do their children a serious disservice in most cases. It does not take a great deal of elaboration to imagine the damage to a child

15. Whitehead, p. 50.
16. David Popenoe, *Life without Father* (New York: Free Press, 1996), pp. 52-78.
17. Popenoe, p. 58.
18. David Popenoe and Barbara Dafoe Whitehead, *The State of Our Unions, 1999* (Rutgers, N.J.: National Marriage Project, 1999), p. 8.

whose parents are publicly struggling over her, where the child herself may have to state a preference in a choice she does not want to make. Since divorce affects close to 1 million children annually,[19] the damage created is enormous.

Moreover, a summary of recent research by Popenoe, Whitehead, and Waite shows that not only are children disadvantaged by divorce, but the very marriage partners it was supposed to benefit also suffer. As previously stated, women lose economically. Both sexes have increased health hazards. Depression is relatively well recognized, but less obvious are the physical hazards of divorce. They range from loss of weight to increased cigarette and alcohol consumption, lower immune function, and a higher risk of dying.[20]

This research has at least corrected the record that divorce is cost-free to all concerned. There is no free lunch in divorce. The cost is more than individual. When multiplied by the over 1.1 million divorces per year,[21] and the 1 million children whose parents annually divorce,[22] there is an enormous cost piled on society every year.

Legal Reforms

There has been some advocacy of resurrecting the fault divorce laws, or at least enacting more restrictive laws, to replace the present no-fault divorce laws. Louisiana in 1997 actually passed into law a covenant marriage that parties may select as a voluntary alternative to the state's ordinary marriage. Louisiana's ordinary marriage permits no-fault divorce after six months' separation; covenant marriage requires the proof of a fault ground to obtain a divorce or requires living apart for a more substantial period of time. Arizona followed suit the next year by enacting a less restrictive covenant marriage alternative by which proof of one of the fault grounds or living apart for a period of time is required for a divorce, unless the parties agree to the divorce.[23]

The theory of these partial returns to fault divorce is that if it is more difficult to divorce, there will be less divorce. But this is simplistic reasoning. It is true that there was less divorce under the fault laws, but as previously stated, this was due to a variety of societal factors that supported marriage but no lon-

19. Popenoe and Whitehead, *State of Our Unions, 2000*, pp. 32-33.
20. Linda J. Waite, "Does Marriage Matter?" *Demography* 32, n. 4 (November 1995): 486-89. See also Waite's contribution to this volume, chap. 1.
21. Wright, pp. 293-95.
22. Popenoe and Whitehead, *State of Our Unions, 2000*, pp. 32-33.
23. Wardle, pp. 783-84, 787-89. Louisiana Revised Statutes Annotated §§9.272-275.1, 307-309; Arizona Revised Statutes Annotated §§25-901-906.

ger exist. Moreover, the fault divorce laws had negative consequences that included discrimination in favor of the wealthy, a skewing of financial allocations that followed supposed guilt and innocence rather than equity lines, and court testimony that may at best have been exaggerated or at worst was untrue.

There is no reason to believe that the widespread reenactment of fault or more restrictive divorce laws by itself would produce good results. The opposite would more probably be the case. Divorce law is largely the creature of state legislation. The expectation would be that not all states would enact the restrictive laws. The wealthy would still travel to divorce. Even in the unlikely event of the passage of uniform legislation, without societal support for the preservation of marriage, and with the public accustomed to easy divorce, the laws would be circumvented, either by agreement after negotiating the cost or by traveling to an offshore jurisdiction that viewed divorce more permissively or by de facto bigamy. Uniform restrictive divorce laws could be as ineffective as was the prohibition of alcohol.

What Will Work?

New Value

There is no easy answer or quick fix to the deluge of divorces that began in 1969 and has persisted for more than thirty years. Divorce has become ingrained in our culture. It is not even clear that the majority of the American people are interested in a change away from the protection of choice for the dissatisfied spouse and toward a greater protection for marriage. There are substantial unanswered questions. For example, if society gives marriage greater protection, what is to be done about adultery? We cannot just presume that it will go away. What would be the mechanism to allow the dissolution of verifiably destructive marriages? The trapped and endangered spouse must be allowed to escape.

The current research is pragmatic in that it stresses the costs of divorce to individuals and to children. The research should help reduce divorce, because we are a society that is interested in individual costs and health. But we have not moved beyond our intense focus on the individual. As Paul D. Numrich notes, the new research has adopted the language of individualism by concentrating on the costs of divorce to the spouses.[24] The very fact that we are expectantly embracing the new research is itself a demonstration of

---

24. See Paul D. Numrich's article in this volume, chap. 14.

Is the Genie out of the Bottle?

the erosion of the traditional religious, moral, family, and institutional supports of marriage that affirm the collective family unit.

We cannot expect the new research results by themselves to deter husbands and wives from divorce. To do that a more fundamental change in the values of society concerning marriage must take place.

Both the successes and the failures of the national campaigns to end cigarette smoking, to eliminate guns, and to eradicate drugs are good paradigms. The costs of those pursuits to individuals and to society are well known and virtually undisputed, but cost and health research, while a good start, has been insufficient by itself for success in any of the campaigns.

To change the divorce equation, which now favors the spouse who wants to leave the marriage, and at least establish a balance between that spouse and a preservation of the marriage for the other spouse and for the children, requires a change in cultural values. Marriage and the collective interests of the family must be invested with at least as much value as the right of the dissatisfied spouse to abandon the marriage.

A spouse, in order to preserve her marriage, either has to know from the time she marries why divorce is unacceptable or be given cogent reasons when she faces divorce. Superficial family values are insufficient to combat current ideas of individual self-fulfillment. It is therefore important that all the disciplines that touch families rethink the value of marriage. Since most of the traditional moral and religious value of marriage has lost its urgent persuasiveness, it is necessary to develop a new coherent resource of marriage value for today's society. There are some tricky contradictions in what the new value must accomplish, but they should not be fatal. The new value must move from the individual to the collective interests of the family. It should preserve the moral, religious, and family precepts of the past. At the same time, it must gain relevance to the individualistic concerns of the present. Men and women entering marriage need a reservoir of current marriage value, which has been carefully taught to them beforehand, from which they can draw during their marriage. Professions that deal with families need to know why they should not be value-neutral on the subject of marriage.

People make sacrifices for pursuits in which they believe. In today's fast-paced society, both spouses are often frenetically devoting large numbers of hours to their jobs. They are variously motivated by money or ambition or status or love of work, for which they give up other endeavors. When there is a divorce, it is often apparent that if the spouse switched his exaggerated devotion from his job to his family, he would soon be unemployed. He cannot therefore be surprised that his marriage failed to survive. The same pattern is true for other obsessions, such as athletics, or whatever. Families require balance in life. Families cannot be left out in the cold. A family must be perceived in a person's range of choices as possessing sufficient value to make it worthwhile for sacrifices to be made on its behalf.

Fidelity in its most beneficial family sense has to deserve as much attention as an individual's right to pursue his own happiness somewhere else. In today's more individualistic society, the individual must be convinced that he can realize his own happiness inside a single marriage. He must be prepared to defend his marriage. The family may be the best place for the realization of happiness. The triumph just could be the preservation of marriage through the vicissitudes of life, not the prosaic search for happiness through different partners.

Where to Begin?

These changes in values are no small order: they cannot just be legislated; they cannot be accomplished by cost-benefit research by itself; and they cannot be accomplished by one of the professions acting alone. Because they deal with a variety of intangibles, it is difficult to know even where to start.

The answer has to be to start everywhere, but to first engage areas that have the best chance of success. For example, recent research shows that cohabitation prior to marriage is not related, and may even be detrimental, to success in marriage.[25] The probable reasons are that cohabitation is usually an informal arrangement in which expectations are restrained and there is a relative ease of ingress and egress. After marriage the expectations of one or both spouses change. Dedication to the marriage is immediately anticipated. There is a promise of children. There is a perceived need to earn more money and to establish better living quarters. There has to be a sacrifice of a sufficient amount of personal time to care for children when they arrive. Fidelity is expected. The easy patterns to which the partners became accustomed in cohabitation are not the best preparation for the greater expectations of marriage. The prior patterns may be difficult to give up in marriage. What was a carefree and happy cohabitation may turn into a sour and burdensome marriage.

Cohabitation prior to marriage appears as an inviting target for many of the marriage reformers. But it is a quixotic notion of nostalgia and probably an unwise allocation of resources to try to restrict cohabitation before marriage in today's society of birth control, coed dormitories, and saturation of sexual images.

A more promising starting place is found in two sentences in the

---

25. Popenoe and Whitehead, *State of Our Unions, 2000*, p. 28.

Rutgers National Marriage Project report: "[M]ost Americans continue to prize and value marriage as an important life goal, and the vast majority of us will marry at least once in a lifetime.... Most couples enter marriage with a strong desire and determination for a lifelong, loving partnership."[26]

These two sentences articulate a strong current of idealized belief in marriage that persists in American culture. The conclusion by the Rutgers National Marriage Project was made in the face of findings in the same reports that the chance of a marriage breaking up is between 40 and 50 percent.[27] The separation between the ideal and the reality is wide. But because the ideal of a loving, lifetime marriage exists in the imaginations of so many Americans, it is a starting point from which individuals may be persuaded to give up a portion of their self-absorption in favor of the collective interests of the family. Most changes in society begin in the minds of women and men.

A practical argument for a stable marriage is that an intact family is the best place to raise children. A concomitant of increasing the value of marriage in society is enhancing the worth of children. Children are entitled to at least as much attention as is paid to commerce. As children are more prized, the family will be more honored and there will be more of an effort to keep families together.

Marriage is a receptacle of family history, and therefore a microcosm of society's history. The family is society's basic and most multifaceted unique unit. To a large extent the success of society depends upon its small family units. The well-being of adults and the nurturing of children are entrusted in the first instance by society to families. Artificial substitutes step in only when the family fails. Family inner workings are far preferable to court supervision of broken homes.

Children of intact families are less likely to divorce.[28] Any family that endures as a good family is the most valuable teaching model its children can have. Its children marry and are more likely to stay married and to have children who are more likely to stay married, who will have children who are more likely to stay married, and so on into more successful future generations. Married-parent families therefore have value in numbers far beyond themselves. They reach out into society as their own messengers.

Instruction in the value and dynamics of the family should involve all the professions, but they must also be joined by the schools, churches, media,

---

26. Popenoe and Whitehead, *State of Our Unions, 1999*, p. 6. See also Popenoe and Whitehead, *State of Our Unions, 2000*, p. 8.

27. Popenoe and Whitehead, *State of Our Unions, 1999*, pp. 22-23; Popenoe and Whitehead, *State of Our Unions, 2000*, pp. 26-27.

28. Popenoe and Whitehead, *State of Our Unions, 1999*, p. 8.

government, and other institutions of society. Ironically, we teach and support commerce better than we do family life.

Restoration of institutional support is important for the increased preservation of marriage. Under the best of circumstances, there will always be marital crises that need outside help. Couples should be able to look to their parents, churches, schools, mental health professionals, lawyers, media, and government for positive support.

The influence of Buddhism, Hinduism, and Islam is a valuable resource that should not be overlooked. In all three religions the interest of the individual yields to the extended family. The divorce rate and percentage of households headed by females in Asian American families are roughly half that of the general American population. The danger is that the salutary influence of these non-Judeo-Christian religions will be lost in the United States because of erosion of their religious marriage practices by traditional Western individualism.[29]

The Role of Legislative Law

Marriage needs reinforcement from every aspect of society in order to survive. It is not a simple matter of legislating it into greater life. Legislation without the mores of society being in agreement will be no more successful than was the prohibition of alcohol.

Montesquieu, the French political philosopher who lived from 1689 to 1755, wrote eloquently about the interaction between laws and the societies they govern. He warned against trying to change the mores of society by the imposition of laws. The manners and customs of a society are better changed, he said, by introducing other manners and customs.[30]

However, this does not mean that legislation has no part in a cultural campaign to change American marriage values. Legislation, rather than just facilitating divorce, can support marriage.

For example, legislation could give a voice to the spouse who does not want her marriage to fail, and to a spokesperson for the children, in deciding

---

29. See Numrich's article in this volume.

30. "We have said that the laws were the particular and precise institutions of a legislator, and manners and customs the institutions of a nation in general. From hence it follows, that when these manners and customs are to be changed, it ought not to be done by laws; this would have too much the air of tyranny: it would be better to change them by introducing other manners and other customs." Montesquieu, *The Spirit of Laws* (Berkeley: University of California Press, 1977), pp. 292-93.

whether there should be a divorce. Legislation can be shaped to add balance: not to just favor the spouse who wants to terminate the marriage, but to insure more protection to the spouse and the children who are left by the divorce.

The Louisiana and Arizona covenant marriage laws are attempts to make legislation contribute to marriage preservation. There is a recent proposal to have couples prior to their marriages commit to mechanisms that would impose penalties or delay on divorce, in order to discourage divorce by making it costly and less impulsive.[31] Another proposal is to have the spouses and children upon a divorce share the wealth that has been accumulated during the marriage in accordance with predetermined guidelines, primarily in order to give children more financial security than they presently receive.[32]

While neither the covenant marriage laws nor the proposals for premarriage commitment and for family sharing of assets upon divorce are panaceas, they are clear evidence that law is seeking a role in controlling the damage of divorce. Particularly useful are the provisions for pre- and post-marital counseling in the Louisiana and Arizona covenant marriage laws.[33] Legislation can support marriage by encouraging counseling, establishing readily available resources for counseling, and allowing sufficient time between the filing of a lawsuit and the entry of a divorce judgment for the spouse who does not want the divorce to have a fair chance through the counseling to preserve his marriage.

With very minor exceptions, the present divorce legal system assumes that the highest value is the individual pursuit of happiness. The scales of justice are out of balance. Is it true that we want a society where the individual pursuit of happiness is elevated to such an untouchable status that other values and the damage created by divorce are shoved aside? That is not the case with other highly protected and cherished rights, such as free speech.

The Role of Lawyers

What part can lawyers play in enhancing the value of marriage in society? They can obviously work to shape more balanced legislation. But there is more to be done in the day-to-day representation of clients.

---

31. Elizabeth S. Scott, "Rational Decision-Making about Marriage and Divorce," *Opportuning Virtue: Lessons of the Louisiana Covenant Marriage Law,* Communitarian Report (1997): 23.

32. Katherine Shaw Spaht, "Family as 'Community': Implementing the 'Children First Principle,'" in *Marriage in America: A Communitarian Perspective,* ed. Martin King Whyte (Lanham: Rowman & Littlefield, 2000), pp. 235-56.

33. La. Rev. Stat. Ann. §9.273; Ariz. Rev. Stat. Ann. §25-901.

Family lawyers who believe in marriage should work to convince other family lawyers of the value of marriage by lecturing, writing, and conversation. Lawyers should encourage and participate in professional seminars that teach support of marriages as well as those that teach the mechanics of taking them apart. This is not different from the cancer doctor who believes in the value of health. Lawyers can be part of and contribute to the building of institutional support for marriage.

Family lawyers should be sensitive to the potentialities for reconciliation in every case. As professionals admitted to the bar, lawyers are obligated to do more than treat a case as a business transaction. Family lawyers should explore with every client the potential for reconciliation and the comparative costs and benefits of staying married and obtaining a divorce. Many clients reach their lawyers' offices in such a pell-mell rush toward divorce that they have hardly considered other possibilities nor the downside of dissolving their marriage and family. Before the divorce dynamic takes over and establishes a life of its own, a lawyer can create a vital pause just by playing devil's advocate, a role to which lawyers should be accustomed. A client's negotiating strength to draw his partner into marital therapy should be analyzed in every case where there is a possibility of counseling. All the while a lawyer must be protective of a family's children.

There is no question that reinvesting value into marriage requires the cooperation of all the professions. The most obvious place where family lawyers interact with other professions is with counselors or clergy who are engaged with the same clients lawyers are representing. Communication among all the participants is critical. This is particularly so where the marriage relation itself is left out of therapy, which happens when only one spouse is in therapy, or even when both spouses are in separate therapies but there is no contemporaneous counseling that considers the marriage itself. The wall of therapist or clerical confidentiality cannot be allowed to interfere with the vital cross-communication concerning the marriage. Preservation of the marriage and the family is at least as important as most individual confidences. This will produce an outcry from the mental health professionals, but undue confidentiality is just another example of favoring the individual over the family group of spouses and children. A balance can and should be struck.

A reformation of the money incentives to lawyers would help. A reward for reconciling couples and a system other than the hourly rate, which encourages prolonged litigation, are not impossible and would be an improvement. But they are unlikely to come soon, and they are unnecessary.

Lawyers are licensed by the state. Marriages are licensed by the state. The state has an interest in marriage. With a license to a family lawyer to practice his trade goes the obligation to assist the state in preserving the marriages that are sanctioned by the state. Lawyers need to be made aware of this obligation and taught how to discharge it. Lawyer support of marriages could produce large benefits to spouses, children, and society at large, but benefits would also accrue to the lawyers themselves. A lawyer who not only spends his time undoing marriages but also offers wise counsel to preserve families is the more respected lawyer whose broader range of ability is more widely sought. Lawyers are seen by society primarily as troublemakers. It was not always so. The perception of family lawyers could undergo a dramatic change if they lent their good offices to the constructive preservation of marriages as well as to the negative activity of dissolving them. Lawyers could resume their former status as something more than creatures of the marketplace.

The Genie Is Out

The answer to the question we posed in the title of this article is: yes, the genie is out of the bottle. America is inundated with divorce and its consequences. Divorce is part of the fabric of our society. Ironically, however, even the pursuit of individual happiness is not fulfilled: second and subsequent marriages have higher divorce rates than do first marriages.[34] A spouse is divorcing a spouse with a short right arm to marry one with a twisted left foot. Recently a small groundswell of protest has focused on the cost of divorce. No single remedy will work. No one of the professions can do it alone. Patchwork with legislation is not enough. There needs to be more of a balance established between the individual and the collective parts of the family. This can only happen by giving the family, the spouse who wants to hold her marriage together and the children, more value so that their side of the scale is at least in equilibrium with the individual's side. It will take a change in the ethos of America. If there are to be new laws, there has to be a working congruency between them and the values of society. As many elements of society as possible have to be mobilized, as they have begun to be in the campaigns against drugs, tobacco, and guns. It is necessary to pursue practical and not quixotic goals. The genie is out of the bottle; but there are many reasons why we should try to push him back in — where he belongs.

---

34. Popenoe and Whitehead, *State of Our Unions, 2000*, p. 27.

Medicine

CHAPTER 5

Health, Marriage, and the Ethics of Medicine

Stephen G. Post

Physicians as well as their patients should be made aware of data indicating that, in general, lasting marital unions are good for health and longevity. Linda J. Waite's empirical generalizations are impressive. For example, marriage enhances emotional health when contrasted with being single; enhances physical health, particularly for men, who are otherwise more prone than women to unhealthful behaviors; increases longevity of life for both husband and wife; improves material well-being with respect to income, assets, and wealth, and the financial circumstances of women in particular. Cohabitation, which lacks the degree of commitment that characterizes marriage, offers fewer benefits in these areas.[1]

These facts provide a context for proper professionalism, which starts with the principle of beneficence, i.e., furthering the good of patients. Beneficence may come into tension with patient autonomy, a value which must be afforded priority. Yet the professional who brings these facts to light does not coerce, but merely enhances the informational basis upon which patients make decisions about their lives and their health.

In contemporary culture the heuristic key of public health epidemiology plays a particularly powerful role in shaping attitudes and practices, although the association between marriage and health is affirmed in the historical tradition of Western religious thought (in this volume see Witte). Pointing out the generally healthful impact of marriage need not obscure the reality of domestic violence, of high-conflict and unhealthful relationships, and of the consequent duty of professionals to help alleviate such harms after

---

1. Linda J. Waite, "Does Marriage Matter?" *Demography* 32, no. 4 (1995): 483-507.

careful and compassionate questioning of the patient.[2] Yet these worst-case scenarios need not obscure the generalization that more lasting marital unions are healthful.

In this chapter I proceed from an initial discussion of the place of the health paradigm in marriage to the subject of the marriage covenant as providing a necessary context for that paradigm. I then turn to a particular case of covenant loyalty in marriage, one that involves a couple caring for a father with dementia, in order to ground the idea of covenant in the world of common experience. This leads inevitably to a discussion of "limit situations" and the connection between circumstances of intense demand on caregivers and spirituality/religion in the family as a covenantal institution of caregiving. I then revisit the health paradigm of Waite, address the problem of domestic violence, and offer some concluding remarks.

Taking the Health Paradigm Seriously

Does attention to data on the beneficial health consequences of marriage and the negative health consequences of divorce (although there are justifiable and necessary divorces) somehow trivialize marriage? Trivialization entails a diminished attentiveness to the deeper features of marriage that cannot be contained within the reigning paradigm of the pursuit of health. I do not think there is any trivialization involved here, although the health data must be contextualized in a balance with those aspects of marriage that require a dutiful commitment to the other in times of serious difficulty with mental illness, progressive dementia, or major disability — times when an informal family caregiver will experience stress and often-related adverse health consequences, both physical and emotional. The deep vow of marriage, "until death do us part," exists as a radical alternative to the notion of a marriage that lasts only so long as each party feels entirely loved, hopeful, joyful, and self-fulfilled. The ideal of lasting marital unions brings with it an inevitable demand for sometimes painful and often exhausting commitment to the other that limits the strictly egoistic or acquisitive expectation for "my" physical and "my" emotional health. The "death" in "until death do us part" is the natural solution to the human problem of solipsism — i.e., our human tendency to see ourselves as the center of the universe and to value others only as they contribute to our own agendas "in orbit around ourselves." Aging,

---

2. Martha B. Holstein, "Women, Religion, and Violence: A Challenge for the Health Care Professional," *Park Ridge Center Bulletin* 15 (May/June 2000): 5-6.

chronic illness, and dying encourage within us an appropriate humility, and for many caregiving spouses the demands of providing care and the realities of frailty will make death appear more as a blessing than a curse, for life may have become a dreary business. The ultimate heuristic key for marriage may be less health than the need to infuse decay, dependency, and death with moral and spiritual value.

Yet the healthful aspects of marriage — which include the benefits of having someone who can be a loyal provider of tender loving personal care in time of need — need to be appreciated. Arguably, marriage contributes to health through a sometimes difficult transformation from egoism to a loyal altruistic love of the other. This freedom from self through discovery of the reality of the other as other is a perennial theological theme. Marriage, in order to last and achieve its full potential, must be based on something spiritually and morally deeper than fleeting romantic infatuations or "tit-for-tat" contractual self-interest. Jewish and Christian traditions get at this deeper notion of freedom through the language of covenants. In such relationships, acquisitive desires may still exist, but they do not rule.

The truly healthy person enters and maintains a marriage not simply on the basis of egoistic interests informed by epidemiological data, but as one who sees worth in the beloved as a child of God independent of the self's own interests. The truly healthy person is willing to make significant sacrifices of self, although this need not imply self-immolation, radical self-abnegation, or a reluctance to accept help from others in time of need. Some social scientists, evolutionary biologists, and economists (especially rational choice theorists) have invested much effort in proving that human beings do only what is in their self-interest, however long-term or "enlightened" it may be. But we need not accept their image of the purely self-interested agent, an image that has never been proven although it has achieved a certain popularity among the so-called realists. As Robert H. Frank writes, "The flint-eyed researcher fears no greater humiliation than to have called some action altruistic, only to have a more sophisticated colleague later demonstrate that it was self-serving."[3] But it is impossible to imagine that lasting marriages could ever exist with nothing more than self-interest as foundation. Yet they do exist, and are often deeper because husband and wife have successfully navigated tough times, and even very tough times.

The pursuit of one's own health and longevity, while valid and important, cannot provide the ultimate moral context that makes for "more lasting

---

3. Robert H. Frank, *Passions within Reason: The Strategic Role of the Emotions* (New York: W. W. Norton, 1988), p. 21.

unions."[4] So we turn now to the notion of covenant love, which, as mentioned above, has played the dominant role in Jewish and Christian thought about marriage. Covenants require a balance between primary altruistic tendencies and secondary but nevertheless important egoistic ones.

Covenant Marriage

The marriage covenant includes the above-mentioned altruistic sense, in contrast to the marriage contract, in which strictly self-interested parties enter into a union-of-a-sort that lasts only so long as the acquisitive desires of both parties are fulfilled, as determined by a calculating mind-set. A covenant begins under a sacred canopy with a promissory ritual intended to shape the future through good times and bad.[5] The promise includes duties that will define the future within an overall fidelity that "extends beyond particulars to unforeseen and unforeseeable contingencies."[6] Husband and wife are each receiving a gift of love not fully deserved. This is not just a love based on an assessment of the particular features of the other that one finds attractive as defined by egoistic interests; it is more crucially a love warmly and generously bestowed upon the other as a human being of equal worth. The covenant affects one's deepest personal identity by creating a lasting community; one essentially becomes a new being within the covenant, distinct from the self that lives in a world of temporary and minimal commitments of self-interested contractors. Covenant *does* also include an important element of self-concern, for it is a blessing in which much will be received as well as given. The blessing of good health is a benefit that requires no apologetics.

The solemnity of the marriage covenant is a key feature. The promise between "I and Thou" is a direct consequence of God's love for the other as well as for self. Solemnity includes a sense of awe before a presence in the universe that is greater than one's own, and in whose sight both husband and wife will walk all the days of their lives together. They must remember this promise of fidelity amidst all the cares and occupations of their daily lives, and in the hardest of times. And those times will come when husband, wife, child, or parent becomes imperiled in vulnerability, or just *inevitably* fails to live up to our full or even partial expectations.

---

4. Stephen G. Post, *More Lasting Unions: Christianity, the Family, and Society* (Grand Rapids: Eerdmans, 2000).

5. William F. May, *The Physician's Covenant: Images of the Healer in Medical Ethics* (Philadelphia: Westminster, 1983), p. 107.

6. May, p. 107.

This altruistic love is central in marriage, but this is not a "pure" altruistic love that requires of the agent a strict disinterest in his or her own health. These egoistic features of legitimate self-concern are in fact important if the agent is to be able to care for the other effectively. The covenant is first of all *agapē*, a genuine self-giving that includes self-sacrifice in the interest of sustained mutuality; it includes as well *erōs*, the love that seeks its own. Covenant, as I have defined it here, resonates well with the Roman Catholic notion of *caritas*, which also includes elements of *agapē* and *erōs*.

The following narrative highlights the unforeseen element in covenant marriage, reaching into the intergenerational context of helping a spouse care for a father whose cognition has been lost to the ravages of dementia. In order to breathe life into this notion of the family as covenant of care, I must avoid abstractions. This narrative should ground the reader in the experience of the family caregiver. It concerns Barbara and Mike McCurry, and Barbara's father. The reader is invited to reflect on this account as a test case of the limits of the health paradigm as a foundation for marriage.

The McCurry Family

On 25 May 1999 I led a daylong program entitled "Ethics in Alzheimer's Disease" for the Carolina Piedmont Chapter of the Alzheimer's Association in Charlotte. Of 250 participants, about half were family caregivers. A wonderful couple, the McCurrys, started us off with a beautiful summary of their experience as caregivers. The McCurrys, in granting permission for me to include this material in my writings, wanted me to use their names and that of Thomas Luther Hodge, Barbara's father, to commemorate him. I am thankful to the McCurrys for grounding their readers in the lived realities they, Mrs. Hodge, and Thomas Luther Hodge faced.

Thomas Luther Hodge

The following is taken from a copy of the McCurrys' written comments:

(Daughter Barbara) "Hi! I am Barbara Hodge McCurry. This is my husband Mike. My mother, Mrs. Hodge, is not here on the panel with us today. The three of us were caregivers to our beloved father and husband, Thomas Luther Hodge. He was a wonderful gentleman in the truest sense of the word. He was kind, gentle, caring, and loving. There was never any question as to how deeply he loved life, his family, friends, country, and the Lord Jesus

Christ. At 73 years of age he was in perfect physical condition. He worked a part-time job three days a week, walked 2 or 3 miles per day and was on no medication. In June of 1992 the four of us celebrated their 50th wedding anniversary by taking a cruise to Alaska. We each had a grand time! However, it was on this trip that we began to notice a slight personality change in daddy. He didn't want to be out of mama's presence and was much quieter than usual. (Up to this point when we traveled he was always the explorer who was finding sights for us to see or suggesting adventures for our enjoyment.)

"Looking back now we realize daddy's battle with this horrible disease called Alzheimer's started in the year of 1992. The battle ended in July 1998.

"For a year or so he didn't exhibit any symptoms worthy of real concern. Only a few times did he run a red light without noticing it, misplace his keys or glasses, or fail to recognize someone he hadn't seen for some time. After all, we all do this, right? Especially in the stressful 90s.

"Suddenly it seemed everything changed. There was pronounced memory loss, confusion, the inability to perform usual activities and duties, frequent misplacement of items, insecurities. Daddy was acutely aware that something was happening to his mind . . . in fact his fear was that he was losing his mind. (At this time I had worked in the medical field for 30-plus years.) There was no denying the so-called classic Alzheimer's symptoms. Fear gripped my heart! Daddy had Alzheimer's! Before long our worst fears were confirmed. Daddy was diagnosed with Alzheimer's disease. I can't begin to tell you the heartache we felt nor will I elaborate on the intensity of that pain in the years that followed.

"We loved him so much we wanted to be there to talk with him through as much of this nightmare as possible."

(Son-in-law Mike) "Our utmost desires were (1) to provide daddy with the best care possible, (2) to allow him to maintain as much dignity as possible during his illness and when the end came to allow him to die with dignity, (3) for as long as possible to allow him to feel he was still a very vital, respected, contributing part of his family and friends' lives, (4) to provide the components needed for the enhancement of his spirituality, (5) for him to always be able to feel our love for him. Like most families, we had a lot of questions: What about our financial and legal status? Would we be sensitive to daddy's feelings when he could no longer drive? When and what medications would be appropriate? In the end stage of the disease would we really have the courage to respect daddy's wishes for no feeding tube or other heroic measures?

"We never dreamed the challenge before us! A caregiver wears more hats than almost any head can hold! There is so much care to be given, so many decisions to be made, so many issues to face."

(Barbara) *Nutritional needs.* "Proper nutrition became a major concern. Daddy could eat a well-balanced meal and in approximately 15 minutes he would be ravenous. It was definitely a challenge to provide three meals per day and numerous nutritional snacks throughout day and night. He went from a size 33 slack to a size 38. We can laughingly ask now — How many 18-wheeler loads of snacks did we purchase during his illness? We're convinced we were responsible for the rise of several stocks on the market during that time."

(Mike) *Support.* "We were going to give daddy all the love and support possible. It wasn't long until we realized how much we needed support also. If it hadn't been for family, friends, pastors, support groups, others in similar situations, wonderful health care givers, the Alzheimer's Association, and certainly the grace of God, we couldn't have made it. We soon learned to reach out and accept help and support from those who were reaching out to us."

Activities. "Daddy was a workaholic. He always wanted to be doing something. As long as possible we gave him little chores to do. We tossed ball. We sang songs, especially the old hymns. We clapped our hands and danced, laughed, exercised, took rides, went to the mall. We had a party with ice cream, cake, and presents for every special occasion. We walked untold miles. After he could no longer walk we resorted to the wheelchair. We were determined he would be active as long as possible."

(Barbara) *Placement.* "Daddy was a pacer and a wanderer. He sometimes would literally pace or try to do so for 24 hours. He would wander away in a second. It became painfully evident for his safety that he needed the security of a long-term care facility (for the longest time none of us could say 'nursing home'). The day he had to leave home was one of the most difficult in our lives.

"We were blessed to have daddy in two very good facilities. The first was out of town. We hated being separated from him! It didn't have an Alzheimer's unit, and therefore, due to his pacing and wandering into other residents' rooms, we needed to find an Alzheimer's unit. In desperation, I called the Alzheimer's Association. I don't remember her name, but 'some angel' gave me the names of local facilities with Alzheimer's units. She also mentioned a beautiful new facility being built approximately two miles from Mike's place of employment. They would have an Alzheimer's unit! Immediately we started the application process. Several months later we were able to bring daddy back to Charlotte to live there just before Christmas holidays. How wonderful it was to have him near us rather than 2 and a half hours away."

(Mike) "Even though we were no longer 24-hour caregivers, we were still caregivers in many ways. We were very active on daddy's care-giving and care-planning teams. Our already heavy involvement there increased as daddy lost the ability to communicate, to feed himself, to walk or basically do anything for himself. We continued to talk with him, hug him, hold his hand, kiss him, and tell him we loved him. Not only did we participate in his care but we were active in volunteer activities, family counsel, and in all phases of life at his new home."

(Barbara) *Hospice.* "The staff at his new home were wonderful to daddy and us during those last days. We also elected to call hospice. They worked hand in hand with the staff to see that all daddy's needs were met. They provided much-needed counsel, reassurance, and support in addition to preparing us for what to expect in the final hours."

(Barbara) *Death.* "On Sunday July 12, 1998, Daddy was cured from Alzheimer's disease. He went quietly and peacefully to heaven! Mike and I were holding his hands. Mama was at his bedside. Special friends were present. His battle was over."

(Barbara) *Conclusions.* "Looking back over the years, we feel we did some things well, some things not so well. We realize times were often difficult. However, there were good times too, seeing his face light up when we walked into the room, seeing his smile, watching him laugh, seeing him enjoying music or some other activity, receiving those big hugs, watching him sleep so peacefully after hours of restlessness, hearing him say 'I love you too!' or when he was no longer able to speak seeing the love in his eyes as he squeezed your hand so tightly! Yes, these and other memories are cherished. We're so thankful we were able to help him during his journey. All who knew him will remember his wonderful smile and Christian integrity. We've been told by many how he positively touched their lives in spite of, and even during his illness. We're convinced an Alzheimer's patient feels and yes, even comprehends, far more than we realize. Personally, we feel they never lose their need to be loved.

"Thank you and God bless you."

Many elements from the McCurrys' testimony brought tears to the eyes of listeners that day. Their depth of care and commitment is obviously sustained by religious faith.

The McCurrys emphasized activities to enhance quality of life rather than aggressive medical means that inevitably are a form of assault for the demented person who lacks insight into the purposes of such invasive acts. The McCurrys went through a great deal themselves as caregivers, including the difficult decision to place Daddy in a nursing home, which is usually the right decision because it ultimately serves the best interests of the person with advanced dementia and the family.

The McCurrys had a clear understanding that Alzheimer's disease (AD) is ultimately a terminal disease, and they established therapeutic goals of comfort care as an alternative to an aggressive and inevitably uncomfortable dying. Thomas Luther Hodge died a comfortable natural dying, including the forgoing of artificial nutrition and hydration, surrounded by love and spirituality.

Any adult child (or elderly spouse) who has cared for an elderly person with a progressive dementia knows what it means to speak of a thirty-six-hour day.[7] Many women are sandwiched between responsibilities to children, husband, and parents; regrettably, women still do most of the direct caring.[8] In the McCurrys' case, however, Mike was very helpful in directly caring ways, and he therefore clarifies a male standard that is altogether fitting. While Barbara no doubt felt a great deal of stress at times, Mike's active participation was obviously a source of respite for her. It is odd that in a society that will pay for virtually any lifesaving technology no matter how expensive, our system does too little to help families with the financial burdens of long-term care, and with respite services. Surely one important role for the faith community is to lend an active hand to families such as the McCurrys, and evidently the community was helpful. Arguably, churches, synagogues, and other religious communities are the key element of support in enabling such families to survive and even to thrive.

The McCurrys had great love for Mr. Hodge. This made their task more agreeable and natural as an act of felt reciprocity and solicitude. Solicitude will often suffice in motivating actions of caring, but it is likely that at some points the more arid sense of duty must be invoked when spontaneity wanes, even if it then waxes again. The affective basis of solicitude may become less central in caregiving than the deontological perception that, because "I am parent, spouse, or adult child of this person," certain obligations exist regardless of a loss of joy and spontaneity. When caregivers can act with joy, spontaneity, and love under trying circumstances, we tend to see a certain saintliness in them that stands out in their tone of voice and in all their attentiveness to small gratifications that become so large in the lives of loved ones.

A spiritual basis for this sort of caring is very often present — i.e., the

---

7. Nancy L. Mace and Peter V. Rabins, *The Thirty-six-Hour Day* (Baltimore: Johns Hopkins University Press, 1991).

8. Elaine M. Brody, *Women in the Middle: Their Parent Care Years* (New York: Springer, 1990).

perception of a solicitude at the heart of the universe that sustains care and from which inspiration is possible. Stephen Toulmin calls this the sense of "cosmopolis," that our actions here on earth in the polis are in harmony with the ultimately loving nature of the cosmos and its creator.[9] Christians have traditionally spoken of the *imitatio Christi*. There is a tendency to consider the hagiography of the great public spiritual saints, but there is also the domestic sphere in which a tremendous idealism can thrive despite immense hardship. Most family caregivers have moments of joyful spontaneity mixed with periods of dutiful despair that can be described as dark nights of the soul.

Ours is an aging society in which the fastest-growing segment of the population is the "old-old" (a gerontological term for those eighty-five years of age or older). Demographers speak of the historically unprecedented transition from the classic demographic triangle with the old-old at the apex and the relatively younger and young filling out the base, to a demographic rectangle with roughly proportionate numbers of relatively young and old. No society in history has had to navigate this transition. Discussion now abounds on the issue of justice between the generations, and some ethicists call for age-based rationing of life-extending medical technologies.[10] It may be that *agapē* is more necessary under these familial circumstances than ever before, and that the role of faith is dramatically important for most caregivers, although they may wonder about the wisdom of continued expansion of the human life span until a cure for AD is discovered.

The moral and institutional role of the family, with public support as needed, is to create a value framework and sphere of care in which all people can be loved and supported. Family members can challenge existing social stigmas against vulnerable loved ones and create a hospitable milieu. Through voluntary associations such as the Alzheimer's Association, they become public policy advocates for the constituency they know best. A loving family caregiver learns what a person in radical dependence needs, and then struggles for the necessary public entitlements and financial support that constitute justice for an identified vulnerable group.

Family caregivers demonstrate a loyalty based on proximity and gratitude without which, according to classical sociologist Georg Simmel, "society

---

9. Stephen Toulmin, *Cosmopolis: The Hidden Agenda of Modernity* (New York: Free Press, 1990).

10. Daniel Callahan, *Setting Limits: Medical Goals in an Aging Society* (New York: Simon & Schuster, 1987); for a rejoinder, see Robert H. Binstock and Stephen G. Post, eds., *Too Old for Healthcare? Controversies in Medicine, Law, Economics, and Ethics* (Baltimore: Johns Hopkins University Press, 1991).

simply could not exist."[11] There is a familial expectation of nonappraisive love and care that professional caregivers may approximate but will rarely equal. People expect the family to be their "haven in a heartless world" — although they may forget how impossible this may be without caregiver respite in wider communities (e.g., neighborhoods, churches and synagogues) that offer strong support.

Realistically speaking, the modern nuclear family — parents and children living as an isolated unit, perhaps with grandparents in the home or nearby — faces a caregiving crisis with the rise of large numbers of people with AD. The nuclear family is the last remnant of the extended family, and public policies for its support are far from ideal. Politics aside, the caregiving within the family is a precious moral resource — so precious that it should not be exhausted. The interests of the person with dementia and of his or her caregivers are practically and ethically interwoven and interdependent. The stories of how family caregivers succeed, day in and day out, with people affected by dementia are remarkably interesting and inspiring. The McCurrys present a somewhat atypical case because, fortunately, both husband and wife were deeply engaged in direct caregiving, and they needed one another in this demanding context. Too often it is just the wife who is so engaged.

For those caregivers who have struggled with frightening and persistent agitation, aggressiveness, and combativeness in affected individuals, life is difficult. It is no easy matter to get a combative and resisting man with advanced dementia into the shower; at some point, sedation may be needed. Hallucination, delusions of suspected theft, depression, aggressive behavior, wandering, and incontinence all make family caregiving very difficult. Yet I am amazed at how often filial and conjugal love rise to the occasion. The patience, humor, and affectivity of caregivers are a tribute to the human spirit. One wonders whether this is ineffable divine grace in action.

The person with advanced dementia who does not recognize others and who can no longer communicate has become now the neighbor who is anyone in need. The personal connections based on a life story of relationship within the family are now resigned to memory. Caregivers sometimes remark that their loved one is "no longer there," "gone," and "absent." Thus, love for the near and dear is finally reconciled with love for all humanity. Care is given now purely to the neediest regardless of relational proximity. This demanding care is anything but self-interested and continues in the absence of reciprocity.

To better define how intensive family caregiving and spirituality often

---

11. Georg Simmel, *The Sociology of Georg Simmel*, ed. K. H. Wolff (New York: Free Press, 1950), p. 379.

conjoin within covenant marriage, I will move in the next section to the well-known theological and philosophical concept of a "limit situation."

Covenant Marriage in "Limit Situations": Spirituality and Caregiving

Families like the McCurrys are in "limit situations." Karl Jaspers (1883-1969), a physician, psychologist, and philosopher, has described a group of situations that are endemic to the human condition: "[H]e [man and woman] is involved, beyond all individual situations, in certain decisive, essential situations, which are the unavoidable condition of finite human existence. . . . These situations, which at the limits of our existence are everywhere felt, experienced, conceived, we therefore call 'limit-situations.'"[12] What are these situations? In his *Philosophy*, Jaspers enumerates several limit situations and elaborates on the description given in *Psychologie der Weltanschauungen*: "Situations such as: that I am always in situations, that I cannot live either without struggle or without suffering, that I ineluctably take guilt upon myself, that I must die — these I call limit situations. They do not change except in their appearance; as applied to our existence they possess finality. . . . They are like a wall against which we butt, against which we founder. They cannot be changed by us but merely clarified, yet they cannot be derived from an Other."[13] Even if we set aside the technical explanation of terms such as "Other," Jaspers's enumeration is by no means complete — nor, in his context, did he intend it to be. Suffice it to say that limit situations are those that are not of our making and from which we cannot escape.

Jaspers finds limit situations doubly important. First, they serve to illumine *Existenz* — i.e., that aspect of my being that gives me absolute uniqueness and by virtue of which I am related to God. As Søren Holm has put it, "*Existenz* without relation to Transcendence (God) has no meaning."[14] Adolph Lichtigfeld, who was active in the rabbinate and an important Jaspers scholar, has expanded Holm's claim: "Principles of religion were disclosed to

---

12. Karl Jaspers, *Psychologie der Weltanschauungen*, trans. Marga Frank and Arthur Newton in cooperation with Eva Reintz Grossman and Maurice S. Friedman, 2nd ed. (Berlin: Springer, 1931), p. 229, reprinted in *The Worlds of Existentialism*, ed. Maurice S. Friedman, 2nd ed. (Atlantic Highlands, N.J.: Humanities International, 1991), p. 100.

13. Karl Jaspers, *Philosophy,* trans. E. B. Ashton, rev. Robert G. Leisey, 3 vols. (Chicago: University of Chicago Press, 1969-71), 2:179. *Philosophie* was published in 1932.

14. Søren Holm, "Jaspers' Philosophy of Religion," in *The Philosophy of Karl Jaspers,* ed. Paul Arthur Schilpp, 2nd ed. (La Salle, Ill.: Open Court, 1981), p. 672.

man in these ultimate [limit] situations, in which he found himself."[15] Second, the experience of limit situations brings one to an awareness of God's presence through an awareness of oneself as foundering and utterly dependent.

Suffering, especially suffering secondary to *chronic, debilitating, and often life-threatening illness, is a limit situation,* one that Jaspers endured from his early adolescence. Of himself he has written: "Not only is the invalid more conscious of man's finiteness and his radical dependence, in his case it is something qualitatively different. Not ever for a day can he depend on himself as existence."[16] The experience of complete dependence, first described by Friedrich Schleiermacher in the nineteenth century and manifested in the personal life and philosophy of Jaspers, leads to an acknowledgment of dependence on God insofar as one is aware of self as *Existenz.* In *Way to Wisdom* he puts it thus: "[T]o ultimate [limit] situations we react either by obfuscation or, if we really begin to apprehend them, by despair and rebirth: we become ourselves by a change in our consciousness of being."[17] Thus, in limit situations, the consciousness of a presence beyond and above ourselves is essentially natural to human existence.

The McCurry family has been to the limit, and will be forever deepened for the experience. The role of the physician is to provide as much support to the family caregivers as possible, knowing full well how intense the challenge of family caring in limit situations can be. Mr. Hodge could not have lived at all well without his daughter and son-in-law, who were with him loyally to the end. The medical professional works with the family and is in many respects beholden to it, with regard both to general caregiving for the chronically ill or dying patient and to the decisions that have to be made about treatments and their limitations in the context of severe dysfunction.

In other words, it is really in the context of those illness scenarios that reach the limit situation that we see the relationship between the family, medical care, and the professional.

This is, however, also precisely the context where spirituality and religion enter into the lives of those with illness and their caregivers.

One of the finest autobiographical accounts of living with the diagnosis and initial decline of AD is Rev. Robert Davis's *My Journey into Alzheimer's*

---

15. Adolph Lichtigfeld, "The Concept of God in Jaspers' Philosophy," in *The Philosophy of Karl Jaspers,* p. 700. Some translators have chosen to render Jaspers's term *Grenzsituationen* as "ultimate situations," but the more literal and common interpretation is "limit situations."

16. *Karl Jaspers: Basic Philosophical Writings: Selections,* ed. Leonard H. Ehrlich, Edith Ehrlich, and George B. Pepper (Athens: Ohio University Press, 1986), p. 534.

17. Karl Jaspers, *Way to Wisdom,* trans. Ralph Manheim (New Haven: Yale University Press, 1954), p. 20. These are lectures Jaspers delivered over Radio Basel in 1949.

Disease. He writes as follows: "One night in Wyoming, as I lay in a motel crying out to my Lord, my long desperate prayers were suddenly answered. As I lay there in the blackness silently shrieking out my often repeated prayer, there was suddenly a light that seemed to fill my very soul. The sweet, holy presence of Christ came to me. He spoke to my spirit and said, 'Take my peace. Stop your struggling. It is all right. This is all in keeping with my will for your life. . . . Lie back in your Shepherd's arms, and take my peace.'"[18] As Rev. Davis "mourned the loss of old abilities," he nevertheless could draw on his Christianity: "I choose to take things moment by moment, thankful for everything that I have, instead of raging wildly at the things that I have lost."[19] Yet as he struggled to find a degree of peace amidst decline, he was also keenly aware of people who "simply cannot handle being around someone who is mentally and emotionally impaired."[20] The journey was made more navigable in his church community, and through the love of his wife, Betty, who helped him write each page of his book, which is really their book together, a tribute to a lasting union in troubled times.

People with a diagnosis of Alzheimer's often pray, for they cling to whatever faith they have in the meaningful and beneficent purposes underlying the universe. They pray because the routine and the control have been taken from their lives, and probably because they fear the future. They are shaken existentially, and must begin a final phase of their journey in remarkable trust. The person with a diagnosis of AD will often desire to pray with family members, in religious communities, and alone. The word "prayer" comes from the Latin *precari*, "to entreat," or ask earnestly. It comes from the same root as the word "precarious," and it is in the precariousness of emerging forgetfulness that the person with dementia is often driven to prayer. Chaplains and clinicians should encourage this propensity to gain strength through prayer in the midst of cognitive decline.

An autobiographical account from my earlier book, *The Moral Challenge of Alzheimer Disease*, demonstrates the search for meaning typified by persons with dementia who are categorically in "limit situations."[21] The following story — only lightly edited — was told by a woman in her midforties with dementia, etiology unknown. She is conversant, although some days she is too mentally confused to engage in much dialogue. She has more difficulty

---

18. R. Davis (with help from his wife Betty), *My Journey into Alzheimer's Disease: Helpful Insights for Family and Friends* (Wheaton, Ill.: Tyndale House, 1989), p. 55.

19. Davis, p. 57.

20. Davis, p. 115.

21. Stephen G. Post, *The Moral Challenge of Alzheimer Disease: Ethical Issues from Diagnosis to Dying*, 2nd ed., revised (Baltimore: Johns Hopkins University Press, 2000).

responding to open-ended questions, but does very well if her conversation partner cues her by mentioning several alternative words from which she might choose, at which point she can be quite articulate.

"It was just about this time three years ago that I recall laughing with my sister while in dance class at my turning the big 40. 'Don't worry, life begins at forty,' she exclaimed, and then sweetly advised her younger sister of all the wonders in life still to be found. Little did either of us realize what a cruel twist life was proceeding to take. It was a fate neither she nor I ever imagined someone in our age group could encounter.

"Things began to happen that I just couldn't understand. There were times I addressed friends by the wrong name. Comprehending conversations seemed almost impossible. My attention span became quite short. Notes were needed to remind me of things to be done and how to do them. I would slur my speech, use inappropriate words, or simply eliminate one from a sentence. This caused not only frustration for me, but also a great deal of embarrassment. Then came the times I honestly could not remember how to plan a meal or shop for groceries.

"One day, while out for a walk on my usual path in a city in which I had resided for 11 years, nothing looked familiar. It was as if I was lost in a foreign land, yet I had the sense to ask for directions home.

"There were more days than not when I was perfectly fine; but to me, they did not make up for the ones that weren't. I knew there was something terribly wrong and after 18 months of undergoing a tremendous amount of tests and countless visits to various doctors, I was proven right.

"Dementia is the disease, they say, cause unknown. At this point it no longer mattered to me just what that cause was because the tests eliminated the reversible ones, my hospital coverage was gone, and my spirit was too worn to even care about the name of something irreversible.

"I was angry. I was broken and this was something I could not fix, nor to date can anyone fix it for me. How was I to live without myself? I wanted her back!

"She was a strong and independent woman. She always tried so hard to be a loving wife, a good mother, a caring friend and a dedicated employee. She had self-confidence and enjoyed life. She never imagined that by the age of 41 she would be forced into retirement. She had not yet observed even one of her sons graduate from college, nor known the pleasures of a daughter-in-law, nor held a grandchild in her arms.

"Needless to say, the future did not look bright. The leader must now learn to follow. Adversities in life were once looked upon as a challenge; now they're just confusing situations that someone else must handle. Control of *my life* will slowly be relinquished to others. I must learn to trust — completely.

"An intense fear enveloped my entire being as I mourned the loss of what was and the hopes and dreams that might never be. How could this be happening to me? What exactly will become of me? These questions occupied much of my time for far too many days.

"Then one day as I fumbled around the kitchen to prepare a pot of coffee, something caught my eye through the window. It had snowed and I had truly forgotten what a beautiful sight a soft, gentle snowfall could be. I eagerly but so slowly dressed and went outside to join my son, who was shoveling our driveway. As I bent down to gather a mass of those radiantly white flakes on my shovel, it seemed as though I could do nothing but marvel at their beauty. Needless to say, he did not share in my enthusiasm; to him it was a job, but to me it was an experience.

"Later I realized that, for a short period of time, God granted me the ability to see a snowfall through the same innocent eyes of the child I once was, so many years ago. I am still here, I thought, and there will be wonders to be held in each new day; they are just different now. . . . Now my quality of life is feeding the dogs, looking at flowers. My husband says I am more content now than ever before! Love and dignity, those are the keys. This brings you back down to the basics in life, a smile makes you happy."

People with AD, as well as their caregivers, can benefit remarkably from pastoral care. Sometimes the patient who has not spoken coherently for several years will suddenly blurt out a prayer or a hymn, for such deeply learned material is the very last to disappear. The beauty of litanies, prayers, and hymns has a certain affective power. I remain open to the idea that, as the capacity for technical (means to ends) rationality fades, more contemplative and spiritual capacities are elevated. Demented people continue to respond to their faith and inner needs through long-remembered rituals that connect them with the present. Prayers and hymns are still familiar in many cases, especially after several repetitions.

My point in this section is simply that in the "limit situations" of severe prognosis and family caregiving, when all the routines of life have been dramatically disrupted, it is frequently the case that faith and spirituality become profoundly important both to the person who is ill and to those who in loyal love are there at the bedside. It is here that the physician must realize the centrality of family spirituality and be supportive of it as a matter of professional beneficence.

Patient and family caregiver expressions of spirituality should be screened for and respected by physicians. Requests for pastoral care should be implemented; those who frequently attend religious services will predictably ask for such referrals. The clinician who hopes to maximize therapeutic efficacy must respect his or her patients and their caregivers in this manner, especially when their spirituality is a critical life factor.

Yet I have without question been too colored by twelve years of constant work and study in the context of family caregivers whose loved ones navigate dementia, retardation, and mental illness. I am convinced that only family members have the knowledge of the imperiled individual's history that makes caregiving personal and ultimately secure. Now, on to the brighter themes of happiness and life extension, which are equally important heuristic keys into the value of lasting marital and family unions! Life in the family is not just snow and cold winds in the dark night of "limit situations," although we all see our fair share of these and hope for the support of loved ones.

Health, Happiness, and Longevity: Neither Trivial nor Sufficient

David B. Larson has already discussed the empirical data regarding the health benefits of more-lasting marital unions (see also his contribution to this book).[22] Since marriage is, from the biblical perspective, counted as a blessing, it should come as no surprise to believers that such benefits might well be quite marked. This is not, of course, to deny the ultimate human reality of "limit situations," the immense challenges they bring, and the importance of spirituality and faith in the lives of many family caregivers who navigate such situations.

If marriage is a blessing, then should we be surprised that Waite finds that more-lasting unions result in enhanced life expectancy? A further question, yet to be examined empirically, is the relationship between religious traditions and the expectation of lasting marital unions. Thus, one would expect that those attentive to such traditional expectations as manifest in religious observance and attendance would be the ones who had longer lives. This is precisely what religious researchers such as Harold Koenig and William Strawbridge have brought to light.[23]

22. David B. Larson, Susan B. Larson, and John Gartner, "Families, Relationships, and Health," in *Behavior and Medicine,* ed. D. Wedding (St. Louis: Mosby, 1990), pp. 135-47.

23. H. G. Koenig, J. C. Hays, D. B. Larson, L. K. George, H. J. Cohen, M. E. McCullough, K. G. Meador, and D. G. Blazor, "Does Religious Attendance Prolong Survival? A Six-Year Follow-up Study of 3,968 Older Adults," *Journals of Gerontology* 54A, no. 7 (1999): M370-M376. Another important study is W. J. Strawbridge, R. D. Cohen, S. J. Shema, et al., "Frequent Atten-

Is it the more-lasting unions themselves or the spirituality underlying these expectations that enhances life expectancy? Assuming that this spirituality, broadly defined, consists in part of a transformation toward altruism and away from egoism, one might also wish to study whether or not the presence of covenantal intentions and motives in entering marriage, rather than merely contractual ones, predicts better emotional and physical health outcomes. In other words, just as health outcomes are associated mostly with "intrinsic" religion (i.e., internal spiritual motives) but not with mere "extrinsic" religion (e.g., attending religious services for social prestige), so perhaps the health benefits associated with marriage will vary along a continuum from egoism to altruism.

The solution to the above questions awaits analysis. One highly productive step would be for demographers such as Waite to consider the religion variable in their studies of marriage and longevity. Similarly, Koenig and others should become familiar with the demographic studies on marriage and mortality in order to better understand how this variable intertwines with his studies of religious attendance. I offer no hypotheses, although one commonality between intrinsic religion and lasting marriage is the presence of genuine altruistic motivations in addition to any egoistic ones.

Society at large should be well informed of the health and longevity benefits of more-lasting marital unions. Western thought affirms the teleological or prudential benefits of this great blessing. Attention to empirical health data can play a part in turning us away from the culture of divorce. Physicians aware of these data ought not promote or easily endorse divorce, although there are cases in which divorce is necessary and salutary. Yet the language of health (and economics) cannot fully handle limit situations, which require covenant love, care, and compassion. I define love here as affective affirmation of the other. Love is to person as care is to person-in-need and compassion is to person-in-suffering.

The Problem of Violence

One can be hopeful that the new data on health benefits associated with marriage will impact the professional culture of health care. This data could provide the sometimes-missing context in which to place the events of domestic violence which most physicians will encounter.

---

dance at Religious Services and Mortality over Twenty-eight Years," *American Journal of Public Health* 87, no. 6 (1997): 957-61.

No ideal of lasting marital unions should include tolerance of physical violence, the presence of which is always a reasonable justification for separation and possibly for divorce. The American Medical Association (AMA) has initiated a National Coalition of Physicians against Family Violence. In a 1998 one-page announcement of the coalition, the AMA begins with the following words in large print: "Millions Victimized by Family Members Every Year!" Child abuse, sexual assault, domestic violence, and elder abuse are all matters that of course should be of concern to any physician. Through the coalition the physician will be informed about local contacts and referrals, become aware of local and regional resources, become aware of treatment guidelines and protocols, and even receive an official membership card and poster. One paragraph points out the staggering proportions of family violence: "Every year 2 million cases of child abuse and neglect are reported, between 2 and 4 million women are battered by their spouses, and between 700,000 and 1.1 million of the elderly population are abused."

First-year medical students at my institution receive a powerful lecture from a woman physician in family practice, along with several articles on why women stay in abusive relationships (financial dependence, small children needing their home, and fear of retaliation are among the documented reasons). Students must begin to learn how to interview an abused patient with compassion and insight, as well as gain the ability to implement alternatives for her.[24] The students role-play interviews based on these four questions:

- How would she describe her spousal relationship?
- What happens when she and her partner argue?
- Do fights result in her being hit, shoved, or hurt?
- Does she have an emergency plan?

The students are taught to look for nonspecific complaints (fatigue, insomnia, anxiety, depression, headaches, muscle aches, pelvic pain, and dyspareunia) and for physical signs such as injuries to the face, burns, bite marks, and the like. Such complaints or signs trigger the assessment interview process. Confidentiality is crucial, and the students are taught to never disclose to an abusive partner that the woman has revealed abuse.

I do not take issue with the physician's attentiveness to abuse. Over the course of my own career on the faculty of a school of medicine, virtually every educational project I have been involved with surrounding the family has fo-

---

24. See G. L. Bundow, "Why Women Stay," *Journal of the American Medical Association* 267, no. 23 (1992).

cused on the themes of neglect and abuse, whether with medical students or through various local voluntary associations or public meetings. Perhaps this is fitting, for defining, identifying, reporting, and intervening in the context of the abused patient are clearly parts of the art of the medical professional, who is as such committed to the patient's good. After all, medical students and physicians so often must grapple with the problem of the patient who has been abused and is subsequently seeking treatment for wounds. Elsewhere I have described the grieving medical student whose first pediatric patient, a toddler, was beaten to death by his mother's boyfriend after returning from the clinic.[25]

I do not wish to assert that medical students and physicians are overly inculcated with the most tragic realities of family violence, nor that they do not appreciate the benefits of good marriages and stable families. Fortunately, it is only rarely that a physician takes the view that the family is the source of all evil. Psychiatrist R. D. Laing, for example, in his writings in the 1960s, went to far as to liken the family to the Holocaust, for he saw the family as the perennial source of psychiatric illness or maladjustment.[26] Yet physicians and other health care professionals are typically the ones society charges with the task of dealing with the sequelae of dysfunctional and abusive families.

Although I am aware of no empirical studies of physician attitudes toward marriage and the family, I would anticipate a strong sense of realism. There is, however, one interesting study conducted by the Religion, Culture, and Family Project, with which this volume is associated. This question was put to 1,035 therapists: "Do you find yourself taking a more conservative approach to divorce in your counseling when children are involved?" Answering yes were 80 percent of female and 73 percent of male psychiatrists, 75 percent of female and 59 percent of male psychologists, 69.9 percent of female and 54.0 percent of male marriage and family therapists, 57 percent of female and 45 percent of male social workers, and 43.0 percent of female and 51.8 percent of male pastoral counselors.[27] It appears from this study that however realistic psychiatrists are regarding the potential of the family for good and evil, they are considerably less biased against it than are social workers and pastoral counselors. I will make no attempt here to interpret these data, an endeavor better left to the researchers themselves.

In general, despite being appropriately on the lookout for abuse, physi-

---

25. Stephen G. Post, Patricia R. Frutig, and James Bennett, "The Moral Challenge of Children at Risk: Protective Policies and Pediatrics: A Report of the Children's Services, Inc. Task Force of Greater Cleveland," *Clinical Pediatrics* 36 (1997): 625-34.

26. R. D. Laing, *The Divided Self* (reprint, New York: Penguin Books, 1992).

27. These data were released from the Religion, Culture, and Family Project in March 2000.

cians for the most part see the remarkable loyalty of family caregivers. It may be this usually presumed and absolutely essential interdependence of family members in time of routine care or severe illness that prevents physicians from becoming jaded about the perennial value of the family as a caregiving institution. The pediatrician sees the everyday solicitude of new mothers and fathers, although there may be cases in which parental love, so deeply grounded in evolutionary biology and psychology, is undermined by substance abuse or overwhelming circumstances. The neonatologist marvels at the parent who cares deeply for the newborn, knowing full well that the child may manifest degrees of retardation or physical disability. The family doctor knows well that in times of illness most families pull together and make sacrifices that are both perfectly ordinary yet perfectly extraordinary. Little is "supererogatory" in the family, the fiber of which is shaped and formed in the experience of sometimes severe health crises for one of its members.

The psychiatrist knows what the families of persons with severe mental illness go through in their efforts to be supportive of a loved one. Geriatricians and neurologists are all well aware of the extent of in-home care in the United States, despite relentless pressures on family caregivers for spouses or parents with chronic illness, including irreversible progressive dementias. Rehabilitation specialists know that the patient's successful adjustment to a radically different quality of life due to a major limb amputation or spinal cord injury is chiefly facilitated through faith and a caring family. In every area of medicine, from surgery to oncology to hospice, the family is the very foundation of what has always been best described as "tender loving care" (TLC). This is the deep, generous, warm affirmation of a loved one coupled with an attentive presence in time of need. I think physicians and other health care professionals see so much of this loving care over the course of a clinical career that they know that the family is that "haven in a heartless world."

Conclusions

The paradigm of marriage as a means toward the enhancement of one's health is empirically validated and therefore highly significant in a culture that is shaped by the newest public health data. What has only now been empirically proven has always, however, been part of the common wisdom of social and religious traditions. It will, of course, do no good for health care professionals to "prescribe" marriage, any more than it will be helpful to tell the patient to "get spirituality." Yet there are many cases in which health care professionals should openly discuss the health data on marriage with patients, who then, in their patient autonomy, can make the life choices that they will. Indeed, a truly informed choice about marriage or divorce must take into account all the facts. Given existing data, health care professionals cannot anymore acquiesce to the culture of divorce, for they must "profess" the best interests of spouses and children, and even of aging parents.

But in basing caring and compassionate discussions with patients on existing data, they must also appreciate the wider context of the covenant of love that accurately reflects human frailty and essential interdependence. Marriage and family are ultimately unique institutions designed to maximize the possibilities of warm and personal care for loved ones in need.

Medicine

CHAPTER 6

The Family as a Clinical Entity

Edmund D. Pellegrino, M.D.

The focus of this volume is primarily on marriage and secondarily on the family. This chapter, however, will reverse that order since the physician's perspective is ordered, in the main, by his encounter with the demands made on the marriage commitment when illness strikes the partners and the offspring of a marriage.

To be sure, physicians may well be consulted premaritally when physical or psychological fitness is at issue. Also, physicians are interested in the facts of greater health and longevity enjoyed by married people. But in this they are more the beneficiaries than contributors. Physicians should understand better why this is a fact, and to the extent medicine can enhance this advantage, they should cultivate it.

When all is said and done, however, what the physician encounters are the strengths, weaknesses, and peculiarities of the human commitment in particular marriages when that commitment is tested by illness, disease, disability, and death. It is this perspective that I shall emphasize without demeaning the roles some physicians may be asked to play in premarital fitness evaluation and counseling.

Marriage is a mutual, voluntary commitment of self-surrender to another human being and, at least in traditional marriage, a commitment for life. The commitment is unconditional, traditionally in sickness and in health until "death do us part." Understandably, few people at the moment of marriage appreciate the awesome implications of this commitment. Fewer still can comprehend in advance the depth of the same commitment to children as yet unborn or relatives as yet unmet. But the commitment is open-ended, a lifelong covenant of mutual trust.

In this chapter the term "family" will not be limited to those who are formally married, children of that marriage, or blood relations. In our contemporary world, any group of persons living together in various states of mutual commitment may regard themselves as a "family." At least from the physician's point of view, their interactions and roles in illness causation, treatment, and prevention may parallel those of more traditional family arrangements. They are de facto part of the medicine *of* the family.

This chapter examines the family from the perspective of the physician who enters the family milieu through the need of one of its members for medical care or counsel. From the physician's point of view, the dynamics of family life can be an asset in therapeutics or a liability capable of producing illness. Physicians therefore seriously compromise their own capacities to help, heal, care for, or cure those who consult them by ignoring or neglecting the reciprocal impact of the family on the patient and the patient on the family.

The family has enormous health effects on all its members. It shapes their nature by the genes with which it endows them. It determines how those genes are expressed by the way it nurtures its members. The family leaves its imprint even if it is long forgotten, at a great geographic distance, or consciously repudiated. No matter how much technological advance medicine enjoys, it remains a human enterprise. As such, medicine can rarely diagnose or heal in the fullest sense without taking the family itself to be a part of, or extension of, the patient's health and illness — physical, mental, or spiritual.

This chapter examines this conception under four headings: (1) "Family Medicine and Medicine *of* the Family," (2) "Genetic Screening," (3) "Chronic Illness," and (4) "Family Surrogacy." This is obviously an incomplete survey of the ways physicians confront families in clinical practice. The subjects are chosen because they emphasize the interrelatedness of the health and illness of individual family members and their collective effects on the family as a microcosm of human health and illness.

Family Medicine and Medicine *of* the Family

Ordinarily when people think of the relationship of the physician to the family, they think of the family doctor, someone who can and will treat any member of the family regardless of age as a *primary* care, or first contact, physician.

Traditionally, in days when medicine was less technically oriented than it is now, this role was fulfilled by a general practitioner. Since the end of World War II, medical knowledge has expanded beyond the capacities of any single physician. In 1969, when the American Board of Family Practice was formed, general practitioners themselves became specialists in family practice. The academic discipline for this type of practice was designated family medicine.[1]

Family practitioners interpret family medicine in several ways: one way sees the individual patient as the focus of attention, with the family as the background against which illness is generated or treated. Another sees family medicine as a specialty that can treat all members of the same family regardless of age or gender. Finally, the family, taken as a unit, can be regarded as itself the patient in need of diagnosis and treatment as a collective organism made up of interacting humans. The scope and depth of the physician's entry into the intimate life of the family will depend on which of these approaches the physician adopts. The narrowest interpretation is simply to regard the patient as an individual with the family as the background to his illness, and the most comprehensive is to see the family itself as the patient, with the individual seeking treatment as the entry point into the health of the family as a family. These approaches cannot in actual practice be separated from each other so neatly. Nonetheless, one or the other will predominate with each physician and each clinical encounter.

In the first approach the patient presents himself to the physician as an individual in need of medical help or advice. The physician enters a personal relationship only with this patient. He neither consults nor confronts other members of the family. Generally the physician will obtain a "family history," only insofar as it has some bearing on this patient's presenting problem. The physician, for example, will ask about certain illnesses known to have a family inheritance pattern, e.g., diabetes, hypertension, colon or breast cancer or coronary artery disease, mental depression, Huntington's disease, etc. This information is sought to assist in diagnosis or for prevention for the individual seeking assistance.

The family history serves as a distant warning system which alerts the physician about present or future possibilities which may affect his patient's health. If the patient is discovered to have a disease with a familial tendency, the patient is then a warning signal which may be of significance for other family members. The physician may suggest that the rest of the family be screened for the disease in question. But he does so through the presenting patient. The other family members may or may not consult the physician who discovers the disease. The physician does not automatically take responsibility for each member or for the whole family.

---

1. John P. Geyman, *Family Practice: Foundation of Changing Health Care* (New York: Appleton-Century Crofts, 1980).

Another version of family practice dates back to an earlier era. In this version the physician cares for most or all members of the same family. In the past, this pattern of practice was often seen as the ideal, especially in rural and smaller communities. More usually the physician today treats individual members independently of each other. Each family member may have his or her own physician. Usually there is little communication between physicians regarding either the clinical or psychosocial dynamics of family life or the ways their respective patients react with each other or the family constellation.

However, when the same physician does treat all the members of a family, he has an unusual opportunity to see the interplay of nature and nurture in each of its members who are his patients. He is ethically bound to protect confidentiality for each family member. But with the permission of each person, he can treat family members as an interrelated nexus of human relationships in which each may have an effect on the wellness or illness of the other.

When he takes this step, the family physician enters the realm of the medicine *of* the family in which he has the possibility and responsibility to treat the family itself as a patient. This version of family medicine is an ideal that academic departments of family practice strive to achieve. In this version the physician can examine the state of a marriage; the way adolescents and parents regard each other; how each member plays his or her role; how roles are assigned; how the parents are faring at work; how the children are doing in school; how family eating habits impact the dietary requirements of each member; how a patient's religious viewpoints may influence a child's acceptance of medical advice; how reproductive technologies are viewed; how a drinking problem, attitudes about alternative medicine, or financial worries can shape compliance with the doctor's advice; etc. The number and variety of factors that can influence family health as well as the illness and the recovery of its members are too broad and complex to be captured in any formula.

Manifestly, the physician cannot hope effectively to confront all these relationships. Some are directly related to the development of illness and the recovery of health. But even this limited number can exceed the time, capacity, or interest of the physician. To treat the family as the patient is a humbling concept for even the most conscientious physician. But it does open up possibilities of help and healing that would otherwise be ignored. It can help to identify impediments to treatment and ways to circumvent them. It can, for example, reveal that a woman's nonresponsiveness to treatment for hypertension, peptic ulcer, insomnia, or migraine can only be understood within the context of her husband's drinking problem, infidelity, or abuse.

Clearly, the physician cannot by himself attend to all these problems. But the practical difficulties do not vitiate the idea of medicine of the family.

To some extent the physician can confront these issues by educating family members so they can help in each other's care. Most often the best physicians can do is to recognize the intricate web of family relationships and assist in ameliorating some of the problems these relationships can produce. The remainder must be referred to those better equipped to help, like social workers, nurses, clergy, friends, etc.

What physicians must not lose sight of is the fact that few people become ill or seek help as isolated atoms. All of us become ill in some unique human context of relationships with others. That context may be the family if we are living with them, or the family at a distance physically or chronologically. In these days of complex and variegated living arrangements, it may be those with whom we are sharing living space, whether we are related to them biologically or not. In actual fact, whether physicians treat individuals, households, or whole families, whether they are specialists or generalists, they will confront the medicine of the family to some degree.

In the remainder of this chapter I want to elaborate on this assertion by examining, in more detail, a few illustrative clinical situations. For this purpose I have chosen three clinical contexts: (1) genetic disorders, (2) chronic disease, and (3) surrogate decision making for adults, infants, and children.

Genetic Screening

Biologically the family leaves an indelible imprint on each of its members through the genetic endowment it confers on each of them. Genes are in one sense held in common by family members, shared by ancestors and by current and future generations. Genes are a unifying force but also a divisive one. Out of the common gene heritage each individual family member has drawn a combination which makes him or her unique yet bound to ancestors and successors in the same family.

This biological endowment is variously affected by environmental influences. In some disorders the genetic component is so dominant that it is expressed with a high degree of frequency in most members of a family almost independent of environmental influences. In other circumstances its expression may be strongly dependent on the strength or absence of environmental factors. Our actual physical makeup, and to some extent our behavior, is the result of the interaction of family biology, family social dynamics, and physical environment.[2]

2. Paul R. Ehrlich, *Human Natures: Genes, Culture, and the Human Prospect* (Washing-

When the genome is thoroughly understood (and this goes well beyond simple "mapping"), physicians will be confronted with many questions in their care of individual patients which will require treating the whole family as a patient as well. Many of the most difficult questions, especially those involving genetic engineering to cure disease, gene enhancement of certain characteristics desired by healthy persons, or modification of future generations by germ cell genetic manipulations, lie in the future. At present, some of the practical problems are manifest in genetic screening. Available techniques now make it possible to detect inherited diseases in the fetus and the asymptomatic person, and very early before a disease clearly manifests itself.

Literally thousands of inherited diseases are currently known, and more are being discovered. Almost daily announcements of location of the genes responsible for some disorder are now commonplace. Methods of detection are already available for a growing number of disorders, e.g., various types of muscular dystrophy, breast cancer, cystic fibrosis, Down's syndrome, sickle-cell anemia, thalassemia of various types, Huntington's chorea, etc.[3] It is estimated that the average person has three to five genetic mutations capable of playing a role in disease incidence. Each of these disorders, if detected in one member of a family, has serious implications of an emotional, physical, fiscal, and social significance for all the members of the family. The probability of appearance of a disease in someone with a genetic "defect" is a matter of probability dependent on the interaction of the gene and environment.[4]

One example, Huntington's chorea, will suffice to illustrate the way the family as a unit is affected and, in its turn, affects a person when he or she is tested. Huntington's is a single gene autosomal dominant. This means that if one parent has this gene, there is a 50 percent chance that each offspring will also have the gene.[5] The disease does not manifest itself until later in life and may do so gradually, slowly and subtly at first. It may begin with slight impairment of judgment and proceed inexorably to dementia, difficulties in lo-

---

ton, D.C.: Island Press, 2000); W. Clark and M. Grunstein, *Are We Hardwired? The Role of Gene in Human Behavior* (Oxford, 2000).

3. Task Force on Genetic Testing of the NIH-DOE Working Group of Ethical, Legal and Social Implications of Human Genome Research, *Promoting Safe and Effective Genetic Testing in the United States: Final Report of the Task Force on Genetic Testing*, ed. Neil A. Holtzman and Michael S. Watson (Baltimore: Johns Hopkins University Press, 1998).

4. K. M. Weiss, *Genetic Variation and Human Disease: Principles and Evolutionary Approaches* (Cambridge: Cambridge University Press, 1993).

5. S. Kessler, "Preselection: A Family Coping Strategy in Huntington Disease," *American Journal of Medical Genetics* 31 (1998): 617-21.

comotion and caring for oneself, and convulsions and death in a severely compromised physical, emotional, and mental state.

When the first case in a family is diagnosed, a series of questions important to every member of that family confronts the physician. Should other, apparently healthy members be tested for the gene? Should pregnant members or their embryos be tested? Who is entitled to the results? Can a test-positive member demand that his status be concealed from others? What advice should the physician give to someone who demands to be tested and to others who refuse? Having the gene is different from having the disease at the time of testing. What benefits and harms result from knowing one is positive or negative for the gene? What are the physician's responsibilities to other members of the family, to prospective members contemplating marriage, to their partners entering the family, and to its pregnant members?[6]

The number, range, and variation of these questions are huge. Let us suppose that one member of the family seeks to be tested to be sure he does not have the disease gene. To his consternation, he finds instead that he is positive for the gene and had not contemplated that possibility seriously. He is shocked and wants to hide the fact from his wife, who is pregnant, and his siblings, since there is no known treatment. He has three siblings, none of whom have been tested, and neither have his several nephews and nieces.

Even though there is no treatment, some of his family members might wish to know what they might be facing and would like the opportunity to make preparations and lifestyle decisions. Others may feel differently. Let us suppose that one brother is an airline pilot who has had several minor lapses in procedure and judgment that were noticed by his copilots. Is he showing the first subtle signs of the disease? Is he endangering his passengers? Are his minor lapses nothing more than that? Should he be tested voluntarily? Involuntarily? Should he receive psychological testing rather than genetic screening? Should he receive both?

It is virtually impossible to separate genetic screening decisions affecting one member of the family from their implications for other members.[7] How the physician himself sees the conflicts best resolved will determine how

---

6. A. Kolker and B. M. Burk, *Prenatal Testing: A Sociological Perspective* (Westport, Conn.: Bergin and Garvey, 1994); R. Plomin, "Genetics and Children's Experiences in the Family," *Journal of Child Psychiatry and Psychology and Allied Disciplines* 36 (1995): 33-68; D. Wertz, J. H. Fanos, and P. R. Reilly, "Genetic Testing for Children and Adolescents," *Journal of the American Medical Association* 272 (1994): 875-81.

7. Neil A. Holtzman, *Proceed with Caution: Predicting Genetic Risk in the Recombinant DNA Era* (Baltimore: Johns Hopkins University Press, 1989); Seymour Kessler, ed., *Genetic Counselling, Psychological Dimensions* (New York: Academic Press, 1979).

he advises his patient and then the patient's family. What are the doctor's responsibilities beyond both family and patient — to the employer and the insurer, to the public health authority?

Few physicians are adequately prepared, either with the requisite genetic knowledge or the skills of group dynamics, to manage the nexus of clinical and ethical conundrums the era of molecular medicine will bring. Few physicians are knowledgeable in the accuracy, precision, sensitivity, specificity, or probability implications of genetic testing.[8] Clearly a new set of obligations must be confronted by any physician who purports to be today's or tomorrow's family physician, even though he necessarily will be assisted by genetic counselors, the clergy, psychologists, etc. The family will often as not turn to him for guidance. In the end the physician will write the order for a test or a consultation, or make a decision to involve other family members.

The implications for medical education, residency training, and continuing education of physicians are profound. The doctor cannot and should not do it all. But if the family doctor is to be the doctor of, and to, the family, he must enter a new way of practice in the era of molecular medicine. The traditional physician-patient relationship will expand to become the physician-family relationship. The matters of family involved in genetic screening are already with us. Today's screening questions will seem simple when the more complex questions of germ cell manipulation, genetic enhancement, germ-line manipulation, and eugenics present themselves.[9] Mapping the genome is the beginning of a much more complex enterprise which will more closely relate environment and genetics with a deeper knowledge of how the information in our DNA is transmitted into structure function and behavior.[10] The problems of helping families to cope with the implications of genetic testing, especially in behavioral and psychopathological disorders, will be immense.[11]

---

8. L. A. Demmer, M. J. O'Neill, A. E. Roberts, and M. C. Clay, "Knowledge of Ethical Standards in Genetic Testing among Medical Students, Residents and Practicing Physicians," *Journal of the American Medical Association* 284 (2000): 2595-96.

9. G. Vogel, "Genetic Enhancement: From Science Fiction to Ethics Quandary," *Science* 277 (1997): 1753-54; Philip R. Sloan, ed., *Controlling Our Destinies: Historical, Philosophical, Ethical, and Theological Perspectives on the Human Genome Project* (Notre Dame, Ind.: University of Notre Dame Press, 2000); W. French Anderson, "Human Gene Therapy: Scientific and Ethical Considerations," *Journal of Medicine and Philosophy* 10 (1985): 288-91.

10. A. B. Hatfield and H. P. Lefley, *Families of the Mentally Ill: Coping and Adaptation* (New York and London: Guilford Press, 1987); F. Goodwin and K. R. Jamison, eds., *Manic Depressive Illness* (Oxford: Oxford University Press, 1990); H. Greenspan, "Understanding the Genetic Construction of Behavior," *Scientific American* 273 (1995): 72-78.

11. Hatfield and Lefley, *Families of the Mentally Ill: Coping and Adaptation;* Goodwin and Jamison, *Manic Depressive Illness.*

Chronic Illness

The impact of the realities of human genetics and the genome project on medicine of the family is as yet largely in the future.[12] More immediate is the impact of chronic, disabling disease on family structure, function, and solidarity. Here we need only think, for example, of the effects of stroke, multiple sclerosis, Alzheimer's or Parkinson's diseases on all the members of the family unit. These are truly catastrophic events, reflecting outward in concentric circles of disruption from those closest to the patient — wife, children — to those at a greater distance who may be pulled into the care relationship in a variety of ways.

In days past Alzheimer's and Parkinson's of course occurred as they do today. They were not singled out for special attention but were subsumed under the general, vague rubric of "senility" or senile "dementia." They were expected to occur as a matter of course as a manifestation of aging. They were accepted as the sign of a life coming to a natural end. The patient was infantilized by his family, kept in the family unit, cared for, nursed, and condescended to as a matter of course or filial duty. Expectations were that similar solicitude would be offered when the caregivers themselves would, in due course, succumb to the inexorable processes of aging.

In the past the family, nuclear and extended, continued to see the demented patient as a worthy, though affected, continuing member of the family. Hospitalization and nursing homes were a last resort for those who were violent or self-injuring. Most were kept at home in the family's ambience. Household routines were altered; turns were taken at giving care; and all was seen as a recognized duty — difficult, yes, but not unfair. Care of a disabled family member was part of life's inevitabilities.

A peaceful, early death might be hoped and prayed for, but intentional interruption of that life to ease the anguish of the caregiver or the putative sufferings of the patient was unthinkable. Family relationships were not so much changed as accommodated to the presence of the afflicted member. Self-pity of the caregiver existed, of course, but it was not justified. Care of an ailing family member was not seen as an unjust infringement on the caregiver's right to a "quality life." Care for one's family members was an inevitable fate all would sooner or later experience, not an assault on the caregiver's pursuit of his own happiness.

Today the role and circumstance of the family in its relationships with a patient with Alzheimer's, Parkinson's, or other chronic disorders are pro-

---

12. Greenspan, "Understanding the Genetic Construction of Behavior."

foundly different. Today, as studies in this volume so amply demonstrate, the nuclear family is eroded by divorce, dysfunction, striving to obtain the goods of this world with both father and mother employed, children at an early age pursuing their own self-fulfillment, etc. All are distracted by pursuit of wealth and the constant fascination with entertainment to fill every spare moment. The "family" is today a dispersed entity, its members living miles apart, with their own friends, communities, or associations. They come together as families only in hardship, weddings, deaths, or carefully planned reunions.

When Alzheimer's or Parkinson's or a stroke or other disability strikes one member of a family, there is often no nearby familial supporting structure. The afflicted person is now not so much a loved one in distress but a problem to be solved. It is true that many families still rally around, sharing the responsibility for care, and act with cooperative solicitude. Usually these are families with strong bonds of ethnicity and culture. Too often their actions are more or less regarded as heroic, but not as routine obligations of familyhood.

Today's realities of geographic separation, the need to pursue jobs to keep up a standard of living and consumption, or the concern for one's own "good" life interrupts this traditional family solidarity around the care of the afflicted person. The demands of one's own life lead to early plans to relieve the family of its "burden." The nursing home and retirement home become the loci for "care." For many families, even visits become a chore and an interference in crowded schedules.

Family debates ensue over who is responsible for the care, for the costs, for the visits, for the decisions to be made. Reawakening of ancient family resentments is all too common. Often one member is more faithful or altruistic than the rest. Guilt afflicts the others, and intrafamilial rancor sours the whole experience. Clearly, a chronic, disabling illness in any senior family member afflicts the whole family. The physician who administers to family members finds himself forced to engage the medicine *of* the family. Without its engagement the opportunities for amelioration of disease and disability and of a "good" death are easily missed.

The central responsibility of the doctor of the family is to act as the patient's advocate — to marshal family resources to the extent possible to support those inclined to help, to marshal local and community services on behalf of the afflicted member. This calls for very close working with visiting nurses, social workers, churches, and pastoral counselors — educating family members who need to be motivated to prevent isolation or abandonment of the incapacitated family member. The physician must be aware of subtler forms of family stress, strife, and conflict which will impact negatively on his patient.

The doctor cannot "cure" pathological or dysfunctional families. But he can buffer the disarray, discontent, and distress of a chronic or disabling illness. Generalist physicians must be educated to realize that a debilitating illness in any family member, especially a senior member, is a problem of medicine *of* the family. The whole family is impaired to some degree, even those with no deep sense of familial solidarity or loyalty.

Clearly, all of this applies to any chronic illness well beyond Alzheimer's and Parkinson's, to diabetes, cardiac failure, pulmonary emphysema, arthritis, etc. With every chronic illness the cooperation of the family, especially the spouse or whoever acts as immediate caregiver, is essential. Diet, exercise, assistance in daily living, and stress reduction are crucial to optimal treatment, quality of life, and the prevention of complications.

To put a husband on a low-fat, low-cholesterol diet, for example, is ipso facto to make his wife a member of the therapeutic team. She would ordinarily prepare the patient's meal and must decide whether to make different meals for herself or adhere to the husband's diet. If, as may be the case in our contemporary world, wife and husband lead independent lives or share cooking duties, the same problems arise. Whether the need is a low-fat diet, abstinence from smoking or alcohol, participation in exercise, limitations regarding sexual intercourse, or help in locomotion, the doctor is treating the whole family via the patient he encounters.

Any prescription or advice that involves changes in lifestyle is therefore a treatment for the family as well as the patient. Success or failure, amelioration or exaggeration of symptom and pathology, are closely related to their effects on those with whom the patient lives. How those persons respond can be therapeutic or deleterious, a source of mutual love and concern or a factor for alienation and divisiveness. Again, the family doctor of the future is challenged to practice medicine *of* the family as much as family medicine for its presenting member.

Family Surrogacy

A final example of medicine of the family is in the realm of ethical decision-making at the beginning and end of life. The most common instance involves the family role as a moral surrogate in decisions about withdrawing or withholding life-sustaining treatment. Here the family can be an advocate for the patient, representing his wishes, or a source of potential harm, conflict, and disservice.

Moral surrogacy is a role almost every family member must take seriously. Today, when life-sustaining technologies can prolong life almost indefinitely, a large majority of deaths, at home or in hospital, result from a deliberate decision to withhold, withdraw, or minimize life-sustaining medical interventions.[13] These decisions are often made when the patient himself has lost the capacity to make his own decision.

Of course, if the patient has intact decision-making capacity, his decision, morally, is the determining factor. He has no need for a surrogate. The patient may willingly delegate this privilege to some other member of his family, but he is free to change that designation as often as he chooses. Other family members may feel hurt by the favoritism they see in the choice of a surrogate. But the patient has the moral and legal authority to choose his surrogate so long as his choice is free and uncoerced.

This changes when a patient loses his capacity to make his own choices and the physician must deal with the surrogates who now have a moral and legal authority to act for the family member. Here a number of serious family conflicts may engage the physician, whose first responsibility, with some modifications to be mentioned below, is to be the advocate for the welfare of the patient.

A decision on behalf of a mentally incompetent patient to withdraw or withhold life-sustaining treatment is a family decision. But it is also a source of tension and conflict in which the physician is often embroiled. For one thing, though it may not be openly expressed, there is the age-old tension among families about inheritance of whatever worldly goods the patient may possess. Some members may be eager to gain access to the dying man's assets and, consciously or not, urge the physician to undertreat or desist from treatment sooner than is in the patient's best interests. For some the opposite tendency prevails, if there is some gain in prolonging life — e.g., the patient is receiving disability checks. Most surrogates are genuinely motivated to discontinuance or continuation on the basis of their estimate of what is best for the patient. But their suitability as morally valid surrogates may vary considerably.

Family members may have different emotional relationships with a dying parent or sibling. Guilt over past disagreements or alienation can lead to a temptation to overreact and to "do everything" to prove to oneself, or to the other members of the family, that one is really well disposed to the dying person. Lifelong resentment or hostility, on the other hand, can consciously or unconsciously lead to a desire to undertreat. Among different members of the

---

13. E. D. Pellegrino, "Withholding and Withdrawing Treatments: Ethics at the Bedside," *Clinical Neurosurgery* 35 (1989): 164-84.

family, these sentiments will often vary and conflict with each other so that the doctor can be caught between opposing surrogate decisions.

For the doctor, a key factor in any surrogate decision is the degree to which it reflects what the patient would want were he able to make his own decision. Most family members will claim they know the patient's "values" and what he would have wanted. Sometimes this is based on the slimmest evidence or on some statement from years past which another family member may interpret quite differently. Indeed, a friend or neighbor might have much more recent and accurate knowledge of the patient's wishes than any family member.

Despite this, the physician must remember that the family must live with the surrogate decision for the rest of their lives. The family is thus a patient as much as, or more than in one sense, the comatose patient himself. The undeniable fact is that asking the family to consent to a do-not-resuscitate order or to withdrawal of a respirator often is, in their eyes, to make them executioners of a family member. Yet, in the current era of patient and family autonomy in medical decisions, there is no alternative to asking their permission.

The problem is especially acute with young parents of a critically or hopelessly ill infant whose inevitable death they have not yet come to accept or comprehend as a genuine reality. Here the physician, in the interest of treating the family as a patient, may continue futile treatment for a period to provide time for some degree of emotional adjustment. In certain instances this may apply to the care of a dying parent or spouse as well. At some point, if treatment is genuinely futile and also disproportionately burdensome, the physician may have to refuse to continue treatment. There is no ethical obligation to provide futile treatment. But physicians may decide to continue such treatment temporarily if it gives the family some time to adjust to the inevitable.

Often complicating this nexus of family interactions are differences in religious or cultural beliefs about death, dying, and the value of human life itself.[14] Family members may disagree on this point with each other or with the physician. Religious motives for decisions to treat or withhold treatment are often the most powerful sources of conflict between family members, physicians, and other caregivers. The minister or pastoral counselor then becomes

---

14. E. J. Emanuel and D. L. Fairclough, "Attitudes and Desires Related to Euthanasia and Assisted Suicide among Terminally Ill Patients and the Caregivers," *Journal of the American Medical Association* 284 (2000): 2460-68; J. Wolfe, N. Klar, H. E. Grier, J. Duncan, S. Salem-Schatz, and J. C. Weeks, "Understanding of Prognosis among Parents of Children Who Died of Cancer," *Journal of the American Medical Association* 284 (2000): 2469-75.

The Family as a Clinical Entity

an essential member of the decision-making constellation to help to resolve deep-seated familial conflict.

The physician herself is the bearer of personal ethical, religious, cultural, and scientific beliefs which shape the way she responds to the dynamic forces in the family. But whatever her own beliefs might be in relation to those of the family, the doctor's ultimate covenant of trust is with the patient. If she has evidence of significant fiscal or emotional conflicts of interest between and among surrogates, she must opt for the patient's welfare. She must therefore perform the futility calculus — relating effectiveness, benefit, and burdens of treatment. If these relationships are disproportionate, there is no obligation to treat. The physician is compelled to explain her position to the family. If they disagree, they may discharge her or she may ask to be relieved. This is another family choice in which conflict can arise.

In the case of infants, whose wishes cannot be known, the physician has particularly complex ethical relationships to disentangle. The physician's responsibility must be the welfare of the infant, who is the most vulnerable member of the family and whose life depends upon the decision of the surrogates. We cannot know how an infant would define its quality of life, or with what disabilities it might prefer to contend rather than dying. On the witness of many disabled people, it is clear that they live quality lives which others may not appreciate.

Families do not universally or always act in the best interests of very sick infants. They may refuse consent to simple lifesaving treatment, for example, because they simply do not want to raise an otherwise normal infant with Down's syndrome or some other condition requiring special care. In such cases the physician may be compelled ethically to refuse the parents' request to cease treatment or resort to the courts to resolve the conflict. The courts cannot resolve ethical issues, but they are a last resort when agreement among decision makers is not possible.

This is not the place to review all the issues in moral surrogacy. I have selected it as simply another example of the way the family response to illness of one of its members may be beneficent or maleficent but is always of significance. The physician, especially in the care of infants and children, is treating the complex organism of the human family in a crisis situation.

While I have emphasized the family physician and the physician of the family, the issues are not confined solely to that specialty. Every specialty confronts the inescapable fact that patients become ill and are cured, treated, or die as members of families, and that those families are involved ineluctably in the predicament of illness of their members and can alter treatment for good or harm.

Other authors in this collection have shown clearly that marriage and life within the family are associated with greater longevity, better health, and less morbidity. This chapter has examined the family as a clinical entity which the clinician confronts in a variety of ways. The family is not always a therapeutic ally of the physician. The family may also be the source of illness through its genetic endowment to each of its members and through the way it responds to the illnesses of its members.

On the whole, however, in the examples I have chosen, genetically transmitted diseases, chronic illness, and moral surrogacy, families can be an invaluable resource in enhancing and facilitating the patient's recovery. Physicians who practice both family medicine and the medicine *of* the family can marshal these resources, prevent the harmful responses, and advance the well-being of all members of the family unit.

CHAPTER 7

Whose Marriage? Whose Health? A Christian Feminist Ethical Response

Christine Firer Hinze and Mary Stewart Van Leeuwen

Introduction

This chapter is by two scholars — one Catholic and one Reformed — who participate in the ongoing tradition of social teaching in our respective churches. We are also beneficiaries and supporters of many aspects of the second wave of feminism that began in the Western world in the 1960s. Thus we support the growing movement to reinstitutionalize marriage, especially in light of recent research showing the generally negative effects of divorce and nonmarital cohabitation and childbearing, and the generally positive effects of marriage for both individuals and society. Yet we have theological and historical reasons for questioning any version of the emerging marriage movement that ignores a major force behind the appearance of second-wave feminism in the 1960s — namely, a widespread dissatisfaction with the cultural separation of spheres for men and women, and its effects on people of all ages and classes.

Other chapters in this volume have highlighted findings in the social and behavioral sciences concerning marriage's demonstrably positive effects on the health of adults, children, and society.[1] This data is cited by various

---

1. See, e.g., Paul R. Amato and Alan Booth, *A Generation at Risk: Growing Up in an Era of Family Upheaval* (Cambridge: Harvard University Press, 1997); David Popenoe, Jean Bethke Elshtain, and David Blankenhorn, eds., *Promises to Keep: Decline and Renewal of Marriage in America* (Lanham, Md.: Rowman and Littlefield, 1996); Linda J. Waite and Maggie Gallagher, *The Case for Marriage* (New York: Doubleday, 2000); and "The Marriage Movement," Joint

groups, including Christian communities, who wish to promote marriage as an institution, usually conceived in its Western, nuclear format. Both Reformed and Catholic Christians have traditionally upheld marriage and family as divinely instituted vocational settings where persons respond to the biblical mandates to be fruitful and multiply, and to till and keep the earth as stewards of the gifts and tasks of creation. Internal differences notwithstanding, Christians approach secular treatments of marriage from a theological and moral perspective rooted in the doctrines of creation and redemption and given expression in particular liturgical and sacramental tradition.

Our theological response to the growing marriage movement is informed by feminism and by dialogue with the social and behavioral sciences. We further contend that understandings of marriage and family, Christian or secular, must be informed by a commitment to justice that challenges unwarranted biases and forms of exclusion. We are especially concerned that promarriage initiatives avoid skewed power relations based on differences such as gender — which we emphasize here — but also race, class, and ethnicity.[2] To this end, family and marriage advocates must be discriminating as they assess the present scene and strategies for the future.

We begin by setting our agenda more explicitly within the context of current research on the differential costs and benefits of marriage to women and men. There is now a substantial literature — recently summarized by demographer Linda Waite and public policy analyst Maggie Gallagher — documenting the health benefits of marriage, on average, for *both* sexes as compared to the risks of divorce, cohabitation, widow(er)hood, and/or never marrying. Married men and women face lower risks of dying at any stage of adulthood than those in nonmarital categories. Both sexes, if married, are less likely to engage in health-threatening behaviors such as substance abuse and dangerous driving. On average, married persons rate their sexual lives as more satisfying both physically and emotionally. And the per capita (not just joint) wealth of married people in the United States is four to ten times higher than for those in nonmarital categories.[3]

Statement of the Coalition for Marriage, Family and Couples' Education and the Institute for American Values (New York: Institute for American Values, 2000).

2. See Maxine Baca Zinn, "Family, Feminism, and Race in America," *Gender and Society* 4, no. 1 (March 1990): 70. Adequate marriage and family analysis must, moreover, attend to the *reinforcing* impacts of gender, race, and class on these institutions — a subject that warrants much greater development. Cf. Zinn, pp. 72ff. Here we concur with what Wall and Miller-McLemore, in their contribution to this volume, name a "liberation" approach.

3. Linda J. Waite, "Does Marriage Matter?" *Demography* 32, no. 4 (November 1995): 483-507; Waite and Gallagher, *The Case for Marriage*.

Still, these benefits are not completely symmetrical for women and men. Men, for example, gain more than women from marriage in terms of improved health. This is partly because even when unmarried, women live healthier lifestyles — which they continue to practice when married — and because wives take responsibility for monitoring their spouses' health habits to a degree that the latter don't. Regardless of marital status, women usually develop wider and stronger friendship networks than men do; they also bring these habits into marriage and draw husbands into them.[4] So married men's net gain in social support is somewhat greater than married women's.

Women experience a greater net gain in wealth than men by being married. However, much of this effect comes from a spousal division of labor that allows men to pursue waged labor more effectively than if they were unmarried. This is because wives assume most of the tasks of "social reproduction" — cooking, cleaning, child rearing, and managing the schedules and general well-being of other family members.[5] This division of labor — a residue of the nineteenth-century doctrine of separate spheres — is problematic for at least three reasons. First, its efficiency in generating joint marital wealth is beneficial to women only as long as marriages last, and today in the United States there is about a 50 percent likelihood that any marriage will succumb to divorce. Second, to the extent that this division of labor is made legally and socially normative — as was particularly the case prior to the second wave of feminism — it is harder for married women to pursue extradomestic vocations. The amount of interaction men have with their families is also seriously truncated. Third, continuing to place greater social and economic value on waged labor than on the reproductive labor performed by women perpetuates a subtle patriarchy. Work deemed "feminine" is culturally sentimentalized but practically devalued, and women continue to be denied social agency and security on a par with men.

There is little evidence that either domesticity *or* waged work per se affects women's health or happiness. The crucial factor seems to be the freedom to choose which (or which mix of) roles to adopt. Married women who are reluctantly in the waged workforce express dissatisfaction with their lives, as do reluctant full-time homemakers.[6] In light of this we will argue that current attempts to reinstitutionalize marriage be accompanied by social policies en-

---

4. The pertinent literature on men's and women's relationship networks is reviewed in Hilary Lips, *Sex and Gender: An Introduction,* 3rd ed. (Mountain View, Calif.: Mayfield, 1997), chaps. 10 and 11.

5. See, e.g., Marjorie L. DeVault, *Feeding the Family: The Social Organization of Caring as Gendered Work* (Chicago: University of Chicago Press, 1991).

6. See Lips, chap. 9.

abling spouses to maximize both role flexibility and material security at various stages of the family life-cycle.

Shifting Norms for Families and Households

Sociologists of the family point out that for most of U.S. history, "Americans have shared with virtual unanimity the following cultural beliefs":

> Adults should be married.
> Marriage is a lifelong commitment.
> Married couples should have children.
> A wife's place is at home as nurturer, mother, caretaker.
> A husband's role is provider and decision maker.[7]

Throughout most of U.S. history, Christian understandings of marriage comfortably dovetailed with this cultural consensus. Christian theologians and pastors portrayed marriage as a lifelong, monogamous, procreative union. Families had their origin and center in the dyad of husband and wife. Spouses were assigned complementary yet overlapping roles, which by the mid-nineteenth century were largely interpreted in terms of the more distinct female-homemaker, male-breadwinner arrangement. Till well past the mid-twentieth century, deviation from such forms was liable to elicit ecclesial and social condemnation, and self-recrimination as well.

Variations on traditional norms concerning marriage and family, including the modern homemaker-breadwinner arrangement, have existed even during periods of great consensus. By the twentieth century's end, however, the consensus itself had deteriorated, disrupting the long alliance between Christian and secular assumptions. And as public acceptance of household diversity grows, debates have emerged within Catholic and Reformed circles concerning the exceptionability, elasticity, and even the continued validity of traditional religious prescriptions concerning marriage. Monogamy, heterosexuality, the restriction of sexual relations to marriage, procreativity, indissolubility — all have come under question.

Along with other religious communions,[8] U.S. Catholic and Reformed Christians seek to develop their traditions concerning marriage and family in

---

7. Maxine Baca Zinn and D. Stanley Eitzen, *Diversity in Families,* 4th ed. (New York: Harpercollins College Publishers, 1996), p. xx.
8. Cf. Paul Numrich's article in the present volume, chap. 14.

light of contemporary circumstances. We believe this requires an analysis of certain dangers and distortions attaching to both traditions' embrace, over the past century, of the doctrine of separate spheres for men and women, and the long shadow this doctrine continues to cast on practices surrounding marriage and family. We next examine some strengths and weaknesses of Reformed and Catholic social teaching traditions relevant to an alternative and more promising doctrine for contemporary marriage and family life — namely, a "critical promarriage stance" coupled with a "critical familism" that balances the virtues of family maintenance with an "ethic of equal regard."[9] The latter term implies "that husband and wife should each in principle have equal access to the privileges *and* responsibilities of both public and private worlds ... [not placing] family togetherness above other values such as equality between husband and wife, the well being of children, and the flourishing of individual family members."[10]

Reformed Teaching on Marriage and Family

The current embodiment of Reformed social teaching, like its better-known Catholic counterpart, began at the end of the nineteenth century in response to challenges of the industrial revolution. That era was characterized by increasing urbanization and bureaucratization, with waged labor in factories and corporations steadily displacing smaller family-run farms and businesses. The era also saw fragmentation of families that had previously lived from generation to generation in smaller and more cohesive communities. Politically, the opposing ideologies of rugged individualism and collectivist socialism were competing for ascendancy in the Western world. Each was a potential secular replacement for the Christian worldview which, in various Catholic and Protestant incarnations, had dominated the West for the previous fifteen hundred years.

In response to these contrasting challenges, parallel streams of Christian social thought developed in Catholic and Reformed circles. In 1891 Pope

---

9. On critical familism and a critical promarriage stance, see, respectively, Don S. Browning, Bonnie J. Miller-McLemore, Pamela D. Couture, K. Brynolf Lyon, and Robert M. Franklin, *From Culture Wars to Common Ground: Religion and the American Family Debate* (Louisville: Westminster John Knox 1997), chap. 11; and William J. Doherty and Jason Carroll's article in the present volume.

10. Don S. Browning, "The Task of Religious Institutions in Strengthening Families," Joint Statement of the Religion, Culture and Family Project (University of Chicago) and the Communitarian Network (George Washington University), 1998, p. 2.

Leo XIII issued his social encyclical *Rerum novarum,* which was the basis for the Catholic notion of "subsidiarity." Around the same time, the Dutch theologian and statesman Abraham Kuyper (1837-1920) developed a roughly parallel concept that came to be known as "sphere sovereignty." By this he meant the right of God-ordained institutions or spheres of life — such as church, family, business, science, and the arts — to develop as creationally intended without being overwhelmed by the state, ignored in the name of individual freedom, or reduced one to another among themselves. In more contemporary parlance, Kuyper envisaged a civil society of autonomous institutions that stood between the extremes of libertarian individualism and state (and nowadays we might add, corporate) totalitarianism.

He also wanted to challenge the dualistic notion — embraced by many Protestant pietists — that certain human activities (such as prayer and religious observance) were "sacred" while others (such as science, politics, art, and even family life) were "secular" and therefore of limited or even no importance to the Christian life. By contrast, Kuyper insisted that all of life's activities were blessed by God in creation and were to be developed and redeemed according to norms discernible in the Hebrew and Christian Scriptures. Thus he advanced a theological rationale for robust Christian involvement in family life, scholarship, the arts, commerce, and government. As a Calvinist who subscribed to the doctrine of pervasive depravity, Kuyper (at least in theory) did not idealize the current functioning of any of these spheres. He realized that they could be perverted both internally (for example, when there is corruption in government, abuse in the family, or worker exploitation in business) and externally (for example, when the church tries to dictate topics or theories to scientists, or when the state tries to replace the family). But for Kuyper such distortions called not for eliminating any of these institutions — all of which he regarded as being rooted in creation — but for their reform and renewal according to scriptural norms.[11]

Both visions — the differentiated responsibilities of various life spheres and Christians' calling to participate in all of them — echoed turn-of-the-century Catholic social teaching, and embodied principles that, if anything, are even more important a century later. But within this movement there hangs a gendered tale, one that makes many women in the Reformed tradition skeptical about the notion of sphere sovereignty. Their unease stems

---

11. A readable source summarizing Kuyper's neo-Calvinist viewpoint is Abraham Kuyper, *Lectures on Calvinism: The Stone Foundation Lectures of 1898* (Grand Rapids: Eerdmans, 1970). See also James D. Bratt, ed., *Abraham Kuyper: A Centennial Reader* (Grand Rapids: Eerdmans, 1998); Luis Lugo, ed., *Religion, Pluralism, and Public Life: Abraham Kuyper's Legacy for the Twenty-first Century* (Grand Rapids: Eerdmans, 2000).

from the fact that Kuyper essentialized a limiting and culturally specific view of gender relations in his concern to maintain the functional integrity of the family. He not only believed in patriarchal marriage, albeit of a benevolent and self-sacrificing sort permeated by the fruit of the Holy Spirit; he also accepted — and read back into Scripture — the nineteenth-century bourgeois dichotomizing of men's and women's activities. Variously known as "the cult of domesticity" and "the cult of true womanhood," this doctrine of separate spheres assigned women the tasks of nurturing family, maintaining the home, and being models of morality, community, and self-sacrifice to husbands and older sons, whose days were to be spent in the competitive and individualistic urban arena.

Kuyper did tolerate the idea of women earning a living as domestic servants, factory workers, and salesclerks, particularly if they were unmarried. Indeed, as a self-styled "social feminist" and an early architect of the welfare state, he insisted that women's interests be protected in the areas of civil law, business, industry, and labor. But such work should be at best temporary, he insisted, since women were created for marriage, motherhood, and domesticity, and women's activity in the public arena should never be extended to include participation in the academy or the political forum. For leadership in these areas, he wrote in a 1914 series of articles entitled "The Women's Place of Honor," "the all-disposing Creator and Master of our life did not give special gifts to women." Nor should men be much involved in domestic activity: "Man and woman are fundamentally different in kind," he wrote in the same series, "and . . . whoever has the man take his place at the cradle and the woman at the lectern, makes life unnatural."[12] Women might have an occasional, subordinate place in public-sphere activities that were extensions of domesticity — in child pedagogy, philanthropy, or orphanage and hospital work. But, Kuyper concluded, "woman's position of honor is most effectively maintained if she can sparkle in private life, and in the public domain, for which the man is the appointed worker, she will never be able to fulfill anything but a subordinate role, in which her inferiority would soon come to light anyway."[13]

---

12. Abraham Kuyper, *De Eerepositie der Vrouw* (Kampen: Kok, 1932); these quotes are taken from pp. 15 and 29 of an English translation by Irene Brouwer Konyndyk, published in 1992; the page references for subsequent citations are also taken from this translation. See also Mary Stewart Van Leeuwen, "Abraham Kuyper and the Cult of True Womanhood: An Analysis of *De Eerepositie der Vrouw*," *Calvin Theological Journal* 31, no. 1 (April 1996): 97-124, and "'The Carrot and the Stick': Abraham Kuyper on Gender, Family and Class," in *Religion, Pluralism, and Public Life*.

13. Kuyper, *De Eerepositie der Vrouw*, p. 28.

We do not wish to be anachronistic in evaluating the doctrine of separate spheres, since most of its apologists, including Kuyper, intended it to elevate women's status. By idealizing women's place in the home, they sought to shield them from the heavy and often dangerous work of many early industrial settings. And as American historian Carl Degler has noted, despite the continuing rhetoric of husbandly headship, "within the home women did gain a new recognition, and in the process broke the ancient hierarchy that had assigned superiority to men in all spheres of activity. By asserting a companionate role for women [this doctrine] implicitly denied patriarchy."[14] But it was a doctrine riddled with inconsistencies and unintended consequences. It was based on a narrowly middle-class notion of domestic life, and failed to acknowledge that among the growing percentage of families dependent on waged labor, a husband's earnings were often not enough to support a wife and children. Yet wives who took on waged work, far from being lauded for their contribution, were regarded as at best falling short of the domestic ideal and at worst perverting a fixed creation norm for gender roles. Moreover, the husbands of such women increasingly came to be seen (and to see themselves) as less than adequate providers.

As the doctrine of separate spheres became an accepted cultural norm, women who embraced it became more isolated intellectually and socially, and increasingly dependent on husbands economically — all of which, in practice, made them more vulnerable to domestic abuse.[15] Reformed social theorists have often noted that Calvin (unlike Luther) did not believe in the immutability of life's social stations, but rather recognized that social structures — not just individual behavior — could be permeated by human sin and thus require change. Kuyper was a thoroughgoing Calvinist in applying this principle of *semper reformanda* in public spheres, for he held that business, government, education, science, and art should be continually scrutinized against biblical norms of justice and human flourishing. But with regard to the domestic arena, he was evidently more Lutheran than Calvinist: women were not to question their divinely assigned roles in the home, even if their gifts might equally suit them for service elsewhere. With limited exceptions they were to embrace domesticity (even if it involved "suffering unjustly")[16]

---

14. Carl N. Degler, *At Odds: Women and the Family in America from the Revolution to the Present* (New York: Oxford University Press, 1980), p. 28.

15. See, e.g., Elizabeth Pleck, *Domestic Tyranny: The Making of American Social Policy against Family Violence from Colonial Times to the Present* (New York: Oxford University Press, 1987).

16. Abraham Kuyper, *Antirevolutie Ook in Uw Huisgezin* (Antirevolutionary also in your family) (Kampen: Kok, 1932). See also Van Leeuwen, "The Carrot and the Stick." The "suffering

in a pattern of gender relations neither open to development nor in need of reform.

As well as underestimating the potential sinfulness of patriarchal family life, Kuyper was guilty of two other inconsistencies. First, in none of his other writings did he go beyond describing sphere sovereignty in terms of *life activities* to identifying spheres with *particular groups of people*. Though he was a nineteenth-century paternalist in his attitudes toward South Africa, he saw the long-term goal of colonialism as giving indigenous peoples "Christianization and training for eventual independence."[17] Unlike his South African Boer cousins, Kuyper was no defender of racial separation; on the contrary, he saw the "commingling of the blood as the physical basis of all higher human development"[18] and argued that it was more likely to occur in Calvinist nations than in others. Yet by endorsing the doctrine of separate spheres (and invoking God to underwrite it), he helped construct what amounted to an ethic of gender apartheid: "The private and public life form two separate spheres, each with their own way of existing, and their own task. And it is on the basis of this state of affairs *which has not been invented by us, but which God himself has imposed on us,* that in public life the woman does not stand equally with the man. No more than it can be said of the man that in married life he is called to achieve in the family that which is achieved by the woman."[19]

Finally (though he never acknowledged this publicly), Kuyper's gender apartheid was at cross-purposes with two other neo-Calvinist doctrines which he otherwise held dear — namely, the *cultural mandate* and *common grace*. The former refers to the conviction that God has placed humankind in the world to open up the potential of creation, that this mandate is in no way changed by the fall, and that people are called to restore all life's activities to their appropriate, God-given norms for functioning. But when we examine the *locus classicus* for this doctrine — namely, Genesis 1:26-28 — we find that *both* mandates — accountable dominion and generativity — are given to both members of the primal pair. This does not preclude the fact that a gendered division of labor may be a just and satisfying way to organize a given family or culture for a specific time. But it does imply that any construction of gender involving an exaggerated or inflexible separation of activ-

---

unjustly" reference is to 1 Pet. 2:18-19, which speaks of slaves' obedience to masters, but which Kuyper appropriated frequently to refer to wives' God-ordained relationship to husbands and children's to parents.

17. Frank Vanden Berg, *Abraham Kuyper* (Grand Rapids: Eerdmans, 1960), p. 249.
18. Kuyper, *Lectures on Calvinism*, p. 35.
19. Kuyper, *De Eerepositie der Vrouw*, pp. 19-20, emphasis added.

ities by sex is likely to run into trouble eventually, because it is creationally distorted and therefore potentially unjust toward *both* sexes. The cultural mandate is a human — not a gendered — mandate.

Common grace refers to the Calvinist conviction that God enables the cultural mandate — with its resulting knowledge and virtue — to flourish even in persons not espousing true faith in God. So strongly did Kuyper hold to this doctrine — at least in his middle years — that he once wryly observed that the unbelieving world often did much better than one would expect, and the church worse.[20] Yet in the movement for women's right to vote and to pursue higher education and public careers he saw little common grace at work, but only the sinful individualism of the French Revolution and the "English suffragette" smuggled onto Dutch soil.[21] In sum, though it was a well-intentioned attempt to preserve the family as a mediating institution and cope with the changes brought by industrialization and urbanization, Kuyper's rendering of the doctrine of separate spheres contained both empirical and ethical contradictions. Empirically, it was insufficiently attuned to class differences, and to the vulnerability of even middle-class women when shifted from the economic family partnership of earlier times to a position of total dependence in more isolated urban settings. Ethically, it correlated spheres of activity with two particular biological groups — something Kuyper otherwise never defended. It also bifurcated the cultural mandate along gender lines in a way not reflected in that mandate's scriptural origins, and gave scant recognition to the possibility that common grace might be at work in the doctrine's secular critics.

Although Kuyper expounded his idea of sphere sovereignty in unique detail, his convictions about the gendered public/private dichotomy were widely shared by late nineteenth- and early twentieth-century thinkers, both Christian and secular.[22] However, by the 1930s some ethical nuancing appeared in the writings of Swiss Reformed theologian Emil Brunner, whose concept of the "orders" or "communities" of creation was similar to Kuyper's sphere sovereignty. Brunner saw family as one of the orders of creation existing alongside the communities of labor, government, science, the arts, and education. But unlike Kuyper, he viewed marriage and family as based neither on natural inclination nor divine command; rather, he said, the natural pas-

---

20. Abraham Kuyper, *De Gemene Gratie* (On common grace), 3 vols. (Amsterdam: Hoveker and Wormser, 1902-4).

21. Kuyper, *De Eerepositie der Vrouw,* p. 30.

22. See, for example, Jean Bethke Elshtain, *Public Man, Private Woman* (Princeton: Princeton University Press, 1981), esp. chap. 5.

sion that leads people to marriage must be enhanced by an ethic of fidelity and mutual sacrifice, rooted in the grace of God.

In addition, Brunner was much less inclined than Kuyper to assign women and men to different spheres of service or to read male headship back into the creation order. Although he maintained some notion of created inequality between the sexes, he also insisted that it was "limited by the knowledge that Redemption has removed this inequality and transcends it."[23] And although he believed that women were somewhat more physically, mentally, and spiritually equipped for nurturing children, he also recognized that women's specialization in domesticity "is not merely the gift of the creator, but also the product of sin." And he meant sin not just on the part of heavy-handed males wanting to keep women confined to the home, but of women who were content to let men relieve them of their mandate to exercise responsible stewardship in other life spheres in return for domestic creature comforts: "It is at this point that the [Women's] Emancipation Movement rightly intervenes. That is why it is absolutely impossible to put down in black and white, as a universal rule, which spheres of activity 'belong' to woman and which do not. This can only become clear through experience, and for this experience first of all the field must be thrown open."[24] Brunner thus recognized that the doctrine of separate spheres was held in place partly by sinful — though differing — impulses in both sexes, a theme that was taken up by feminist theologians several decades later.[25]

Roman Catholicism on Marriage and Family

As one traces U.S. Roman Catholic thought and practice concerning marriage and family during this same period, three points stand out.[26] First, Catholics have typically combined theological and sacramental traditions with popular sensibilities to portray marriage and family life as a locus for encountering the sacred. Second, a strong emphasis on juridical and institutional norms

---

23. Emil Brunner, *The Divine Imperative: A Study in Christian Ethics* (Philadelphia: Westminster, 1947), pp. 357-58.
24. Brunner, p. 380.
25. For example, Judith Plaskow, *Sex, Sin, and Grace* (Lanham, Md.: University Press of America, 1980); Mary Stewart Van Leeuwen, *Gender and Grace* (Downers Grove, Ill.: Intervarsity Press, 1990).
26. Cf. Christine Firer Hinze, "Unity and Diversity in the Body of Christ: Catholic Families 1945-90," in *Faith Traditions and the Family,* ed. P. Airhart and M. Bendroth (Louisville: Westminster John Knox, 1996), pp. 53-72.

surrounding marriage has coexisted with a pastoral flexibility and tolerance for the nonideal among everyday people. Third, in the face of threats from modern individualism and industrial market economy to traditional social bonds, Catholics, like their Reformed counterparts, supported a gendered division of family and economic life. Unreflective acceptance of this dual-sphere ideology — though less blatant at century's end — has distorted Catholic analyses of the domestic and public arenas and impeded the changed approaches to marriage and family flourishing that late-modern circumstances may require.

Pre–Vatican II Teaching and Practice

Pre–Vatican II Roman Catholic teaching and practice valorized marriage and family as the normal arenas for persons to live out their temporal callings while preparing for their supernatural destiny. Among U.S. Catholics, most with recent immigrant backgrounds, marriage was never reified as the only path for adults. Indeed, popular piety and official teaching evinced higher regard for celibate priesthood and religious life.[27] But most Catholics married, embracing marriage as a sacrament instituted by Christ and constituted by monogamous sexual fidelity, openness to children — often described as the "primary end of marriage" — and a commitment to lifelong, loving partnership reflecting Christ's indissoluble love for his church.[28]

U.S. Catholic marriage and family practices over the past century wed an in-the-bones appreciation for the sacramentality of daily life with a strong emphasis on law and institutional conformity. Marriages among Catholics of European, Hispanic, and African heritage were certainly lived out in culturally rich and diverse familial settings.[29] At the same time, to be married "in

---

27. Hence children's catechisms often pictured a bride and groom at the altar, labeled "This is good," offset by an illustration of a behabited religious nun and cassocked priest, labeled "This is better."

28. Besides procreativity, the secondary aims of marriage were taught to be mutual aid and comfort of spouses — especially aid in reaching their supernatural destinies — and the quieting of concupiscence. See, e.g., Pope Pius XII, "The Apostolate of the Midwife" (1951), in *Papal Pronouncements on Marriage and the Family from Leo XIII to Pius XII (1878-1954)*, ed. Alvin Werth and Clement S. Mihanovich (Milwaukee: Bruce Publishing, 1955), p. 63. Pope Leo XIII (1878-1903) and Pope Pius XI (1922-39) both promulgated influential statements on marriage within an Augustinian framework that highlighted the goods of children, conjugal fidelity, and indissolubility. Cf. John Witte's contribution to this volume, chap. 3.

29. Such diversity failed to translate into interethnic or interracial harmony or neighborliness among U.S. Catholics, however, as a long-standing history of separate parish and neigh-

the church" meant complying with strict canonical requirements which in cases of "irregularity" or "invalidity" required action by official representatives of the clerical hierarchy. Against modern trends, pastors emphasized the absolute prohibition of divorce as a particular hallmark of Catholic discipline.[30] As in other areas of Catholic piety and practice, being a Catholic in good standing meant living up to these organizational expectations; those who failed to do so risked institutional marginalization or sanctions, most poignantly excommunication and barring from reception of the Eucharist.

But alongside this juridical framework and widespread consensus about Christian marriage, actual Catholic marriages and families showed considerable plurality and nonconformity. Cultural diversity was accommodated in a capacious spirituality embracing a wide range of popular devotional piety. Nonconformity, though strictly dealt with on the canonical side, found a more tolerant and sympathetic response within pastoral ministry through the sacrament of penance and in the everyday functioning of Catholic communities.

A third identifying feature of Catholicism's marriage and family ethos has been its framing within a social doctrine known as subsidiarity. This doctrine, elaborated in papal teaching from Leo forward, ascribes specific, nonsubstitutable functions to marriage and family, and relates them to larger civic and economic institutions within a hierarchical and organically interdependent conception of society.[31] In articulating the social purposes of marriage and family, Catholics grafted traditional teachings to a modern, gendered division of household and public spheres. Women were regarded as naturally suited for child rearing and homemaking, and men for public-

---

borhood enclaves attests. See, e.g., John T. McGreevy, *Parish Boundaries: The Catholic Encounter with Race in the Twentieth-Century Urban North* (Chicago: University of Chicago Press, 1996).

30. Pope Leo XIII inveighed against a rising tide of divorce: "[D]ivorce, which is born of the perverted morals of a people, . . . leads . . . to vicious habits in public and private life, [and] is particularly opposed to the well-being of the family and of the State. . . . [O]nce divorce has been allowed, there will be no sufficient means of keeping it in check within any definite bounds. . . . [I]t cannot but happen that divorce and its consequent setting loose of the passions should spread daily and attack the souls of many like a contagious disease or a river bursting its banks and flooding the land." Pope Leo XIII, *Arcanum divinae sapientiae* (1880), quoted in Pius XI, *Casti connubi* (1930), in William J. Gibbons, S.J., ed., *Seven Great Encyclicals* (New York: Paulist Press, 1963), p. 105.

31. The notion of subsidiarity is elaborated by Wall and Miller-McLemore in their contribution to this volume (chap. 9). See also Jonathan Chaplin, "Subsidiarity and Sphere Sovereignty: Catholic and Reformed Conceptions of the Role of the State," in *Things Old and New: Catholic Social Teaching Revisited*, ed. Francis P. McHugh and Samuel M. Natale (Lanham, Md.: University Press of America, 1993), pp. 175-202.

involvement breadwinning. Gender roles within marriage and family were distinct and hierarchical; woman was "queen" and "heart" of the home, and man the "head."[32]

The thought of John A. Ryan (1869-1945), priest-economist and progressive reformer whose work compares interestingly with Kuyper's, and Pope John Paul II's more recent writings on family and marriage illustrate this latter facet of Catholic thought. Ryan was best known for his treatises defending a family living wage and distributive justice and his public activism on behalf of economic justice for workers and families. His generation's foremost interpreter of papal social teaching for American Catholics, Ryan also successfully articulated a natural law–based vocabulary of economic justice to wider public audiences.[33]

In defending "the worker's" right to a decent livelihood, Ryan refers specifically to adult male workers, "since nature and reason have decreed that the family should be supported by its head."[34] Though unmarried women should receive a wage sufficient to support a single person, Ryan follows Pope Leo XIII in regarding home as the normative arena for women: "The welfare of the whole family, and that of society likewise renders it imperative that the wife and mother should not engage in any labor except that of the household. When she works for hire she can neither care properly for her own health, rear her children aright, nor make her home what it should be for her husband, her children and herself. . . . 'The wife become a wage worker is no longer a wife.'"[35] Ryan's Catholic gender-role script intertwined traditional sources with contemporary cultural trends. Marriage, on this view, fosters the health of its members and society by enabling men and women to express their "natural" identities and capacities. For men this involves activating propensities for household-headship and providing. For women it means embracing "woman's true functions, those of wife, mother, mistress of the home, and molder of the moral and spiritual life of the race."[36] In this way men and

---

32. See, e.g., *Casti connubi* #26-27, #74-77, in *Seven Great Encyclicals,* pp. 84-85, 98-99. Witte details the development of Catholic thought on marriage through the early modern period in *From Sacrament to Contract: Marriage, Religion, and Law in the Western Tradition* (Louisville: Westminster John Knox, 1997), chap. 1.

33. John A. Ryan, *A Living Wage* (New York: Macmillan, 1906), and *Distributive Justice* (New York: Macmillan, 1916, 1924, 1942). Useful analyses include Harlan Beckley, *Passion for Justice: Retrieving the Legacies of Walter Rauschenbusch, John A. Ryan, and Reinhold Niebuhr* (Louisville: Westminster John Knox, 1992); Charles E. Curran, *American Catholic Social Ethics* (Notre Dame, Ind.: University of Notre Dame Press, 1982), chap. 2.

34. Ryan, *A Living Wage,* p. 119.
35. Ryan, *A Living Wage,* p. 133.
36. Ryan, *A Living Wage,* p. 137.

women could enact a complementary, mutually beneficial partnership. In practice, unfortunately, this discourse of complementarity legitimated the greater economic and social status and public power given to men, and the definition of women who followed the dictates of domesticity as economic dependents.[37]

Ryan's thought demonstrates a pattern common in official church teaching of the day. On the one hand, he vigorously defends just treatment for workers and advocates measures to assure the social and economic well-being of all citizens. On the other hand, women's natural roles in marriage and family are prioritized in a romanticized, even sentimentalized way.[38] Ryan's economic advocacy for women thus highlighted protective measures such as shorter hours and less strenuous working conditions, and policies such as a universal family living wage that would enable husbands to financially support their wives, who could then make home and hearth their primary vocation, as their nature dictated.

Post–Vatican II Catholic Teaching

Through the Second Vatican Council, Catholic teaching on marriage and family consistently affirmed the value and dignity of men's and women's roles within a dual-spheres ideology. The later twentieth century saw greater emphasis on the rights and participation of women in both home and public arena. However, as the writings of Pope John Paul II illustrate, a romantically tinged portrayal of women as naturally and particularly suited for domestic-

---

37. On the "unproductive housewife," who became classified as a "dependent" on U.S. census tracts only in the late nineteenth century, see Nancy Folbre, "The Unproductive Housewife: Her Evolution in Nineteenth-Century Economic Thought," *Signs* 16, no. 3 (spring 1991): 463-84.

38. Ryan's speeches to women's groups exemplify this combined respect for women's public contributions and a sentimental insistence on domesticity and motherhood as woman's highest calling. He repeatedly concluded such addresses by quoting Archbishop John Spalding: "Into her arms we are born, on her breast our helpless cries are hushed, and her hands close our eyes when the light is gone. Watching her lips, our own become vocal; in her eyes we read the mystery of faith, hope and love; led by her hand we learn to look up and walk in the way of obedience to law. We owe to her, as mother, as sister, as wife, as friend, the tenderest emotions of life, the purest aspirations of the soul, the noblest elements of character, and the completest sympathy in all our joy and sorrow. She weaves flowers of Heaven into the vesture of earthly life. In poetry, painting, sculpture, and religion, she gives us ideals of the fair and beautiful. Innocence is a woman, chastity is a woman, charity is a woman." Baccalaureate Sermon, Trinity College, 3 June 1923, in John A. Ryan Archives, Box 37, Catholic University Library Archives, Washington, D.C.

ity and motherhood persisted.[39] Though the hierarchy of women's and men's places found in earlier writings on subsidiarity is no longer promoted, the impact of dual-sphere thinking continues. In sum, appreciation for the sacramentality of the ordinary, exacting rules and boundaries, and a gendered, hierarchical understanding of family organization together defined a widely accepted Catholic vision of marriage and family in the first half of the twentieth century. Ecclesial reforms and social changes during the 1960s, including the rise of second-wave feminism, contributed to rethinking in each of these areas of Catholic teaching and practice.[40] This period witnessed greater emphasis on the partnership of spouses over the procreative purposes of marriage, selective flexibility concerning rules affecting marriage and divorce, and closer demographic similarities between Catholics and non-Catholics on most marital indicators, including women's participation in the waged workforce. Evolution on each of these fronts continues; however, the triumvirate of sacramentality, institutional juridicism, and a complementary differentiation of familial and public spheres remain identifying continuities in Catholic understandings of marriage and family.

From Dual Spheres to Social Partnership: An Agenda for the Twenty-first Century

The modern separate spheres ideology, and Catholic and Reformed support for it, has persisted in part because it performs certain socially valued functions, with some success. This arrangement protected socially reproductive purposes of households that the modern market economy threatened in un-

---

39. So, the pope writes, "It will redound to the credit of society to make it possible for a mother . . . to devote herself to taking care of her children. . . . Having to abandon these tasks in order to take up paid work outside the home is wrong from the point of view of the good of society and of the family when it contradicts or hinders these primary goals of the mission of a mother." Pope John Paul II, *Laborem exercens* (1981), #19. Through motherhood, women "first learn and then teach others that human relations are authentic if they are open to accepting the other person . . . because of the dignity which comes from being a person. . . . This is the fundamental contribution which the Church and humanity expect from women." *Evangelium vitae* (1996), #99. See also Leonie Caldecott, "Sincere Gift: The Pope's 'New Feminism,'" in *Readings in Moral Theology #10: John Paul II and Moral Theology*, ed. Charles E. Curran and Richard A. McCormick, S.J. (New York: Paulist Press, 1998), pp. 216-34, esp. 220-21.

40. Vatican II's pastoral and liturgical reforms altered Catholics' experiential milieu, prompting fresh perspectives on extraecclesial trends and values. See, e.g., Patrick Carey, *The Roman Catholics in America* (Westport, Conn.: Praeger, 1996), chap. 8; Mark S. Massa, *Catholics and American Culture* (New York: Crossroad, 1999), esp. chap. 7.

precedented ways.⁴¹ Distributing household-reproductive and waged-productive activities according to gender, with its naturalistic and embodied connotations, assured continued attention to the noncommodified and intimate interpersonal features of family life. The two-spheres solution held both religious and cultural appeal because it provided a way to maintain and connect spheres of work, leisure, and relationship that most people sensed were crucial to human welfare. Tragically, this arrangement also maintained a long-standing pattern of according lesser social, economic, and public power and value to women and their activities.

Dual-sphere ideology and practice attempted to guard the health of individuals, families, and society in a modern economic climate. As Christians ponder the health of marriages and families in a new century, they must ask how to move forward in ways that preserve or reclaim the values residing in traditional arrangements, while isolating and eliminating elements that have inflicted questionable side effects on more vulnerable participants. Marriage advocates must be sensitive to an ideological undertow that reinforces the devaluation of nonmarket family labor and of women. And along with combating sexism, Christian analyses must address other forms of injustice that debilitate marriage and family flourishing.⁴²

Beyond Reentrenchment and Functional Equality

Four decades after the advent of second-wave feminism, advocates for just and wholesome family forms face a more complicated set of challenges than were evident in the 1960s. Women's vocational opportunities have expanded, and their economic independence has been increased by new social insurance programs. Changes in divorce law and in social attitudes have made it easier for women to leave dissatisfying marriages, and even to bear and rear children alone, and for men to treat responsibility for children more as a lifestyle option than as a moral obligation. Yet, as other essays in this volume demonstrate, both children and adults of divorce and nonmarital cohabitation are at increased risk of physical and psychological disorders, as well as economic

---

41. Nancy Folbre points out: "One of the functional aspects of traditional patriarchal structures of constraint [on both men's and women's roles and duties] lay in the incentives they provided for care of the very young and the very old." *Who Pays for the Kids? Gender and the Structures of Constraint* (New York: Routledge, 1994), pp. 115-16.

42. On interlocking injustices within dual-spheres approaches to socially reproductive household labor, see, e.g., Phyllis Palmer, *Domesticity and Dirt: Housewives and Domestic Servants in the United States, 1920-1945* (Philadelphia: Temple University Press, 1989).

downward mobility. Divorce and unwed parenting contribute to increased public expenditures to fund ongoing remedial programs. Neither divorce nor cohabitation appears to lead to happier or more stable marriages; in fact, each increases the likelihood of divorce in subsequent marriages.[43]

These negative trends have tempted some to advocate restabilizing marriage by recovering some form of the doctrine of separate spheres, particularly as a way of protecting the welfare of children, who are arguably the most serious casualties of the divorce and nonmarriage revolutions. But we cannot solve today's problems by resurrecting dubious solutions of a previous era. The separate spheres arrangement has entailed costs, and not only for women. While romanticizing women's moral and nurturing superiority, its removal of fathers from domestic involvement has contributed to an intergenerational cycle of misogyny on the part of underfathered boys.[44] The current challenge, then, is this: How can we put the needs of children and families first without putting women's needs last, and without putting men on the sidelines of family life? In other words, how can we promote institutional marriage and honor the need for stable, nurturing families without lapsing back into patriarchal headship or the questionable practice of gender-separate spheres?

As critics of certain features of second-wave feminism have argued, it is no mark of liberation for women (or for men or children) to be shunted from one set of restrictive options to an opposite but equally confining one. This is the upshot of the model of "functional gender equality" that has been incorporated in the policies of some European countries, and has also been influential in U.S. thinking and practice over the past several decades.[45] This model is organized around four tenets that often operate in as doctrinaire a

---

43. The Marriage Movement Statement summarizes and references the pertinent literature very thoroughly. Related research suggests that among cohabiting Generation X couples, many women are now more career-focused and responsible than their male partners, sometimes to the extent of carrying two jobs and greater domestic responsibility while their partners contribute less, both financially and domestically. See National Marriage Project, *The State of Our Unions, 2000* (Rutgers, N.J.: State University of New Jersey, 2000), esp. pp. 6-20, "Sex without Strings, Relationships without Rings."

44. The relevant literature is reviewed in Scott Coltrane, *Family Man: Fatherhood, Housework, and Gender Equity* (New York: Oxford University Press, 1996).

45. This model, and the social partnership model, is described by Neil Gilbert in "Working Families: Hearth to Market," in *All Our Families: New Policies for a New Century*, ed. Mary Ann Mason, Arlene Skolnick, and Stephen D. Sugarman (New York: Oxford University Press, 1998). See also Mary Stewart Van Leeuwen, "Faith, Feminism and Family in an Age of Globalization," in *Religion, Globalization, and the Spheres of Life*, ed. Max Stackhouse, Peter Paris, and Diane Obenchain, 4 vols. (Harrisburg, Pa.: Trinity Press International, in press).

fashion as the ideology of separate spheres that preceded it. The first is the elimination of all gender roles as an essential step for achieving justice for women. The second is the devaluation of domestic activity, which is seen as a tedious necessity to be divided equally between spouses or absorbed by (usually ill-paid) third parties. The third is the celebration of waged labor, which is assumed to bestow "autonomy and self-respect as it liberates women from the repressive confinement of child care and household chores."[46] Fourth is the assumption that the individual should be the primary focus of welfare and taxation policies. Thus, in Sweden, working couples can qualify for subsidized day care to a total of some $12,000 per year but do not have the choice of taking the subsidy as a cash grant to enable one or both parents to care for children at home. Countries embracing a functional equality model also tend to keep tax and pension policies tied strictly to individual persons, regardless of marital status.

Needed: A Social Partnership Model

By contrast, we support a third way: a "social partnership" model which rejects the one-size-fits-all rigidity of the functional equality model while ensuring that any division of marital labor does not render one spouse less socially valued or more economically vulnerable than the other. Thus, instead of tax-subsidized day care on a take-it-or-leave-it basis, this model calls for direct cash subsidies or refundable tax credits that can be used to replace the outside wages of a stay-at-home parent (or adult providing primary care for an ill or frail elderly relative) and/or to pay for child care or nursing assistance.[47]

A social partnership model calls for both public and private retirement pension accounts to be credit-shared between spouses, with all contributions — whatever their source and amount — going into an account over which spouses have joint title. Such credit sharing may be of little practical significance in stable marriages, but it constitutes an important safety net in cases of divorce where one spouse (still usually the wife) has less independent earning capacity as a result of having spent time out of the labor force doing family work. The social partnership model is neutral as to *how* couples divide waged work and family responsibilities. But it acknowledges that time taken out of the waged labor force by either spouse will reduce any pension account that

---

46. Gilbert, p. 195.
47. So far Finland is the only Western democracy that provides for such flexibility. See Gilbert, p. 195, for a more detailed description.

depends on accumulated time in the workforce. Thus, this model also calls for something like homemakers' pension credits covering years spent in nonwaged domestic activity. The accumulated funds and interest might be left in a pension account until retirement, or withdrawn earlier without tax or penalty to finance a homemaking spouse's eventual return to school or even the start-up of a small business.

Finally, a social partnership model requires both a cultural consensus that actively supports marriage and family life and social policies that allow rhetoric about the value of domestic work and activity to grow real economic teeth. This means that recent forays into "family-friendly workplaces" must push dramatically further. Access to status-bearing and career-advancing part-time work, with appropriate health care and pension benefits, needs to become the norm rather than the exception. We also need a substantial retreat from the addictive "work-and-spend" climate that is the hallmark of consumerism.[48] We should embrace instead an ethos of shared family and breadwinning duties, a renewed sense of what it means to "have enough" and to "work enough," and limit work outside the home to fifty to sixty hours per week for married couples with young children and thirty for single workers with primary caregiving responsibilities for other dependents.[49]

In sum, we follow the social teaching traditions of our respective churches in regarding the family as a creation-based sphere of life whose functional integrity parallels respect for other spheres of activity that together form a strong and just civil society. But justice must operate within the spheres as well as between them, and neither the older doctrine of separate spheres nor the newer model of functional equality makes for the most just policy or healthiest setting for persons or groups. The most promising vision of marriage and family relations, we contend, is a version of the social partnership model coupled with a strong ethic of lifelong monogamy.[50] The part-

---

48. See, e.g., Juliet Schor, *The Overworked American: The Surprising Decline of Leisure* (New York: Basic Books, 1994), and *The Overspent American: Upscaling, Downshifting, and the New Consumer* (New York: Basic Books, 1998).

49. This would enable a gender-equitable retrieval of the equilibrium between domestic and public economies that Reformed and Catholic teaching attempted to preserve by the dual-spheres doctrines. Similar policy proposals characterize the platforms of religious-civic initiatives such as the Marriage Movement Statement and the 1998 joint statement issued by the Communitarian Network and the Religion, Culture and Family Project entitled, "The Task of Religious Institutions in Strengthening Families." See the Religion, Culture and Family website, www2.uchicago.edu/divinity/family, for the complete text of this statement.

50. This critical promarriage stance acknowledges that chronic problems such as abuse, adultery, addiction, or financial irresponsibility may make it impossible, in certain cases, for a marriage to survive. Cf. Doherty and Carroll's contribution to this volume.

nership model allows spouses flexibility in the division of waged and unwaged labor while ensuring that the fruits of joint labor are equally valued and shared, and economic and vocational compensation of some sort accrues to either spouse who takes time from the waged workplace to specialize in domesticity. We believe this model represents a logical development — not a contradiction — of the agendas of nineteenth- and early twentieth-century Reformed and Catholic social thinkers, and one to which they might well have contributed had they lived today.

Conclusion

We have argued that Christian support for a critical promarriage approach needs to incorporate a social partnership model of marriage within the familial and wage-earning spheres. We urge religious communions to reject a social scenario in which men and women are systematically accorded asymmetrical status, roles, and power, but also to reject a situation where elite men and women have identical civil rights and social expectations while class and ethnic inequalities persist. We propose instead a social norm in which men and women across race and class lines have flexibly similar responsibilities for supporting families through domestic and waged work. In this genuine partnership of the spheres of home and work, economist Nancy Folbre predicts,

> [M]en would substantially increase their hours of unpaid work, devoting more time to home, children and community. Their formal labor force participation rate would decline to levels more typical of women today. Forms of work that women once specialized in, such as child care and teaching, would be re-valued. High skill levels, as well as high wages, would be required. The family would remain an important economic institution, and common commitments to certain kinds of unpaid household labor would reduce class and race inequalities.[51]

Further, satisfactory Christian approaches will not support any effort to reinvigorate the institution of marriage that intentionally or unintentionally reifies hidden injustices that have marred family theories and practices over the past century. We have highlighted one key pattern to which Christian theology has lent its support: a sexual division of labor between public and private economies, the assumption of distinctive personalities according to gender, and consequent segregation of men's and women's aspirations and

---

51. Folbre, *Who Pays?* p. 103.

opportunities. By simultaneously romanticizing and marginalizing women's activities, this ideology has nourished a gender-based occupational hierarchy that especially harms women.[52]

A Christian social-partnership model of marriage and family seeks renewed ways to cherish marriage while acknowledging and honoring the equal value of the spheres of home and public economy, and the pluralism and diversity of expression and practice that have existed even in the most marriage-supportive cultures. In pursuing these aims, Reformed and Catholic communions have made positive strides. Yet the rich analyses of marriage and other spheres of life represented by Kuyper and Ryan continue to be in need of reshaping and pruning. Christians therefore should join new efforts to promote marriage with both vigor and circumspection, championing what is wholesome but combating whatever may erode marriage and family as a vital locus of God's creative and redemptive work.

---

52. Evelyn Nakano Glenn illumines how the devaluation of socially reproductive work contributes to gender, class, and racial-ethnic injustice in "From Servitude to Service Work: Historical Continuities in the Racial Division on Paid Reproductive Labor," *Signs* 18, no. 1 (autumn 1992): 1-43.

CHAPTER 8

Health, Marriage, and the Practice of Ministry

Richard A. Hunt

The chapters in this volume by Linda Waite, by David Popenoe and Barbara Dafoe Whitehead, and by David Larson and James Swyers clearly demonstrate that good health and successful marriage are positively related and that marital disruption has many negative consequences for all areas of health.[1] These findings challenge clergy and religious groups to proactively support man-woman covenantal coequal "social partnership" marriage as beneficial to health by reaching couples in every area of society and enabling marriages to maximize love, care, and justice.

The relationships between marriage and health are multidirectional. Healthy persons are more likely to stay married, probably due to higher energy, resources, and skills. Married persons are more likely to have built-in supports for a healthy lifestyle. Successful marriage encourages spouses to give positive supports for better physical and mental health and cooperate in equal power relationships with each other. Both good health and successful marriage have common causes, such as supportive family and community networks, and more skills for negotiating life's challenges and dangers. These skills are more likely to bring individuals into religious and secular communities with similar values, goals, and skills.

Defining Health

"Good health" is a holistic system involving genetic, physical, biochemical, mental/emotional, spiritual, and relationship factors (or subsystems). Health

---

1. See chaps. 1, 2, and 13 in this volume.

is both a condition (i.e., to "be" in good health) and a process (i.e., all subsystems functioning at optimal levels to maintain the system's health). The same level of health in different individuals may be produced by different combinations of contributions from their subsystems, since to some extent some components may compensate for the lower functioning of other components.

Marriage health is also a holistic system of continuing relationships between a man and a woman involving all the personal health factors plus social interaction competencies for successful marriage. While not a guarantee of health, marriage utilizes factors that contribute to health. Marriage transforms the ways spouses act toward each other, their children, and others, as well as the ways others act toward the couple.[2] The public, legal side of marriage increases couples' confidence that their partnerships will last. Religious faith helps to deepen the meaning of marriage and provides inspiration and support in times of difficulty.

Defining Marriage

The equalitarian concepts of "critical familism" and "social partnership," described by Van Leeuwen and Hinze in chapter 7 of this book, and "progressive familism" apply to all dimensions of marriage, including legal contract, financial partnership, sacred promise, sexual union, personal bond, and a productive institution for society.[3] Focusing on mainline denominations in the past fifty years, W. Bradford Wilcox traces "progressive familism" in support of egalitarian married two-parent households in contrast to "expressive liberation" that diminishes the role of marriage.[4] In support of marriage and health we must not fall back into unjust marriage structures such as patriarchalism and/or gendered divisions of roles.

Healthy marriage requires a coequal "social partnership" composed of a husband and wife in radical gender equality that affirms both the uniqueness of each gender and their mutual cooperation. The complex crucible of marriage reaches inward into the innermost depths of personal development and outward into many areas of society.

An "ethic of equal regard" replaces the "sphere sovereignty" of Kuyper

---

2. For example, see Steven L. Nock, *Marriage in Men's Lives* (New York: Oxford University Press, 1998).

3. "The Marriage Movement: A Statement of Principles," available at http://www.marriagemovement.org.

4. See his "For the Sake of the Children?" (manuscript draft prepared for the "Public Role of Mainline Protestantism" project, Robert Wuthnow, principal investigator, June 2000).

and seeks equal freedom for both genders to eliminate any unjust power relations. Marriage is a fully coequal "social partnership"[5] of wife and husband as spouses in relation to their household and society. Each couple must work out their own unique lifestyle, responsibilities, and patterns that best express equal regard and justice for themselves and for women and men in society.

Marriage defines the home and forms the faith and virtues of those who live therein, especially the children. Every home is a "twenty-four hour per day/seven day per week" (24/7) school teaching values that form the faith of each participant, who impacts both society and religious institutions through his or her actions at work, school, leisure, and community.[6]

Principles for good marriage transcend all cultures and have much more convergence than divergence across nations, races, and religions. The underlying principles that enable good marriage, such as safety, peace, respect, social skills, and cooperation, may be expressed in many different, perhaps contrasting, ways. Most religious traditions acknowledge the positive relations between good health and successful marriage, as noted by Numrich.[7] "Whether it is the deep metaphors of covenant as in Judaism, Islam and Reformed Protestantism; sacrament as in Roman Catholicism or Eastern Orthodoxy; the yin and yang of Confucianism; the quasi-sacramentalism of Hinduism; or the mysticism often associated with allegedly modern romantic love, humans tend to find values in marriage that call them beyond the mundane and everyday."[8]

Defining the Practice of Ministry

"Ministry" is both a profession and a calling to serve (vocation). The practice of ministry includes both ordained clergy and other professional leaders in churches, synagogues, temples, mosques, and other religious groups as well as all members of the congregation. The "practice of ministry" refers to what religious institutions do through their clergy, lay leaders, participants, and ad-

---

5. From Don Browning, noted by Mary Stewart Van Leeuwen and Christine Hinze, chap. 7 in this volume.

6. See Mary Ann Glendon and David Blankenhorn, eds., *Seedbeds of Virtue: Sources of Competence, Character, and Citizenship in American Society* (Lanham, Md.: Madison Books, 1995); Cameron Lee, *Beyond Family Values: A Call to Christian Virtue* (Downers Grove, Ill.: InterVarsity Press, 1998); "The Marriage Movement."

7. See Paul Numrich's contribution to this volume, chap. 14.

8. Don Browning, "What Is Marriage? An Exploration" (paper presented at the Institute for American Values Marriage Consultation, New York City, 25 January 2000), p. 11.

herents in response to the mounting evidence that successful marriage is vital for individuals, families, and society. Ministry includes basic education and preventive, remedial, and enhancement tasks.

Some Implications of Health and Marriage for the Practice of Ministry

Clergy and religious institutions should promote marriage as a means to health, a "laboratory for learning to love" in which spouses can further develop positive loving goals and actions that are conducive to better health. The historic marriage promise (vow) of "better, worse, richer, poorer, sickness, and health, till death us do part" calls spouses to long-term growth in all situations. As valuable as health is, it is ultimately only a means to higher values such as love, care, fairness, kindness, and other qualities. Commitment, obligation, and sacrifice both serve the goal of love and result from deep love. Sacrifice is needed and may transcend health, yet genuine love gives unconditionally, not counting it as sacrifice nor expecting any reward.

Health rationales for marriage complement traditional religious and legal understandings of marriage. Marriage education techniques express traditional wisdom about marriage, such as mutuality, safety, respect, equality, appreciation, thoughtfulness, dependability, and more. Scientific evidence for the positive relationships between constructive behaviors and health corroborates the finest descriptions of married love that come from religion, literature, and cultural traditions. Research on communication patterns of couples is producing refined techniques to coach couples in specific means to change their conversations in positive ways.[9]

Professions should be interested both in the individual wishes of their clients and in the health and welfare of all marriages. Decisions and actions of individuals have consequences for their family, friends, neighbors, and work associates. Although more complicated, treatment care of any individual must also consider others who are involved with that individual. Clergy and other religious persons need to encourage other professions (medicine, law, therapy, business, and others) to better understand spiritual dimensions and religious institutions. Other professions need religious leaders who can describe how religion fits in the "health, marriage, and religion" trilogy.

---

9. For examples, see John M. Gottman, *What Predicts Divorce?* (Hillside, N.J.: Lawrence Erlbaum, 1994); Howard Markman, Scott Stanley, and Susan L. Bloomberg, *Fighting for Your Marriage* (San Francisco: Jossey-Bass, 1994).

Attitudes and Value Priorities of the Clergy and Other Congregation Leaders

Since there are many good programs available, what keeps religious groups from using them? Churches and leaders may have little commitment to the importance of marriage in their tradition or denomination. They may lack knowledge of programs. The cost of programs or time required may deter their use, although the costs of such marriage preparation and support programs are insignificant compared to a couple's huge lifelong investment of time and money in marriage.

Proactive ministries begin with answers to these three challenges:

1. *Clergy and other religious leaders must commit themselves to boldly proclaim truths about marriage and family health,* since these have implications beyond the private concerns of the couple. This replaces any sense of despair, any fear of hurting nonmarried persons, and/or any reluctance to address marriage issues.[10] We must counter the false claim that mentioning, teaching, or celebrating marriage will offend others or make them feel sad or guilty.

Leaders can assert God's presence in marriage and emphasize essential qualities for a good marriage, such as commitment, mutuality, compatibility, companionship, intimacy, sexuality, primacy, exclusivity, fidelity, and permanence.[11] For Roman Catholics, marriage is a special sacrament through which husband and wife "learn what it means to love God and neighbor by learning what it means to love one another completely and faithfully."[12] For most Protestants marriage is a combination of sacrament, vocation, covenant, and communion.[13] Even a secular perspective affirms marriage as the primary relationship within which a community socially approves sexual intercourse and the birth and rearing of children.[14]

With compassion and sensitivity clergy need to implement the positive

---

10. David Popenoe and Barbara Dafoe Whitehead, *The State of Our Unions* (New Brunswick, N.J.: National Marriage Project, 1999), p. 12.

11. Blu Greenberg, "Marriage: A Jewish Perspective," in *The Family Handbook,* ed. Herbert Anderson, Don S. Browning, Ian S. Evison, and Mary Stewart Van Leeuwen (Louisville: Westminster John Knox, 1998), pp. 3-9.

12. Paul J. Waddell, "Marriage: A Catholic Perspective," in *The Family Handbook,* pp. 10-12.

13. William J. Everett, *Blessed Be the Bond: Christian Perspectives on Marriage and the Family* (Lanham, Md.: University Press of America, 1990).

14. David Popenoe, Jean Bethke Elshtain, and David Blankenhorn, eds., *Promises to Keep: The Decline and Renewal of Marriage in America* (Lanham, Md.: Rowman and Littlefield, 1996), pp. 17-20.

truths expressed in statistical comparisons and marriage research. There would be fewer divorced persons if congregations gave more effective and sustained help to couples at earlier points in their marriage. Just as it takes a man and a woman to create a marriage, it also takes both spouses to produce a divorce. It is essential to ask, in kindness and love, how each spouse unwittingly used criticism, contempt, defensiveness, and stonewalling to get the other spouse to leave the marriage.[15]

2. *We need to enable every clergy member and leader to be satisfied and successful in his or her own personal decisions about marriage and about health.* Leaders' personal experiences in their own households influence how they minister to other households. This involves two dimensions. One is whether clergy and other leaders embody home/household/family lifestyles that are affirmed by their congregation and polity, and the other is whether leaders are satisfied, happy, and healthy in their chosen lifestyle.

While clergy may complain about being scrutinized by their congregations, most members want to see real-life examples of faith in action in homes. If the leaders, who are presumed to know more about these matters than others, are unable to implement them in their own homes, then where can persons who are trying to learn how to live in love at home successfully find models to guide them?

Congregations need to distinguish between the clergy's lifestyle being merely different but acceptable and being of such a nature that most consider harmful or unacceptable. In most congregations the majority may not care whether their clergy leaders attend ball games or opera, but may be rightly concerned if these same leaders physically abuse their children or engage in nonmarital sexual intercourse.

Leaders must value marriage ministries. Leaders dissatisfied with their own family situations are less likely to be positive about marriage and family ministries. As a result, they may blame the institution of marriage for failures rather than use effective resources to improve and strengthen marriage relationships. This is akin to devaluing the driver's license because some licensed drivers have accidents.

3. *We need to research, understand, clarify, and proclaim the fundamental reasons for defining a valid marriage as a "one woman, one man" unit.* The

---

15. Gottman describes these as the "four horsemen of the apocalypse" in *What Predicts Divorce?* and in a more popular version, John M. Gottman, *Why Marriages Succeed or Fail . . . and How You Can Make Yours Last* (New York: Simon & Schuster, 1994).

profound ways in which marriage implements society's vision of health and well-being for children, women, and men are receiving renewed support from many sources.[16] In the United States the challenge to marriage from same-sex couples is parallel to the marriage challenges over a century ago from those who attempted to legalize polygamous marriage.[17] We need to give clear rationales to strengthen the legal definition of marriage as "two persons, one woman and one man." Alternate domestic arrangements of two or more persons may be legally permitted, but these cannot be called "marriage."

Let us now look at some practical actions churches, synagogues, and other religious groups can initiate, enact, and expand.

Possibilities for Any Congregation: Church, Synagogue, or Other Religious Group

Marriage Ministries in the Congregation's Administrative Structure

A congregation's marriage ministries begin with establishing a family ministries committee or task group with the mandate and support to do the job. "Family ministries" includes ministries with marriages, parents, and other nuclear and extended family relationships. This places marriage in the context of family systems as well as being the key relationship that organizes the family. Because each home is an essential unit in the educational and pastoral care ministries of every congregation, in the administrative and budget pro-

---

16. For details see John Witte, Jr., *From Sacrament to Contract: Marriage, Religion, and Law in the Western Tradition* (Louisville: Westminister John Knox, 1997); Popenoe, Elshtain, and Blankenhorn, *Promises to Keep;* Carl E. Schneider, "The Law and the Stability of Marriage: The Family as a Social Institution," in *Promises to Keep,* pp. 187-214; Richard A. Hunt, Larry Hof, and Rita DeMaria, *Marriage Enrichment: Preparation, Mentoring, and Outreach* (Philadelphia: Brunner/Mazel, 1998), chap. 3; Linda J. Waite and Maggie Gallagher, *The Case for Marriage* (New York: Doubleday, 2000).

17. In 1862 the U.S. Congress first passed a series of laws to prohibit polygamy. After some twenty-five years of conflict, the federal definition of marriage was finally firmly established in 1887 when the U.S. Supreme Court declared the Reynolds-Tucker Act constitutional (*Encyclopedia Americana,* 19:459-60). This clear definition of marriage was compromised in 1996 when Congress decided that the definition of marriage will be left up to each state. In this vacuum over thirty states have passed some type of law declaring that legally sanctioned marriage consists of one man and one woman, and more states are working toward this goal. See also Charles C. Kroeger, "Are Gay Unions Christian Covenants?" in *Caught in the Crossfire* (Nashville: Abingdon, 1994), pp. 132-40.

cess congregations need to make family ministries equal with the education task groups concerning children, youth, and adults.

The family ministries task group can work with the clergy to support the congregation's pastoral and educational work with marriages, parents, and other elements of the family households in the community. Its membership should include the congregation's clergy (and other staff, if a larger congregation), married couples, representatives for single parents and other household types in the congregation, and professionals who service families (if they are members of the congregation; if not, then at least seek to have professionals as consultants for the committee).[18]

Specific Ministries of Congregations

The basic focus of family ministries is twofold: marriage and family relationships in the home and educational activities for marriages and families in group settings of the congregation. A family ministries task group can provide these marriage ministries by using any leadership combination of clergy, mentor couples, and professionals.

1. Links to Existing Ministries and Professional Services

Many clergy already minister to couples and families through counseling and other pastoral contacts they have with them. Pastoral care ministries can be expanded to support healthy marriage by training married couples as lay cocounselors and pastoral mentors for couples and families.[19]

2. Training Mentor Couples

Trained mentor couples provide positive images of marriage by making both men and women available to any marriage and family situation. Couples can

---

18. More details may be found in Richard A. Hunt and Joan A. Hunt, *Caring Couples Network Handbook* (Nashville: Discipleship Resources, 1996). Including clergy, married couples, and professional therapists as members of the family ministries team links these ministries to the education and pastoral care work of the congregation and to the available professional expertise.

19. See Siang-Yang Tan, *Lay Counseling: Equipping Christians for a Helping Ministry* (Grand Rapids: Zondervan, 1991).

begin training by attending marriage enrichment events for their own growth and as an initial screening of their potential competence.[20]

3. Engagement/Prewedding Preparation for Seriously Dating Couples

As a minimum a pastor needs to meet with every couple and make available basic resource guides with exploratory activities and questions for discussion to enable the couple to clarify their values, goals, priorities, and commitments. The pastor and mentor couples may utilize marriage inventories and/or couple communication programs. Since no one program has everything, clergy and other leaders should obtain training in at least two different programs.[21]

Mentor couples can offer support and services to engaged couples and assist in follow-up concerning special needs, professional treatment, community agencies, and other resources. Group sessions may be led by married couples, clergy, marriage counselors, physicians, attorneys, financial consultants, and other professionals. Where cost is a factor in whether a couple can participate, program expenses may be supplemented by a gift to the couple from their parents, friends, other relatives, or the congregation. Leaders need to stress marriage education and enrichment as a normal part of marriage.[22]

---

20. See Hunt and Hunt, *Caring Couples Network Handbook;* see also the sponsor/mentor couple guidelines in Jane Ives and Clifford Ives, *Pastor's Manual for Growing Love in Christian Marriage* (Nashville: Abingdon, in press), and Les Parrott III and Leslie Parrott, *Mentoring Engaged and Newlywed Couples: Building Marriages That Love for a Lifetime Curriculum Kit* (Grand Rapids: Zondervan, 1997).

21. Among basic couples guides is Richard A. Hunt and Joan A. Hunt, *Growing Love in Christian Marriage, Couples Book* (Nashville: Abingdon, 1981; rev. ed., in press). Among marriage inventories are the Life Innovations series (Prepare, Enrich, Mate; see David H. Olson and Amy K. Olson, *Empowering Couples: Building on Your Strengths* [Minneapolis: Life Innovations, 2000]) and Foccus (Rudy Buettner and Faith Buettner, *Mentors' Guide for FOCCUS: A Premarital Inventory* [Bethesda, Md.: Marriage Savers, 1999]). Among communication programs are Couples Communication (Sherod Miller, Phyllis Miller, Elam W. Nunnally, and Daniel B. Wackman, *Talking and Listening Together* [Littleton, Colo.: Interpersonal Communications Programs, 1991]) and PREP and Christian PREP (Markman, Stanley, and Bloomberg, *Fighting for Your Marriage*). The "Great Start" program at Country Club Christian Church in Kansas City combines a marriage inventory and a couples communication program.

22. See the Marriage Movement Statement at www.marriagemovement.org for states that are changing marriage license fees to encourage couples to get premarital education.

4. Ministries with Postwedding Couples in Their Early Years of Marriage

Postwedding events are essential follow-up during the critical first two years of marriage when spouses are establishing their patterns and facing the realities of differences, stresses, and pressures. Many congregations have couples classes and fellowship groups. These face-to-face groups provide mutual support, personal contacts, and a sense of belonging in congregational life, an important positive factor for marriage and health success. Congregations also need to adapt programs to reach couples who are married in other communities or settings.

Mentor couples may give special attention to couples with higher risks for dysfunction or divorce. Among these risks are the following: one or both spouses are younger than twenty; spouses have been involved in one or more previous marriages; parents of spouses are divorced; divorces have occurred among the couple's relatives and friends; spouses lived together before marriage (especially with more than one partner); and presence of addictions, very low income, lack of job training, wide educational or values differences between spouses, socioeconomic background, and personality disturbances.

5. Transitions to Parenthood

Parents include couples in their first marriage with the birth of their children, couples entering marriage already pregnant, and couples with children from previous marriage(s) or relationships. Congregations can provide information and classes on parenting, child and adolescent development, and other dimensions of family life. Concern for children extends to support systems for those who parent the children, including single parents, foster parents, and grandparents, some of whom must become parents to their grandchildren. The congregation's marriage ministries need to include making contacts and follow-ups with unmarried new mothers since they also face issues of marriage and man-woman relationships.

In traditions that provide for infant and/or child baptism or dedication, the congregation can affirm child, parents, and extended family. Mentor couples could be included as sponsors to the child and parents in the dedication service. Through follow-up contacts with parents and child, sponsors help link the child and family to the congregation and can advocate for ministries with children and their parents.

6. Foster and Adoptive Parents

The transition to parenthood also includes foster and adoptive parents. With society's increasing need to find homes for children who are abused, neglected, or abandoned, congregations can develop ways to encourage those who become foster parents, adopt children, or provide other child care services. Classes could help train foster parents. A support group could help a foster/adoptive couple in child care, additional family expenses, legal matters, and other ways.

Clergy and congregations can work with community agencies concerning adoption, foster family care, shelters for abused women, domestic violence, and other matters that affect the stability of the home. Professionals involved with these situations can help sensitize the congregation to local community needs and create specific ministries to address them.

7. Marriage Crises: Abuse, Affairs, Separation, Divorce, and Other Crisis Points

Clergy and other leaders can provide both preventive education and crisis intervention ministries to address major marriage stresses, crisis points, difficulties. Preventive helps, information about how to contact resources, and education about early warning signs of marital distress and dysfunction can be disseminated through classes, support groups, newsletters, websites, and other channels.

Ministries with couples and families in crisis can be related to the congregation's lay counseling program (if any), such as Stephen Ministry, and to pastoral counseling agencies in the community, such as a Samaritan Center. McManus describes many ways that religious groups can minister to hurting couples in crisis.[23] With appropriate training, couples who have weathered a stormy period in their marriage can help others cope with similar stresses and transform crises into learning opportunities.

A congregation can minister to individuals and couples who are affected by any crisis, such as alcohol, drug, and other substance abuses; extramarital sexual affairs; job losses; financial crises; trauma from accidents, illness, or violence; separation, divorce, and postdivorce. Professionals trained in crisis intervention can be especially helpful as consultants in designing cri-

---

23. Michael J. McManus, *Marriage Savers: Helping Your Friends and Family Avoid Divorce* (Grand Rapids: Zondervan, 1995), pp. 201-11.

sis ministries, in training and supervising mentors and lay counselors, and for referrals for couples who need professional help. Busy clergy can multiply the availability of pastoral care and counseling through supervising trained mentor couples who supplement clergy contacts with distressed couples. With supervision, mentor couples can be very effective in reaching couples in crises. The family ministries task group can establish details for these crisis and outreach ministries.

Retrouvaille offers a lifeline for troubled marriages. Rooted in Marriage Encounter, this program begins with a weekend retreat in which husbands and wives acknowledge difficulties, reestablish communication, seek new understandings of themselves and each other, and recommit to working on their marriage rather than divorce. Leader couples share their stories of pain, reconciliation, and healing. Follow-up sessions and support are scheduled for several months after the initial retreat. Couples who have experienced healing through Retrouvaille could become mentor couples for other couples in crisis.

8. Celebrating Achievements and Transitions across the Lifetime Marriage Journey

How a congregation publicly celebrates marriages and families creates a general atmosphere of appreciation for homes and families. The family ministries task group can help couples create rituals that signify their commitment. These can include activities to bring together children and other family members as "stakeholders" in their family, perhaps with a ceremony of recommitment to each other and their congregation.

Renewing visions and recommitment should be part of marriage celebration events. With their clergy and other leaders, the family ministries task group can schedule events around annual themes that relate to marriage and family, such as Valentine's Day, Mother's Day, and Father's Day. Each month or quarter couples with anniversaries during that time could be recognized in the congregation and listed in the congregation's newspaper. An annual "marriage celebration" event can be adapted to congregation and community needs. Announcements of births, deaths, and other transitions among families in the congregation can affirm marriage also.

In addition to these large public celebrations, a congregation can give practical helps to couples. Where grandparents or other relatives are not available to care for their grandchildren so the parent couple can have a night out as a couple, a congregation could provide child care.

9. Marriage Support and Enrichment

Individually or in cooperation with other groups, a congregation can sponsor at least one marriage enrichment activity each year. A "marriage checkup" could be part of a marriage enrichment or other marriage celebration, analogous to a health checkup. Many churches provide classes and fellowship groups for couples for face-to-face fellowship of mutual support in crises and transitions. Although these usually assume that both spouses are members of the same church or synagogue, increased support for interchurch and interfaith couples is being encouraged.[24] Small groups of couples can band together to support one another, help each other to cope with life events and transitions, and renew their mission in the world. Sometimes these emerge as a follow-up to a marriage enrichment event.[25]

10. In-Home Ministries

Visits to couples and families in their homes can provide very effective ministries because a well-trained parish visitor has opportunity to see the family in action and can adapt information and services to their home environment. Given today's high-security environments and great emphasis on the Internet and E-mail, personal visits to couples and families in their homes convey a special valuing of the persons visited.

To be effective, those who visit need training in theology and marriage and family dynamics, and knowledge of resources. Visits need to be planned at times convenient to those who are contacted. It is helpful to provide informational materials on topics of interest or concern to the home.

The principles of home visits also apply to visits to persons in hospitals, prisons, extended treatment facilities, and other institutions. A home with a spouse, family member, or relative in any institution for any purpose is affected by shifts in the family power structure, additional financial obligations, and other factors. Phone calls, letters, and E-mails are extensions of personal visits and can utilize home visit principles.

In addition to visits by well-trained clergy and volunteer home visitors,

---

24. See "Ministry to Interchurch Marriages," available from the Center for Marriage and Family at Creighton University, at www.creighton.edu/MarriageandFamily/.

25. The number and variety of marriage enrichment events are expanding rapidly with a wide range of formats, models, and exercises (for examples see Hunt, Hof, and DeMaria, *Marriage Enrichment*; ACME at www.marriageenrichment.org; CMFCE at www.smartmarriages.com).

a congregation can reach homes through a staff parish nurse or nursery/preschool home visitor. A parish nurse with medical and pastoral care training can be alert to home needs, offer encouragement, and help connect the home to appropriate community resources. A nursery home visitor focuses on younger children in the home and can encourage parents as couples to strengthen their marriage as basic to parenting.

11. Studies about Marriage, Parenting, and Families

A congregation could sponsor a study class on a topic such as "Marriage, Health, and Society," using a substantial textbook such as *Promises to Keep*[26] or *The State of Our Unions*.[27]

A congregation can survey its own membership and its surrounding community to assess the composition of its households. The process could increase sensitivity to marriage and health issues, especially if brief information about marriage were included in the survey. Among key questions might be how many adults and children are in the household; whether it is headed by a married or unmarried couple, single parent, or other head; and on what topics the home would like to have more information or help.

Ecumenical Cooperation in a Local Community

1. Community Marriage Agreements and Policies

Clergy, churches, synagogues, and judges can establish community marriage policies and agree that they will only marry couples who have fulfilled basic preparation requirements. These guidelines describe basic marriage preparation as well as ways to strengthen existing marriages and save troubled ones. Guidelines typically include at least ten to twenty hours of marriage preparation over at least a four-month period, including meeting with a mentor couple and participating in engagement and postwedding workshop events.[28]

---

26. See n. 14 above for bibliographic information.
27. See n. 10 above for bibliographic information.
28. See McManus, *Marriage Savers*, or www.marriagesavers.org.

2. Training Mentor Couples

Training marriage mentors can be done across religious groups, with each group adding its particular resources and policies as needed. Ecumenical cooperation broadens the range of available mentor couples who share their marriage successes and challenges as well as makes mentoring community-wide in relation to community marriage policies.

3. Professional Networks, Discussions, and Support

As noted above under "Some Implications of Health and Marriage for the Practice of Ministry," conversations between professions that impact marriage and family through ecumenical, professional, and service club associations can be facilitated at community levels. Interested persons from each of the five fields discussed in this volume could use the chapters here as a basis for planning action at the community level. These informal groups might provide panel discussions on selected marriage and health topics and stimulate cooperative efforts for improving the community's services with marriages and families.

4. Community Media

Ecumenical community groups can work together to create news stories and other special reports about healthy couples for publication through newspapers, television, websites, and other channels. One goal is to raise the profile and awareness of how religiously involved faith-based homes are more successful, healthy, stable, and beneficial to the community, than are non-faith-based homes.

5. Cooperation with Community Agencies Serving Marriages and Families

Churches and synagogues can multiply their ministries with couples through mutual support of and cooperation with other agencies that serve families, such as the human services professions (psychologists, counselors, social workers, etc.), schools, government agencies, and law enforcement. Since most agencies serving families are overloaded, understaffed, and underpaid, an ecumenical support group could offer support and appreciation to the many dedicated persons who, on behalf of the entire community, must daily cope with major family issues, often in conflict or violent situations.

Outreach to business personnel who often are asked for help on family matters can be cooperatively designed. Among these workers are beauty operators, loan officers, restaurant operators, bartenders, cabdrivers, police, secretaries, personnel managers, community recreation leaders, hospital personnel, day care workers, and others to whom persons in family trouble may turn for encouragement or advice. Input from these persons may be the difference in whether a reluctant couple seeks needed therapy or interventions. Clergy and church-sponsored ministries can be available to receive referrals as well as give referral information and support.

6. Public and Private School Systems

Through ecumenical channels pastors, therapists, and mentor couples can work with school boards, administrators, teachers, and counselors to identify needs, create solutions, support implementation, and encourage courses and presentations on marriage, family, and parenting issues. Religious groups can cooperatively train successfully married couples to serve on panels and be available as volunteer consultants.

Ecumenical Cooperation beyond the Local Community

Some strategies are more effectively implemented by an ecumenical approach at regional or national levels, although individual churches, synagogues, or other groups could implement them. The "Marriage in America" report by the Council on Families in America[29] clusters many fine suggestions for congregational and ecumenical cooperation into four broad goals: (1) reclaim the ideal of marital permanence; (2) decide that out-of-wedlock childbearing is wrong; (3) increase the proportion of children who grow up with their two married parents; (4) increase the time that parents spend raising their children.

---

29. In Popenoe, Elshtain, and Blankenhorn, pp. 307-15, see esp. 308.

1. Website to Evaluate and Disseminate Current Information about Successful Marriage and Family Ministries

Although much information is available via the Internet, couples and leaders may not take time to search and evaluate details. An independent, impartial, faith-based website could continuously summarize and provide constructive critiques of marriage resources and monitor media treatments of marriage. Among possibilities are viewer guides to movies and other media, annual awards for positive treatments of marriage in each medium, and cooperation to improve media treatments of marriage.

2. Create Training Programs for Leaders for Churches and Agencies

Materials for training clergy, mentors, and professionals in issues affecting marriages and families are constantly needed. Excellent resources are available.[30] More ecumenical study and leader guides are needed.

3. Facilitate Interaction between Professions

Clergy can bring together other professions in this symposium — law, medicine, therapy, and business. Each can contribute to basic education, preventive and remedial, and enhance ways of strengthening marriage and improving health. Ongoing cooperation between professions at regional, state, and national levels will produce a clearer vision, resources, and opportunities to facilitate marriage and family action at local levels.

4. Incentives for Marriage and Health

Incentives are essential to produce positive changes in society. Some are already in place or emerging, such as requiring premarital education before granting a marriage license and using antipoverty funds for interventions that teach couples to succeed in marriage. National efforts can establish and report on effective programs to help local communities.

---

30. See "Propositions" and "Marriage in America: A Report to the Nation," from the Institute for American Values, and *The State of Our Unions, 1999,* from the National Marriage Project at Rutgers.

Compare the "cost of divorce" to the "cost of marriage maintenance." If a couple spends as much time, energy, and money on strengthening their marriage as they spent on producing a big wedding or getting a divorce, their success would bring many by-products.[31] A creative insurance company could design a "marriage assurance" product that provides marriage enrichment as "preventive maintenance" for families and pays benefits when the couple succeeds in marriage.

Now to Action . . .

Many answers are needed, yet we know enough to implement some positive actions. Invite others into a discussion on marriage and health. Initiate discussion with your spouse, relatives, friends, and colleagues. Religious leaders can encourage members of the professions included in this book to discuss common concerns about marriage and family.

Commit yourself to at least one positive change you can do now. Invite your congregation to join you in study to formulate your plan of action. Let us know (www.Family-project@uchicago.edu) how you are implementing your vision, overcoming obstacles, and reaching your goals of ministry for the improved health of marriages as a key influence on families, congregations, and society.

SELECTED INTERNET RESOURCES

www.marriagemovement.org   Full text of "Marriage Movement: A Statement of Principles."
www.Family-project@uchicago.edu   The Religion, Culture and Family Project website with information on marriage programs and conferences.
www.americanvalues.org   Institute for American Values emphasizes scholarship and policy making in government, media, and private sectors.
www.smartmarriages.com   Information about resources, professionals, political efforts, programs, research, and media concerning marriage, parenting, and family concerns, by the CMFCE (Coalition for Marriage, Family and Couples Education).
www.marriageenrichment.org   ACME, Association for Couples in Marriage Enrichment.

31. Waite and Gallagher, *The Case for Marriage.*

www.marriagelovepower.net   An ecumenical Christian perspective, offers LovePower inventory profile, interactive exercises, and resources for marriages and mentor couples.

http://marriage.rutgers.edu   Reports from the National Marriage Project at Rutgers, the State University of New Jersey.

www.creighton.edu/MarriageandFamily/   Reports from the Center for Marriage and Family, Creighton University.

www.marriagesavers.org   Information on community marriage policies.

www.fmef.org   Resources concerning family, marriage, and faith matters.

CHAPTER 9

Health, Christian Marriage Traditions, and the Ethics of Marital Therapy

John Wall and Bonnie Miller-McLemore

Social critics frequently charge therapists with undermining marriage. While in the 1950s and 1960s many people saw marital therapy as liberating deeply unhappy couples, now many suggest that this movement has gone too far, as the chapters in this volume by Muller Davis and by William Doherty and Jason Carroll suggest. Marital therapy often seems to encourage a reckless pursuit of individual desires whatever the outcome. Moreover, some people question the therapeutic maxim that meeting a parent's needs automatically promotes what is best for the children.

These accusations, regardless of their accuracy or distortion, reflect a profound crisis in the core professional identity of marital therapy. This crisis arises directly from its conflicted origins in a psychotherapeutic movement that has been concerned chiefly with the health, not of institutionalized relationships like marriages and families, but of individuals. Marital therapy is in the difficult position of promoting *individual* well-being while at the same time somehow dealing with the fact that these individuals, at one point at least, chose to commit themselves to marriage and family as *social institutions*. Now that individuals can exit marriages with less stigma, the crisis of identity in this profession has surfaced with special vigor.

Can this crisis be addressed and alleviated in any way? We suggest that the language, attitudes, and practices of marital therapy would be greatly enriched by a serious conversation with a diversity of Christian traditions' approaches to marriage. Specifically, the dominant therapeutic language of health and personal well-being needs to be brought into a richer conversation with the languages of commitment, covenant, mutual responsibility, and social goods. A couple's judgment about the value of their marriage should not be limited to its immediate health benefits for either partner, important as the insights in this volume of Linda Waite, Barbara Dafoe Whitehead and David Popenoe, and David Larson and James Swyers are. The therapeutic profession should also consider the more public, social, and relational dimensions of marriage, including the wide range of goods fostered by marriage, the importance of marital responsibilities and gender justice, and the relationship between marriage and the wider community.

Our case for the enrichment of marital therapy will proceed in three stages. First, we look at how the moral language of "health" has come to dominate the professional self-understanding of marital therapists in the therapeutic movement at large and most recently in the marriage education movement. Second, we examine three major models of marriage that have emerged in the Christian theological traditions and explore how, despite problems of their own, they provide useful perspectives from which to critique and reshape this health ethics. These models of marriage are Roman Catholic subsidiarity theory, a Protestant covenant view, and a more recent liberation theology perspective, all of which have today been largely forgotten or overlooked. Third, on the basis of a conversation between these three traditions and contemporary marriage therapy, we propose a revised understanding of marriage therapy's professional identity.

Our thesis is that therapists should balance concern for married partners' personal well-being with a broader perspective which also treats marriages as involving important social, intergenerational, and public dimensions. We support a "critical familism" similar to but even richer than that described in Doherty's chart.[1] Such a critical familism, rather than advocating any one of the above three Christian perspectives alone, includes a layering of these ideals that recognizes the hazards of each while drawing out their respective strengths. This Christian critique helps us understand marriage as private and social at once. Our view encourages therapists to help couples explore the meaning of their marital commitment, connect their personal well-being to marriage's wider social goods, and work toward a relationship of shared power and radical mutuality.

---

1. See Don S. Browning, Bonnie J. Miller-McLemore, Pamela D. Couture, K. Brynolf Lyon, and Robert M. Franklin, *From Culture Wars to Common Ground: Religion and the American Family Debate* (Louisville: Westminster John Knox, 1997), esp. pp. 2-3.

Health in the Emerging Therapeutic Movement

How has the profession of marital therapy come to support and adopt a "health" ethics? Some would suggest that the notion of an "ethics" guiding the marital therapy profession is an illusion, since therapists seek only to promote the psychological well-being of their clients. But this position, we suggest, is precisely part of what this profession's ethics is all about, namely, the promotion of whatever the client believes is in her or his individual interests. A number of critics have convincingly put the idea of therapists' value neutrality to rest. Therapists, we now see, do steer their clients toward one or another conception of a worthwhile human life whether they realize it or not.[2]

The view that therapists should be "value-neutral" has its origins in the methods of modern science and in Freud's reaction to the narrow and repressive Victorian notions of moral duty of his day, particularly around marriage and family. But this Freudian legacy ignores the considerably broader meanings of the term "ethics" that both traditional and contemporary ethicists use. No doubt therapists are right to root out *moralism* or the rigid, parochial, or destructive enforcement of moral rules and regulations. But this does not mean they aren't guided by ethical images of how human life ought to be lived. This is most especially the case for marital therapists, who are faced with the task of helping couples change behaviors which affect both each other and any children they may have. While each particular therapist brings a different moral background to his or her work, as members of a defined profession, therapists also accept and are trained to understand certain general beliefs about the basic ingredients of a "good" client outcome.

It is not insignificant that the founders of today's therapeutic profession, Freud and Jung, came out of modern medical backgrounds. The original meaning of client "health" was developed explicitly in analogy to the biological health of the person's body. It might not be too much to say that therapeutic individualism arose first out of a body-oriented understanding of the psyche. Freud clearly was less interested in his clients' actual relations to their parents and to others around them than in the psychobiological reactions these relations instilled in the individual's inner being.[3] Likewise, Jung

---

2. Most recently, see William J. Doherty, *Soul Searching* (New York: Basic Books, 1995). For an earlier example of this argument, see Susan Sturdivant, *Therapy with Women: A Feminist Philosophy of Treatment* (New York: Springer, 1980).

3. See, for example, Sigmund Freud, *New Introductory Lectures in Psychoanalysis*, in *Standard Edition of the Complete Psychological Works of Sigmund Freud*, vol. 22 (London: Hogarth Press, 1953-74), pp. 5-182.

viewed the process of "individuation" leading to human well-being as involving archetypes instilled in our bodies' very genetic makeup.[4]

But more than this biological individualism, Freud and Jung developed visions of the kind of client outcome they desired around notions of individual *psychological* health as well. Ernest Wallwork has argued that Freud was quite explicit in promoting an ethics of maximizing the analysand's personal capacity for freedom.[5] The purpose of Freudian therapy was to free the individual from internalized social repressions so that the ego could act with the maximum possible autonomy. Jung, although perhaps having a more favorable view of culture than Freud, nevertheless sought for clients to achieve maximum "individuation" by overcoming the oppressions of the "mass."[6]

While these founding perspectives were perhaps appropriate responses to the repressive Victorian ethics of the day, they have persisted and arguably even grown in the therapeutic profession since. One could point in particular to Carl Rogers's influential humanistic school of psychology, which sought after such therapeutic goals as individual self-sufficiency and personal self-fulfillment.[7] This kind of therapy, which rose to prominence in the 1960s and 1970s, is the primary object of critique by the influential book *Habits of the Heart*, which argues that the therapeutic profession undermines persons' sense of belonging to families and larger communities.[8] But even more recent therapeutic models like D. W. Winnicott's object-relations theory and Heinz Kohut's self-psychology assume that the primary therapeutic goals are not intersubjective or relational but rather have to do with such things as "ego integration"[9] and "self-cohesion."[10] Broadly speaking, other persons and social institutions are of significance primarily insofar as they promote inner psychic health and self-esteem over inner psychic conflict and repression.

---

4. See, for example, C. G. Jung, *Two Essays on Analytical Psychology*, trans. R. F. C. Hull, 2nd ed. (London: Routledge, 1992).

5. Ernest Wallwork's *Psychoanalysis and Ethics* (New Haven: Yale University Press, 1991).

6. Jung, *Two Essays on Analytical Psychology*.

7. Carl Rogers, *Client-Centered Therapy: Its Current Practice, Implications, and Theory* (Boston: Houghton Mifflin, 1951).

8. Robert Bellah, Richard Madsen, William Sullivan, Ann Swidler, and Steven Tipton, *Habits of the Heart: Individualism and Commitment in American Life* (New York: Harper and Row, 1985).

9. D. W. Winnicott, *The Maturational Processes and the Facilitating Environment: Studies in the Theory of Emotional Development* (New York: International Universities Press, 1965).

10. Heinz Kohut, *The Analysis of the Self: A Systematic Approach to the Psychoanalytic Treatment of Narcissistic Personality Disorders* (New York: International Universities Press, 1971).

Health and the Growth of Relational Therapies

This overall ethics of individual health in the therapeutic profession has been qualified in the past several years, however, by increasing attempts to understand client health in relational or intersubjective terms. Social critics of psychology often overlook this trend. This shift is especially evident in Erik Erikson's ego psychology, feminist therapy, and systems theory, each of which attempts to capture something of what therapy should seek to accomplish when it comes to interpersonal relationships.

Despite the label he applies to his school of thought, Erikson understands "ego psychology" to include not only building up inner structures of the mind but also developing healthy and productive relations with others. This is especially true as one moves into adult stages of life where the central psychological issues have to do with intimacy and generativity. Erikson's theory of "cogwheeling" nicely describes the mutual dependency of generations upon one another, older persons like parents and teachers depending as much for their psychological health on younger persons as younger persons do on them.[11] Here the individual health of one's inner ego is viewed as inextricably linked to the health of one's relations to significant others in one's life.

Likewise, more recently feminist therapeutics has developed a concern for healthy relationality. Feminist psychology evolved out of the conviction that personal complaints in individual and family therapy are intimately linked to larger political constraints. A wide range of feminists in psychoanalytic, humanistic, and marriage and family circles all generally agree that conventional therapy erroneously lifts the individual out of history and society altogether, thereby reducing political and social problems related to women's oppression to technical operations upon the psyche.[12] Feminist therapists argue instead that healthy development requires recognizing the mutual interdependency of self and other. Individual health is also seen as dependent on gender justice in marriage and parenting as well as society. In particular, when the mother bears sole responsibility for home and child, boys grow into men incapable of loving, girls grow into women incapable of selfhood, and both women and men struggle with the interpersonal demands of sustaining family life today.

11. Erik Erikson, *Childhood and Society* (New York: Norton, 1950).
12. See, for example, Sturdivant, *Therapy with Women;* Mariam Greenspan, *A New Approach to Women and Therapy: How Psychotherapy Fails Women and What They Can Do about It* (New York: McGraw-Hill, 1983); Louise Eichenbaum and Susie Ohbach, *Understanding Women: A Feminist Psychoanalytic Approach* (New York: Basic Books, 1984); and Harriet Lerner, *Women in Therapy* (London: Aronson, l988).

As early as the 1960s, family systems theory also shifted the goal of individual therapy from personal fulfillment to securing the health of the wider family system as an interlocking set of patterns and processes. The very premise of systems theory — that individuals themselves are constituted by the interactions of larger systems — implodes upon itself. That is, over the years systems theorists have simply continued to stretch the boundaries of the therapeutic session irreversibly beyond itself to wider and wider social spheres, from analysis of generational patterns through genograms to political advocacy in public health-care networks to consciousness-raising about ethnicity.

It is interesting to note, however, that these three approaches to therapy — ego psychology, feminist therapy, and systems theory — finally do not fundamentally question or alter the supremacy of the moral language of health. Although each aims at a therapeutic goal that includes relationships to others, they also on the whole still understand this relationality in terms of the language of health. Relationships on the whole are judged "good" insofar as they are good *for me*, not because they might have some intrinsic social value or fulfill some basic set of moral commitments or responsibilities. Erikson wants clients to raise children, enter into sexual relationships, and become leaders and teachers in their professions because this will enrich, deepen, and more adequately fulfill *their own ego identity*. Relationships are admitted into the therapeutic task chiefly on the grounds that they speak to the individual's different stage-specific "needs," the needs for intimacy, a sense of self-worth, and a meaningful part to play in the world.[13] Feminist critics in particular have pointed out the limitations of a stage theory built primarily around achieving autonomy and individuation rather than around building connections and relationships.[14]

The issue with feminist and family systems therapy is arguably somewhat more complicated. Some feminist theorists have actively promoted values at odds with individual self-fulfillment, such as mutuality, reciprocity, and interdependence in democratic family structures. By definition feminist

---

13. Erikson, *Childhood and Society*. For an insightful discussion of the ethical underpinnings of Erikson's psychology, see Don Browning, *Generative Man: Psychoanalytic Perspectives* (Philadelphia: Westminster, 1973).

14. See Bonnie J. Miller-McLemore, *Also a Mother: Work and Family as Theological Dilemma* (Nashville: Abingdon, 1994), chap. 3; Carol Gilligan, *In a Different Voice: Psychological Theory and Women's Development* (Cambridge: Harvard University Press, 1982); and Carol E. Franz and Kathleen White, "Individuation and Attachment in Personality Development: Extending Erikson's Theory," in *Gender and Personality: Current Perspectives on Theory and Research*, ed. Abigail Stewart and Brinton Lykes (Durham, N.C.: Duke University Press, 1985), pp. 137-68.

therapists have been invested not simply in individual women but in women as a group. Similarly, systems theory is by definition concerned about more than individual health. Moreover, feminist therapeutic theory has included within itself a self-critical moment, asking from the beginning about the implicit values and worldviews promoted by various schools of psychology, particularly as these affect women's lives. In the preface to *Feminist Family Therapy,* Rachel Hare-Mustin claims, "family therapy is a moral endeavor, one based on a vision of human life, and the moral questions should not be obscured," particularly when it comes to women's subordination, trivialization, and the harm of blaming women for family problems.[15] Some systems theorists are especially explicit about their moral assumptions. Therapists, says Ivan Boszormenyi-Nagy, have "an imperative of accountability" to the welfare of all those affected by therapeutic intervention, with consequences for children and future generations being of particular relevance.[16]

This has not necessarily meant, nonetheless, that the basic priority of securing individual health itself is challenged. Nor does it mean that feminist psychology and family systems theory as social sciences have within themselves the means or the history to question the primacy of self-fulfillment. It simply means that personal health is placed into relationship with the wider good. While perhaps not completely sufficient from our point of view, this is at least a step in the right direction. Personal problems, including marital dissatisfaction and dissolution, can be resolved only as wider forces such as sexist gender socialization, workplace discrimination, and generational pathologies are challenged and changed.

Health and the Marriage Education Movement

The most powerful new approach to marriage therapy is the so-called marriage education movement, a movement which includes a diverse group of therapeutic professionals and researchers who believe that the best way to help people in their marriages is to promote healthy marriage practices *before*

---

15. Rachel Hare-Mustin, foreword to *Feminist Family Therapy: A Casebook,* by Thelma Jean Goodrich, Cheryl Rampage, Barbara Ellman, and Kris Halstead (New York: W. W. Norton, 1988), p. viii.

16. Ivan Boszormenyi-Nagy, "The Field of Family Therapy: Review and Mandate," *AFTA Newsletter,* winter 1995-96, p. 34; Ivan Boszormenyi-Nagy, "Commentary: Transgenerational Solidarity — Therapy's Mandate and Ethics," *Family Process* 24 (December 1985): 454-56. See also Ivan Boszormenyi-Nagy and D. N. Urich, "Contextual Family Therapy," in *Handbook of Family Therapy,* ed. A. S. Gurman and D. P. Knistern (New York: Brunner/Mazel, 1981).

major conflicts start to arise. Therapists in this movement counsel couples prior to marriage, help couples already married to strengthen marriage skills, and even sponsor premarriage programs in high schools and colleges.[17] These therapists focus on marriage "education" (not just "preparation") as a way to teach couples the *communication skills* they need to deal with marriage's inevitable conflicts and problems. Prominent among these skills are "the speaker-listener technique," in which couples learn during disagreements to give each other the floor and take turns hearing each other's perspectives;[18] separating problem discussion from problem solution;[19] engaging in a "fair fight for change";[20] softening one's "start-up" in raising a difficult marital issue;[21] using "I" rather than "you" when expressing difficulties;[22] and even simply taking a break when issues start to escalate.[23]

This approach has a distinct advantage over traditional marriage therapy in that it views marriage as something one can get better at, something in which one can become educated and therefore more skilled. In addition, it tends to take a more long-term approach to marriage, since rather than focusing on the content of present problems, communication skills education gives couples the methods to handle conflicts in the future. Despite these advances, however, the marriage education movement retains from its traditional therapeutic starting point both a view of therapy as teaching abstract techniques and a view of marriage as oriented chiefly toward each partner's individual health. Let us take up each of these points in turn.

First, the marriage education movement retains its roots in traditional marriage therapy by focusing less on marriage as a social institution and more on marriage as a network of communicative *techniques*. Marriage is understood in chiefly functional or utilitarian terms. Partners are encouraged to work on the quality of their relationship so that they may eventually reap greater personal gain out of it. A "good" marriage is one in which partners are

---

17. One prominent example of a high school and college program is *Connections,* in which students learn about relationship skills and the legal and economic dimensions of marriage.

18. Markman et al., *Fighting for Your Marriage: Positive Steps for Preventing Divorce and Preserving a Lasting Love* (San Francisco: Jossey-Bass, 1994), pp. 63-72.

19. Markman et al., pp. 82-88.

20. Lori Gordon and Jon Frandsen, *Passage to Intimacy: Key Concepts and Skills from the Pairs Program Which Has Helped Thousands of Couples Rekindle Their Love* (New York: Simon & Schuster, 1993).

21. Gottman, *The Marriage Clinic: A Scientifically Based Marital Therapy* (New York: W. W. Norton, 1999), pp. 224-25.

22. Gottman, *The Marriage Clinic,* pp. 224-25.

23. Gottman, *The Marriage Clinic,* pp. 225-33.

skilled in such things as active listening, de-escalating tension, and avoiding negative start-up. Whatever the partners in a marriage wish to use therapeutic techniques *for* — whatever, substantively, they think a good marriage should in fact aspire *toward* — are on the whole questions considered to lie outside the purposes of therapy. Therapists again remain in a basic sense "value-neutral" about concrete marriage ideals. It is enough that couples learn to negotiate their own particular purposes and goals for the marriage — whatever they are — with skill and effectiveness.

But this leads to our second point. The marriage education movement does in fact advance some images of the components of a good marriage, even if it does so on the whole implicitly and unreflexively. Marriage education inherits from its therapeutic background a strongly *private* or *individualized* conception of the therapeutic outcome it seeks. One of the leading and best-selling books in the movement, Howard Markman et al.'s *Fighting for Your Marriage: Positive Steps for Preventing Divorce and Preserving a Lasting Love*, ends with the following summary: "We've tried to provide tools that you can use to build a relationship that brings long-term fulfillment, and to protect your relationship from naturally occurring storms. But, like anything, once you have the tools, it's up to you what you do with them. As the ad says, 'Just do it.'"[24] Is the only purpose of marriage each partner's individual long-term "fulfillment"? Is there nothing that can be said about the goods which marriage may bring besides that they are "up to you"? Can marriage as an institution promote any substantive goods different from, for example, those pursued in friendships, relationships with coworkers, or relationships between parents and children?

Generally speaking, marriage educators operate with thin definitions of what constitutes a "good" marriage. They suggest that a good marriage should be defined as one which promotes personal aims like satisfying sex, fun, and emotional fulfillment.[25] One prominent researcher in the field, John Gottman, describes "happy couples" as those who, in one way or another, "have a 5 to 1 ratio of positive-to-negative exchanges." Such couples build up an "emotional bank account" creating "very rich climates of positivity."[26] "Positivity" here means whatever contributes to each individual partner's psychological, emotional, spiritual, and physical health. Marriage educators strongly endorse Linda Waite's claim that marriage should be valued because in all kinds of ways it can be *good for you*.[27] In fact, in a book blurb, Diane

---

24. Markman et al., p. 315.
25. Markman et al., *Fighting for Your Marriage;* Gottman, *The Marriage Clinic.*
26. Gottman, *The Marriage Clinic*, p. 88.
27. Linda Waite, "Does Marriage Matter?" *Demography* 32, no. 4 (November 1995): 483-507.

Solle, the director of the Coalition for Marriage, Family, and Couples Education, actually calls Waite's *The Case for Marriage* — which provides "scientific evidence" that marriage promotes health, wealth, and happiness — the "new bible for every smart marriage educator." Our point that marriage education and therapy on the whole need a far more substantial foundation for their ideals of marriage than can be obtained from psychology and scientific evidence alone could not be better illustrated than through this remarkable comparison. Is there anything lacking in this new "bible" for marriage? Is there anything that the Bible itself or, more exactly, the longer religious traditions might have to offer as a corrective and an embellishment?

Marriage and Christian Traditions

In our view, a fruitful conversation between marriage therapists/educators and the Christian traditions should, in the great twentieth-century theologian Paul Tillich's term, be a two-way conversation or "correlation." A correlational approach means that Christianity and modernity are brought into mutually critical dialogue so that thinking and practice on an issue may be furthered and enriched in new ways.[28] This stands in contrast to an approach that is merely *confessional,* that is, which simply asserts the Christian witness of the Scriptures without undergoing a process of interpretation and historical contextualization, or without respect for a diversity of opinions about "the gospel." A confessional approach is, unfortunately, the kind taken up by most Christian writers on the therapies, whether they are for or against them. Several marriage educators, for example, have placed themselves in what in our view is the untenable and unhelpful position of claiming that marriage education techniques are presaged by, and accord harmoniously with, images of marriage in Scripture (on the grounds that both describe the "truth" about human relationships).[29] A far better approach, as we hope to show, is to initiate a critical conversation between the marital ethics presupposed in the therapies and that developed in different ways in the various Christian traditions. Our failure to enter into this kind of dialogue is a sign of how much Christians have forgotten the complexity and richness of their own marital traditions.

Marriage "therapy" and "education" have in fact, in different ways, been

---

28. Paul Tillich, *Systematic Theology* (Chicago: University of Chicago Press, 1951-63).
29. Scott Stanley, Daniel Trathen, Savanna McCain, and Milt Bryan, *A Lasting Promise: A Christian Guide to Fighting for Your Marriage* (San Francisco: Jossey-Bass, 1998), pp. 6-8.

a central concern throughout most of the Christian theological tradition. How to support marriage, how to address its possible dissolution, and how to understand its central meaning and purposes have been pondered at length by theologians from Augustine to Thomas Aquinas, from Martin Luther to John Calvin, and from Karl Barth to Reinhold Niebuhr. There is much about these traditions which should rightly be rejected. However, there is much about the dominant contemporary therapeutic discourse on marriage that is problematic as well. The theological traditions have a rightful and valuable place in helping us move toward a deeper appreciation of marriage's meaning, purpose, and social significance.

Three major contemporary Christian approaches to marriage could be said to have emerged from the centuries of Western Christian thought about marriage: Catholic subsidiarity theory, a Protestant covenant view, and a more recent liberationist perspective. While numerous other theological perspectives could be drawn out of the Christian traditions (not to mention the rich approaches in Judaism, Islam, and the other major world religions), these illustrate what in our view are three major defining options significant for marriage therapy today. They are proposed as beginning points to what we hope is a much larger correlation or conversation between the therapies and the Christian marriage traditions as well as other religious traditions.

The Catholic Model of Subsidiarity

The term "subsidiarity" first became official doctrine in Roman Catholic teachings in 1931 with Pope Pius XI's encyclical about the well-being of workers.[30] Subsidiarity theory has its deepest roots in Thomas Aquinas's concept of natural law. It affirms a diversity of natural institutions in society in which more powerful institutions like government and businesses should "furnish help" *(subsidium)* to smaller social institutions like families, schools, and religious congregations, but without taking over the natural functions which these less powerful institutions are uniquely able to perform.[31] The principle of subsidiarity promotes and protects the diversity of social institutions on the grounds of their various capacities to contribute to society's common good.

---

30. Pope Pius XI, *Quadragesimo anno* (Forty years after [*Rerum novarum*]) (1931). This encyclical is largely based on ideas in Pope Leo XIII's encyclical *Rerum novarum* (On the condition of workers) (1891).

31. For a good definition of "subsidiarity," see National Conference of Catholic Bishops, *Economic Justice for All* (Washington, D.C.: U.S. Catholic Conference, 1986).

Subsidiarity theory does not exhaust what the Catholic tradition has to say about marriage, but it does provide a useful angle on it. This view is promarriage. It affirms marriage as conferring on couples and children unique goods — benefits and rewards — and it demands that larger social institutions, like communities, businesses, professions, and government, furnish marriages with the appropriate needed help. As in Aquinas, the individual goods and purposes of marriage are understood to be more than merely private or personal. As John Witte's chapter in this volume suggests, for most of the Christian tradition, an individual's goods have been understood as deeply related to larger natural, divine, and social goods.[32] Sex, for example, is a good pursued in part for one's own personal fulfillment. But also, through marriage, sex serves such social goods as long-term loving union with another, the procreation and raising of the next generation, a remedy for licentiousness, and, overall, the vitality of the family as one important building block of society. Subsidiarity is one way to interpret the classic Catholic idea of family as "domestic church."[33]

What is more, subsidiarity theory supports the notion of marriage as a sacrament. In classic Catholic terms, marriage is one form of symbolic participation in the union of Christ and the church.[34] A couple's mutual fidelity in marriage is a sign of Christ's actual presence, just as the Eucharist and baptism are also active vehicles of grace. In the marriage ceremony, a real and fundamental change occurs and God is seen to dwell not just in the relationship but also in the goods that flow from this unity. This is another way in which marriage fulfills more than just private health goods. Marriage links the most personal and intimate natural tendencies of individuals — for sex, love, and companionship — to the sacred goods intended by God's larger mysterious order. As a sacrament, marriage is affirmed as a key element in God's purposes for the natural order of society. It evokes life's mysteries and serves as a channel of God's grace. In this sense, Catholic views of marriage are similar to the Hindu and Muslim perspectives described in this volume by

---

32. Thomas Aquinas, *Summa Theologica* 2.2 (London: R. & T. Washbourne, 1917), q. 26; *Summa Theologica* 3, "Supplement," trans. Fathers of the English Dominican Province (New York: Benziger Brothers, 1948), q. 41; Aquinas, *Summa contra Gentiles*, trans. Dominican Fathers (London: Burns, Oates & Washbourne, 1928), 3.2.

33. For an insightful discussion and critique of the Catholic idea of family as "domestic church," see Lisa Sowle Cahill, *Sex, Gender, and Christian Ethics* (New York: Cambridge University Press, 1996), chap. 6.

34. Thomas Aquinas, *Summa Theologica* 3, "Supplement," q. 42; see also the following papal encyclicals: Pope Leo XIII's *Arcanum* (1880), Pope Pius XI's *Casti connubi* (1930), and Pope John Paul II's *Familiaris consortio* (1981).

Paul Numrich, in that they view marriage as furthering various social and sacred goods.

Subsidiarity theory would find much to agree with in the marriage therapeutic goal of health. One of the central natural purposes of marriage, which other social institutions are on the whole less well equipped to perform, is the combined sexual, relational, and emotional health of its members. What is more, subsidiarity theory ties in nicely with the marriage education movement in particular in its emphasis on marriage as a union for the long term. It is no accident that the Catholic Church has been a leader in incorporating the new marriage education techniques into its marriage ministry.

But subsidiarity theory also raises the question of whether marriage therapists and educators understand marriage adequately in its unique connection to larger social goods, as well as its dependency on wider social institutions to furnish it with help. The good of "health" is on this view more than each individual's sexual, psychological, and spiritual well-being, or even a couple's mutual self-dedication in love. Marriage education should promote also the "health" of vital *social* goods. Thus, for example, it might help couples not only have more gratifying sex, but also explore how they see themselves as partners in the social good of parenting. Or it might help couples not only provide each other with a safe refuge from the demands of the world, but also enrich their appreciation for their marriage as a vital source of work support and the capacity to effect changes in the community. Finally, marriage education could help couples explore their marriage as a basis for connection to what is ultimate and sacred. This expanded view of marital goods, far from crippling individual self-fulfillment, opens up the therapeutic process to exploring couples' deeper participation in the larger social order.

The other critique or qualification that a subsidiarity view offers the marriage therapies is that marital health, whether narrowly or broadly conceived, depends on more than instilling good communication techniques. Marriages are not isolated from the rest of society, but depend on the help furnished by a diversity of civil institutions, including the extended family, communities, schools, churches, synagogues, and the government. It is in fact damaging and counterproductive to suggest that marriages stand or fall, thrive or decline, solely on the basis of the partners' personal skills in communication. Rather, a necessary component of a healthy and happy marriage is the couple's ability to contribute to and find support from the myriad social institutions on which their marriage depends. For example, couples could be trained in how to reform or limit the demands of their workplace so they can find the time and energy for their relationship. Or, if they plan to have children, they could be provided help in anticipating what they may need from grandparents, neighborhoods, and schools, or what they have to offer the wider community.

The Protestant Covenant View

The notion of marriage as a "covenant" has grown in the public consciousness since the passage of Louisiana's covenant law option for marriage.[35] However, covenant marriage is generally viewed, both legally and culturally, as simply a more stringent version of regular contract marriage. In a covenant marriage one commits oneself to significant marriage education upon entry and more stringent grounds for marriage exit. But the notion of "covenant" marriage as developed in the Christian tradition, particularly by Protestant Reformers like John Calvin, was not just more stringent than contract marriage today. More importantly, it took the revolutionary view — revolutionary both then and now — that marriage lies at the center of the very structure of society. The Protestant Reformers believed that the covenant of marriage was not just one social institution among others, but rather was ordained by God as one of the primordial "orders of creation," alongside and equal in importance to the church and the state.[36]

The notion of covenant comes from the Hebrew Bible and has been used by many of the great Christian theologians to understand the divinely sanctioned promise of sustained commitment between humans and God. What the Protestant Reformers accomplished, however, was to apply the term not only to our *vertical* relation to God, but also, and in conjunction with this, to the *horizontal*, or human-to-human, relation of marriage. In Calvin, marriage was not a grace-filled emblem of Christ's union with the church, as it was in the Catholic sacramental view. Rather, marriage was a social institution in which God covenanted to join together both the marriage partners with each other and the married couple with the state, the church, their families, and their wider community.

---

35. In 1998, Louisiana became the first state in the United States to institute a bilevel legal structure to marriage in which couples can choose to marry under traditional marriage law, which provides for marriage exit on grounds of "no fault," or under "covenant" marriage law, which legally requires marriage education training and more restrictive conditions for marriage's exit.

36. See, for example, *Calvin's Commentaries*, 47 vols. (Edinburgh: Oliver & Boyd, 1843-59), *Comm. Eph.* 5:22 and *Comm. Mal.* 2:14. For an excellent discussion of Calvin's development of a covenant theology of marriage, see John Witte, Jr., *From Sacrament to Contract: Marriage, Religion, and Law in the Western Tradition* (Louisville: Westminster John Knox, 1997).

The marriage covenant instituted a new center of social order in which God formed a spiritual bond of mutual responsibility and trust between the couple and their social environment. For example, the couple covenanted to support each other in sickness, the state covenanted to protect the couple in their joint properties, the church covenanted to provide spiritual counsel, and families and community members covenanted to lend economic and moral assistance.[37] It was indeed the Protestant Reformers who made marriage in the West into not just a spiritual union but also a social institution, with all the attendant legal requirements, family obligations, and social responsibilities this entails. Pre-Reformation marriages did not involve the state, and indeed Catholic canon law condoned so-called secret marriages formed with no family, community, or ecclesial involvement at all.[38]

The notion of covenant marriage provides another way, different from what we found in subsidiarity theory, to evaluate contemporary marriage therapies. A covenant theology of marriage is not, as in subsidiarity theory, chiefly concerned with the larger natural, social, and spiritual goods which marriage is uniquely able to promote. Marriage in this case is less a source of a variety of social goods and more a duty and responsibility. Although this sense of created duty in marriage has often played into patriarchal inequalities, at bottom it affirms that marital love is good and right in itself as part of God's fruitful creation into which humans are placed.[39]

Moreover, like all parts of creation, marriage and its fallen participants, on this view, always stand in need of redemption. From this vantage point, it is unreasonable and unrealistic to assume that marriage can or ever will satisfactorily meet all individual or social goods. Not all marriages promote health or promote health equally at all stages of the family life-cycle. Counting the benefits of marriage can never fully justify getting married. Given the ambi-

---

37. See Witte, pp. 94-98.

38. The requirements for marriage in many places prior to the Reformation entailed only that the couple be baptized Christians and consent to the union. The church blessed marriages, but it was not necessary for their formation. See Jack Goody, *The Development of the Family and Marriage in Europe* (New York: Cambridge University Press, 1983); Witte, pp. 32, 80.

39. It is our view that the use of covenant theology to support patriarchal views of marriage today is a mistake. Such an approach is arguably taken by groups like the Promise Keepers and James Dobson's Focus on the Family. Recent scholarship suggests that patriarchal language in the Bible, while certainly present, is more a reflection of the Bible's Greco-Roman historical context than it is a unique biblical value. In fact, the New Testament has convincingly been shown overall to have pressed for significantly greater gender equality than existed anywhere at the time, under the rubric of all people as radically equal "children of God." See Carolyn Osiek and David L. Balch, *Families in the New Testament World: Households and House Churches* (Louisville: Westminster John Knox, 1996).

guity of human existence, it is more honest to assume that marriage and children will both enhance and detract from human fulfillment. However, blessing marriage as a distinctive covenant and being receptive to correction and reconciliation in the midst of its inevitable failures make the fruition of its personal and social benefits more likely.

It should not be surprising that, with this background, many Protestants today would find it harder on average than Catholics to join their marriage theology with marriage therapy's ideals of health. The language of "health" does not necessarily blend well with that of social "responsibility" and "obligation." Nor should it be surprising that the notion of "covenant marriage" as used today has been voided of virtually all the social dimensions to which the original Reformation use of the term was attached. However more stringent today's secular version of "covenant" marriage may be as compared to "no fault" marriage, it remains principally limited to a covenant between the consenting partners alone. It is entirely possible that one reason for the recent cultural success of therapeutic models of marriage in predominantly Protestant countries is that they provide an alternative to traditional covenant ideas of marriage which have the potential to entangle the marriage partners in enormous social pressures, not to mention affirming biased and patriarchal sex roles.

Despite these potential drawbacks to Protestant covenant marriage, however, we believe it merits deeper reconsideration and reconstruction. For one thing, marriage therapy and education arguably presuppose something like a covenant responsibility in marriage without clearly understanding it. Marriage educators in particular are fond of the word "commitment," and it is now commonplace for marriage therapists and educators to speak of the necessity of commitment in order to have a strong marriage. However, therapeutic discourse today has difficulty, in our view, explaining what such a commitment exactly means. In addition, marriage educators generally do not conceive of the marital commitment as depending on any kind of third party, be it familial, social, legal, or religious. Nor do they consider it a commitment to anyone or anything beyond the couple, such as children and extended family.

Let us take the example of marriage educators Markman et al., who make a famous and oft-quoted distinction between "dedication commitment" and "constraint commitment." *Dedication* commitment refers to an ideal state in which couples express "loyalty, trust [and] devotion" toward one another. *Constraint* commitment, by contrast, means a less than ideal (although sometimes necessary) state in which couples are held together by a sense of "obligation, . . . covenant, and [feeling of being] trapped."[40] Exam-

---

40. Markman et al., pp. 169-70.

ples of the more favorable dedication commitment include "wanting the relationship to continue into the future," giving "priority" to the relationship over other things, "participat[ing] in their relationship as a team," and feeling "a sense of satisfaction in doing things that are largely or solely for their partner's benefit."[41] Constraint commitment, on the other hand, includes belief in the "immorality of divorce," not wanting to lose "irretrievable investments" like one's house, "social pressure," "economic dependence," "unavailability of [alternative] partners," and, most tellingly of all, "concern for children's welfare."[42] In the end, constraint may be able to "stabilize" one's marriage, but dedication "is the side of commitment that's associated with healthy, satisfying, and growing relationships."[43]

Why do these authors make this distinction? In part they need to explain why, as therapists and researchers concerned with promoting individual and personal fulfillment, they are speaking of such a thing as "commitment" at all. Whatever they mean by it, they are claiming, it is *not* any of those negative and old-fashioned ideas of "obligation" and staying "trapped" in an unhappy marriage. This is precisely what "the triumph of the therapeutic," in Phillip Rieff's famous phrase, consists in, at least when it comes to marriage: the loosening of the moralistic collar that seemed to hold people in social bondage.[44] On this score it is revealing that "covenant" is placed under this kind of commitment, since this suggests a rejection of the previously dominant Protestant paradigm of social duty and obligation against which marriage therapies partly developed.

But what of "dedication" commitment? Here we must ask, exactly what is each marriage partner supposed to be dedicated *to?* And, more importantly, *why?* Why should partners commit themselves to each other? The authors respond essentially by fudging. Yes, you are supposed to dedicate yourself to the relationship, to its long-term viability, and to your partner. But the reason for this is that it will pay off in the end for your own personal satisfaction and fulfillment. It is especially instructive that almost all larger social concerns — social mores, economic responsibilities, and especially "concern for children's welfare" — fall on the side of constraint rather than dedication commitment. The implication is that these might be obligations that could hold a troubled marriage together, but they are less than ideal as reasons for being in a marriage in the first place. The only kinds of commitments that should be consid-

41. Markman et al., pp. 176-78.
42. Markman et al., pp. 170-75.
43. Markman et al., p. 182.
44. Rieff, *The Triumph of the Therapeutic* (New York: Harper and Row, Harper Torchbooks, 1968).

ered positive ones in a marriage are those that have a very good chance of increasing one's own personal well-being. Here we are reminded of the ultimate vacuousness of the marriage education goal of "positivity." It is indeed telling that these same authors go on to compare marriage at length to the stock market, arguing that success in both rests on the skill of balancing the "risks" and "rewards" of one's "investment."[45]

The Protestant view of marriage as a covenant, despite its potential drawbacks, is able to shed a more helpful light on the kind of "commitment" which marriage seems to involve. First, a couple's commitment to each other is more than a long-term, utilitarian or stock market–like bargain aimed at two people's simultaneous personal satisfaction. The marriage commitment is made not just to oneself or to another isolated individual, but also to a social *institution* embedded within a wide range of similar institutional supports. Marriage is not just another kind of individual legal contract, like a fishing license or a business deal. It is a fundamental and necessary component of society. In marriage, money and assets can be consolidated, basic sexual and psychological needs can be met, the next generation of children can under most circumstances most effectively be raised, and extended families and communities can find greater integration and unity.

Second, a couple's commitment to each other cannot be sustained productively without being understood as also a responsibility toward, and a dependence upon, a range of third parties to the marriage. *Pace* Freud, there are more than just six people in the marriage bed (the couple plus each partner's parents). There are also any children the couple may have (and grandchildren), bosses and coworkers, friends and community members who make up the marriage's web of support, and more indirectly, various representatives of religious institutions and the state (the last becoming particularly evident in the event of divorce).

Marriage educators and therapists should not shy away from helping couples explore the many ways in which their marriage both benefits from and is responsible toward the great number of people and social institutions on which its success depends. Marriages should be supported with an eye toward the complex networks of social institutions in covenant with which people pursue their deepest and richest goals. The marriage covenant is not just "constraint" from personal fulfillment; nor can it be reduced to "dedica-

---

45. Markman et al., pp. 191-97. This analogy betrays the marriage education movement's captivity to the rational choice mentality of late-twentieth-century culture, as for example in Gary Becker's book explaining marriage as an entirely economic calculus (*A Treatise on the Family* [Cambridge: Harvard University Press, 1991]).

tion" to long-term reciprocal satisfaction. More profoundly, it should be understood as the commitment of taking on a set of unique private and public responsibilities. Given the fallen nature of this world, marital responsibilities are bound in various ways to be broken. But their deeper purpose is to open partners up to greater and unique possibilities for social and cultural participation.

Health and Marriage Liberation

A third possible model of marriage is based in liberation theology. Liberation theology began in the early twentieth century in South America and was at first primarily Catholic and concerned with liberating the poor from systematic economic oppression. It claims to recapture a dimension of Christian existence which classic Catholic and Protestant perspectives have lost. Since its inception, liberation theology has been taken up by Protestants as well and, what is more, applied to many other kinds of social oppression besides poverty, including racism,[46] sexism,[47] and the neglect of children.[48]

Liberation theology can be defined broadly as seeking to free or liberate those who suffer from structural social inequalities and cultural exploitation and oppression.[49] It is based on the Christian view that all persons have a radical and sacred dignity as brothers and sisters in God's intended kingdom. No liberation theologian to our knowledge has applied this perspective to marriage, although many have demonstrated extensive concern about the family as a social, and sometimes harmful or even dangerous, institution. In our view, a liberation angle can help bring out a further theological point that marriage therapists should consider. Specifically, despite its original intentions of freeing individuals from the potential sufferings of marriage, marriage therapy and education risk increasing marital oppression by failing to address adequately marriage's relation to larger and potentially onerous social and political structures. Quite distinct from the libertarian position that

---

46. See, for example, James Cone, *A Black Theology of Liberation*, 20th anniversary ed. (Maryknoll, N.Y.: Orbis Books, 1990).

47. See, for example, Rosemary Radford Ruether, *Sexism and God-Talk: Toward a Feminist Theology* (Boston: Beacon Press, 1983).

48. See, for example, Adrian Thatcher, *Marriage after Modernity* (New York: New York University Press, 1999), chap. 5.

49. See Gustavo Gutiérrez, *A Theology of Liberation* (Maryknoll, N.Y.: Orbis Books; London: SCM Press, 1973); and Leonardo Boff and Clodovis Boff, *Introducing Liberation Theology* (Maryknoll, N.Y.: Orbis Books, 1987).

Doherty describes, liberation theology plays an essential role in moving us toward the kind of "critical promarriage" position he himself advocates.

Marriage is potentially an oppressive institution in several different respects. First, and perhaps most obviously, marriage can play into social and cultural forces which bring about suffering for women. For example, marriage often locks women into a situation where they become dependent on the income of their spouse, especially in a culture like ours in which women are expected to leave paying jobs to raise children. Such dependency also makes women more vulnerable to physical abuse. Politically, marriage still generally reinforces expectations that women hold primary responsibilities for housework, child and elder care, and school and community involvement.

Second, marriage can also be oppressive toward children and men. Children in particular are vulnerable in marriages that are not able, for economic and political reasons, to create sufficient time or resources for child rearing. Children are also vulnerable to the same violence and abuse suffered by women obliged to submit to male authority and power. Men are vulnerable to economic pressures that ground their value in purely materialistic terms and take them away from family life, and to legal structures that may cut them off from their children after divorce.

Third, marriage can be oppressive in the larger sense of creating responsibilities for partners that are nevertheless not valued or supported by a capitalistic, market-oriented economy. For example, couples need so-called free time to develop their relationships, yet the demands and norms of today's economy often make this very difficult. Couples with children may need extended family help, which our mobile culture makes increasingly problematic.

In each of these different ways, marriage must be viewed as not just an interpersonal but also a political institution. Liberation theology raises the stakes even further than subsidiarity and covenant views do about what it means for marriage to be tied up with larger social structures. Unlike in subsidiarity theory, marriage is not only directed toward social and public goods, but is also shaped and conditioned by economic and political inequities, exploitations, and damaging constructions of reality. Unlike in covenant theology, marriage is not only dependent upon the state, the economy, the church, and the community, but is also deeply affected by each of these larger institutions' powerful and sometimes detrimental social purposes and expectations. Liberation theology requires that marriage be viewed within a political context that has yet to resolve deep problems of sexism, racism, classism, and heterosexism, making strong marriages sometimes near impossible under some circumstances. It may even demand a certain activism in marriage as a grassroots institution able to model and engender changes in the very social fabric of society.

On a certain level liberation theology, like subsidiarity theory, can affirm marriage therapy's aim of its members' greater individual health. What else does "liberation" mean than freedom from suffering in order to lead a more fulfilled existence? Indeed, the liberation metaphor of "suffering" is borrowed from the same medical language as is the term "health." However, liberation theology suggests that health and freedom from oppression are shaped not just by interpersonal relations but also by larger political attitudes and currents. For example, good communication skills can help a husband understand that his wife is angry because she does the bulk of the housework. However, this understanding is not necessarily in itself enough to change his actual behavior, nor to free her from these expected responsibilities. This is because an unequal division of marital roles in the home is powerfully and structurally supported by our still patriarchal culture (the wife will still get blamed for a messy house) and by our economy (the workplace doesn't recognize men as needing time for such tasks).

Communicative skills can provide the techniques to begin to address these kinds of issues, but they cannot in themselves provide substantive ideals that can help couples liberate themselves from the deep-seated social structures which play into marital distress. In some cases, the focus on communication colludes with the perpetuation of injustice. It distracts and prevents attention to the ways in which sexism, racism, homophobia, or poverty may spawn marital conflict. The "kingdom of God" for marriage therapists and educators consists in little more than a society of highly skilled communicators. In order to change deeply embedded social practices, like women taking primary responsibility for housework and child care, therapists should help couples develop their consciousness of marriage's deeper political dimensions. This requires not just active listening but also exploring together alternative images of the kingdom of God, images of ideal social arrangements which critique the way contemporary culture is currently structured and call for a more radical mutuality internal to family life.

Unfortunately, marriage therapists and educators all too often view marital oppression as caused only by the relationship itself. While partners certainly have responsibilities for treating each other with dignity and humanity, they would be better able to do so if the therapeutic environment looked also beyond their immediate relationship to the cultural and economic structures which condition it. This does not mean that marriage therapists and educators should impose their own cultural beliefs on the couple. This would only deepen social oppression. In fact, without much self-consciousness, many therapists already impose political ideals on couples, such as individualism, that it would be useful to explore openly. Rather, to take up the liberationist task in marriage therapy is to help couples explore their own marriage's larger political dimensions. This task has as its goal not just greater communicative openness, but also helping couples develop critical perspectives on the basis of which they can learn to contest, resist, and overcome the deeper cultural and political oppressions which play into marital suffering.

Conclusion

A theological analysis of marital therapy does not mean replacing ideas about promoting individual health and well-being with separate theological values. A more helpful approach is to correlate the insights of marriage therapy and education with the relevant perspectives offered by the Christian tradition. We hope our suggestions, tentative and sketchy though they have been, can be meaningful to marriage therapists and educators broadly, whether they consider themselves "Christian" or not. Since the therapies grew up in the West, insight into the Christian traditions can at the very least serve the function of helping us understand some of the deeper historical underpinnings to our views of marriage today.

Rather than recommending the greater value of one or another of the three theological perspectives we have looked into, we prefer to suggest that each proposes a new *layer* in how marriage therapists could better reenvisage their professional identity. As we argued at the start of this paper, marriage therapy has the problem of balancing the traditional therapeutic ethic of promoting individual health with the fact that married partners are also part of a larger social institution. Each of our three Christian perspectives enriches what it means for this balancing of individual and social dimensions of marriage to take place.

Specifically, the Catholic view challenges therapists to broaden their understanding of the *goods* of marriage — its benefits and rewards — so that couples may better integrate the private side of marital goods with the complex interpersonal, social, and intergenerational sides. The Protestant view challenges therapists to deepen their perspective on marriage's *responsibilities,* so that partners' responsibilities toward themselves may be related more carefully to those they take on toward each other, each other's families and lives, and children. And the liberationist view challenges therapists to embrace a more radical and wide-ranging approach to marital *justice,* so that couples may better resist powerful political and cultural threats to their marital mutuality. All three dimensions, we suggest, are necessary if marriage therapists are to develop an ethic of truly critical familism.

Therapy and Counseling

CHAPTER 10

Health and the Ethics of Marital Therapy and Education

William J. Doherty and Jason S. Carroll

The histories of marital therapy and marital education reflect larger trends in how Americans have viewed marriage and individual health over the past century. In the origins and development of psychotherapy during the first half of the twentieth century, marriage was rarely a focus of sustained attention. As in the culture at large, marriage was viewed as one of many stages on which the drama of individual life and personal psychology played out, but not worthy of focused attention. Interestingly, the dynamics of parent-child relationships were analyzed in great depth by most schools of psychotherapy, but marital relationships were not examined in any depth, perhaps because psychological development was considered pretty much set in place by adulthood.

This chapter recounts how professionals came to be concerned with helping married couples, how the fields of marital therapy and education developed in the second half of the twentieth century and then were influenced by the social revolutions of the last third of the century. We then offer a typology of ideological stances toward marriage in order to understand the divisions among professionals and in society. Finally, we offer a preliminary version of an ecological view of marriage and its moral stakeholders.

It was professionals outside the mental health field who first turned their attention to fostering the well-being of marriages. As concerns about the state of American marriages grew in the 1930s and 1940s, clergy, gynecologists, and educators began to develop counseling methods to help individuals in their role as married persons.[1] These professionals conspicuously referred to their work as "counseling" and not "psychotherapy," reflecting the separation of the social realm from the individual health realm. They also avoided running afoul of the psychiatric profession that controlled psychotherapy as a mental health specialty. Counselors, in this way of thinking, dealt with personal adjustment problems and not health problems. Since the field now uses the term "marital therapy," we will use it here.

Reflecting the power of the individual psychotherapy models, the preferred method of marriage counseling, until the 1960s, was for the counselor to meet with an individual spouse or for the two spouses to meet with separate counselors. Conjoint marriage counseling (with both spouses present) was considered unethical because it would compromise the individual relationship between the client and the counselor. It was not until the development of family therapy as a practice specialty in the late 1950s and 1960s that it became customary to work on marital relationships directly, with both spouses in the room.

However, for a period of twenty years or more, family therapy developed separately from marriage counseling, with family therapy focusing on working with two-generational family systems in order to treat a psychological or behavioral problem of an individual family member, often a child or adolescent.[2] It was not until the 1980s that marital therapy established its own body of theory and research to support clinical practice, and took its place alongside family therapy.[3] In the 1980s the field began its ongoing (and only partly successful) effort to establish marital therapy as a bona fide mental health intervention, with third-party reimbursement.

The field of marriage education has developed in tandem with marital therapy, but about a decade or so behind. Although sociologists began teaching practical marriage courses at the college level as early as the late 1920s, marriage education with couples did not begin in an organized fashion until the 1960s and did not take hold in the United States until the 1970s.[4] Marriage education developed in parallel to marital therapy, but from its begin-

---

1. Carlfred B. Broderick and Sandra S. Schrader, "The History of Professional Marriage and Family Therapy," in *Handbook of Family Therapy*, ed. Alan Gurman and David Kniskern, vol. 2 (Philadelphia: Brunner/Mazel, 1991), pp. 3-40.

2. Rony Berger and Mo Therese Hannah, eds., *Preventive Approaches in Couples Therapy* (Philadelphia: Brunner/Mazel, 1999).

3. Neil S. Jacobson and Alan S. Gurman, eds., *Handbook of Marital Therapy* (New York: Guilford Press, 1986).

4. Larry Hof and William Miller, *Marriage Enrichment: Philosophy, Process, and Program* (Bowie, Md.: Brady, 1981).

nings has had even more involvement of theologically trained professionals and religious institutions. As it has evolved, marriage education involves work with groups of couples more than with individual couples, and is more oriented to prevention than treatment.[5] Its practitioners are not necessarily health professionals and generally do not seek insurance reimbursement for their work.

Marital therapy was born with a strong interest in helping spouses achieve stable, satisfying marriages and avoid divorce. But as the field coalesced into a professional discipline in the 1970s, its leaders tried to dispel the notion that they were "marriage savers" oriented to saving marriages at any cost.[6] Instead, the field moved in the direction of general support for marriage (why else be a marital therapist?) but of neutrality about whether particular couples stayed together or divorced.[7] In this new way of thinking, some marriages are not healthy for one or both of the spouses, and individuals should not be pressured to stay in a marriage they think is bad for them. In fact, a literature on "divorce counseling" emerged in the 1970s and 1980s to help people make a good decision on marriage versus divorce and to deal with the aftermath of a decision to end a marriage. In 1981 the eminent psychologist Arnold Lazarus wrote an article titled "Divorce Counseling or Marriage Therapy: A Therapeutic Option" for the major journal of marital therapy. Although he came down on the side of a "happy marriage" over an "amicable divorce," Lazarus contended that "divorce if properly orchestrated by a specially trained therapist, can be a liberating experience that promotes, rather than undermines, family solidarity."[8]

In the 1980s the feminist critique of marital therapy led to a good deal of soul-searching among marital therapists about their previous neglect of domestic violence against women and of unequal power and division of labor in marriage.[9] Therapists became more sensitized to the dark side of marriage, and even abandoned the idea of conjoint counseling sessions in cases that involved domestic violence. These concerns, along with the growing cultural and professional consensus that individuals should not feel obliged to stay in

---

5. Berger and Hannah, *Preventive Approaches in Couples Therapy.*

6. Frederick Humphrey, *Marital Therapy* (Englewood Cliffs, N.J.: Prentice-Hall, 1983).

7. Esther Fischer, "A Guide to Divorce Counseling," *Family Coordinator* 22, no. 1 (1973): 55-61.

8. Arnold A. Lazarus, "Divorce Counseling or Marriage Therapy: A Therapeutic Option," *Journal of Marital and Family Therapy* (January 1981): 15.

9. Virginia Goldner, "Generation and Gender: Normative and Covert Hierarchies," *Family Process* 27 (1988): 17-31; Marianne Walters, Betty Carter, Peggy Papp, and Olga Silverstein, *The Invisible Web: Gender Patterns in Family Relationships* (New York: Guilford Press, 1988).

unhappy marriages for the sake of their children, moved many marital therapists to take a stance of neutrality, and sometimes even skepticism, about marriage as a venue for individual health and well-being.

Evidence for our claim that contemporary marital therapists now take a neutral stance toward marriage and divorce comes from two sources. A national survey of members of the American Association for Marriage and Family Therapists found that over 60 percent of therapists said they are "neutral on divorce." Only one-third said they are "committed to preserving marriage and avoiding divorce whenever possible." Two percent "often recommend divorce."[10] These findings from therapists are supported by a poll of divorced individuals in Minnesota, conducted as part of a random-sample survey of adults in the state. When asked to "think about the counseling you received," only 35 percent of respondents believed their therapist "wanted to help save [the] marriage." Forty-one percent believed their therapist "was neutral about whether or not to stay together or to get a divorce," and 14 percent said the therapist "encouraged [them] to get divorced." (The outstanding 11 percent fell in the "other" category.)[11] It appears that most therapists who work with married couples have embraced neutrality as a values and clinical stance.

When therapists abandoned advocacy for marital commitment and stability, marriage educators were alone in holding a promarriage perspective. But even in marriage education there emerged a split between educators whose goal is to equip couples with the skills for happy marriage — but who do not take an advocacy stance for marital commitment and stability or focus on marriage as a social institution[12] — and those who have an explicit agenda to promote marital stability and marriage as an institution.[13] Furthermore, some marital therapists are skeptical about marriage education on three grounds: the skills approach is seen as not dealing explicitly with power imbalances between the genders, the procommitment approach is viewed as po-

---

10. John Wall, Thomas Needham, Don S. Browning, and Susan James, "The Ethics of Relationality: The Moral Views of Therapists in Marital and Family Therapy," *Family Relations* 48 (1999): 139-49.

11. Unpublished data available from William J. Doherty, based on a random-digit telephone survey of 384 adults in Minnesota during the winter of 2000.

12. For example, Lori Heyman Gordon and Carlos Durana, "The Pairs Program," and Sherod Miller and Peter Sherrard, "Couple Communication: A System for Equipping Partners to Talk, Listen, and Resolve Conflicts Effectively," in *Preventive Approaches to Couples Therapy*, pp. 217-36 and 125-48, respectively.

13. For example, Michael J. McManus, *Marriage Savers: Helping Your Friends and Family Avoid Divorce* (Grand Rapids: Zondervan, 1995); Rhoderick J. Elin, "Marriage Encounter: A Positive Preventive Enrichment Program," in *Preventive Approaches to Couples Therapy*, pp. 55-72.

tentially trapping people in bad marriages, and promarriage rhetoric is believed to marginalize gay and lesbian couples.[14] In fact, the major professional association of marriage and family therapists has kept an arm's-length relationship with the growing marriage education movement.

A Typology of Ideological Perspectives on Marriage

In struggling to understand and address the splits and controversies in the professions about marriage, we have developed a typology of ideological stances (see table 1 on p. 213). These represent ideal types rather than fully developed models, and in practice individuals and groups might hold to aspects of more than one type. The three types represent a dialectic process, with the third offering a synthesis of the first two opposing approaches to marriage. The noncritical promarriage perspective had characterized much of Western thinking about marriage until the last third of the twentieth century. The neutral/skeptical perspective then emerged as an antithesis focusing on individual autonomy and the dangers of traditional marriage. We believe it continues to hold sway in the social sciences and among many marital therapists and some marriage educators. The critical promarriage perspective is a recent effort to retain the promarriage, procommitment, and communal dimensions of the noncritical promarriage position, but with sensitivities to the critiques of the neutral/skeptical proponents.

In this section we briefly review the core philosophies of these ideological perspectives and present a comparative analysis of how they differ on several crucial issues that are debated in the current cultural and professional dialogue on marriage. We give particular attention to articulating the critical promarriage stance that has emerged within the current marriage movement and in the writings of Don Browning and his colleagues in this volume and others in the series. One payoff from this typology is a way to address the fears of neutral/skeptical advocates that any promarriage stance is tantamount to a return to a patriarchal, prefeminist view of marriage. Instead, we see the critical promarriage perspective as embracing the best of both of the previous models.

---

14. Joan Laird, "The Politics of 'Smart Marriage,'" *American Family Therapy Association Newsletter* (fall 1999): 43-44.

Table 1: Contemporary Ideologies about Marriage

	Noncritical Promarriage	Neutral/Skeptical	Critical Promarriage
Core Philosophy	Authoritarian	Libertarian	Communitarian
Value of marital commitment and stability	Absolute value, few exceptions	An individual choice, based on personal values	An ideal to be promoted, but not feasible in every case
Decision to divorce	Divorce stigmatized, except for adultery, abuse, or abandonment	Divorce equally valued with staying married, based on personal choice	Divorce tragic, to be prevented if possible, but sometimes unavoidable
Two parent versus one parent families	Two-parent families always preferable	No privileging of two-parent families over one parent	Two-parent ideal, but one-parent families preferable to high-conflict two-parent families
Cohabitation	Condemned	Equally valued with marriage as lifestyle option	Valued less than marriage, viewed with caution
Marriage education	Viewed cautiously; commitment should be enough	Viewed cautiously; fear of traditional gender roles and divorce prevention	Strongly encouraged to promote both satisfaction and stability
Feminism	Not embraced	Embraced enthusiastically; concern about male power and women's well-being; skepticism about marriage	Gender equality embraced, but not feminism's emphasis on male power and skepticism about marriage
Religion versus social science	Religion strongly preferred; social science viewed warily	Religion viewed warily, social science embraced with feminist and multicultural slant	Religion and social science both valued, but critically
Sacrifice versus personal satisfaction	Sacrifice emphasized more strongly	Personal satisfaction emphasized; sacrifice seen as dangerous	Satisfaction and sacrifice both valued and mutually intertwined
Public versus private emphasis	Public face of marriage emphasized	Private face of marriage emphasized	Private and public emphasized

The Noncritical Promarriage Stance

The dominant view of marriage until the last third of the twentieth century, and still held among some conservative religious groups, is the noncritical promarriage perspective. In this view marriage is a permanent bond between man and woman and a centrally important institution for the well-being of adults, children, and society. Depending on the theological tradition, marriage is viewed as a natural institution governed by natural law as well as a divinely ordained institution governed by religious doctrines.[15]

We label this stance "noncritical" for three reasons: (a) the virtues of marriage are largely assumed and celebrated via an understanding of the natural order and the divine order; (b) problematic features of marriage such as patriarchal authority patterns and physical, sexual, and emotional abuse are not examined or are de-emphasized; and (c) the tension between individual well-being and marital stability is not dealt with in a systematic fashion. This is not to say that religious beliefs that view marriage as a natural and/or divinely ordained institution are inherently noncritical in their orientation, but that historically these beliefs have been filtered through cultural norms and practices that support a hierarchy of male privilege in the familial and social realms. For this reason, until recently even sophisticated theological and philosophical discussions of marriage, such as those described by Witte in this volume, have lacked a critical discussion of marriage.

The noncritical promarriage perspective is not confined to religious worldviews. The structural functionalist school of family sociology, dominant in the mid-twentieth century, can be characterized as having a noncritical stance toward marriage because it largely assumed the functional "goods" of marriage and of contemporary marital roles, it accepted traditional gender roles as part of the natural order of social relations, and it ignored the dark side of marriage that could create tensions between individual health and marital stability.[16]

It is important to stress that scholars who have taken a noncritical promarriage position are not necessarily simplistic thinkers. Thomas Aquinas and Talcott Parsons can hardly be accused of lacking analytical skill. But their views of marriage can still be labeled "noncritical" for the reasons listed

---

15. See John Witte's contribution to this volume, chap. 3.
16. See Talcott Parsons, "The Normal American Family," in *The Family's Search for Survival*, ed. Farber, Mustacchi, and Wilson (New York: McGraw-Hill, 1965), and Nancy Kingsbury and John Scanzoni, "Structural-Functionalism," in *Sourcebook of Family Theories and Methods: A Contextual Approach*, ed. Pauline Boss, William J. Doherty, Ralph La Rossa, Walter Schumm, and Suzanne Steinmetz (New York: Plenum), pp. 195-217.

above. Indeed, it was what many saw as the critical blind spots of conservative theological and structural-functional views of marriage that fueled the backlash of the neutral/skeptical perspective.

The Neutral/Skeptical Stance

The social movements of the late 1960s, 1970s, and 1980s ushered in feminism, multiculturalism, and postmodernism, all of which offered profound criticisms of conventional ways to think about marriage, family life, and social relations in general. Feminism in particular shone a bright light on the dark underbelly of marriage: the prevalence of physical and sexual abuse, the gap between egalitarian norms for marriage and the actual division of labor and decision making between the sexes in the family, women's assumed greater responsibility for the quality of marriage and parenting, the impact of the greater earning power of husbands relative to wives, and the stigmatization of single mothers. Thus emerged the neutral/skeptical stance toward marriage, which is now prevalent in the professions.

At best, this stance views marriage in neutral terms and regards it as one of a number of viable lifestyle arrangements an individual can personally choose, with the marriage-based, two-parent family form being neither more nor less deserving of support from professional and community resources. Marriage is seen ultimately as a personal lifestyle choice, and as such, should be regarded as a private contract whose terms should be set only by the partners themselves. At a policy level, being neutral about marriage means treating all coupling forms as equal — in particular, cohabiting couples and gay and lesbian couples who are currently denied access to legal marriage — and interprets the decision to divorce as a strictly personal decision that should not be encumbered by outside pressures. As a well-known therapist colleague of ours likes to say, "The good marriage, the good divorce — it matters not."

Some professionals move past neutrality to open skepticism about marriage relationships and worry that efforts to promote marriage and prevent divorce may be inflicting more harm than good on individuals. Those espousing this position point out that the reality of marriage relationships often departs significantly from the idealized notions portrayed in noncritical promarriage dialogue. This position is wary of the potential dark side of marriage and questions if marriage, as traditionally defined, is an inherently hierarchical institution that oppresses women and serves to reinforce patriarchal power structures in our society. Those who hold this view see marriage as a major context in which sexism, heterosexism, and racism are fostered and reinforced.[17] They therefore oppose efforts to support marriage as a social institution and are wary of interventions for married couples that do not focus on power inequities.

The Critical Promarriage Stance

The third, and most recent, ideological perspective on marriage is the "critical promarriage" stance. For its formulation we owe a debt to Browning et al.'s work on developing a model of "critical profamilism" and to Amitai Etzioni and colleagues' articulation of a communitarian approach to marriage and the family.[18] If the noncritical promarriage stance has authoritarian philosophical roots (in culturally based interpretations of natural law or divine revelation), and the neutral/skeptical stance has roots in social libertarianism (individuals are free to choose their lifestyle), the critical promarriage stance is communitarian (trying to balance individual needs and society's needs).

This perspective has the promarriage elements of the noncritical promarriage stance. Marriage is viewed as an ethical vocation, not just a lifestyle choice. Marriage promotes social and communal goods in addition to personal goods. But, having learned from the neutral/skeptical critique of marriage, it is also "critical" because it acknowledges the historical injustices of marriage for women and the prevalence of abuse and inequality. It goes beyond both previous perspectives by acknowledging the inevitability of tension at times between the needs of individuals for autonomy and personal happiness and their marital, family, and community obligations. In the critical promarriage perspective, this tension is not resolved by saying either "do your duty" or "do your own thing." Both sides of the dialectic are held, along with an attempt to resolve them by showing how duty and autonomy are mutually intertwined in the complexities of married life.

We next discuss how these three perspectives deal with certain core aspects of marriage.

---

17. Kristine M. Baber and Kathrine R. Allen, *Women and Families: Feminist Reconstructions* (New York: Guilford Press, 1992).

18. See Don S. Browning, Bonnie J. Miller-McLemore, Pamela D. Couture, K. Brynolf Lyon, and Robert M. Franklin, *From Culture Wars to Common Ground: Religion and the American Family Debate* (Louisville: Westminster John Knox, 1997), and Jean Bethke Elshtain, Enola Aird, Amitai Etzioni, William Glaston, Mary Ann Glendon, Martha Minow, and Alice Rossi, *A Communitarian Position Paper on the Family,* Communitarian Network, http://www.gwu.edu/~ccps/pop_fam.html.

Marital Commitment and Divorce

Much of the current marriage debate has emerged in response to varied interpretations of the causes and consequences of the high rates of divorce of the last three decades. Within a noncritical promarriage perspective, marital stability is a near-absolute value. Divorce is often stigmatized except for cases of adultery, abuse, or abandonment. In some religious communities, divorce is not recognized or seen as a viable option, leaving divorced individuals feeling like second-class citizens even if they have remarried. There is little attention paid to the problem of the stable but highly conflicted marriage or to the social and economic consequences of the stigmatization of divorce, especially for women. The current high divorce rates are seen as disastrous for families and society.

Within the neutral/skeptical perspective, divorce is equally valued with staying married, as long as individuals have made free choices. While the ending of a relationship might be seen as regrettable, the decision to divorce is ultimately made on the basis of whether the marriage meets the needs and expectations of the spouses. No one should be legally or psychologically pressured into staying in an unsatisfactory marriage out of a sense of duty or responsibility. Historically high divorce rates are not viewed as a sign of decline, but rather as an evolution in family patterns that have resulted from removing barriers that kept individuals of past generations trapped in unsuccessful relationships. In the realm of therapy, the neutral position comes down solidly on the side of promoting individual happiness as opposed to the institution of marriage. Arnold Lazarus writes: "For me, the worth of a marriage is weighed solely in terms of human happiness. Marriage is not a sacred entity to be preserved for its own sake."[19] Some scholars move past this neutral stance toward divorce to posit that high divorce rates are a confirming sign that "the traditional institution of marriage is deeply, if not fatally flawed."[20]

Within the critical promarriage position, permanent marital commitment is seen as very important for marriage to promote the well-being of individuals, couples, children, extended families, and communities. This is particularly true when the role of wife or husband is intertwined with the role of mother or father. Divorce is seen as tragic and to be prevented if at all possible. But the critical promarriage perspective recognizes that some marriages cannot and should not be salvaged, especially when there are danger and

---

19. Lazarus, p. 20.
20. Baber and Allen, p. 34.

harm to spouses or children. This perspective is reflected in a communitarian statement on marriage which notes that, "though divorces are necessary in some situations, many are avoidable and are not in the interest of the children, the community, and probably not of most adults either."[21] Staying married is clearly held as a more desirable outcome than divorce. Divorce can be viewed like an amputation — to be prevented and avoided with all vigor and persistence and embraced only after all other solutions have been attempted — which is sometimes unavoidable for survival.[22]

Two-Parent versus One-Parent Families

Another issue that distinguishes ideological perspectives on marriage is how they regard single-parent families versus two-parent families. Within the noncritical promarriage perspective, two-parent families are seen as always being a preferable arrangement for raising children. This is the natural order of family life, and, from some theological perspectives, the divinely ordained order. Not infrequently, single-parent families are assigned responsibility for a host of social ills, but the pathologies of two-parent families are not emphasized.

As we noted previously, neutral/skeptical perspectives hold that no family form or arrangement should be privileged above others. Therefore, there is strong opposition to the privileging of two-parent families over one-parent families. For those with a neutral view of marriage, there is concern that promoting marriage and two-parent families stigmatizes single and divorced parents, many of whom are raising children under difficult circumstances. Likewise, since single parents are more prevalent in African American communities, a promarriage agenda may seem particularly insensitive to their concerns and realities.[23] Those who move past neutrality to skepticism about marriage often embrace and promote intentional single parenting, a stance that only a generation or so back would have been seen as unthinkable. In this way of thinking, getting married and becoming a parent are separate and unconnected life decisions, each to be made on its own merits as seen by the individual.

Within the critical promarriage stance, there is a two-parent family

---

21. The Communitarian Network, *Responsive Communitarian Platform* (Communitarian Network, 2000), p. 4.

22. William J. Doherty, *Soul Searching: Why Psychotherapy Must Promote Moral Responsibility* (New York: Basic Books, 1995).

23. Theodora Ooms, *Toward More Perfect Unions: Putting Marriage on the Public Agenda* (Washington, D.C.: Family Impact Seminar, 1998).

ideal but a recognition that in particular cases when the family environment is emotionally, verbally, and physically hostile, one parent is preferable to two parents. The ideal is held because marriage is seen as the best environment for the raising of children psychologically, economically, and socially. Marriage is also valued because it promotes responsible fathering. Most proponents of the critical promarriage stance support social programs for single-parent families, since many children grow up in these households, but insist on maintaining the ideal of a married, two-parent family, and believe that society should promote the viability of this family form.

Cohabitation

Based generally on religious beliefs, the noncritical promarriage stance sees cohabitation as one of the primary indicators of marriage decline. This living arrangement is morally inappropriate and condemned because it violates natural and theological laws about the proper place for sexual behavior. Generally, distinctions are not made as to the motive for the cohabitation or the nature of the commitment between the partners.

Holding to the principle that no family form should be privileged above others, neutral and skeptical perspectives view cohabitation as a personal lifestyle option equally valued with marriage. Some even hold up the flexibility and freedom of cohabitation as virtues of the lifestyle arrangement and see the rise in rates of cohabitation as a sign of progress, especially for women, who are regarded as having been traditionally limited within obligations of marital relationships.

Within the critical promarriage perspective, cohabitation is viewed with caution and skepticism but not condemned. Drawing on the research literature, advocates of this perspective are concerned about the association of cohabitation with later divorce and poorer marital quality. It is particularly seen as a bad arrangement for children. Another concern is that since many religions disapprove of cohabitation, couples who choose this form of union are distanced from organized religious communities, which are potentially strong support networks for their relationship and family.[24] It should be noted that there is some variance on views of cohabitation among proponents of the critical promarriage stance. Citing the research literature on the differential impact of different kinds of cohabitation, some make a distinc-

---

24. Linda J. Waite, "Cohabitation: A Communitarian Perspective," *Communitarian Network*, http://.gwu.edu/~ccps/Waite.html.

tion between prenuptial or engaged cohabitation, where the couple have a solid commitment and a planned wedding date, and cohabitation where the couple live together without a permanent commitment. Others see all types of cohabitation as ultimately an inferior imitation of marriage and something to be discouraged.

Marital Therapy and Education

The noncritical promarriage perspective is cautious about secular approaches to assisting marital relationships, preferring to focus on biblical and other theological perspectives. Recently, however, the challenge of high divorce rates in all faith communities has moved conservative faith communities to develop initiatives to prepare couples for marriage, to support married couples, and to help troubled couples. However, there is still wariness in many circles about adopting secular models of marriage education and therapy. It should be noted that there are grounds for this wariness, given the historical skepticism of social scientists and therapists about religion.

The neutral/skeptical perspective takes a generally positive view of marital therapy, as long as the therapist is neutral on marital stability versus divorce and is attentive to problems of abuse and inequality for women in marriage. Therapy is seen as a way to clarify individual desires and to promote communication and problem-solving skills to allow couples to overcome their problems and shape their marriage in a more egalitarian direction. When it comes to marriage education, however, neutral/skeptical advocates are wary of the procommitment stance of many marriage educators, and they criticize the absence of an explicitly egalitarian stance toward marital roles in most of the marriage education movement.

The critical promarriage stance is strongly supportive of marital therapy and marriage education, both premaritally and after marriage, as a way to promote both stability and satisfaction in marriage. It differs here from the noncritical promarriage perspective on marriage education by positing that even couples who are religious and deeply committed to their relationship need to be intentional in growing their marriage to develop good communication and problem-solving skills. The critical promarriage perspective joins the skeptical/neutral perspective in recognizing that equality and mutual regard are necessary for satisfying marriages in the contemporary world, and that marital therapy can be helpful. It differs from the neutral/skeptical stance by being more positive about marriage education's emphasis on stability. It also differs about marital therapy, having the opposite concern that therapists are often not supportive enough of couples' commitment. Finally, this perspective has a unique emphasis on the larger community's responsibilities in promoting lifelong marriage education and support for troubled couples.

Feminism

With regard to feminism, the noncritical promarriage perspective historically has been skeptical, for reasons that should be clear. The neutral/skeptical stance has been enthusiastic about the contributions of feminism to the understanding of marriage, while the critical promarriage stance embraces feminism's emphasis on gender equality but does not emphasize patriarchy and male power as priority areas for discussion and intervention. The critical promarriage stance also does not embrace feminism's skepticism about marriage.

Religion versus Social Science

As mentioned before, the noncritical promarriage stance has historically been wary of social science, especially when its moral neutrality is seen as threatening the institution of marriage. The neutral/skeptical perspective, for its part, views religion warily and embraces social science, especially social science that has feminist and multicultural emphases. The critical promarriage perspective values both religion and social science but takes a critical stance toward both: each is viewed as making important contributions, but each has limitations and blind spots when it comes to understanding and supporting marriage. Stated simplistically, religion is strong on the issues of commitment and the public dimension of marriage but tends to lack sophisticated ways to understand and promote the well-being of modern companionate marriages. Social science is strong on understanding contemporary marital relationships but is generally poorer in the areas of commitment and community in marriage.

Sacrifice versus Personal Satisfaction

The notion of self-sacrifice in marriage is a key dividing point among the three ideological views of marriage. Sacrifice for the good of the marriage is at the heart of the noncritical promarriage perspective, while it is anathema to the neutral/skeptical perspective because sacrifice is seen as compromising individual well-being. The critical promarriage perspective values both sacrifice and individual satisfaction, and sees them as necessarily intertwined. This both/and stance is reflected in the following quote from Browning and colleagues, in which the ideas of sacrifice and equal regard/mutuality are viewed as intertwined: "One of the greatest tasks of our time is to create a spirituality of marriage which links sacrificial love and the experience of the transcendent in ways that reinforce a steadfast love in the service of equal regard and mutuality."[25]

Public versus Private Emphasis

The noncritical promarriage perspective has a strong emphasis on the institutional, community dimension of marriage, which views personal relationships as strongly connected with public purposes. The personal side of marriage was often less strongly emphasized in these traditions, but in recent decades it has come into greater prominence as conservative churches have become more active in promoting marriage. The neutral/skeptical perspective, reflecting its social libertarianism, strongly emphasizes the private side of marriage over the public. The critical promarriage perspective, once again, attempts to embrace both dimensions of marriage. Marriage is a highly personal relationship to be shaped by spouses, and it is also a relationship that is embedded in two-way influences with community. Communities support or undermine marriage, and the quality and stability of marriages build or detract from community.

Views of Health in Marital Therapy and Education

This discussion of ideological models of marriage sets the stage for the following discussion of health in marital therapy and education. Since the 1970s, the field of marital therapy, reacting against its precritical roots, has absorbed feminist and other critiques which saw traditional marital therapy and education as denigrating the health and well-being of individuals.[26] The mainstream of the field became neutral/skeptical toward marriage, for the

---

25. Browning et al., p. 292.
26. See chap. 3, "The Contemporary Context of Family Therapy," in Michael P. Nichols and Richard C. Schwartz, *Family Therapy: Concepts and Methods* (Needham Heights, Mass.: Allyn and Bacon, 1995).

most part avoiding the term "marriage" in books, articles, and conference presentations. In so doing, the field by and large adopted the "thin view" of individual and marital health described by Wall and Miller-McLemore, that is, health viewed as a private, personal good and marriage viewed as a private, skilled relationship aimed at promoting personal well-being. The good marriage, from this perspective, is one that "works" for the two individuals involved. Other voices have emerged in recent years to present a more communitarian view of health and marital well-being.[27]

The newer field of marriage education shows a more complex picture. On the one hand, leaders in marriage education clearly embrace a promarriage perspective. They see their programs as giving couples the knowledge and skills to negotiate marital relationships that work for both parties. Beyond these core areas of agreement, however, marriage educators divide into two major ideological positions. One has elements of the noncritical promarriage position. As exemplified by Marriage Encounter and Marriage Savers,[28] two religiously based organizations, "traditionalist" marriage educators stress the sacredness and permanence of the marital bond and oppose strongly what they see as today's culture of easy divorce. They see marriage as a divinely ordained institution that nevertheless can be enhanced by knowledge of modern approaches to communication skills. Religiously grounded commitment is the cornerstone of marriage, with skills, mentoring, and religious community serving as valuable ways to keep that commitment alive. Cohabitation is condemned and two-parent families strongly preferred. Traditionalist marriage educators deal relatively little with the concerns of the neutral/skeptical advocates in areas such as gender roles and gender equality, domestic abuse, and justifiable divorce. In fact, traditionalist marriage educators keep an arm's-length relationship with feminism. They also differ from more radical noncritical promarriage advocates by their openness to the role of social science and their efforts to help couples in their private relationships.

The other major group of marriage educators tends to be secular professionals or liberal religious professionals. This can be called the "skills" group of marriage educators who base their work on social science theories and research on the psychological knowledge and interpersonal skills needed

---

27. See William J. Doherty's *Soul Searching* (1995) and *Take Back Your Marriage: Sticking Together in a World That Pulls Us Apart* (New York: Guilford, in press); Blaine J. Fowers, *Beyond the Myth of Marital Happiness* (San Francisco: Jossey-Bass, 2000); and Scott Stanley, *The Heart of Commitment* (Nashville: Thomas Nelson, 1998).

28. McManus, *Marriage Savers,* and Elin J. Rhoderick, "Marriage Encounter: A Positive Preventive Enrichment Program," in *Preventive Approaches to Couples Therapy,* pp. 55-72.

to maintain a viable companionate marriage in today's world. They share elements of the critical promarriage and neutral/skeptical stances. They are critical promarriage in their embrace of marital commitment as a positive value, their embrace (at least implicitly) of the idea of gender equality, and their willingness to work collaboratively with religious organizations.

They share with the neutral/skeptical stance an emphasis on individual well-being as the goal of marriage and individual autonomy as the main consideration in divorce decisions. For skills-oriented marriage educators, marriage is a personal relationship far more than a social institution. Cohabitation is not devalued relative to marriage; the skills can help any couple succeed. Skills-oriented marriage educators want people to be happy in their marriages, with the assumption that if they are happy they will stay committed. As Fowers has pointed out, most of the marital problem–solving skills focus on individuals getting what they want through clear, focused, and democratic negotiation.[29] Notions of the common good of the marriage, the children, the family, and the community are generally not discussed.

Some marriage educators have recently moved more fully into the critical promarriage stance by embracing moral commitment as central to marriage and emphasizing the public, common-good face of marriage.[30] And documents coming out of the broader marriage movement (as distinguished from marriage education) are taking a critical promarriage position that lines up with column 3 in the table describing the three models.[31]

The Ecology of Marriage

We concur with our companion authors' call for an expanded perspective of "marital health" that encompasses "the wider range of social goods that evolve from good marriages" and defines the health benefits of marriage in individual, relational, and social terms. We also agree with Wall and Miller-McLemore's assertion that an important task for marriage therapists and educators is "to explore each marriage's implicit and explicit dependencies on larger social institutions" and how these relations contribute to a marriage's

---

29. Fowers, *Beyond the Myth of Marital Happiness.*

30. For examples, see Doherty, *Take Back Your Marriage;* Fowers, *Beyond the Myth of Marital Happiness;* and Stanley, *The Heart of Commitment.*

31. See *The Marriage Movement: A Statement of Principles* (Coalition for Marriage, Family, and Couples Education; the Institute for American Values; and the Religion, Culture, and Family Project, 2000); Ooms, *Toward More Perfect Unions;* and Elshtain et al., *A Communitarian Position Paper on the Family.*

greater fulfillment and meaning. The ecological view of marriage that we present is consistent with the critical promarriage perspective described above. It goes beyond standard models in marriage education and marriage therapy by emphasizing the institutional as well as relational dimensions of marriage, and the interplay of influence between marriage and its ecology.

Toward an Ecological Model of Marital Health

Ultimately, an expanded perspective of marital health entails recognizing and appreciating the ecology of marriage and the moral stakeholders who both benefit from and support marriage relationships at each level of the system. As marital therapists and educators, we have found that an effective way to expand clients' views of marital health is to ask about and discuss the moral stakeholders whose well-being is intertwined with their marital relationship. This type of therapeutic dialogue illuminates the *moral ecology of marriage* and encourages couples to view their relationship as a community-based covenant rather than a private, contractual relationship that involves only their personal well-being. It is our experience that as therapists and their clients think about the various levels of moral stakeholders of marriage, they are ultimately challenged to expand their considerations of what is truly involved in assessing marital health. Marital health becomes more than one's individual fulfillment or well-being, but ultimately the well-being of a network of interconnected and interdependent stakeholders who all benefit from and provide certain goods to the marriage relationship. The promotion of marital health by therapists and other professionals is then defined as an ongoing process of balancing the mutually interdependent needs of the moral stakeholders in the marital ecosystem.

We conceptualize "marital health" at four ecological levels: (1) the individual level, (2) the family level, (3) the community level, and (4) the societal level (see table 2 on p. 226). Each level comprises various moral stakeholders whose well-being both influences and is influenced by the marriage relationship. In the individual and family levels, this bidirectional influence is often explicit and direct (e.g., children's welfare, personal health), but in the community and society levels it is more implicit and indirect in nature (e.g., social goods, financial productivity, well-being of future grandchildren, etc.).

A core principle of this model is the idea that the health and well-being of the stakeholders at the various levels are interconnected and interdependent. Therefore, when viewed with an ecological lens, the promotion of individual health or community well-being should benefit the other stakeholders

Table 2: An Ecological Model of Marital Health

Ecological Level	Moral Stakeholders	Benefits: "What marriage gives"	Provisions: "What marriage receives"
SOCIETY LEVEL	Civic institutions Corporate institutions Educational institutions Criminal justice system Religious organizations	Productive citizens Productive employees Productive students Less crime/delinquency Moral socialization	Policy support Financial support Education Protection/security Spiritual guidance
COMMUNITY LEVEL	Neighborhoods Faith communities Children's peers	Shared support Shared support Socialization	Role models Community network Friendship
FAMILY LEVEL	Children Extended family Children's marriages Future grandchildren	Secure environment Socialization Financial security Parental involvement Strong kin network Trust of the institution of marriage Sense of heritage	Purpose/Meaning Child care Family ties
INDIVIDUAL LEVEL	Spouse Self	Physical health Mental health Spiritual health Personal growth	Purpose/Meaning Sense of belonging Emotional support Sense of community

in the ecosystem and vice versa. Like all ecological systems, the goods of various levels exist in tension, and at times compete, with each other. Rather than trying to avoid this tension by focusing on only one level or by telling ourselves that what is good at one level automatically becomes what is good for another (e.g., "if a parent is happy, that is what is best for the child"), true ecological health involves balancing the needs of all the stakeholders at all the levels. (This is why our perspective is "critically" promarriage.) Marriage and family life involves moral decisions that, at times, will involve prioritizing some stakeholders' needs over others. But such decisions should be made with a conscious recognition of the consequences of such choices. Not acknowledging the moral ecology of marriage has short-term consequences that appear to free individuals to make unfettered, self-interested choices, but it ultimately limits the horizon of significance of marriage itself in human life. No marriage is an island.

Table 2 outlines some of the two-way influences in the ecology of marriage. It is intended to exemplify some of the major influences involved, and not to be exhaustive. One difference between this ecological model and traditional top-down, structural-functional models is that we see the decisions of married couples influencing their larger environment and not just their microenvironment. For each ecological level, we specify the moral stakeholders and describe the benefits that marriage potentially offers and receives. Of course, these reciprocal influences can also be negative, as when social institutions undermine marriage through legal provisions such as a marriage tax penalty. The table does not show indirect influences that can also be important, such as when marital breakdown influences certain societal norms which contribute to the deterioration of local community bonds.

Toward a Conceptual Ethic of Marriage Promotion

We share our companion authors' concern that unless the professions of marriage therapy and marriage education incorporate an expanded perspective of marital ethics and health into their professional identities, they will continue to contribute to the contemporary crisis in the meaning and purposes of marriage. To this end, we believe that the professions of marital therapy and marital education, and the other professions as well, would be greatly benefited by the development and articulation of a conceptual ethic of marriage promotion. Dollahite and Hawkins define a conceptual ethic as "a framework intended not primarily to model or describe reality — although it may do that — but mainly to suggest what is possible and desirable."[32] Such an ethic could provide a vision for professional support of marriage and define an ideal to be promoted. We realize that the development of a conceptual ethic that is widely accepted may be difficult to achieve in our diverse society, but we feel that even the process of engaging in such a discussion could prove very beneficial. This process may be seen as an ongoing discussion that is never complete. But we believe that some common ground is possible, as exemplified by our own coauthoring process involving a committed Mormon (J.C.) and a committed Unitarian-Universalist (W.D.). On the basis of the foregoing analysis in this chapter, we propose several central components of a conceptual ethic of marriage promotion.

---

32. David C. Dollahite and Alan J. Hawkins, "A Conceptual Ethic of Generative Fathering," *Journal of Men's Studies* 7, no. 1 (1998): 109-32.

1. Marriage therapy and education should be guided by an ethical vision of marriage that is rooted in the moral responsibilities of spouses to each other, their children, and the other stakeholders of their marriage relationship.

Marital therapists and educators need to develop a deeper vision of what constitutes a good marriage. Within the last several years there have been a handful of solid examples of attempts to define such an ethical vision of marriage. Drawing from a Christian critical familism perspective, Browning and colleagues have proposed an "equal regard marriage" ethic of marriage life that is based in equal regard of spouses, self-sacrifice in the service of mutuality, and the subordination of families to the larger social good.[33] Fowers has promoted a vision of "partnership marriage" based in appropriate expectations of marriage, meaningful shared visions and goals, and the virtues or character strengths of spouses.[34] Drawing on Mormon theology of marriage, Hawkins and colleagues have articulated an "equal partnership" ethic of marriage based in shared family leadership, personal growth, and the interdependence of father and mother roles.[35] There is a need to infuse these and other ethical views of marriage into the marriage movement discourse and into the literatures on marital therapy and education.

2. Marital therapists and educators should embrace their role as moral consultants in promoting a marriage ideal and moral responsibility in marriage.

Caught in the current neutral/skeptical ideology of the field, many therapists fear that promoting a marriage ideal and moral responsibility in marriage is beyond the scope of their profession. This is true even when they highly value marriage in their personal lives, often holding deep spiritual beliefs about the importance of marriage. In fact, it was these deep beliefs that drew them into the profession to begin with. As a result of this value-neutral ideology, the profession is currently dominated by a reflexive morality that ultimately reflects the individualistic and consumer orientation of contemporary society.[36] Doherty has developed a model for therapists to move beyond values neutrality in working with marriage and other issues.[37] The therapist becomes a moral consultant who works sensitively to help clients unearth and examine their moral sensibilities about issues of commitment,

---

33. Browning et al., *From Culture Wars to Common Ground.*
34. Fowers, *Beyond the Myth of Marital Happiness.*
35. Alan J. Hawkins and colleagues, "Equal Partnership and the Sacred Roles of Mothers and Fathers," in *Strengthening Our Families: An In-depth Look at the Proclamation on the Family,* ed. David C. Dollahite (Salt Lake City: Bookcraft, 2000).
36. See Doherty, *Soul Searching* and *Take Back Your Marriage.*
37. Doherty, *Soul Searching.*

justice, truthfulness, and social responsibility. Doherty delineates specific ways that a therapist can support and challenge clients to practice the responsibilities they embraced in their marriage vows.

3. Marriage therapy and education need to view marriage in more expansive terms than a network of communicative techniques.

As noted by our companion authors in their chapter, much of marital therapy and education is based in a private or individual conception of marriage that views a good marriage as one in which partners have sufficient mastery of communicative techniques to negotiate their own goals and purposes of marriage, and thus to achieve personal happiness. The last twenty-five years of marital research have consisted primarily of descriptive studies which have focused on observable conflict-oriented behavior in a relatively atheoretical way.[38] Although this line of research has yielded valuable insights and important behavioral tools for enhancing marriage, its paradigm is based on a skills-deficit perspective that assumes that marriage difficulties are primarily the result of marriage partners' inadequate communication and conflict resolution skills. This approach has recently been critiqued,[39] and a call has gone out for new model development that includes a broader array of psychological, interpersonal, and moral dimensions.[40] Therapists and educators will need to deepen their ideas of what is required to develop and maintain successful marriage relationships. For example, without moral commitment to the spouse and the marriage, communication skills are likely to falter as a basis for long-term marriage, and without the virtue of justice or fairness, marital problem-solving skills can descend into business negotiations between two self-interested parties.

4. Marital therapy and education need to define the health benefits of marriage in individual, relational, and social terms and should seek to promote marriage from all the levels within the ecology of marriage.

The ecological nature of marriage has several implications for marriage therapists and educators. First, therapists and educators should help clients see

38. F. D. Fincham and S. R. Beach, "Conflict in Marriage: Implications for Working with Couples," *Annual Review of Psychology* (1999): 47-77.

39. For an example see Brant B. Burleson and Wayne H. Denton, "The Relationship between Communication Skill and Marital Satisfaction: Some Moderating Effects," *Journal of Marriage and the Family* 59 (1997): 884-902.

40. For examples see Fincham and Beach, "Conflict in Marriage," and Thomas B. Holman and Associates, *Premarital Prediction of Marital Quality or Breakup: Research, Theory, and Practice* (New York, Plenum, 2000).

how their behavior and choices in marriage have consequences for others. Doherty described this perspective as the heart of the moral domain of therapy.[41] Second, when seen through an ecological lens, strengthening marriage needs to take place at all levels of the ecosystem of marriage, as described below.

Individual Level: Promote Marital Capacity

Many models of marriage therapy and education focus almost exclusively on couple negotiation in some form or another and operate on the assumption that all people, more or less, have equal capacity for developing and maintaining a strong marriage relationship. These assumptions seem shortsighted, in that they do not adequately emphasize the personal virtues needed to practice such skills and to sustain a relationship during the inevitable times of miscommunication. At the individual level, therapists and educators should strive to *promote marital capacity* in current or prospective spouses. This should include the promotion of marriage virtues and character strengths (loyalty, generosity, justice, courage, etc.)[42] and personal development and maturation (e.g., identity development, self-validation, etc.),[43] as well as marriage skills (e.g., communication skills, consensus building, problem solving, etc.).

Couple Level: Promote Partnership in Marriage

The benefits of marriage are most profound when couples can develop a sense of partnership in marriage. At the couple level therapists and educators should strive to *promote ethical partnership in marriage*. This should include helping couples develop a partnership based in shared goals and projects, a common commitment to equity, couple communication skills, mutual growth, and the successful navigation of life transitions.

Community Level: Promote Promarriage Communities

At the community level therapists should find ways to actively *promote communities that support marriage*. We have become interested in the role thera-

---

41. Doherty, *Soul Searching*.
42. For a rich description of the importance of practicing virtue in marriage see Fowers, *Beyond the Myth of Marital Happiness*.
43. For examples see Luciano L'Abate, *The Self in the Family* (New York: John Wiley and Sons, 1997), and David M. Schnarch, *Constructing the Sexual Crucible: An Integration of Sexual and Marital Therapy* (New York: Norton, 1991).

pists and other professionals can take in developing partnerships and tapping the natural, existing resources of communities. We believe that this type of community work presents a new paradigm for therapists and educators. Doherty and colleagues have begun to articulate a families and democracy model that could serve as the basis for marriage therapists and educators to involve themselves in grassroots efforts to build communities that are deeply nurturing of marriage.[44]

Societal Level: Promote a Promarriage Culture

Therapists and educators should take an active role in promoting social policy, corporate policy, and other measures that will *promote a promarriage culture*. Active participation in the current marriage movement would be one way to do this.

5. Marital therapy and education should take a life-cycle perspective that recognizes the importance of marriage promotion at the various stages of development.

Marriage education is currently concentrated at the premarital stage, where it is often mandatory. The knowledge, skills, and virtues needed for a marriage after the birth of a first child or in the middle years may differ in kind or intensity from those needed by newlyweds. Likewise, adequate preparation for marriage requires age-appropriate learning throughout childhood, adolescence, and young adulthood. Different kinds of community supports aimed at marriage promotion should be linked together across the life span.

Conclusion

Marital therapy and education are at new crossroads as American culture changes from a focus on individual welfare, narrowly construed, to a more communitarian perspective that transcends individualism and embraces the moral stakeholders in marriage but maintains contact with the important critiques of marriage that emerged in the 1960s and 1970s. Ironically, the new emphasis on the importance of marriage as a social institution, and not just a

---

44. William J. Doherty, "Family Science and Family Citizenship: Toward a Model of Community Partnership with Families," *Family Relations* 49, 3 (July 2000): 319-25, and William J. Doherty and John M. Beaton, "Family Therapists, Community, and Civic Renewal," *Family Process* 39, 2 (Summer 2000): 149-61.

personal relationship, returns the field of marriage therapy to its roots in the concerns of non–mental health professionals about the state of marriage in the first half of the twentieth century. Similarly, the emerging communitarian or critical promarriage perspective on marriage is fully consistent with the implicit values of most marriage educators, even those whose explicit statements reflect neutrality about issues such as marital commitment.

Value neutrality about marriage has been exposed as the disguised embrace of individual self-interest. Our field cannot be intellectually honest or professionally responsible unless we openly grapple with the deeper moral, spiritual, and communal meaning of marriage. We believe that the creative futures of both marital therapy and marital education lie in the synthesis of three powerful elements: knowledge emerging from social science about the psychosocial ingredients of healthy marriage; traditional religious views of marriage as a sacred covenant and central social institution; and a contemporary ethic of equality and mutual regard in marriage, an ethic that looks squarely at the dark side of marriage without lapsing into neutrality or skepticism, and that sees the revival and reformation of marriage as perhaps the central challenge facing the next generation.

CHAPTER 11

Familial, Social, and Professional Integrity in Relationship to Business

Max L. Stackhouse

The dynamics of work, religious ethics, and family are inevitably intertwined in contemporary economic life, although the linkages are sometimes below the surface. We can see them, however, if we trace key historical developments where they were obviously joined and identify those that have altered and obscured the relationships while not obliterating them. One place to see the connections is, of all places, in obituaries. The public summing up of a business leader's life recounts a record of providing goods or services to the community over a sustained period of time (along with notable achievements in introducing new products or techniques); of involvement in various communities of commitment, especially religious ones; and of family relationships and survivors. What is revealed in death is not always obvious in contemporary life; yet work and professional activities, social and community commitments, personal and familial relationships, and faith are together constitutive of a person's, and a society's, integrity. They are nearly always honored as a whole in assessing a life.

Yet, most of the time people in business live segmented lives. They go out of the home to work. The connection of weekends with the family and of worship to the workweek is not always clear. Customers know little about the familial attachments of those with whom they do business. Suppliers and clients take scant notice of the faith or the social or political commitments that are often a major part of a business leader's life away from work. In fact, family members and members of religious or community organizations often have only a rough idea of what people's business life is all about. What one does as a member of the key organizations in civil society — church, for example, or "nonreligious" associations where cultural, social, or political convictions about the meaning and well-being of human life in society are made manifest — involves still different behaviors. Different values are built into these activities, different circles of acquaintances are involved, different ends are pursued — even if certain first principles such as honesty, trustworthiness, commitment, and mutuality offer a moral integrity to them all, and even if the plural parts of a person's life involve a federated network of involvements that are integrated into one distinctive identity and lend integrity to the fabric of the civil society.

Moments to Remember

To understand the simultaneous integration and separation of such profound areas of our lives as work, family, community, and faith, we must do some social archaeology with an eye to the role that key values and commitments have played in shaping why we live as we do. Historically, the connections were dense and transparent, and although the visibility and interdependence of these connections are today less obvious, they are personally and professionally decisive for healthy and wholesome lives, lives of integrity, as we shall see. This is true even though the move from small, traditional, organic cultures to modern, complex, industrial societies — and now toward a postmodern global, info-tech civilization — has thinned and obscured the connections.

Traditionally, one's place in the tribe, clan, village, or caste was determined by family connection, and that social location determined also the kind of work one did and the kind of cultural role into which one was socialized. Economic responsibilities were scripted by sex, birth order, age, and inherited status, and reinforced by both political authority and religious creed, cult, and code.[1] The household was the center not only of intimate affection

---

1. The transition from traditional cultures, studied especially by anthropology, to modern societies, studied especially by sociology, has been a main topic of modernization theory for a century. From Sir Henry Maine's distinction between those forms of social organization governed by "status" and those governed by "contract," in *Village Communities in the East and West* (British ed., 1985; U.S. ed., New York: Henry Holt & Co., 1989), and Ferdinand Tönnies's famous *Community and Society* (Ger., 1987; Eng.: East Lansing: Michigan State University Press, 1957), a host of scholars in the twentieth century have treated the shift, especially in the West, from "traditional" to "modern" life. See the overview of the various ways of construing this in John C. McKinney and Charles P. Loomis, "The Application of *Gemeinschaft* and *Gesellschaft* as

and reproduction but also of production and consumption, and was also the determinant unit of religious and social membership. To be sure, exchange took place between households, and peddlers, traders, caravans, and craftsmen carried goods and skills across the seas and deserts, bringing exotic wares to occasional markets — often at or near sacred sites at festival times. But those merchants with unfamiliar parentage or religious background were treated with suspicion. How could one trust such anonymous people? *Caveat emptor.*

Of course, all businesses were not always so disconnected or suspect. Crafts were largely local businesses and had both familial and religious connections. One was born into a guild family, took training to become a master craftsman, and took part in that craft's communal celebrations. The guilds, indeed, were not only standard-making bodies with regard to probity in craftsmanship and pricing; they also defended hereditary rights and formed worshiping communities of those in the alliance. The familial and worship connections were among the factors that excluded Jews from certain kinds of economic activities in the Christian West, reinforced occupation-based caste and clan identities in Asian and African cultures, and relegated peoples of distinctive ethnicity and religiosity to subordinate functions in societies as different as Hindu India, Islamic Arabia, and Buddhist Japan.[2]

However, under the impact of modern industrialization and postmodern globalization, these guilds were increasingly displaced in "developed" lands by technologies that have made their crafts obsolete, their products less standard and relatively more expensive, and their organizations as much a hindrance to development as a help. Their demise has also been hastened by the separation of religion from economics and the incapacity of some religious traditions to provide guidance to the kinds of work people did in complex, technological societies. The guilds, after all, usually had a patron saint (in the West) or distinctive deity (in the East or South), and thus eco-

---

Related to Other Typologies," in the introduction to the Harper Torchbook edition, 1963, of *Community and Society.* Émile Durkheim's view of "mechanical and organic solidarity," Robert Redfield's "folk-urban continuum," P. A. Sorokin's treatment of "familistic, contractual, and compulsory relations," and Talcott Parson's elaboration of "pattern variables" are all seen as largely compatible efforts to chart this transition. The key assumptions are gathered into what has been widely held to be the case for several generations in Myron Weiner, *Modernization* (New York: Basic Books, 1966).

2. This is one of the most important, if most neglected, contributions of Max Weber's "post-Marxist," and in some ways "postmodernist," sociology, and is seen both in his studies of comparative religion and in his massive *Economy and Society* (Glencoe, Ill.: Bedminster Press, 1962; Ger., 1925), esp. vol. 2, VI, and vol. 3, XVI.

nomic production and community were linked to cultic life as it had been in hunting, gathering, and agricultural societies also. When the locus of work shifted to entrepreneur-owned factories and now to publicly held corporations, the means of production were not only removed from the household, but the economic identity group was split from solidarity with a religious institution. Around the world, even today, people who are losing their traditional jobs, familial-neighborhood connections, and religious associations at the grass roots due to economic change experience dis-integration and turn out to be those most resistant to modernization and most angry about globalization, in spite of evidence that they and their societies will benefit from such changes over time.[3]

Moreover, the policies of the great regulatory bodies of modernity — the modern nation-states for several centuries, and now also the postmodern transnational agencies (e.g., the International Monetary Fund, World Bank, and World Trade Organization) — sometimes seek to help those who are in cultures that rely on the solidarity of familial, religious, and political ties but are being left behind by globalization. For the most part, however, they offer encouragement to those who are able to form corporations, go into business, and join the international bazaar.[4] Functionally, this reduces the importance of familial, religious, and political connections even where they remain as centers of loyalty.

It is widely acknowledged that the separation of church and state made an enormous difference in the social history of the West, but a more significant step for our question was the separation of economic institutions from familial and religious communities as the course of history meandered toward pluralistic, complex, technological societies. The differentiation of church from family or ethnic group gave a new, nonfamilial center to civil society. On the basis of that distinction, the economic center of activity also gradually was distinguished from family life — in a complicated but fateful history. To be sure, family farms and family firms continue to play a notable role in every economy, and people everywhere tend to marry, celebrate holidays, and do business with those to whom they are related by familial and religious ties. As Max Weber pointed out a century ago, one can identify many

---

3. These themes are treated, in various ways, in Anthony Giddens, *Runaway World* (New York: Routledge, 2000); James Mittelman, *The Globalization Syndrome* (Princeton: Princeton University Press, 2000); and John Micklethwait and Adrian Wooldridge, *A Future Perfect: The Challenge and Hidden Promise of Globalization* (New York: Crown Publishers, 2000).

4. See World Bank, *Assessing Globalization* (Washington, D.C.: World Bank, 2000), and Robert Gilpin, *The Challenge of Global Capitalism* (Princeton: Princeton University Press, 2000).

of the religious dynamics of a culture by studying the patterns of *connubium*, *commensalium*, and *commercium*.[5] Those with whom one marries, eats (especially at celebrative feasts), and does business are revealing of a religiously informed cultural ethos.

What appear to be formal and distant structural changes deeply influence personal commitments and values. And they have parallels in public policy debates. Advocates of marriage and the family see economic policies as a way of developing support for families in the context of civil society, and they can show that financial resources make at least a statistical difference in family viability. Those who would celebrate the autonomy of the individual advocate policies that accent the state's responsibility to care for persons irrespective of their familial relationships. In the recent debates about welfare policy, for example, it has often been argued that some social assistance programs which gave more aid to single mothers than to poor married couples have contributed to family instability and, arguably, to higher divorce rates, especially among lower-income people.[6] Others argue that they have allowed persons in abusive situations to gain an independence. Moreover, how much difference in divorce rates the so-called marriage tax has made at the higher-income levels, while not conclusively proven, is hotly argued. It does make it more expensive for a dual-career, professional couple to live together than for them to live separately.[7] Certainly people make very complex judgments about affection, bonding, moral principles, costs, benefits, and loyalty.

In the bigger picture, the rise of the corporation made such decisions more complicated because it brought about the separation of the institutions of production and distribution from those of reproduction and consumption and the segregation of business accounts from familial coffers. This generated another center of social activity outside the household. It brought people of different religious and familial backgrounds together into common economic endeavors. In the industrial, corporate environment, in principle, one's parental and religious heritage is supposed to make no difference. The relative independence of individuals from communal definitions of faith, from parental authority, from shared definitions of propriety with regard to sexual

---

5. Max Weber, *Economy and Society*, vol. 3, *The City*.

6. The Australian policy analyst, Alan Tapper, was one of the first to treat these issues in a cross-cultural comparative way. See his *The Family in the Welfare State* (Canberra: Oxford University Press of Australia, 1992).

7. However, in families where pressures from the social environment could easily invite the youth to criminality, the interdependence of family life, strong religious conviction, and economic mutual assistance reinforce stronger families and greater stability and achievement on the part of young people.

behavior and marriage, and from the impact of inherited economic status was reinforced.

The corporations also became the locus of technological innovations for mass markets, and these innovations themselves reshaped family life. The impact of the car and the mass media, especially film and television, was most dramatic; but household appliances that removed much of the drudgery from dawn-to-dusk housework were also notable. The roles of the wife and the daughters in the peasant's cottage, and of the maids and the cooks in the manor, were fundamentally altered, even if most of the responsibilities of child care and household management remained the assigned duty of women. Still, larger and larger percentages of women have joined the paid or salaried workforce, a fact that made them less obligated to and dependent on the household and on husbands for their economic status, even if many are willing and eager to contribute their income to the common household's well-being.[8]

The segregation of both affectional-familial and religious spheres of social life from business had other unintended consequences. For centuries fathers and older sons had sometimes marched off to war on behalf of the regime, but now they regularly marched off to the factory or the office, no longer producing in the household but producing for the company and taking wages home to the family. Later the older daughters and increasingly the mothers did too, in spite of "glass ceilings," all-too-frequent harassment, and often an evening shift of housework. That was made possible in part by the corporation's technology-based production and the availability of higher levels of education. Political, church, and business leaders founded schools and colleges, and the higher levels of learning in turn allowed the extension of technology-based production in the workplace and the possibility of the technological control of reproduction at home. "The pill" joined the car, the media, and the washing machine as life-changing technologies. As a result, neither production nor the transmission of economic skills is a primary function of the home. Family life becomes more exclusively devoted to consumption and affectionate recreation, with less frequent reproduction, or to getting people restored to face school or work, the real business of life.[9]

Today people from those cultures in which family, faith, and economic function are directly related and deeply interdependent feel the fracturing

---

8. See Gwendolyn Wright's unsurpassed *Building the Dream: A Social History of Housing in America* (Cambridge: MIT Press, 1993).

9. See Colin Campbell, *The Romantic Ethic and the Spirit of Modern Consumerism* (Oxford and New York: Basil Blackwell, 1987).

impact when these disentangle. Immigrants into more developed countries feel the pressure, and urbanizing families around the world where globalization is most clearly manifest and adopted do too.[10] The economic skills mastered by the parents are soon obsolete and generally less decisive for the well-being of the children than "impersonal" interdependencies guided by (supposedly) kinship-free and religion-neutral principles of management and technological competence.[11]

The kids begin to make their own decisions, and are given the time and space to do so. Peer culture expands with the increase of the number of years in formal education, and no few businesses have found ways to cater to these new consumers. More young people have their own rooms in the home, equipped with their own telephone, TV, radio, and computer with E-mail. They also have their own schedules and join the family for meals or common activities less often than in the past. It is quite unsurprising, thus, that they choose not only "love marriages" with premarital "dating" instead of "arranged marriages" and premarital "purity," but also their own religious orientation and values instead of adopting those inherited from parental communities of religious identity. Many either drop out of religious activities or join groups that organize into communities of commitment or support based on voluntary associations (congregations, fellowship groups, social clubs, or service organizations) that aid their development of personal identity, rather than that of the people of their heritage.[12]

Religion and its ethical emphases thus became less a matter of socialization into a pre-given tradition and more a matter of personal exploration and voluntary commitment — sometimes by a decision to opt out of organized religion in favor of a more purely "private spirituality." The place of clergy is reduced in the horizon of many, as larger segments of the lives of young people are spent under the care of guidance counselors, teachers, and professors — at least until they are able to participate more fully in the processes of economic production, at which point they are spent increasingly under the guidance of managers, engineers, and accountants — plus, as necessary, therapists.

---

10. See Peter Stalker, *Workers without Frontiers: The Impact of Globalization on International Migration* (Boulder, Colo.: Lynn Rienier Publisher, 2000). Three great periods of immigration flow have taken place across national borders that have shaped our present history: in the first half of the nineteenth century, in the early twentieth century, and at the end of the twentieth century continuing into the twenty-first.

11. Allan Carlson, *From Cottage to Work Station: The Family's Search for Social Harmony in the Industrial Age* (San Francisco: Ignatius Press, 1993).

12. See Nancy T. Ammerman and W. C. Roof, *Work, Family, and Religion in Contemporary Society* (New York: Routledge, 1995).

In a number of religious traditions, we find concerned elders and newly convicted youth resisting these developments by turning again to traditional, religiously saturated cultures of delayed gratification and self-control, as religious conservatism and fundamentalism become vocal and visible. But it is not at all clear whether such groups can long compete with the open relationships, optional convictions, wealth opportunities, and mass entertainment that the larger cultural shift invites. Much of the modernization of the West, and now of the postmodern globalization of the world well beyond the West, suggests that life in the future may well be increasingly conducted outside the traditional connections and with decreasing reference to them.[13]

Business as a "Profession"

In the global economy, to run a business on terms that privilege family members or comembers of a common religious group is viewed as nepotism or discrimination. In spite of the fact that small and medium businesses have been the primary area of economic growth and employment for half a century, and that many of these start as family firms, high percentages of such firms fail or fold within five years, and many which do survive longer than a generation are later bought out by public corporations. Integrity is redefined, less in terms of a status sustained by religious solidarity or family-based ties, and more in terms of a personal and religiously-neutral "professionalism" — which is to say, by quality expertise at competitive prices with fairness to all stakeholders and attention to customers' and suppliers' concerns civilly given with honest disclosure, on-time delivery, and efforts to make things right if they go wrong.[14]

Business, of course, is not necessarily a "profession" in the classical sense. Clergy, lawyers, doctors, and professors were long identified as "true professionals" in the sense that they gained specified advanced training, joined associations with examinations on theoretical and practical matters as standards of admission, took formal oaths to follow standards of conduct, and made claims about a dedication to values (respectively: faith, justice, health, and wisdom) that were beyond material gain. Architects, engineers, accountants, pharmacists, nurses, teachers, psychologists, certain military and police officers have also developed patterns comparable to those of the

---

13. Ammerman and Roof, *Work, Family, and Religion in Contemporary Society.*
14. David H. Maister, *True Professionalism: The Courage to Care about Your People, Your Clients, and Your Career* (New York: Free Press, 1997).

classic professions. Indeed, the term "professional" has become quite recently applied to any occupation where people live off a skill, from athletes to beauticians, and do so with excellence.

Something, however, is lost if "expert" is all one means by "professional." Two biblical themes that shaped the deeper history of the professions were "vocation" and "covenant." With regard to the one, God "called" (Latin: *vocare*) by giving special talents; the proper human response was a profession of faith and the leading of a disciplined life and the cultivation of these talents in accord with the highest principles and purposes, for the good of all. This set of ideas took root in the social history of the monastic communities during the Middle Ages. Many were called into a community of faith to profess the faith, but some were set aside by special gifts, opportunities, and training to undertake special professions and lead exemplary lives. The Reformation applied these ideas to all persons, and particularly advanced the notion of a dedication to principles and purposes beyond the quest for gain and honor as a part of being a professional.[15]

Although contemporary economic theory is today replete with the notion that people make their economic decisions entirely on the basis of a cost-benefit analysis, according to the push of evolutionary drives and the pull of egocentric interests that ought not be interfered with at all by religion, morality, or government regulation, life in the business world only partly operates by that logic. In fact, a number of pressures today invite business leadership toward a professionalism of the more classic "vocational" sort. One development stands as a symbol of this change, and perhaps its simultaneous betrayal. With roots in the early-twentieth-century introduction of business management and efficiency studies (the application of technology to human systems) into college curricula, the MBA has become an academically honored degree conferred by business schools at leading universities. While some exceptional beginnings were made, management became a major center of professional consciousness only after World War II. Indeed, before that most business education occurred on the job or in practical business courses or secretarial schools that were marginal to the central work of colleges and universities. It was only in the 1950s that it began to develop into a major force, especially after the publication of two landmark studies.[16] Since then there

---

15. See the debate over this matter between Roels and Camenisch in Shirley J. Roels, Barbara H. Andolsen, and Paul F. Camenisch, *Organization Man, Organization Woman: Calling, Leadership, and Culture* (Nashville: Abingdon, 1997).

16. Early efforts to professionalize business were inaugurated at Dartmouth at the beginning of the twentieth century. The potential development of this profession was also anticipated in the 1912 Brown University commencement address by Justice Louis D. Brandeis, "Business

have been many efforts to raise the quality of such education at both the undergraduate and graduate levels. Business, in short, is a latecomer to the circle of professional education.

The business schools now attract some of the most promising young talent of the future, and have begun to certify that well-trained business managers are equally qualified experts as those who graduate from a divinity school, medical school, law school, or many doctoral programs,[17] although something of a contempt for business remains in many of these institutions. When they complain about what is wrong today with the "classic" professions, they say, "It is merely becoming a business!" This charge reveals the erosion of a sense of vocation as a basis for profession in many centers. However, it is increasingly mandatory that people in such programs have at least one course in professional ethics. Although some of these courses may be narrow in focus and shallow in social, philosophical, and religious depth, the topic is again on the curricular agenda.[18]

This new professional degree marks a potential new chapter in the history of the professions, for it brings the prospect that business is developing internal standards of performance and excellence that are still neither universally practiced nor widely recognized. Still, business remains a more open potential profession than the classical ones. It is unlikely that states will conduct the kind of qualifying exams that doctors, lawyers, clergy, professors, architects, and others are required to take in order for managers to practice their profession. Still, the ripple effect of this development means that business, commerce, and management courses in colleges and universities are adopting standards of scholarship, discipline, and values orientation that can also be found among those who are in premedical, prelaw, and other preprofessional courses of study.

— as a Profession." A. A. Berle and Gardiner Means saw the emerging importance of management in *The Modern Corporation and Private Property* (New York: Commerce Clearing House, 1932), reprinted several times after World War II, as did Kenneth Boulding, *The Organizational Revolution* (New York: Harper, 1953); but it was Robert A. Gordon and James E. Howell, *Higher Education for Business* (New York: Columbia University Press, 1959), and Frank Cook Pierson, *The Education of American Businessmen* (New York: McGraw Hill, 1959), that established business education as a profession. I am grateful to Shirley Roels for drawing these last two studies to my attention.

17. See the prizewinning work of Alfred D. Chandler, Jr., *The Visible Hand: The Managerial Revolution in American Business* (Cambridge: Harvard University Press, 1977), esp. pp. 464-68.

18. See Max L. Stackhouse, Dennis McCann, Shirley Roels, et al., *On Moral Business: Classical and Contemporary Resources for Ethics and Economic Life* (Grand Rapids: Eerdmans, 1995).

At the same time that overt religious or familial (ethnic) content declined, it became difficult to avoid ethical issues having to do with matters of religion and sexuality in the workplace, with the privileges of race and sex (both influenced by familial and religious considerations), and with the creation of a responsible corporate policy that aids the families of employees, protects religious freedom, and assumes that the professionals of tomorrow will have responsibility for preserving the viability of the community.

The MBA or business major may form his or her own corporation, or may join a family firm, get appointed to a department of government, or work for a nonprofit organization — a religious, charitable, community, or political institution; but for the most part, this new kind of professional is employed by a profit-oriented corporation to manage other people's resources. And all of these require a distinctive form of ethically laden expertise, one in which overriding concerns for family ties and behaviors are necessarily and properly removed from what one does at work. They demand a kind of responsible stewardship characterized by a prudent balancing of short-term gains; long-term viability; transparent planning and coordination in the face of potential investors, donors, or users; and alertness to the actions of competitors and the inventors of new techniques. As the truly professional clergy is trusted and is trustworthy in regard to faith, the doctor in regard to health, the lawyer in regard to justice, and the professor in regard to wisdom, the genuinely professional manager is trusted with regard to the productive wealth of the society.[19] This is all the more striking since the decline of state capitalization in its several socialist and liberal forms has increasingly turned over the management of the society's assets to corporations through "privatization." The uncontrolled character of the result has led to many parallels to the laissez-faire economies of the robber barons of the nineteenth century, and the criticisms of unbridled capitalism are as many and as sharp as the desires to get in on the opportunities it brings.

The Global Complication

These internal developments in business education and the external relative decline of the centrality of the nation-state in economic planning are made obvious in the fact that business is increasingly global. The intellectual, technological (and for that matter, medical, legal, and religious) dynamics of life

---

19. David Krueger, Donald Shriver, and Laura Nash, *The Business Corporation and Productive Justice* (Nashville: Abingdon, 1997).

are generating the conditions in which the prospects of a global civil society could develop. Not only are the giant transnational corporations involved, but many small and medium-sized businesses and more families are also dependent on what happens at the global level. In consequence, a multitude of families around the world are dependent on decisions they cannot make or understand.[20]

In our geo-economic era, no single world government or central international agency is able to control business activity in ways that were attempted with mixed results over the past several hundred years by nation-states. Efforts to control everything from the throne of political power by fascism, communism, and liberationist one-party states, over the last century, have met with great disaster. Most of the world's 192 nations have decided not to have government be the central agent in capitalization and in managing the economy. We are quite unsure of the results of this decision, but it obviously puts a greater weight of responsibility for general human well-being on managers.

Wide-visioned professionals today know that while the market is indispensable to a viable economy and must have relative degrees of freedom to work, a totally free market, one without law or conscience, is inevitably a license for exploitation, corruption, and the pathological forms of modern business life that can still be found in abundance around the world — mafia capitalism, crony capitalism, samurai capitalism, and mercantilist capitalism. All the skills business professionals are developing and all the ethical perspicacity they must develop will be foiled if their activity does not have inner moral integrity and does not take place in an open and justly ordered society.[21] Indeed, the very fabric of civilization is more dependent on them at this juncture of history than in any other known period of history. What they do not have is a generalized concept of how to organize the institutions they manage and the multiple associations of the civil societies (city, regional, national, and global) in which they operate. The notion of a political economy regulated by the nation-state is still powerful, but is likely to erode even more in the future. And the notion of a market economy, that everything should be done by voluntary contract without governmental interference or social pressure, has led many to grave anxieties about forms of individualism and con-

---

20. See Kofi Annan, *Millennium Report*, at www.un.org/millennium/sg/report. Compare World Bank, *Assessing Globalization*.

21. My own views of these matters are set forth in Max L. Stackhouse, Peter Berger, Dennis McCann, and Douglas Meeks, *Christian Social Ethics in a Global Era* (Nashville: Abingdon, 1996).

sumerism that entail the loss of any moral models of community in work, family, and society.

The need for concerned and committed managers and highly skilled workers comes at a time when loyalty to corporations is not high. Not only does the general residual distrust of "capitalism," a term still laden with the residues of the thought of Adam Smith or Karl Marx, make many intellectual and religious leaders reluctant to engage business too closely, but downsizing has meant that many previously dedicated "company men" have lost confidence in the institutions into which they poured decades of their lives. An institution is less often seen as a social organism to which one gives loyalty and from which one draws sustenance in order to build enduring communities, as it is an artificial mechanism of convenience, to be used when it fits individual wants and felt needs and abandoned when it does not.

The indirect effects of these changes were that the perceived roles of husbands and fathers, and the well-being of many middle- and lower-middle-class families, were undercut. They further eroded the confidence in society in general. In the face of these conditions, neither governments nor unions can protect persons for long. Indeed, confidence in the government's and union's ability to protect families in need eroded also, and in the most economically developed nations the popular support for expanded welfare, social services, and safety nets has declined. Those companies that failed to respond and adapt to these new conditions became increasingly unable to compete in the global economy, while those which did adapt by making difficult choices have, ironically, helped expand the entire economy. This brought the unemployment rates to the lowest peacetime levels in half a century. At the same time, many nations exhibited the greatest differential in incomes in nearly a century. The latter result is partly due to higher incomes among the professionals, managers, and highly skilled technical workers.[22]

Contemporary business is flourishing today in spite of the fact that it remains deeply distrusted by many religious, moral, and academic leaders. The best of its management, meanwhile, have begun to recognize that business requires what it cannot itself supply. It needs a reliable currency and water, road, and police systems. In short, it needs government, although it is generally opposed to expanded governmental roles in social policy. It needs educated and dependable workers and managers, and it needs customers and suppliers who will not cheat, lie, and steal at every turn. It needs community organizations to nurture arts, sports, cultural values, and human creativity

---

22. Former Labor Secretary Robert Reich seems to have correctly identified these trends early. See his *The Work of Nations* (New York: Alfred Knopf, 1991).

that make for a more fulfilling life. It needs the dedication of doctors and nurses in well-furnished hospitals and clinics, and the diligence of skilled lawyers and independent advocates who will see that the conflicts of ordinary life are adjudicated fairly. This means also that it needs a legal system able to accommodate dynamic change while preserving a tolerable level of law, order, and peace. It needs also communities of commitment — religious, charitable, social, and familial — that inculcate enduring values and call people to justice, the service of others, and the common good.[23] In short, business depends upon integrity in the civil society that hosts the corporations which produce effectively and manage the society's wealth.

The shopkeeper who supports school projects, contributes to fund drives for the Scouts, helps sponsor a concert series, serves on the board of the regional hospital, or belongs to the local human rights committee already knows this. Moreover, the benefits are fairly direct — the shopkeeper's children go to these schools, meetings, and concerts, and the fabric of health and law enforcement in the community is improved by dedicated volunteer service. Something similar takes place when the owners of a great corporation form a foundation dedicated to the well-being of the society in which the corporation does business. And all such activities have implications for the well-being of families in the community, although the benefits are often less direct or immediate.

All truly professional managers will find ways to deploy a reasonable portion of the resources that their business helps produce and steward to pursue such directions also, and will do so in ways that enhance not only the integrity of the corporation but also its host society and the citizenry — even in an age of global business. But if the business leaders in society are to have integrity in their relationships, if the community itself is to have integrity, and if the corporations are to gain and advance integrity, they will have to have a basic concept to guide them. If it is not supplied by the bureaucratized regulation of a political economy, and if it is not present in the libertarian ideology of the market economy, where shall we find it?

It is at this point that the other biblical concept besides "vocation" is being introduced by some to guide contemporary economic and social institution building. This is the idea of "covenant." This is a notion of bonded loy-

---

23. The debate over the relative health of such organizations has been renewed by Robert Putnam's *Bowling Alone: The Collapse and Revival of American Community* (New York: Simon & Schuster, 2000). The main points of the argument have been recognized for some time. Useful perspectives can be found in Wilhelm Roepke, *The Moral Foundations of Civil Society* (New Brunswick, N.J.: Transaction Press, 1996; Ger. ed., 1946), or Alan Wolfe, *Whose Keeper? Social Science and Moral Obligation* (Berkeley: University of California Press, 1989).

alty, voluntarily chosen and accepted (and in this way protodemocratic) but governed by a disciplined loyalty to first principles of right and wrong and the adoption of those virtues, practices, and policies, as proximate ends, that point to and enhance an ultimate good end. Such a bonded loyalty builds institutions — stable yet flexible, open but with special responsibilities and duties, mutually enhancing but exemplifying qualities that sustain the common life more than any individual effort can. These institutions will inevitably be linked into federated networks to form a pluralism of communities, a society of associations that are more than the parts and that expose the deep links between religion, personal identity, and civilizational fabric, if we are to have a wholesome and healthy life at each level.

Business Needs the Family

I have argued that the professional values of business in a posttraditional society must entail a redefinition of integrity. They will be less constrained by direct familial and religious relationships and more defined by certified expertise and an understanding of business morality. These values will involve an increasingly impersonal fairness to employees, clients, customers, and suppliers with on-time delivery of quality products and services, and good relationships to all stakeholders with civil pleasantness, honest disclosure, and reasonable efforts to make things right if they go wrong. We have also argued that integrity for business professionals demands a renewed sense of vocation and social vision of the relationship of the company to the wider covenantal fabric of the civil society on which good business depends — not only for its viability, but for the human and cultural resources that it cannot and ought not itself provide. And we have implied that this entails a strengthening of the family. Ironically, the separation of familial ties and professional obligations means we have to rely more directly on the people who manage and the people who work under management.

The separation of family and work does not mean that there is no influence on job performance and human relations at work by forces that are outside the ordinary scope of the company's and the manager's control. The "personal" life of those in business is still integral to what people do, what they can concentrate on, how well they get along with coworkers, and how often they are ill or absent. Simply for reasons of the well-being of the corporation, it becomes prudent to develop policies that secure the loyalty, health, and welfare of employees, customers, clients, and wider community. That entails fomenting stable family life in society. The recent work of Linda Waite and Maggie Gallagher argues convincingly that happily married persons and their children do better in all these various areas of life, and are personally and socially healthier.[24]

A great debate has erupted in the last generation and is related to just this point.[25] In part because the historically intertwined support systems of religion, social and political institutions, and family life that mutually reinforced each other are no longer bound so intimately together, and in part because increasingly pluralistic societies have fewer immediately recognizable and authoritatively shared values, the most developed societies have, largely without intending to, embarked on a great new experiment with regard to family. It is indeed a potential tragedy in the ancient Greek sense of the term. A virtue turned to excess becomes a fatal flaw.

Rather than seeing the whole of life as constituted by overlapping and interacting webs of relationship, organized into sustaining institutions and sanctified by sacrament, sacred covenant, or enduring commitments, we have begun to think of society and all its institutions in terms of individuals who may choose to join in temporary contractual relationships.[26] This has brought with it a high degree of individual freedom and evoked a great deal of individual initiative. Yet it has also brought an anti-institutional element that has an eroding effect even on those institutions that form and sustain strong and creative individuals able to make and keep serious long-term commitments and to sustain dynamic and enduring institutions. The anti-institutional sentiment that is widespread in regard to governments, parties, corporations, unions, churches, and voluntary associations also spills over into views of the family. Our relationships to these groups, even to marriage, are seen as properly subject to the fluctuating calculations of costs and benefits to the individuals involved. The business model of making temporary, private contracts by the voluntary construction of terms out of the will of the participants has been radicalized and now dominates the idea of how one relates to all the institutions of civil society, including the family.[27]

The idea of the voluntary contract has, of course, long been an aspect of

---

24. Linda Waite and Maggie Gallagher, *The Case for Marriage: Why Married People Are Happier, Healthier, and Better Off Financially* (New York: Doubleday, 2000).

25. The most balanced current volume treating this debate is Don S. Browning, Bonnie J. Miller-McLemore, et al., *From Culture Wars to Common Ground* (Louisville: Westminster John Knox, 1997).

26. See John Witte, Jr., *From Sacrament to Contract: Marriage, Religion, and Law in the Western Tradition* (Louisville: Westminster John Knox, 1997).

27. See my *Covenant and Commitments: Faith, Family, and Economic Life* (Louisville: Westminster John Knox, 1997), written with the help of Deirdre Hainsworth.

marriage life, and the taking of spouses by force, purchase, or duplicity has long been forbidden in most religions, morality, and law. But the dramatic increase of freedom for the individual sparked by the technological, economic, and social changes mentioned above, all expanded by the modern corporation, has made marriage increasingly contractual and temporary. It is precisely the resulting understanding of family life and the experience of people in regard to marriage life that has caused such a dramatic ideological battle about "family values" for a generation.[28]

Many of the heated religious and political debates around "family values" have been focused on abortion, homosexuality, welfare-dependent mothers, sex education and birth-control devices in the schools, "promise keeper" pledges, and access to the legal benefits of marriage by same-sex partnerships. While each of these reflects a major issue that needs continued debate until a morally valid, intellectually coherent, and politically viable resolution is reached, these are only sometimes the key issues facing business professionals. The central issues for business leaders who have the long-term stewardship of the economy in their hands are centered around the fact that it is very doubtful that a viable business environment, a healthy workforce, and the most creative professionals can be formed and sustained over time if people are not nurtured by and engaged in relationships of enduring commitment and intimate support. Those who are abused, neglected, abandoned, inadequately socialized, struggling to survive, or subject to repeated family crises are unlikely to be either reliable workers, responsible suppliers, focused professionals with a deep sense of vocation, or decent customers.

Of course, the forms that these enduring relationships will take sociologically and the kinds of occupations that are likely to become attractive in a high-tech geo-economy will surely modulate and must become appropriate to the kind of society in which people want to live and to the vocations they are called to pursue. It is pure nonsense to think we can return to the family of the village and farm, to the Victorian ideal, to the Norman Rockwell family dinners, or even to the sitcom images of the 1950s. But it may be possible to enhance personal inclinations, pursue social projects, and engender business policies that will help people form and maintain reliable and creative families able to shape a next generation of citizens, workers, and managers by contributing creatively to the contexts in which people live and work. This requires

---

28. Many of these topics are treated with nuance in Anne Carr and Mary Stewart Van Leeuwen, eds., *Religion, Feminism, and the Family* (Louisville: Westminster John Knox, 1996). This volume and those cited in notes 25, 26, and 27 are in a series, The Family, Religion and Culture, edited by Don S. Browning and Ian S. Evison.

forming a social and a moral environment in which family life that is private, just, voluntary, and lasting can flourish and simultaneously nurture the kinds of people with whom one would want to work and to whom we can confidently entrust the stewardship of the future.[29] It also invites us to ask whether such durable relationships demand a spirituality rooted in fidelity and sustained by love.

The evidence is quite overwhelming. People who have deep family problems, especially the children of those marriages that end in divorce, are more likely to be alcohol and drug abusers, neglectful or violent toward their own children, frequently absent at school or work, distracted on the job, and unpleasant to coworkers.[30] At the same time, those who abuse alcohol and drugs, are violent toward others, are unable to focus on tasks at hand, and are unreliable at work have the most marriage problems. Whether family problems cause problems at work, or low levels of work performance, reliability, and income reinforce tendencies toward family problems, is not easy to determine. The best research on family life suggests the former; the best research on social discrimination on racist, sexist, and classist grounds suggests the latter.[31] Few dispute the correlation. What is more certain is that those who come from broken and problematic families often manifest the more severe problems in their own families, at their work, and in their relationships to the wider society.

It is terribly important to be careful here. Some marriages are harmful to partners and to children and must be ended. All religions and moral philosophies agree on this point, even if they also say "God hates divorce," to quote the biblical prophet. Further, some who come from terrible backgrounds find their way to successful and enduring relationships in love, positions in economic life, and responsible engagements in community life. It helps no one to blame the victims. But we know what often helps victims: a heroic parent or loving mentor nurtures the person through the crises of the

---

29. This is the central point made by Linda Waite and Maggie Gallagher, that married people are happier, healthier, and more successful economically, as mentioned in note 24 above.

30. See David Popenoe, Barbara Dafoe Whitehead, and Nowal Glenn of the National Marriage Project, *The State of Our Unions: The Social Health of Marriage in America* (New Brunswick, N.J.: National Marriage Project at Rutgers University, 1999). The data they summarize confirms the groundbreaking work by Sara McLanahan and Gary Sandefur, *Growing Up with a Single Parent* (Cambridge: Harvard University Press, 1994).

31. Popenoe, Whitehead, and Glenn, *The State of Our Unions*. This debate has often been focused on public policy questions as it bears on family assistance issues. The two sides are well articulated in contrary but mutually regarding series of books and articles over the last decade by Lawrence Mead, Jr., and William Julius Wilson.

early years; a religious experience or profound intellectual-vocational commitment in the adolescent years becomes a reference point for the psychological, social, and spiritual direction of a person's life; and open social opportunities allow a person from an otherwise unpromising background to develop in ways that would otherwise remain hidden or repressed.

Realism, Trust, and Integrity around the World

It is not a good idea for business leaders to seek to be social workers in trying to carry out their vocation professionally. But it is an aid to realism, not a blinkering of it, to suggest that at certain levels it is better to acknowledge that trust is indispensable to an integrated life. Several studies have argued this point rather convincingly. Recently, the sometimes controversial social theorist, Francis Fukuyama, has traced some of the deeper dimensions of the relationship of family life to the creation of social prosperity in the emerging global economy. In his cross-cultural study, he identified trust as a, if not the, critical factor in the social well-being of societies and of persons.[32] He studied eight societies, half in the West, half in the East, and the ways in which they characteristically nurture or inhibit trust in various kinds of groups. It is family life in relation to pluralistic institutions of civil society that almost always plays a decisive role.

Those societies that trust only family members are not able to form and sustain trust in complex groups outside the family, and the total "social capital" of these persons is small.[33] The associations from which they come and which they tend to generate are small, limited, and based on common ethnic bonds or long-term personal relationships, or chains of relationships. Independent voluntary associations, democratic political parties, and complex corporations have a difficult time flourishing in such a familistic environment.

---

32. F. Fukuyama, *Trust: The Social Virtues and the Creation of Prosperity* (New York: Free Press, 1995).

33. Fukuyama is interested in how familial, religious, and cultural values are able to engender and sustain what scholar James S. Coleman identified as "social capital," a term that has been adopted widely to refer to the ability of people to work together in social groups and organizations for common purposes ("Social Capital in the Creation of Human Capital," *American Journal of Sociology* 94 [1988]: 95-120). The key point is that capital is, under present conditions, less and less centered in land or factories or gold reserves, and more and more in human knowledge and skill. Among the kinds of knowledge and skill that are decisive are those which can discover shared values and invite a willingness to subordinate private short-term interests to those of larger, long-term associations.

Only some kinds of families nurture the kinds of persons who will be empowered to form or find independent associations and social and political groups, generate complex economic institutions, and inspire others to bring their knowledge and skills into play in those groups. At the same time, those families that do not nurture much trust tend to doom individuals to a grave suspicion of outsiders. They may do a very limited, tightly prescribed job perfectly well, but one cannot expect technological, economic, or social innovation from them. They have not cultivated, and are unlikely to cultivate, trusting and trustworthy communities of cooperation. Moreover, those societies that develop internal trust and build a capacity to participate trustingly in social, political, and economic groups outside the home find their capacities to contribute to a complex, postindustrial, global economy highest.

While he is not notably religious in his orientation or argument, Fukuyama is clear that the kind of religious and moral training given by families and by the families' participation in religious groups plays a decisive role here. The implications seem obvious for professionals who expect the next generation — their own or other people's kids — to sustain those blends of moral fiber, trust, trustworthiness, and realism that form creative leaders for the common good and for the long run.

The capacity of persons to cultivate trust in a personal sense, specifically in regard to the big picture of what life is about, requires the kind of integrity that many people think is found, finally, only in profound religious trust. After all, unless there is another dimension to being beyond visible and material existence, life has no destiny beyond that of death and dissolution. Even the strongest and most necessary institutions fade, organizations grow ineffective, products become obsolete, or leaders turn to corruption, and finally all is left in the clutter of ruins. And whole societies, even the best societies, are marked by conflict and decline. Although, under certain conditions, there are relatively long epochs when networks of covenantal trust and federated networks of institutions provide relatively sustained good living for large numbers of people, the annals of history are littered with the ruins of societies that could not face the economic, political, and moral-spiritual threats that beset them from inside and out. Even the cosmos is governed by the law of entropy — everything that does not explode or implode will run down and fall apart.

In the face of this dreary list of probabilities, one can either cynically seize every advantage of the day and accumulate what one cannot take with one or seek to find a spiritual path to integrity. And if that path is wide and deep and not selfish, it will imply efforts to extend the integrity into society at large — into the networks of personal and familial relationships, into the immediate communities of which one is a part, into the character of the next generation, into every professional interaction, and thereby into the very large, new civilization emerging due to globalization. That involves not only the direct concerns about health care benefits for those who have none, just liability laws to constrain the manufacture and distribution of those products that harm people, and reasonable, enforceable environmental protections. These are a matter of good business. But it also means being a business professional for good — in the double sense of contributing to moral and spiritual betterment of the whole civil society and for the permanent future.

In brief, genuine business professionals in their family, social, and religious life will seek to find new models of "covenanted" integration of that which is necessary to holistic living and a holistic view of life, and to make these effective in the dynamic, threatening, and exciting global society into which we are being plunged. They will seek to develop the kinds of communities of commitment and intimate networks of trust that can creatively deal with, and not become mere victims of, the high-tech, incredibly differentiated and complex geo-economic worldwide civilization which key streams of religion, ethics, technology, earlier professional developments, international law, and pluralistic politics have produced. This we must mediate to our children and help others to mediate to their children. The true business professional will manifest that in his or her personal life and at work, and will seek to influence the society at large, that it too may be enabled to manage the massive changes that the emerging global future is likely to bring.

Business

CHAPTER 12

Reconstructing Home: Business Responsibility for the Family

Shirley J. Roels

Introduction

Going home is important. As Robert Frost wrote, "Home is the place where when you have to go there, they have to take you in."[1] No matter how men and women mature, we want special human places to which we can return, to people who know us now and have known us then. We need committed intimate circles that contribute to personal identity, continuity, meaning, and value. Don't all of us hope someone will take us in when we need to go there? We need home, and we need business professionals who emphasize its importance.

The sad problem is that for many in North America, going home and finding someone to take you in is not possible. There is no functional home, no operational family to which to return. Instead, home is often a fragmented network of dysfunctional relationships. Spouses, bitter from marital stress, loathe homecoming. Single parents break down under the weight of handling a household alone. Children's academic and economic achievements are affected by the disruptions of a mother and father who can't be home together.[2] Divorced parents may find that continuity and purpose related to their chil-

---

1. Robert Frost, "The Death of the Hired Man," lines 118-19 (written in 1914).
2. Sara McLanahan and Gary Sandefur document these effects in chap. 3, "Which Outcomes Are Most Affected," of *Growing Up with a Single Parent: What Hurts, What Helps* (Cambridge: Harvard University Press, 1994), pp. 39-63.

dren have diverged. Grown children feel little responsibility for aging separated parents in whose destructive wake they have developed.[3] For too many, there is no place of identity, warmth, encouragement, teaching, and faith development called home.

Over the latter half of the twentieth century, North American families split up and reconfigured themselves at troublesome rates. This progressive implosion of home occurred for many reasons. Divorce is a much larger variable than it has historically been. According to the National Marriage Project, "[T]he divorce rate was level for about two decades after World War II. . . . By the middle of the 1960s, however, divorce started to increase and it more than doubled over the next fifteen years to reach an historical high point in the early 1980s. Since then the divorce rate has modestly declined, a trend described by many experts as 'leveling off at a high level.' . . . Overall, the chances remain very high — close to 50% — that a marriage started today will end in either divorce or permanent separation."[4]

Besides divorce, cohabitation has significantly shifted the frame of marriage and divorce. By the mid-1990s, those in the prime ages to marry, between twenty-five and thirty-four, were more likely to cohabit than in the middle of the twentieth century. While 20 to 24 percent of Americans in that age group now cohabit, research indicates that such relationships tend to be relatively short. These arrangements either fall apart quite quickly or move into marriage.[5] According to new research by Popenoe and Whitehead, cohabitation has not had positive effects on the dating and mating culture of adults in their twenties. Their studies show that those who cohabit remain more individualistic in their orientations. As these relationships fail, as they so frequently do, men maintain unrealistic ideas about meeting women they deem marriageable. By contrast the women simply become depressed. They don't anticipate marrying after having been "dumped" several times and don't expect commitment.[6] Thus cohabitation does not provide the security that many men and women are seeking or a clear segue into a healthy marriage.

In addition to the number of men, women, and children affected by divorce or cohabitation, the percentage of children living in single-parent fami-

---

3. Barbara Dafoe Whitehead, "Dan Quayle Was Right," *Atlantic Monthly* 271, no. 4 (April 1993): 47-84.

4. National Marriage Project, *The State of Our Unions, 1999: The Social Health of Marriage in America* (Rutgers, N.J.: Rutgers, the State University of New Jersey, 1999), pp. 21-22.

5. Linda Waite, "Does Marriage Matter?" *Demography* 32, no. 4 (November 1995): 483-507.

6. David Popenoe and Barbara Dafoe Whitehead discuss these concerns in depth in their contribution to this volume, chap. 2.

lies has grown tremendously. Since 1960 there has been a sixfold increase in the percentage of babies born to unwed mothers. By the mid-1990s about a third of all births were out of wedlock. The percentage of children who live apart from their biological fathers increased from 17 percent in 1960 to more than 35 percent in the 1990s.[7] By 1980 only half of American children could expect to spend their entire childhood in one intact family.[8] By the 1990s it was estimated that some 12 or 13 percent of American children live with a stepparent.[9]

Thus, for many, even if they can wend their way to a physical address, there is no one there who can psychologically receive them. The web of complex family relationships and competing loyalties woven over the years distracts and distresses family members. For too many when you have to go there, "there" can't be found.

Perhaps in the short term, individuals can live without home. But if home is the most feasible place to cultivate continuing life stories, purpose, meaning, and value, then how will a society with a large number of dysfunctional families develop? The prospects are frightening.

While business by itself cannot reconstruct home life, it must bear some responsibility for the redevelopment of a larger network of healthy marriages and families. As a profession, businesses must care about the quality of home life. While business will struggle in reconstructing a higher quality of family life, there are several appropriate avenues for business responsibility.

Why Should Business Care about Marriage and Family Quality?

If we acknowledge the dysfunctional state of many marriages and families, the remaining question is why businesses should bear responsibility for reconstructing the quality of home. Why should they shoulder a task that does not relate directly to customers, products, and profitability? There are several reasons why business organizations should contribute to the development of effective marriages and families. They are historical, practical, social, political, and pragmatic.

---

7. National Marriage Project, p. 25.
8. Whitehead, "Dan Quayle Was Right."
9. National Marriage Project, pp. 21-22.

The Workplace Affects Family Life

The location, organization, and purpose of work, historically and currently, affect family life. Historically, a change in the location and nature of work, from family cottage industries to factories of the industrial revolution, greatly affected the family. Prior to the industrial revolution the family was a unit for both production and consumption, making items such as shoes, tools, candles, and bedding to sell to their neighbors. Van Leeuwen and Hinze as well as Stackhouse describe, in this volume, the subsequent shift of productive labor to larger nonfamily work units, separating family production from consumption, splitting work and home into public and private spheres respectively.[10] Now families are principally consumption units. Shifting the foundations for production out of the family has had a significant effect on family purposes. The economic ties that bind families are weaker than they were 250 years ago because of business developments.[11] Historically, therefore, business has been a driving force in family change.

Similarly, the organization of work by businesses today affects the purpose and structure of family life. The location and technology of work continue to evolve. Businesses are globalizing production, marketing, and personnel, and they also experiment with home office options. While the effects of working in Daghestan or the former family den are different, still, in both cases, business decisions are intimately intertwined with family function. Organizational life shapes daily household operations. Hours for paid work affect schedules for sleeping, waking, child care, parent-teacher conferences, meals, and social events. Pressures from work go home with the worker. Working colleagues and office climate are discussed over dinner, and unresolved challenges are mulled over a 3:00 A.M. cup of Ovaltine. Business continues to be a driving force in family life.

Workplaces also affect families because they have become important

---

10. Mary Stewart Van Leeuwen and Christine Hinze specifically consider the relationship between industrialization and women's work at the end of the nineteenth century in their chapter of this volume (chap. 7). Max Stackhouse, in his chapter (chap. 11), also examines the emergence of the public/private split with the rise of the business corporation. For a more detailed discussion of these issues, see several readings in Anne Carr and Mary Stewart Van Leeuwen's *Religion, Feminism, and the Family* (Louisville: Westminster John Knox, 1996) that explore these topics. In that volume author Bonnie J. Miller-McLemore, in particular, explores some of this history in her chapter "Family and Work: Can Anyone 'Have It All'?" (chap. 14, pp. 275-93).

11. Max Stackhouse, *Covenant and Commitments: Faith, Family, and Economic Life* (Louisville: Westminster John Knox, 1997). In chapter 1 Stackhouse explores how changes in economic structure have affected family functions.

sources of individual meaning for most people.[12] When people dedicate their primary energies each day to a product, a service, a customer group, and an employee team, the workplace greatly affects their sense of purpose, self-knowledge, and moral decision-making. By nature business intertwines economic performance and rewards with social identity and location. In social settings, the "and what do you do?" question establishes one's status in relationship to the group; and when an expected promotion doesn't materialize, the gap between self-definition and company expectations can prompt someone to look for another job. Moral value is also interwoven with business. For example, a restaurant manager can believe that serving a good, hot meal at a fair price is a valuable contribution to society, but that same restaurateur can also be morally jarred when a served meal results in food poisoning. An automotive executive can believe that providing transportation for society is worthwhile, but that same leader can struggle morally over excessive energy consumption for gas-guzzling SUVs. The meaning and value of their paid professions influence the restaurant manager and automotive executive. The moral value created in the workplace, or lack thereof, goes home with these professionals and affects their families too.

Workplaces have more power over personal and family life than in prior decades for several reasons. Other defining influences such as neighborhoods, extended families, faith communities, and civic associations have declined. As Americans move more frequently, local communities have a smaller impact on meaning and continuity. Work-related mobility causes nuclear family members, either individually or together, to separate from their extended families more readily. Higher education also contributes to separations from home since it often occurs in different communities than those of our birth families. For all the value gained from advanced learning, it shapes minds, perspectives, and experiences in ways that may well be quite different from those of the family.[13] Houses of worship and religious denominations have also declined as close networks of meaning, value, and continuity. Many North American religious shoppers pick places of worship by style and program. When the factors that drew them change distastefully, they rarely hesitate to shift their worship locations. For these consumers, specific worshiping

---

12. C. William Pollard, chairman of the Service Master Corporation, explores this topic in "Mission as an Organizing Principle," in *Leader to Leader* (New York: Drucker Foundation; San Francisco: Jossey-Bass, 2000), pp. 17-18.

13. Peter Berger, Brigitte Berger, and Hansfried Kellner, *The Homeless Mind: Modernization and Consciousness* (New York: Vintage Books, 1973). These authors document the effects of mobility related to higher education during the early 1970s. Since that time mobility related to higher education has become even greater.

communities are addenda, not centers, of meaning and purpose.[14] Finally, as Robert Putnam so carefully documents in *Bowling Alone,* participation in a vast array of civic groups that developed early in the twentieth century has been replaced by more isolating activities such as television watching.[15] For such reasons the extended family and the local community are less influential sources of identity and social location.

Historically, workplaces had an effect on family life because they were the principal sources of income. That is still true. However, as neighborhoods, extended families, religious traditions, and local civic life become less compelling sources of identity and purpose, the workplace fills this vacuum and becomes an even greater source of personal definition. Because our culture uses paid employment as a principal means to determine societal status and personal meaning, Americans are now more socially as well as economically dependent on their sources of employment. Business workplaces are now more powerfully positioned to affect the family sense of identity, contribution, and place.

Family Life Affects the Workplace

However, the relationship of work and family life flows both ways. Marriage and family life have implications for business life as well. Men and women do not step outside their marriages and families when they enter the workplace. Because people are whole beings, for good or ill, they cannot completely segregate personal and business life. Working with employees inescapably means managing the intersection with their households. For example, a happy marriage creates a balanced perspective on work, but a spouse's illness, substance abuse, or death drains focus, energy, and well-being on the job. Healthy children create little early morning stress, while sick children are a significant source of worker absenteeism. Family medical problems create pressures for wage increases, or healthy spouses may add another source of insurance coverage. Adults and children who have been devastated by divorce bring their shaken self-images to the office, while forgiveness within the intact family can bring that value to a workplace team. It is impossible for human beings to funnel their lives into disconnected streams. The human body, heart, and mind are all one system.

14. Martin E. Marty, "Denominations Near Century's End" (two speeches delivered as the Stob Lectures of Calvin College and Seminary, 1990-91).

15. Robert Putnam, *Bowling Alone: The Collapse and Revival of American Community* (New York: Simon & Schuster, 2000). Putnam documents the decline of civic involvement through substantial research in his book.

Recent research strengthens the links between marriage and the workplace. Despite the stresses of marriage, Linda Waite's studies provide strong evidence that getting married is causally related to better health.[16] Because marriage has strong organizing effects on the life patterns of both men and women, they are emotionally and physically healthier if they commit to marriage and stay married. In turn, emotional and physical health affect employee capacities to be pleasant and productive.

At times businesses may wish that employees could compartmentalize home and work. Yet the business effects of such compartmentalization are unhealthy in the long run. Employee family stresses may not go away; they may simply be rechanneled to a less obvious current. If employees segregate personal and paid life, employers run great risks of being characterized as cold, hard, and uncaring. The long-run damage to organizational culture and employee motivation could be major.

Business performance depends on the everyday motivation and competence of real people. In mighty ways, what happens at home affects the desire and capacity to work.

Business Interests in Community Life Are Tied to Family Quality

There are also reasons for business responsibility beyond the interactions with individual employees. Professions typically claim that they have a moral commitment to society that is not directly attributable to self-interest.[17] Thus most business professionals believe they should be responsible for the communities and regions in which they operate. Some of that responsibility is legal in nature, involving laws of taxation, consumer rights, zoning, and environment. Yet many businesses believe their participation should spread beyond basic legal adherence to a sense of social responsiveness. These business leaders view communities as an important business stakeholder.[18]

---

16. Linda Waite describes the relationship between marriage and health in her chapter of this volume (chap. 1).

17. Paul Camenisch, "Men and Women in Business: On Professional Ethics and the Limits of Theology," in *Organization Man, Organization Woman: Calling, Leadership, and Culture*, by Shirley J. Roels with Barbara Hilkert Andolsen and Paul F. Camenisch (Nashville: Abingdon, 1997), chap. 3, pp. 97-118. Camenisch discusses the nature of a profession and related commitments.

18. Thomas L. Wheelen and David J. Hunger, "Issues in Social Responsibility and Ethics," in *Strategic Management and Business Policy*, 4th ed. (New York: Addison-Wesley, 1992), chap. 3, pp. 61-87.

Community participation has several goals. Businesses want to be seen as good community citizens. They wish to improve community life so local communities will be supportive of business in leaner as well as fatter times. Some businesses simply want to do good because such fits their vision of business responsibility in society. Businesses that embrace their communities of operation as important stakeholders may, for example, contribute earnings to arts organizations, become partners with local schools, or set up teams to renovate inner-city houses.

If businesses go one step further in their thinking, they will quickly realize that the quality of community life is intimately intertwined with the health of marriages and families. Healthy marriages and families are primary factors in any community's economic well-being, neighborhood ambience, educational achievement, and crime rate,[19] while crumbling home relationships shake a community's moral and spiritual tone.

Without enough marriage and family glue, any community can fall apart. Therefore attention to the quality of life in community homes can be a significant component in business responsiveness to local stakeholders. If a business believes it has responsibility to the communities in which it operates, then it cannot escape responsibility for the lives of the families that compose them.

Business Has Responsibilities Because of Changing Welfare Policy

As a profession, business also intersects with governmental structures to jointly improve the well-being of citizens. During the 1990s, one of the most important intersections was in the reform of social welfare policy. Responsible businesses will be the principal providers of work for former welfare dependents, and particularly in labor markets with low unemployment, businesses need these citizens as employees.

By the mid-1990s the U.S. government reconfigured public welfare policy to emphasize welfare-to-work programs. Society is now grappling with the effort required to reconstruct those being pressed to leave long-term welfare. This is a task that government can't principally or singularly do. Having lived through prior decades of government-related welfare dependency, policy framers now assume more limits on government capacity to develop work and family life for those who have been chronic welfare cases. They agree that

---

19. Whitehead, "Dan Quayle Was Right."

good government can provide economic assistance, but because of its inherently bureaucratic nature, it is not a good vehicle for investing in the intricacies and nuances of reconstructing family health.[20]

The shift in welfare policy presumed that other societal parties would shoulder more responsibility for the poor than they had since the 1950s. Business and religious institutions were particularly cited as organizations that could be partners in implementing new social welfare strategies. Communities of faith are working to fill some of the family support gap. They provide food, clothing, and temporary shelter as needed. Some groups adopt families working to leave welfare, providing them with job counseling, employment training, and family budget advice. Yet the missions of these faith communities do not typically include significant employment within their own circles. Thus businesses become important partners in the reconstruction of productive family units for those working to leave welfare dependency. They provide jobs. These jobs bring businesses closer to the daily problems of those leaving governmental welfare programs.

For example, a Milwaukee business leader tells the story of a parent hired from the welfare case ranks. She had never held a job for more than four weeks in her life. From the first employment day, her efficiency was less than half the company's standard. After a month of no improvement this businessman asked her to the manufacturing office to discuss her underperformance. When asked about it, she said, "Your light is so bad in the shop. It's hard to see the parts." Because this businessman knew the lighting was sufficient, it dawned on him that his employee had serious vision problems. Her life on welfare had not demanded that she see well. She strenuously denied needing glasses, but an eye exam led to her first set of lenses, productivity that exceeded the company standard, and a job held for several years. This employee had never known that she couldn't see.[21]

Without intimately connected business support, former welfare recipients may never know what they haven't previously seen, either physically or metaphorically. They may not understand commonly assumed standards for paid employment. Some may never have been exposed to culturally accepted expectations for work performance and work-related behavior. Others may not understand how to schedule household life in conjunction with paid em-

---

20. Stackhouse, *Covenant and Commitments*. Chapter 4 of this work provides a detailed history of U.S. government welfare policy and its effects in the last decades of the twentieth century.

21. Milton Kuyers, Milwaukee business leader, told this story during a conference entitled "Business: An Outstanding Christian Calling," held on the campus of Calvin College in May 1997. It is used with the permission of Mr. Kuyers.

ployment. Business will find that its task with former welfare recipients may involve the crafting of both physical and mental lenses through which these new employees can see what they may never have seen before. Without such assistance, this change in governmental welfare policy will not beat the blight of intergenerational welfare dependency.

Businesses are among the institutions best positioned to address the challenges of welfare reform by providing employment, training, opportunity, and basic life advice. Yet being a partner in welfare reform will require that businesses also engage the marriage and family situations of those trying to leave long-term welfare dependency. Households once enmeshed in the public welfare web are likely to be among those least able to segregate their family situations from employment life. Many have become welfare recipients because of single parenthood or divorce.[22] Often they have primarily known struggle, pain, and a highly disrupted sense of personal and social identity. Without close attention, their limited vision and personal struggles will be barriers to productive work lives. How can business employers meet their professional commitments in relation to changing social welfare policy unless they involve themselves in improving the quality of marriage and family life?

Business Viability for the Long Run

Some businesses may suggest that the above arguments for business involvement in marriage and family needs are idealistic or moralistic. Such premises presume that business, as a profession, will have some concern for the broader society. However, some in the business community may wash their hands of responsibility for shifting government welfare policy, the communities in which they function, and the intersection of business and family living.

Yet, for pragmatic reasons these businesses cannot afford to presume that the plight of the family is someone else's problem. Business must be concerned with family life because it affects the long-term viability of business itself. Even assuming that business has no direct responsibility for the quality of home life, in its own self-interest business should shoulder more of the marriage and family challenge.

Businesses need continuing generations of skilled, educated workers with solid work habits, psychological balance, good teamwork abilities, and a capacity for lifelong learning related to their work. As the knowledge economy grows, the demand for workers who can continue to learn is expanding.

---

22. Stackhouse, *Covenant and Commitments,* chap. 4.

As the networked economy mushrooms, the expectations for teamwork will become even greater than they are now.

However, evidence accumulated by the 1990s indicates that generations of youth from disrupted families will never have the same focus, attitude toward education, sense of long-term commitment, and team sensitivities so desired in business employees. They are more likely to be unfocused individualized tumbleweeds.[23] For their own sakes businesses cannot afford to let younger generations stumble into such limited futures. Marriage and family situations provide lessons about commitment, obligation, and sacrifice, one way or the other. If families, through their actions, teach that basic commitment is highly limited, that promised obligation is not binding, and that sacrifice is not honored, what types of employees will their offspring be? By comparison, if children learn, through example, that family promises ought to be kept and that sacrifices are needed to keep the team together, aren't they more effectively prepared for the commitments, obligations, and sacrifices required in business?

Similarly, members of younger generations that do not focus on the development of high-level reading, writing, math, science, and computer knowledge will not match the needs of the new economy. Children from dysfunctional families as a group are educational underachievers. They are much more likely to drop out of high school and much less likely to finish college even if they enter it.[24] They are not as prepared to contribute to the emerging economy. If business does not help to cultivate marriage and family life, its decline will undercut the base of business values, knowledge, and skill needed to function effectively in a global market economy.

Businesses should also be well aware that the quality of community life affects their capacity to attract mobile, talented employees to their organizations. If businesses do not pay attention to marriage and family health, the quality of communities to which they want to attract new employees will decline. Why would talented new recruits wish to join a company in a local environment replete with marriage and family dysfunction?

Businesses operate in the context of civil society. Their capacity to operate well is highly dependent on the lessons learned by those who participate in society. For their own sakes businesses can't ignore the fostering of healthier marriages and families that sustain healthy employees and generate healthier youth and community contexts for business. As Frances Hesselbein so eloquently states, "[L]eaders must look beyond the walls of the corpora-

---

23. Waite, "Does Marriage Matter?" pp. 483-507.
24. McLanahan and Sandefur, "Which Outcomes Are Most Affected."

tion . . . knowing that there is no hope for a productive enterprise within the walls if the community outside the walls cannot provide the healthy, energetic workforce that is essential in a competitive world."[25]

For all these reasons — the intertwined nature of business and family living, community involvement, the changing role of government welfare policy, and its own self-interest — business must take greater professional responsibility for the quality of marriage and family life.

Business Struggles in Reconstructing Home

The case for greater business responsibility related to the quality of home life is a weighty one. However, businesses must be well aware of the challenges that will confront them when they grapple with these responsibilities. They will quickly discover that making strategy is a challenge because businesses differ in models for their goals, families and firms have some opposing dynamics, the public disagrees about the definition of the family, and there are divergent business types. Business work on the reconstruction of home life is hands-on and messy.

The specific challenges before business are compounded by the recognition that "business as a profession" is a fairly young idea. While the legal, medical, and theological communities have long histories as professions, the conviction that business should be similarly characterized has emerged primarily in the last third of the twentieth century. Lawyers, doctors, and clergy members have a history of seeing themselves as self-regulating independent experts whose principal goal is client service that improves society's well-being. The business community is still growing into the idea that business professionals have great responsibility for the interaction between their specific services and the broad welfare of society.

Contrasting Models for Business Goals Affect Marriage and Family Involvement

An older model for business goals makes it more difficult to emphasize the professional responsibility of business. If business is framed as a profit-

---

25. Frances Hesselbein, "Managing in a World That Is Round," in *Leader to Leader*, a Drucker Foundation book edited by Frances Hesselbein and Paul M. Cohen (San Francisco: Jossey-Bass, 1999), p. 14.

maximizing venture that makes choices based principally on economic rationality, the limitations on its role are significant. Under this model the principal goal of the business is to balance consumer demands with the most efficient production and distribution possible to maximize profitability, the wealth of shareholders. Businesses that operate with this model may have greater struggles arguing that the firm should invest in marriage and family support for its employees and its communities of operation. Those who operate with this model may question whether programs to support a healthier marriage and family culture contribute obviously to the firm's profitability and shareholder interests.

However, those who see business as a profession can adopt a different model for its role in civil society. Instead of seeing the goal of business as profit maximization, they can espouse a stakeholder framework. In this alternative model, business is responsible to a variety of stakeholders, including customers, suppliers, employees, communities (local, national, and international), and stockholders. Business must continually balance the needs and interests of these various groups in ways that produce a satisfactory profit. Profit becomes not a goal but a means for proper investment in the future viability of the firm. In this model profitability is a necessary but insufficient means to determine the effectiveness of the business. A better measure of evaluating professional success is the balanced satisfaction of the stakeholders. Under such a model it is much easier for business to tackle marriage and family challenges. Since businesses using this model have already identified employees and communities as two important stakeholder groups, the task of marriage and family development is already within the normal bounds of business responsibility.

Yet the model for business goals adopted is a matter of worldview and ethics. Such perspectives will vary depending on whether business professionals acknowledge a divine Creator whose purposes encompass those of business organizations. The choice of a business model therefore involves religious beliefs and their connection to business frameworks.

Business and Family Dynamics Differ

If one uses the stakeholder model, however, businesses still should not assume that families can or should function like business organizations. Marriage and family life have different dynamics. Legally, businesses are encouraged to serve customers and shareholders through arm's-length transactions. This perspective protects them against favoritism, encourages a sense of fair competitive play, and promotes equitable treatment of parties in a transaction.

By comparison, families operate at a much different level of intimacy and focus. Families who provide for life needs are not based on abstract, arm's-length transactions. Family life can be lived only in the particular, not the universal. It is in families that we come to grips with concrete and daily physical, psychological, and spiritual needs. Addressing such needs for particular family members requires inherently biased care. Businesses presume that those who come to work have eaten, are appropriately clean and clothed, have typically slept at home, and have had sexual desires fulfilled in ways that are specific to individual employees. Those who hate oatmeal are typically allowed to eat cornflakes. Those who dislike red can wear blue. Those who like to sleep cuddled next to a spouse or those who need space to escape the great snore are treated in ways that favor their special desires. Society expects that families shape their care in light of the particular desires and quirks of their members.

Family systems are also much more quickly affected than business systems by a change in one member's status. Since families are much smaller entities, the effects are more direct, immediate, and particular. For example, families sense the direct and immediate effect when the one assigned to load the dishwasher is in bed with the flu, or when an infant feeding turns dinner from pork chops to pizza, or when an alcoholic parent is too inebriated to help with homework. Particularly for single-parent families, any change in daily life, be it child-care provider, school schedule, or location of work, can provoke a crisis. While businesses are also affected by changes in the roles, circumstances, and schedules of their employees, most businesses are buffered by their larger size. Others can more easily step in for sick employees or fill schedule gaps. Most likely, business systems are not as dramatically affected by a change in one employee's situation as our families are by the change in one member's status.

Furthermore, families are bound by person-to-person commitments, not cyberspace transactions. As technological capacity accelerates, more business transactions are virtual ones. A customer will likely never see someone from Amazon.com but will still expect his or her merchandise to show up as promised. The bargainer who bids in eBay's virtual auction, be it for baseball cards or basalt, never expects to meet an on-line executive. Such virtual contractual transactions are often appropriate and sufficient as business connections. Businesses and individuals need not exceed such boundaries to achieve the intended results.

It is hard to imagine that families could ever operate so virtually. Real experience requires the touches, the tears, and the smells of direct interaction. Can a quality marriage or family exist without any face-to-face, person-to-person living? Could parents raise a child virtually and expect good results, or could web-transmitted pictures sufficiently replace a personal visit to an elderly parent? To fully be a family, its members must see, hear, touch, and smell particular family members for significant periods of time. While it might be possible for business to conduct a great share of its transactions in virtual settings, families are not highly virtual entities. Their deep needs don't fit the frame of the virtual business contract.

The factors that establish the rhythms of life also differ between businesses and families. As businesses globalize, the rhythms of work can change because of worldwide time and schedule variations. The North American broker may rise early to check Nikkei stock exchange results. A corporate manager accumulates E-mail problems from a subsidiary in Hungary while he's asleep. The virtual meeting over videophone occurs during the dinner hour to link up with employees in New Delhi just starting their day.

By comparison, most families live in close conjunction with the rhythms of local schools, places of worship, and community activities. They participate in shaping the everyday civil society around them and are, in turn, affected by it. Teaching young children is particular and local, as is participation in school plays and team sports. Even social outlets for families, with or without children at home, typically involve civic theaters, regional symphonies, local museums, and city-sponsored recreation teams. The local rhythms of living to which most families are tied are quite different from those of global business.

As businesses grow, managers deal less and less with individual customers, stockholders, and employees. Business professionals manage more generalized systems of marketing, finance, and human resources. Concrete operations and systems management are separated. As businesses globalize and the number of virtual transactions grows, the level of abstraction in such businesses multiplies. Such developments are not to be decried; they are necessary in a global economy and spread benefits to those with great economic need. However, businesses must remember that families continue to be bodily, operational, and intimate spaces tied to the rhythms of local living.

So, while business concern for the quality of marriages and family life may grow, business life also tugs its participants in different directions. Families move to particular, everyday, and local rhythms. Businesses, particularly large corporate ones, move to the beat of abstracted, organizational, and global rhythms. Connecting these different and often opposing dynamics will not be easy for businesses.

Business Sizes and Types Require Different Solutions

Business/family dynamics must also be shaped in relationship to business size and type. One solution cannot fit all. It is more difficult for small businesses to address family challenges on a systemic basis. Often they cannot gain some of the economic advantages that come with business size. For example, a small business has less influence over the cost of family health care coverage than does a large corporation that can partner directly with a regional health maintenance organization. Less access to capital and a greater concern about cash flow also affect small business abilities to promise and deliver on comprehensive compensation packages that include life insurance, personal leave days, and extensive retirement benefits. Furthermore, when, for tax and regulation purposes, governmental entities classify businesses according to size, this also affects the capacity of differently sized businesses to support families.

However, smaller businesses may have a more connected understanding of the specific marriage and family situations of their employees as well as more flexibility in addressing such needs. Smaller businesses may be able to create particular solutions for individuals with less worry about charges of either unfairness or violation of company policy. They may be operationally closer to the daily lives of their employees, may have less abstracted company policies, and may understand the dynamics of particular local communities in which employees live. Thus, business size provides both advantages and disadvantages in addressing family life.

Businesses also vary substantially in type. A start-up business cannot have the flexibility of a matured corporation; nor does the reorganizing business always have the creative capacity of a growing firm. The product or service rendered also affects how a business intersects with families. For example, flexible starting times may assist families, but businesses with direct daily customer service may find it difficult to offer such flexibility; or an agricultural business may find it challenging to limit overtime during prime harvesting season.

This wide variety of business sizes and types will not allow standardized business recommendations to fit all of them. Business solutions must be intertwined with the nature of each individual business in different ways. Yet different business types may also offer unique opportunities. Direct customer service firms may be able to employ part-time workers; the agricultural business may be positioned to offer seasonal employment to at-risk youth. If business and society abandon the idea that one set of solutions can fit all businesses, there is opportunity to create solutions specific to different companies, communities, and employees. Yet if solutions are not interchangeable and cannot easily be borrowed from other firms, finding them will require hard thinking on the part of business professionals.

Establishing a Definition of Family Is Challenging

A final challenge for business will be in defining the family. After several decades of diversifying North American definitions of the family, finding a workable business consensus about what constitutes a family will not be easy. In any organizational environment, the definition of family is now a political question.[26]

At one extreme, some define family as any committed people whose lives are supported in the same household. For them a functional family does not involve blood ties, marriage ties, or the typical presence of the two sexes. For some in Western culture, family is now primarily a unit of political and psychological preference. At the other extreme, on the global scene, the family is often viewed as an extended network of blood relatives who must necessarily work or even occasionally go to war together.

In North America, post–World War II assumptions about the family unit were easier for business to manage. Family patterns were still greatly influenced by the historically dominant Judeo-Christian culture. That culture espoused sexual activity only within marriage, guarded monogamy, and saw children as a divine gift to be nurtured into God's service. High marriage and family formation rates more readily conformed to one pattern during the late 1940s through the mid-1960s. Both women and men married at a younger age, and divorce rates were lower. Single adults over the age of twenty did not constitute near the volume they do fifty years later. Thus businesses could and did assume that the family involved the provision of wages and benefits for male and female married adults. The male was typically considered the economic head of the household. The female contributed, at most, a secondary wage, particularly after children were born into this family.[27] Business decisions regarding wage and benefit adequacy and equity were far simpler in a more standardized family climate.

This description does not imply that all changes in the family since the 1940s have been bad ones, or that the mode in which families function should

---

26. Whitehead, "Dan Quayle Was Right."
27. Betty Friedan, *The Feminine Mystique* (New York: W. W. Norton, 1963). This book is widely regarded as an important analysis of women's roles and functions in the post–World War II era of the United States.

never be altered. Women have greatly benefited from the wider variety of social, economic, and family choices available in the past few decades. Furthermore, families in the 1950s mold were not problem-free. Many, then and now, ponder whether the gap between the nuclear and extended families that developed after World War II has, on balance, been beneficial. Many men in these families, feeling substantial economic responsibility, readily conformed to employer demands to perform stultifying tasks and uproot their families upon corporate command.[28] Many women in these families struggled with social isolation, a panoply of boring household tasks, and fear that death or divorce could quickly undercut their economic well-being.[29] Yet, despite concerns such as these, the frame for the family thirty to fifty years ago was more standardized and coherent than in current times. It was easier for businesses to develop policy for families knowing that the majority of families had a certain configuration. For businesses to work with families now requires a much more sophisticated understanding and analysis of family variety.

Business Decision Foundations in Reconstructing Home

Such a variegated garden of business and family types does not obviate the requirement that businesses make value-based choices about marriage and family. Throughout the twentieth century, businesses made such choices in determining what constituted an adequate family wage, what business should provide for employee families when the primary provider was injured or died, how business should handle layoffs in economic downturns, and the amount of business responsibility for retirement income. Ethical questions for business concerning marriage and family existed then just as they do now. Yet, while businesses made many value judgments about what portion of their resources to devote to employee well-being, the debate then was more about the adequacy of the resources and less about the nature of the receiving family unit.

A business interpretation of what now constitutes a marriage or family unit is a messy political undertaking. It asks businesses to evaluate the choices that employees and communities have made about what constitutes their family. Such judgments seem to violate the going assumption that businesses

---

28. William H. Whyte, Jr., *The Organization Man* (New York: Simon & Schuster, 1956). Whyte documents the struggles and stresses of corporate business life in the era after World War II.

29. Friedan, *The Feminine Mystique*.

should corporately be value-neutral on such individual employee decisions. Yet on issues of meaning, value, and morality, businesses will not find a neutral, amoral place to stand. Business decisions, particularly those involving its employees, involve moral choice. While the data on which decisions are based may be amoral in character, such business decisions and activities are inherently value-based. They always have been. The difference is the greater diversity of values among postmodern business stakeholders. In such an environment, finding and operating from a shared value base is a greater challenge.

While businesses are not legally founded on any particular religious faith perspective, there are some faith-based perspectives from the major monotheistic world religions that should influence the frameworks business uses for its work with family. First, families are not a human invention that we can radically reconstruct outside the boundaries of divine intent. Instead, marriages and families should operate within God's design. That design has some variety, as Max Stackhouse describes in his discussion of the global nature of family life.[30] Yet in Christianity, Judaism, and Islam, it is the Creator's intent that marriages be permanent unions of females and males and that children be nurtured in the context of those continuing unions. Second, children are an inheritance from God and are principally the responsibility of their parents, while a broader community must still care about their nurture and future. Third, "the family . . . is at every point an ethical and a spiritual association as well as a material and a biological institution."[31] Christianity, Judaism, and Islam, and for that matter most forms of Hindu, Buddhist, and Confucian ethics, are not reductionistic in their understandings of the family. While Paul Numrich argues that non-Western religions see marriage in different ways, these traditions still place marriage within a broad context of extended associations. Even when such religions do not see marriage and family as sacred, they see them as part of the broad fabric of a society. Such belief systems still view marriage and family life as multifaceted and ethical in nature.[32]

Beyond these foundations provided by the world's religions, there are unique contributions from specific faith expressions. For example, Christianity contributes particular frames through which to understand the family and has historically dominated the Western worldview. From a Christian viewpoint, not all families look like God's grand design. The entrance of evil into the world has made humans intent on being their own designers of family

---

30. Max Stackhouse describes the anthropological history of the family in his contribution to this volume (chap. 11).

31. Stackhouse, *Covenant and Commitments*, p. 3.

32. Paul Numrich describes the role of marriage and family in Buddhism, Hinduism, and Islam in his contribution to this volume (chap. 14).

through any means available, whether polygamy, slavery, family violence, gene manipulation, public protest, or a host of other channels. Humans in their family life can be determined rebels as well as the sad victims of others' rebellion. They can also be repressors of the creative family variety allowed and celebrated within God's design. Christianity also posits marriages and families as units that are bound together by sacred covenants, rites, or sacraments. These form the basis for a binding agreement over the length of human life. Within such agreements God is a continuing active participant in the creation, maintenance, and development of these commitments.[33] Finally, while humanity falters, God does not. In the salvation offered through God's Son, a sacrifice for humanity and all of creation, there is redemptive hope for marriages and families. Christians believe that the Spirit of God continues to move in this world through human agents and organizations to restore families and take care of those for whom families cannot be a central part of their lives. For businesses the challenge will be to intersect this Western Christian worldview with the perspectives of other religious faith communities.

In sum, business policy makers who come from a variety of spiritual traditions, and particularly from the more dominant Western Christian traditions, must grapple with developing a moral business viewpoint on the nature of the family. The perspectives above are some of the bases that a business should consider as it develops its framework for the nature of the family and responsibility for its improvement. There will be challenges and differences of opinion in articulating any firm's public perspective on the family. Yet, given a multitude of connotations attached to the word "family" during the past half-century, businesses can't avoid value choices about either the resources directed toward families or the definition of the family unit that business will engage. If businesses don't consciously choose an understanding of home and family, societal differences could easily overwhelm them. All political, cultural, economic, and global family definitions presented by any public audience will be on the table. They will all compete for a favored place within the business. With few foundations for a moral, just, and equitable path through the morass, the good intentions of business could easily flounder. If businesses are to make a positive contribution in reconstructing home, they cannot avoid the development of a moral, and therefore theological, perspective from which to shape policy and practice. The only question is what value bases businesses will use.

---

33. Stackhouse, *Covenant and Commitments*. In chapter 5 Stackhouse describes a range of historical and religious understandings of covenant and applies the meaning of covenant to the nature of family life.

Avenues of Business Responsibility for the Family

If business professionals accept responsibility to redevelop marriages and families as sacred and binding units within civil society, how should business shape its role? There are at least four areas in which businesses can have a significant influence on the reconstruction of home. They are organizational policy and culture, compensation, human resource programs, and employee training.

Organizational Policy and Culture

First, businesses shape family life through the organizational policy and culture that they create. Through business policy a company inculcates certain perspectives on work and its balance with the rest of life. Organizations can tighten or loosen the boundaries for work in terms of its rhythm, time commitment, intensity, and duration. Paid work is no longer bounded by a geographic place in which work is engaged. The knowledge economy and virtual networks destroy traditional physical boundaries. Paid work, accessible through cell phones and laptops, can travel anywhere, including the beach or the backyard.

Real people still need boundaries to allow time and space for their families. So a key task of business is to think through and articulate appropriate time and space expectations in a world of borderless interactions. For example, does a business affirm employees who check global stock markets at 3:00 A.M., or does it choose to set up structures that don't provide such incentives? Does the office culture dangle promotional opportunity before the employee who works seven days a week, or does it support employees who preserve regular time for personal, family, spiritual, and community life? Does the business manage global travel expectations so that those who must travel are home for important family occasions and balance their time away with extended stretches nearby? Does the organization control the pace of technological change so that the learning of yet another software package or telecommunications system can be absorbed while employees sustain other commitments in their lives? The organizational culture created through incentives, rewards, policy, and the pace of change can either enhance or inhibit the needed time and space for marriages and families. These factors shape the urgency and importance of paid work in comparison to unpaid commitments in other areas of life.

In addition to formal business policy, informal understandings created through stories, symbols, celebrations, and examples are just as important. For instance, what is the manager's reaction when the story of Jennifer's corporate weekend work binge is shared over lunch? Do supervisors routinely acknowledge marriages, anniversaries, births, deaths, and other important family happenings? Do managers commend and reward those staff members who seem to know about everyone's special family occasions? What kinds of conversations about family events are encouraged during the course of the workday? What type of social life is encouraged when the workday concludes? Do company socials sometimes include employee children? Answers to such questions create norms and expectations that are powerful shapers of informal organizational culture toward the family.

Personal examples in the business context also matter tremendously. Senior executives in business are role models who set the tone for the organization. How they treat their spouses, their family elders, and their children affects the standards for every other employee with whom they intersect. Compare the difference in organizational effect between the executive who leaves early to see her son in the school basketball finals and the married senior partner whose assistant must wire a dozen roses to his girlfriend. Both acts communicate a standard of behavior, but they send very different messages. The examples established by business professionals affect organizational perspectives on marriage and family in substantial ways.

Formal organizational policy and informal organizational culture are powerful forces in their effect on marriages and families. Homes are affected, for good or ill, by their shaping power.

Employee Compensation

Since many compensation issues are prescribed by law, it would be easy to overlook important nuances in the provision of employee compensation that greatly affect the needs of households in both the short and long term. Yet business responsibility for adequate compensation in relationship to household needs is a second area in which it can improve the quality of marriage and family life.

During the twentieth century, many of the wage-related struggles in industrialized nations were resolved in ways that provided for more stable, consistent, and adequate family incomes. Christine Hinze describes the passionate work of John A. Ryan, a Catholic priest-economist at the beginning of the twentieth century, to establish the idea of a family living wage.[34] A minimum

---

34. Christine Hinze describes the work of John A. Ryan in the chapter in this volume that she coauthored with Mary Stewart Van Leeuwen (chap. 7).

wage was introduced and has become a basic part of the employment landscape. Indirect benefits such as health insurance and funded pension plans, while not ubiquitous, are now more routine. Cafeteria benefit plans now allow more employees to choose benefits matching family situations and thus provide greater compensation equity. Legal requirements now address, though not perfectly, issues of employment and wage discrimination based on race, ethnicity, national origin, and sex. Legal protections have also helped limit discrimination related to pregnancy and childbirth.

Yet there are still compensation challenges that affect the quality of life at home. Positions at or just above the minimum wage may be inadequate for single parents with children. Paltry hourly pay in developing countries may not provide employees with economic security or a foundation for marriage in their cultures. Benefits may need to be reconfigured to create more justice and equity for employees for a broader range of family situations over the family life-cycle. Stock options may need to be thoughtfully balanced with other types of compensation in weighing risk and family need. Retirement benefits must be rethought as longevity increases. Businesses should regularly review their compensation structures to insure that both direct wages and indirect benefits most effectively meet the needs of employees and their families.

Providing Human Resource Services beyond the Legal Requirements

Human resource professionals within firms also have other creative opportunities to enhance the quality of marriage and family life. There are many means through which businesses can reshape work and services to support healthy marriage and family relationships. During the 1980s, many businesses began to introduce job sharing and flextime as ways to reconfigure work. Some are also exploring the idea of the sixty-hour family workweek. Such an approach allows both spouses flexibility in their work commitments so that the total hours of paid labor for the family does not exceed sixty. Other firms are exploring the sense of Sabbath, either through regular provision of one day a week on which work is not expected or scheduled, or through sabbaticals employees can earn for their years of service. Such options help adults who need or wish to continue working in the paid labor force while being responsive to their families and communities. The developments of the home office and telecommuting options have similarly provided many family units with greater flexibility to integrate paid work with family life.

Companies can also develop a range of supports for child and elder care. Depending on the size and type of business, there may be an in-house child care center, a contracted care arrangement, or a network of recommended child care providers. Most female adults spend almost as many years caring for elderly family members as they do for children. Given this situation, businesses should also consider how to help employees as they support senior family members. Human resource professionals can incorporate flexibility in working hours, unpaid leave options, and access to daily care centers for those responsible for aging relatives.[35] With careful analysis and coordinated efforts, care stresses on employees can be reduced.

Businesses can also create a wide variety of employee resources for family life counseling and education. For example, since alcohol and drug abuse are such significant contributors to family breakdown, employee referral programs for those with abuse problems can contribute significantly to the preservation and redevelopment of families. Some businesses have also developed programs that provide easy access to business-related chaplains. These types of interprofessional collaboration can provide early intervention and a broader network of support in times of trouble. Small-scale family life resource centers for employees can provide books, tapes, CDs, and other materials about major family transitions such as new marriage, the birth of children, blended families, and death in the family. Business can actively counsel employees about retirement to increase their well-being and also prevent them from unnecessarily burdening their working children.[36]

Law does not limit business responsibility for family life and the reconstruction of solid homes. Legal requirements provide a foundation for certain operations, but there is much more that businesses, working through their human resource professionals, can do to provide workable jobs, family support, and useful knowledge that serves employees and their families.[37]

Developing Managers to Support Marriages and Families

However, no matter how many services are provided directly by a company's human resource office, there are always some employees and families who

---

35. Barbara Schwarz VanderKolk and Ardis Armstrong Young, *The Work and Family Revolution: How Companies Can Keep Employees Happy and Business Profitable* (New York: Facts on File, ca. 1991).

36. Randall S. Schuler, *Managing Human Resources*, 5th ed. (New York: West Publishing Co., 1995). Chapters 11, 12, and 13 explore compensation, both direct and indirect; see pp. 381-498.

37. Schuler, pp. 474-81.

easily fall through the cracks. A central personnel office does not see people at work every day. The only ones who do are their supervisors, peers, and team leaders. Thus it is not enough for businesses to assign responsibility for the family to their human resource departments. Instead, they must take a more decentralized approach to encouraging and supporting healthy marriages and families. It is with direct supervisors and teammates that healthy family life can be most easily celebrated and challenging family situations most readily addressed. Particular spouses, children, and parents are more likely to be known in these decentralized smaller settings. If direct supervisors and business teammates are corporately encouraged and enabled, they can help to celebrate family milestones, provide flexibility in meeting family needs, accept those with family struggles, and challenge those who defect from their spouses and children.

The involvement of supervisors and teammates must be carefully framed. Most business supervisors and team leaders have not been educated as family counselors. Such is not their primary function. However, since marriage and family living are so intimately tied to work performance, it is worthwhile for business to train its supervisors and team leaders in understanding family dynamics. Trained supervisors can tell employees that involvement in a community of faith will likely strengthen their family but know how to avoid persuasive tactics that are religious harassment. With training, they can know how to watch for potential problems during the high stress associated with new marriage, childbirth, teenagers, family illness, death, or family relocation. Educated supervisors and team peers can identify work/family balancing challenges, substance abuse problems, marital difficulties, or troubled parent/child relationships. If managers and fellow team members know they have responsibility for the family health of their business associates, and if they exercise it, perhaps family challenges can be contained and addressed before they become major crises. They can work with their associates to acknowledge problems and connect them with appropriate assistance. Then if work teams learn how to reincorporate team members after a period of family struggle, all can benefit.

In summary, there are many avenues for business in its regular ongoing operation to address the reconstruction of home in both American and global society. Doing so doesn't necessarily require a business to step far beyond the bounds of its regular operations. However, the reconstruction of home does require businesses to understand themselves as organizations that will develop an explicit viewpoint about marriage and family and then act on it. Raising the quality of marriage and family life requires that businesses incorporate their viewpoints into formal policies, informal culture, compensation, human resource support services, and developmental training for employees.

Conclusion

In 1987 Max DePree, now retired chair of the Herman Miller Corporation, predicted that the era ahead would be one in which business would need to take on more responsibility for family life.[38] Now, over a decade later, his prediction still rings true.

Given the state of marriage and family life, reconstructing home is everyone's business; but business professionals are important players in this process. A descent into the slough of homeless living has occurred all too easily because current generations have not understood and developed important family foundations for living life together. Families are one of the smallest but most basic units in a healthy civil society; without them, it will be exceptionally difficult to sustain a healthy culture over time.

A business choice to be responsible for marriage and family life improvements will involve challenges. It depends on the model for business that business professionals adopt. Defining the family as a basis for action will be controversial. Decisions about family support will raise equity and justice issues close to the heart. Business responsiveness will require hard thinking about what contributions can best be made by businesses of different sizes and types. There's nothing easy about this undertaking. Yet if business professionals believe they should play a morally shaping role in society, they need to influence marriage and family life.

We all need home, that place that will always take us in, not because of what we do but because of who we are in relationship to others in that home. With the help of businesses and many other professions, may we reconstruct marriages and families that generations to come may find to be havens of identity, meaning, faith, learning, and renewal.

---

38. Max DePree made several observations about the responsibilities of business for family life during task force meetings sponsored by the Council for Christian Colleges and Universities to discuss the possibilities of publishing a book exploring Christian perspectives on business. He also weaves these themes into his later publications, *Leadership Is an Art* (New York: Doubleday, 1989) and *Leadership Jazz* (New York: Dell Publishing, 1992).

PART III

WIDENING THE DISCUSSION

CHAPTER 13

Do Religion and Spirituality Contribute to Marital and Individual Health?

David B. Larson and James P. Swyers

Introduction

Do religion and spirituality contribute to marital and personal health? If so, how do they do this, and is the association always beneficial? Furthermore, do the effects of religion/spirituality on marriage somehow impact or interact with personal health? In this chapter we will examine research on the relationship between religion and spirituality and several aspects of marital health. We also will examine the research linking religion and spirituality to several physical and mental health domains. Finally, we will examine the potential overlap between religion and spirituality and both marital and personal health.

Religion, Spirituality, and Marriage

Despite the fact that religion and spirituality have long been believed to be beneficial and even protective of marriages, this area has not been well studied by marriage and family researchers (Weaver, Koenig, and Larson 1997). Only in the late 1960s and early 1970s, when social and demographic researchers began noticing a relationship between a waning of people's involvement in religious activities and surging divorce rates, did scientists begin to conduct studies specifically designed to examine the relationship between religion and marital stability (Shrum 1980). Although the number of high-quality empirical studies in this field is still not extensive, evidence continues to emerge suggesting a strong, beneficial influence of religious and spiritual practices and beliefs on marital stability as well as the quality of marriages.

The following examines studies conducted over the past several decades on the relationship between religion and spirituality and several marriage variables, including: (1) marital stability, (2) marital adjustment, (3) marital satisfaction, (4) marital longevity, and (5) marital reconciliation.

Religion and Marital Stability

One of the earliest empirical studies to confirm a relationship between religious involvement and marital stability was conducted by McCarthy (1979), who analyzed data collected from a nationally representative sample of people in the 1973 National Survey of Family Growth (NSFG). This study found that after five years, 17 percent of couples who attended church once a year or less were separated or divorced, compared to only 7 percent of the couples who attended church once a month or more. At the fifteen-years follow-up, more than twice as many infrequent churchgoers were no longer married, compared to the frequent (once a month or more) churchgoers (37 percent versus 14 percent, respectively).

Religious Commitment and Marital Stability

In a slightly later study, Shrum (1980) analyzed data collected from 1972 to 1977 during six separate surveys of primarily Protestant and Catholic populations. Similar to McCarthy (1979), this study found that more frequent religious participation was clearly linked with increased marital stability. Conversely, those who attended church activities less frequently were more likely to have experienced marital problems. Furthermore, this positive relationship between increased church attendance and increased marital stability was not lessened when five additional variables known to affect marital stability were introduced into the analysis. Thus, religion's effect on marital stability appeared to be fairly direct rather than being mediated through some intervening variable, such as age at marriage or income.

Religious Participation and Personal Commitment to Marriage

A number of studies suggest that there are indeed direct effects of religious commitment on marital stability through, for example, personal commitment to marriage. In one such study, Larson and Goltz (1999) examined data from a random survey of 179 married couples that asked about several religious factors, including religious affiliation, religious homogamy (i.e., whether or not partners were affiliated with the same religious denomination), and frequency of church attendance. In addition, the survey asked the couples about their personal commitment (i.e., commitment to stay in a marriage no matter what the cost) and structural commitment (i.e., commitment to marriage in general, based on social proscriptions, particularly those of one's religion) to marriage.

This study found no significant relationship between religious homogamy and personal marital commitment for both husbands and wives. In addition, personal commitment was not significantly related to the religious affiliation of either the husbands or the wives. On the other hand, personal commitment *was* positively related to church attendance for both husbands and wives. Structural commitment, likewise, was significantly correlated with church involvement for both husbands and wives. Therefore, the more frequently husbands and wives attended church, the more personally and structurally they were committed to staying married.

The investigators also found that the duration of the marriage and the couples' satisfaction with family life were positively associated with structural marriage commitment. In other words, the longer the couples were married and the happier they were with their family life, the greater was their structural commitment to marriage. Larson and Goltz (1999), thus, concluded that commitment to marriage arises from more than experiencing a good marriage. "Instead, commitment is the individual and relational source of making a good [or even weak] marriage better," they suggested.

Coparticipation in Religion and Marital Stability

Recently, Vaughn and Heaton (1997) analyzed data from another extensive and nationally representative sample of people, the National Survey of Families and Households (NSFH). In examining the marital stability of 4,587 U.S. couples who were married at the time of the original NSFH survey in 1987/88 and were then reinterviewed approximately five years later, Vaughn and Heaton found that when both spouses attend church regularly, the couple has the lowest risk of divorce. On the other hand, if there was a substantial difference in the frequency of the spouses' church attendance, their marriage was more likely to have broken up five years later.

Religion, Spirituality, and Marital Adjustment

What is it about religion and spirituality that helps keep marriages together? One explanation may be that, in addition to increasing one's personal commitment to marriage, it also may promote marital stability by helping couples adjust to the rigors of marriage (Albrecht 1979; Bahr and Chadwick 1985; Schumm, Bollman, and Jurich 1982). Research indicates that the length of time it takes people to adjust to married life correlates closely with happiness in marriage (Landis 1946), and that failure to adequately adjust to marriage can be a predictor of psychological problems, such as depression (Merikangas et al. 1985). Therefore, factors that enhance marital adjustment are likely also to enhance marital stability and emotional well-being.

Religious Commitment and Marital Adjustment

The degree of spouses' commitment to their religious beliefs appears to be instrumental in enhancing marital adjustment. In one study, for example, Wilson and Filsinger (1986) analyzed data obtained from a survey of 190 married Protestant couples. This survey included a multidimensional, thirty-seven-item conceptualization of religion which included the couples' degree of (1) religious ideology (e.g., conservatism or liberalism), (2) religious experience (e.g., repentance, forgiveness, etc.), (3) ritualistic involvement (e.g., frequency of church attendance, etc.), (4) religious knowledge, and (5) religious morality. Marital adjustment was measured by the couples' degree of (1) agreement on issues of importance to the relationship, (2) satisfaction with and commitment to the relationship, (3) engaging in activities together, and (4) satisfaction with expressions of affection and sex. To control for other explanatory variables, the investigators also factored in the couples' socioeconomic status, length of marriage, and number of children.

This study found a strong pattern of positive relationships among several dimensions of both religiousness and marital adjustment. Specifically, the higher the couples' (1) ritualistic involvement, (2) reported religious experience, and (3) conservative religious beliefs, the greater was their marital adjustment. These three dimensions of religiousness also predicted the degree of each couple's agreement on issues of importance to the relationship, satisfaction with and commitment to the relationship, and how much they engaged in activities together.

Spirituality and Marital Adjustment

In addition to an outward commitment to one's faith, such as frequently attending church and engaging in religious practices, an "inward" commitment also appears to impact on marital adjustment. Roth (1988), for example, examined the relationship between the subjective "inner experiences" related to being religious and several dimensions of marital adjustment. Specifically, Roth asked approximately 150 married people who regularly attended church about their existential well-being (EWB), religious well-being (RWB), and spiritual well-being (SWB), as well as their degree of marital satisfaction, cohesion, consensus, and expression of affection.

Roth found a significant relationship between EWB (i.e., an individual's sense of self, that is, knowing who he or she is and what he or she needs to focus on) and all four marital adjustment subscales. In addition, there also was a significant relationship between SWB (i.e., degree to which an individual has internalized the beliefs that his or her faith or religion teaches) and all four marital adjustment subscales for wives. In contrast, for husbands, only two of the four marital adjustment factors — marital satisfaction and expression of affection — were significantly related to SWB. On the basis of these results, Roth suggested that a religious belief alone is not enough to ensure marital stability. Rather, such beliefs need to be integrated into the "self." Again, this study underscores the need for multidimensional measures of both religion and spirituality and marital adjustment.

Prayer, Bible Reading, and Marital Adjustment

Private prayer and Bible reading also have been found to have significant effects on marital adjustment. In one study, Gruner (1985) examined the relationship between private prayer and Bible reading at home and marital adjustment among several different groups of Christians, including members of (1) a sect,[1] (2) a conservative-evangelical denomination, (3) a liberal denomination, and (4) an institutional-authoritarian denomination (i.e., Roman Catholic). The respondents also were asked about other potentially confounding factors, such as their age, how long they had been married, their social class, and their race.

This study found that roughly half of those involved in sects reported

---

1. A sect is typically defined as a religious organization with traditional beliefs and practices that has different, or deviant, doctrines, symbols, and icons from the main religious body from which it had split.

high marital adjustment. Among conservative-evangelical Christians, there was a more even distribution among those reporting high, medium, and low levels of marital adjustment (about one-third for each). For the theologically religious liberals and Catholics, however, only about a quarter in each group reported high marital adjustment, with the remaining three quarters almost evenly divided between low and medium marital adjustment.

In assessing the relationship between private prayer and marital adjustment, Gruner found that most liberal Christians and Catholics did not use prayer at all when addressing marital adjustment problems. On the other hand, 50 percent of those affiliated with a sect reported using prayer frequently to address marital adjustment problems. Those affiliated with evangelical religions also reported frequent use of prayer for this purpose.

This study found, however, that across all groups a significantly greater percentage of those who scored high on marital adjustment used prayer quite extensively in connection with marital adjustment problems, compared to those who scored low on marital adjustment (53 percent versus 17 percent, respectively). Further, an even greater percentage (59 percent) of those who extensively read the Bible to deal with marriage problems reported high marital adjustment. This contrasted with only 12 percent of those who read the Bible to deal with marriage problems reporting low marital adjustment. Thus, this study found a fairly strong relationship between both private prayer and Bible reading and enhanced marital adjustment.

Religion, Spirituality, and Marital Satisfaction

Although religion and spirituality appear to have a positive relationship with marital adjustment, what about their relationship to marital satisfaction? Although studies in this area tend to be somewhat contradictory, the available evidence suggests that aspects of both religion and spirituality can enhance marital satisfaction.

Religion and Marital Satisfaction

In a groundbreaking study in the late 1970s, Glenn and Weaver (1978) analyzed data collected from three large-scale surveys conducted in the United States to estimate the effects of ten independent variables (one of which was church attendance) on the marital happiness of white men and women ages eighteen through fifty-nine. They found that frequent church attendance had a positive and statistically significant association with marital satisfaction.

However, because they were unable to control for the reported tendency of more conventional people to be more likely to attend church frequently (or say they do) as well as to exaggerate their marital happiness, the investigators suggested that this positive relationship could be at least partially due to this "marital conventionalization" factor (i.e., the extent to which spouses might describe their marital situation in socially desirable rather than realistic terms).

Although marital conventionalization has been proposed for a number of years as a major factor in the relationship between religion and marital satisfaction (e.g., Edmonds 1967), carefully controlled studies have tended to discount it as a significant explanation for this relationship. Schumm and colleagues (1982), for example, randomly surveyed eighty-three rural and ninety-eight urban families on three items of marital satisfaction — (1) their degree of satisfaction with their spouse, (2) their degree of satisfaction with their marriage, and (3) the quality of their relationship with their spouse. Respondents also were asked about the importance of church and religion in the quality of their lives as well as their importance compared to other factors such as family, friends, community, leisure and recreation, housing, financial security, work, and education.

In the initial analysis of the relationships between all the variables, Schumm and colleagues found that the marital conventionalization argument was "at least partly valid" in explaining the positive impact of religion on marital satisfaction. However, a more detailed statistical analysis found that even among those who scored low for marital conventionalization, religiousness was an "important" predictor of marital satisfaction. This finding led Schumm and colleagues to conclude that the positive association between religiousness and marital satisfaction definitely was not a spurious, or accidental, relationship. They, therefore, strongly encouraged researchers to re-examine their evidence on this topic.

Spirituality and Marital Satisfaction

As previously noted, there is evidence that the internalization of religious beliefs appears to be a key factor in religion's role in affecting marital satisfaction. If one defines spirituality as the internalization of religious belief, then studies of spirituality tend to confirm this internalization phenomenon. For example, Bell and colleagues (1987) assessed the relationship between perceptions of the "quality" of a variety of maintenance activities (i.e., strategies for increasing personal closeness, or affinity) and marital satisfaction within the marriages of 109 women. Each woman completed the Marital Adjustment Test and then rated (1) how frequently she and her husband used each strategy, (2) how personally important it was that her husband use the strategy, and (3) how important she thought it was to her husband that she regularly use the strategy. This study found the women's marital satisfaction was most strongly related to their perception of the frequency of their husbands' use of the five specific strategies: (1) sensitivity, (2) spirituality, (3) physical affection, (4) self-inclusion, and (5) honesty.

In a further exploration of this topic, Mahoney and colleagues (1999) recently conducted a study of ninety-seven couples to develop a clear understanding of the link between marital satisfaction and spirituality. This study found that spirituality (defined as viewing marriage as having "sacred" attributes) did contribute *directly* to marital satisfaction. In fact, this study found that religiously active couples who held more sacred views of marriage not only had higher ratings of marital satisfaction but also had fewer marital conflicts than did couples who had less sacred views of marriage. In addition, couples who held more sacred views of marriage felt that marriage benefited them more individually. As a result, this more spiritual group tended to engage in more constructive, collaborative means of problem solving than did the less spiritual group. Another significant finding of this study was that perceiving one's marriage as having sacred, spiritual significance and joining in religious activities together had *more* impact on improving marital quality than whether the couple were each individually religious or were of the same denomination.

Religion and Marital Longevity

Only in the past twenty years or so have investigators begun to examine the dynamics of religion and the length of marriages. Although most of these studies have been small and have relied on personal accounts from groups who were, for the most part, genuinely religious, they do point to religion as one of a core set of key ingredients involved in many successful long-term marriages.

Importance of Religion and Marriage Longevity

Sporakowski and Hughston (1978) interviewed forty couples who had been married fifty years or more to determine what they believed were the "most important" factors for marital happiness. Wives mentioned "importance of religion" most frequently as a key ingredient to a happy marriage, followed by

(1) love, (2) give-and-take/talking things through, (3) home/family/children, (4) it takes two to make a marriage work, and (5) understanding and patience. In contrast, husbands mentioned "it takes two to make a marriage" most frequently, followed by (1) honesty and trust, (2) give-and-take, (3) marriage is for life, and (4) importance of religion. The investigators noted that although the key factors mentioned were different between husbands and wives, the top five key ingredients, which included importance of religion, were essentially the same.

In another study, Robinson and Blanton (1993) found that among fifteen couples who had been married more than thirty years, intimacy, commitment, communication, congruence, and having a similar religious orientation were the most consistent factors cited as contributing to marital satisfaction. In a follow-up study, Robinson (1994) asked fifteen long-term married couples (between thirty-five and forty-eight years) to discuss the strengths of their marital relationship. Most respondents mentioned "religious faith" as one of the most important assets in enhancing their marital relationship. Indeed, some of them indicated that religion was "primary" in their marriage and enhanced other key ingredients as well, including marital intimacy, marital commitment, and marital communication. Also, they stated that their faith provided them with moral guidance, facilitated decision making, and helped minimize marital conflict.

Additionally, Kaslow and Robinson (1996) studied fifty-seven couples who had been married between twenty-five and forty-six years to determine which factors they believed were the greatest contributors to their marital satisfaction as well as the longevity of their marriage. This study found that love, mutual trust, mutual respect, corresponding religious beliefs, loyalty and fidelity, mutual give-and-take, similar philosophy of life, enjoyment of shared fun and humor, shared interests in activities, and shared interests in their children were the most frequently cited factors (each was endorsed by more than 50 percent of respondents) as contributing to marital satisfaction and marital longevity.

Finally, Fenell (1993) investigated characteristics of "1st marriages" that had lasted over twenty years by asking 147 couples about the "10 most important" characteristics their spouses possessed in helping to ensure a long-term marriage. The couples' responses revealed these: (1) lifetime commitment to marriage, (2) loyalty to spouse, (3) strong moral values, (4) respect for spouse as best friend, (5) commitment to sexual fidelity, (6) desire to be a good parent, (7) faith in God and spiritual commitment, (8) desire to please and support spouse, (9) being a good companion, and (10) willingness to forgive and be forgiven.

Religion and Marital Reconciliation

In addition to buffering against a marital breakup and keeping marriages running more smoothly, research suggests that religion and spirituality may play a role in successful reconciliation of troubled marriages. For example, Wineberg (1994) examined data from the 1987-88 NSFH to determine both the prevalence of successful marital reconciliations among white women and the key ingredients to those reconciliations. This study found that in about 30 percent of cases where women attempted to reconcile their marriages, the woman was still with her husband one year after the reconciliation began. However, the probability that an attempted reconciliation would be successful varied among the subgroups of women.

Specifically, women who had the same religious denominational affiliation as their spouse had a significantly higher probability of having a successful reconciliation than did women with a different denominational affiliation than their spouse. Conversely, if one spouse converted to the other's religious denomination, there was a significantly greater probability of a successful reconciliation.

Summary

The studies highlighted in this section suggest that religion and spirituality are indeed significantly associated with several important aspects of marital health. There is evidence that religious commitment, as measured by the frequency of church attendance, is associated with personal commitment and structural commitment to marriage. Additionally, evidence suggests that certain aspects of religion and spirituality contribute to and enhance marital satisfaction. Religious and spiritual factors also appear to be key ingredients to the success of long-term marriages as well as to healing marriages that have been fractured. In sum, it appears that more religious and/or spiritual individuals may have more stable marriages because they are better able to adjust to marriage, to find more satisfaction and meaning in their marriages, and to take steps to make their marriages better.

Religion, Spirituality, and Health

There has recently been a heated debate over the linking of religious and spiritual beliefs and practices to health outcomes. Indeed, it is suggested in this book and by others (Sloan et al. 2000) that medicalizing religion, that is, linking religious and spiritual practices to health outcomes, has the potential to "devalue" both religion and science. That certainly may be true if one were to put forth that the only potential benefit from being religiously or spiritually committed was in obtaining better personal physical and mental health. The potential health benefits of religious or spiritual beliefs are but a small part of what the religious traditions of the world have provided and continue to provide for mankind and societies.

On the other hand, if one argues, on the basis of surveys demonstrating that patients strongly believe that their religious and spiritual beliefs have a role to play in helping them cope with and recover from serious illness (Ehman et al. 1999; King, Sobal, and DeForge 1988; Maugians and Wadland 1991), that health care providers need to become more aware of and sensitive to the religious and spiritual beliefs and concerns of their patients, then both science and religion are enriched, not devalued. Indeed, in view of the principles of beneficence, it would be unethical for health care professionals not to take into account patients' spiritual or religious beliefs if such beliefs have the potential to impact on treatment (Post, Puchalski, and Larson 2000) or the course of their recovery.

To date, several hundred empirical studies have investigated the effects of some aspect of religious or spiritual involvement in physical or mental health. Although some types of religious and spiritual beliefs and practices have been shown to be harmful for physical and mental health, the vast majority of studies have suggested a beneficial effect for religious and spiritual variables in each of these areas (see Levin 1994 and Larson, Swyers, and McCullough 1997 for a review of this literature). Since the body of literature on the relationship between religion/spirituality and health is so large and diverse, it is beyond the scope of this section to delve into studies in all the areas of personal health in which religious and spiritual beliefs and practices have been found to play a role. Rather, we have chosen to focus on the relationship between religion and spirituality and three well-studied areas of personal health: (1) mortality, (2) morbidity, and (3) depression.

Religion, Spirituality, and Mortality

Similar to the studies in religion/spirituality and marriage, early findings of an association between religious and/or spiritual factors and death rates, or mortality, were largely accidental. For example, in the early 1970s Comstock and Partridge (1972) found, in an epidemiologic study of the role of social factors in death rates, an association between weekly church attendance and significantly lower rates of coronary disease, emphysema, cirrhosis, and suicide. Unfortunately, because this study did not deal specifically with religion, its results went relatively unnoticed for a number of years. However, in the past few years a number of large-scale studies that *have* dealt specifically with religion have confirmed an association between a greater frequency of religious participation and lower mortality.

Strawbridge et al. (1997), for example, recently analyzed the association between frequent church attendance and mortality over twenty-eight years for 5,286 individuals. This study found that people who attended church frequently had lower mortality rates than infrequent attenders, and the relationship was stronger for women than for men. Interestingly, factoring in health behaviors, such as smoking and exercise, had little impact on this relationship, whereas adjustments for "social connections" reduced the relationship significantly but did not eliminate it. The authors concluded, therefore, that mortality rates are lower for frequent church attenders than for infrequent attenders and that these lower mortality rates are only partly explained by improved health practices, increased social contacts, and more stable marriages occurring in conjunction with church attendance.

In another study, Oman and Reed (1998) analyzed the prospective association between attending religious services and all-cause mortality among almost two thousand elderly residents of Marin County, California. The purpose of this study was to determine if there was an association between religion and mortality, and if so, whether it was explainable by six confounding factors: (1) demographics, (2) health status, (3) physical functioning, (4) health habits, (5) social functioning and support, and (6) psychological state. This study found that persons who attended religious services frequently had a 24 percent lower risk of mortality compared to nonattenders. After adjusting for the six potential confounding variables, this relationship was reduced only slightly, primarily by including physical functioning and social support. However, contrary to the investigators' expectations, religious attendance tended to be slightly more protective for those individuals with high social support.

More recently, Koenig and colleagues (1999) demonstrated a 46 percent decrease in relative hazard of dying for frequent church attenders compared to infrequent attenders. This finding was independent of demographics, health conditions, social connections, and health practices. Hummer and colleagues (1999) likewise analyzed data from the *National Health Interview Survey — Multiple Cause of Death Survey* and found that people who *never* attend church had almost *twice* (1.87 times) the risk of death in the follow-up period of the study compared with people who attended church more than once a week. This translated into a clinically important "seven-year difference" in life expectancy between those who never attend church and those who attend more than once a week, according to the researchers.

Finally, a meta-analysis conducted by McCullough and colleagues (2000), which analyzed data from forty-two published and unpublished data sets (representing nearly 126,000 people), found that religious involvement was *indeed* associated with a 29 percent greater odds of survival (or conversely, lower risk of death) during the follow-up periods of the studies.

Religion, Spirituality, and Morbidity

A number of studies in a variety of populations have found that persons who attend church frequently, and for whose lives religion is of major importance, have lower rates of illness, or morbidity, than their less religious counterparts. Graham and colleagues (1978), for example, analyzed data from the Evans County Cardiovascular Epidemiologic Study (ECCPS), a National Institutes of Health–funded survey conducted in Georgia in the late 1960s. This study examined the relationship between blood pressure and a number of sociological factors, including religious involvement, among 771 white males. It found a consistent association between frequent church attendance and lower systolic and diastolic blood pressures. This association was present among smokers and nonsmokers as well as among white-collar and blue-collar skilled workers. Although this data was cross-sectional and care must be taken in drawing conclusions about causal relationships between religion and blood pressure, the consistency of the data among these different demographic groups is noteworthy.

In a follow-up of this study, Larson and colleagues (1989) reanalyzed the data for the original 771 subjects who had participated in the ECCPS to examine the relationship between their blood pressure and their frequency of church attendance as well as the relative importance of religion in their lives. This study found only a nonsignificant trend toward lower blood pressures among those who attended church frequently, compared to infrequent attenders. The relationship between "importance of religion" and blood pressure followed the same trend, but again did not reach statistical significance. However, when the two religion items — importance of religion *and* frequency of church attendance — were combined and analyzed in relation to blood pressure, those with both high religious importance *and* high frequency of church attendance had significantly lower diastolic blood pressures compared to those with both low religious importance and low frequency of church attendance. Systolic pressures followed the same trend but did not reach statistical significance. Although adjusting for confounding factors (age, smoking, etc.) did decrease the magnitude of this relationship, statistical significance was retained for diastolic pressures. Interestingly, for smokers, diastolic and systolic blood pressures were significantly lower in the high religious importance group compared to the low religious importance group, suggesting that religion had a protective effect against smoking in the former group. Indeed, among smokers, those with *low* religious importance had 4.3 greater times likelihood of having an abnormal systolic and 7.1 times greater likelihood of having abnormal diastolic pressure than did those with *high* religious importance.

In addition to lower blood pressure, studies have found that religious and spiritually involved individuals also may have better functioning immune systems than their less religious or spiritual counterparts, and thus are better able to fight off infectious and chronic diseases. For example, Koenig and colleagues (1997) analyzed data on 1,718 randomly selected older adults participating in the National Institute on Aging–sponsored Established Populations for Epidemiologic Studies of the Elderly (EPESE) and found that persons who attended religious services to any extent were only about one-half as likely as nonattenders or rare attenders to have high serum levels of interleukin-6 (IL-6), which is a common marker for immune system dysfunction. For example, immune-compromised patients, such as people with AIDS (acquired immunodeficiency syndrome), have high levels of IL-6, as do people with lymphoma, osteoporosis, diabetes, and Alzheimer's disease. Koenig et al. found that better immune functioning among those who attend church persisted even after they controlled for a number of potentially confounding variables, including age, sex, race, chronic medical illness, depression, stress, and functional status.

Religion and Recovery from Disability

Obviously, participation in religious and spiritual activities is not a guarantee that one will not become sick. However, the evidence does suggest that the spiritual or religious beliefs and practices of those who do succumb to illness may help them recover more rapidly than those who profess little or no religious or spiritual beliefs. For example, Koenig and Larson (1998) found that hospitalized medical patients who reported an affiliation with a church or place of worship spent an average of eleven days in the hospital compared to an average of twenty-five days for non-church-affiliated patients. Interestingly, this association strengthened when physical health and other potentially confounding factors were controlled for (Koenig and Larson 1998).

Harris and colleagues (1995) reported that religious beliefs and practices among heart transplant patients (assessed at the time of transplantation) predicted improved physical functioning, enhanced adherence to medical regimens, higher self-esteem, and diminished anxiety and health worries one year after surgery. Furthermore, McSherry et al. (1987) reported that heart surgery patients with higher than average personal religiousness scores on admission and postoperatively had lengths of hospital stays 20 percent shorter than those with lower average scores.

Additionally, studies indicate that spiritually focused interventions also speed recovery from illness. For example, studies indicate that post–heart attack patients who were shown how to meditate had a reduced risk of both fatal and nonfatal repeat heart attacks (Friedman, Thoresen, and Gill 1986; Ornish et al. 1990). Spiritual interventions also have been shown to help in the recovery of patients being treated for breast cancer (Spiegel 1994). It is believed that such interventions help speed recovery by reducing anxiety, increasing hope, and improving coping skills among patients (Kaczorowski 1989; Fehring, Miller, and Shaw 1997).

Religion, Spirituality, and Depression

Given that religious and spiritual beliefs and practices appear to reduce one's risk of illness and early death, it is not surprising that there is an inverse relationship between greater religiosity and decreased depression. This inverse relationship has been confirmed in several recent studies that have looked specifically at the association between religious involvement and depression. However, these same studies suggest that not all religious and spiritual beliefs are protective against depression. Indeed, some may actually contribute to or exacerbate depression.

Ellison (1995) examined the relationship between religion and depression among approximately three thousand individuals and found that the (1) frequency of church attendance is inversely associated with depressive symptoms among whites but not among blacks; (2) absence of a religious denomination is positively associated with (i.e., increases) depressive symptoms among blacks but not among whites; and (3) frequency of private devotional activities is inversely associated with depressive symptoms among both racial groups.

Similarly, Braam and colleagues (1997) examined the association between religious involvement and depression in almost three thousand Dutch citizens aged fifty-five to eighty-five who had participated in a multifaceted health study of older adults. This study, which assessed symptoms of depression, the frequency of church attendance, and strength of church affiliation, found that religious involvement was inversely associated with (i.e., decreases) depression, both on symptom and syndrome levels. Furthermore, the researchers found that introducing other potentially depression-causing factors into the analysis, such as low income and lack of education, physical impairment, and lack of social support, did not substantially affect this association, particularly among subjects aged seventy-five to eighty-five. This inverse association between religious involvement and depression was no more pronounced among older people with physical impairments than the rest of the study sample. However, the association appeared to be most specific for subjects with a small social support network and those with a low "sense of mastery" (i.e., feelings of control over their own fate).

More recently, Strawbridge and colleagues (1998) used a survey of more than 2,500 people between 50 and 102 years of age to analyze associations between depression and two forms of religiosity: (1) *nonorganizational religiosity* and (2) *organizational religiosity*. Nonorganizational religiosity included prayer and the importance of religious and spiritual beliefs, whereas organizational religiosity included attendance at services and other activities. The investigators also assessed the extent to which religiosity buffers relationships between stressors and depression.

This study found that both forms of religiosity buffered associations with depression for nonfamily stressors, such as financial and health problems. However, nonorganizational religiosity exacerbated associations with depression for child problems, and organizational religiosity exacerbated associations with depression for marital problems, abuse, and caregiving. The authors thus concluded that religiosity may help those experiencing nonfamily stressors but may worsen matters for those facing family crises.

Koenig et al. (1997) recently examined the relationships between religious activities, physical health, social support, and depressive symptoms in a sample of 4,000 people age sixty-five and over. Religious activity was examined first as a single component and then split into three individual components: (1) frequency of church attendance, (2) frequency of private prayer/ Bible reading, and (3) frequency of watching religious TV and listening to religious radio. As expected, religious activity as a single construct was correlated with both social support and better physical health but was unrelated to depression. When split into individual components, however, the three types of religious activities had differential effects on physical health and depression. In fact, frequent church attendance was beneficial to physical health and buffered against depression but was surprisingly unrelated to social support.

More importantly, frequent churchgoers were about half as likely to be depressed as infrequent churchgoers.

In contrast, private prayer/Bible reading was nonbeneficial to physical health and improved social support but was unrelated to depression. Religious TV watching/religious radio listening was unrelated to social support, negatively related to good physical health, and unexpectedly, positively associated with (i.e., increased) depression.

Religion and Recovery from Depression

In addition to protecting against depression, certain kinds of religious beliefs and activities appear to speed the recovery from depression. Koenig and colleagues (1998), for example, examined the effects of religious belief and activity on remission of depression in hospitalized older patients. During the follow-up period of this study, forty-seven patients (54 percent) had remissions; the median time to remission was thirty weeks. Intrinsic religiosity (i.e., internalizing and practicing one's religious beliefs) was significantly and independently related to time of remission, but church attendance and private religious activities were not. Thus, depressed patients with higher intrinsic religiosity scores had more rapid remissions than patients with lower scores.

Summary

A number of studies in a variety of populations have found that a high level of religious commitment is associated with reduced mortality and morbidity in a variety of different populations (see Larson, Swyers, and McCullough 1997 for a more detailed discussion of this literature). The religious also tend to be less prone to depression, a major mental health problem in the United States, compared to the nonreligious. On the other hand, it appears that some religious practices can increase the risk of depression in certain situations.

Discussion: The Potential Overlap between Religion, Marriage, and Personal Health?

To answer the questions posed at the beginning of this chapter, there does appear to be a moderately strong association between religion and spirituality and both marital and personal health. For example, religion and spirituality have been shown to impact marital stability as well as adjustment to marriage, including people's ability to cope with the stressors associated with marriage. Likewise, religious and spiritual beliefs and practices can directly influence physical and mental health by increasing people's abilities to cope with debilitating and life-threatening illness.

In examining the research highlighted in this chapter, it is noteworthy that the findings on the relationship between religion/spirituality and marital health in many ways parallel the findings on the relationship between religion/spirituality and physical health. For example, the observation that internalization of religious and spiritual beliefs is key to the observed benefits of religion and spirituality for marital health also holds true for personal health. Furthermore, as we have demonstrated, religion and spirituality often are found to be "key ingredients" among those who have successfully reconciled their marriages as well as those who have recovered from serious physical or mental conditions, such as depression.

Another interesting finding from an examination of the personal health literature discussed in this chapter, is that social, demographic, and health behaviors account for only a small portion of the observed benefits of religion and spirituality on health. Is it possible that better marriages among those who are more religiously or spiritually committed contribute significantly to the observed benefits of religion/spirituality on personal health? The only evidence for this connection that we are aware of comes from the Strawbridge et al. (1997) study that was previously discussed in the chapter (see "Religion, Spirituality, and Mortality"). This study found that health behaviors, such as smoking and exercise, had "little" impact on the observed benefits of religion and spirituality for reduced mortality, whereas "social connections," including increased social contacts and more stable marriages occurring in conjunction with frequent church attendance, did have a "significant" impact on this relationship.

Although this is only a single epidemiologic study, the fact that it is longitudinal and included such a large sample size suggests that this is an area worthy of increased scientific scrutiny. Indeed, in light of the strong relationship between stable marriages and significantly better mental and physical health outcomes (see Larson, Swyers, and Larson 1995 for a review of this literature), it would seem that a thorough investigation of the religion/spirituality-marriage-health connection should be an urgent priority.

REFERENCES

Albrecht, S. L. "Correlates of Marital Happiness Among the Re-married." *Journal of Marriage and the Family* 41 (1979): 857-67.

Albrecht, S. L., H. M. Bahr, and K. L. Goodman. *Divorce and Remarriage: Problems, Adaptations, and Adjustments.* Westport, Conn.: Greenwood, 1983.

Bahr, H. M., and B. A. Chadwick. "Religion and Family in Middletown." In *The Religion and Family Connection: Social Science Perspective,* edited by D. L. Thomas, pp. 51-65. Provo, Utah: Religious Studies Center, Brigham Young University, 1985.

Bell, R. A., J. A. Daly, and M. C. Gonzalez. "Affinity-Maintenance in Marriage and Its Relationship to Women's Marital Satisfaction." *Journal of Marriage and the Family* 49, no. 2 (1987): 445-54.

Braam, A. W., A. T. Beekman, D. J. Deeg, J. H. Smit, and W. van Tilburg. "Religiosity as a Protective or Prognostic Factor of Depression in Later Life; Results from a Community Survey in the Netherlands." *Acta Psychiatry Scandinavia* 96, no. 3 (1997): 199-205.

Comstock, G. W., and K. B. Partridge. "Church Attendance and Health." *Journal of Chronic Diseases* 25 (1972): 665-72.

Edmonds, V. H. "Marital Conventionalization: Its Definition and Measurement." *Journal of Marriage and the Family* 29, no. 4 (1967): 681-88.

Ehman, J. W., B. B. Ott, T. H. Short, R. C. Ciampa, and J. Hansen-Flaschen. "Do Patients Want Physicians to Inquire about Their Spiritual or Religious Beliefs If They Become Gravely Ill?" *Archives of Internal Medicine* 159, no. 15 (1999): 1803-6.

Ellison, C. G. "Race, Religious Involvement and Depressive Symptomatology in a Southeastern U.S. Community." *Social Science and Medicine* 40, no. 11 (1995): 1561-72.

Fehring, R. J., J. F. Miller, and C. Shaw. "Spiritual Well-Being, Religiosity, Hope, Depression, and Other Mood States in Elderly People Coping with Cancer." *Oncology Nursing Forum* 24, no. 4 (1997): 663-71.

Fenell, D. L. "Characteristics of Long-Term First Marriages." *Journal of Mental Health Counseling* 15, no. 4 (1993): 446-60.

Friedman, M., C. E. Thoresen, J. Gill. "Alteration of Type A Behavior and Its Effects on Cardiac Recurrences in Post-myocardial Infarction Patients: Summary Results of Recurrent Coronary Prevention Project." *American Heart Journal* 112 (1986): 653-65.

Glenn, N. D., and C. N. Weaver. "A Multivariate, Multisurvey Study of Marital Happiness." *Journal of Marriage and the Family* 40, no. 2 (1978): 269-82.

Graham, T. W., B. H. Kaplan, J. C. Cornoni-Huntley, S. A. James, C. Becker, C. G.

Hames, and S. Heyden. "Frequency of Church Attendance and Blood Pressure Elevation." *Journal of Behavioral Medicine* 1, no. 1 (1978): 37-43.

Gruner, L. "The Correlation of Private, Religious Devotional Practices and Marital Adjustment." *Journal of Comparative Family Studies* 16, no. 1 (1985): 47-59.

Harris, R. C., M. A. Dew, A. Lee, et al. "The Role of Religion in Heart-Transplant Recipients' Long-Term Health and Well-Being." *Journal of Religion and Health* 34, no. 1 (1995): 17-31.

Hummer, R. A., R. G. Rogers, C. B. Nam, and C. G. Ellison. "Religious Involvement and U.S. Adult Mortality." *Demography* 36, no. 2 (1999): 1-13.

Kaczorowski, J. M. "Spiritual Well-Being and Anxiety in Adults Diagnosed with Cancer." *Hospice Journal* 5, no. 3-4 (1989): 105-16.

Kaslow, F., and J. A. Robinson. "Long-Term, Satisfying Marriages: Perceptions of Contributing Factors." *American Journal of Family Therapy* 24 (1996): 154-70.

King, D. E., J. Sobal, and B. R. DeForge. "Family Practice Patients' Experience and Beliefs in Faith Healing." *Journal of Family Practice* 27 (1988): 505-8.

Koenig, H. G., J. J. Hays, L. K. George, D. G. Blazer, D. B. Larson, and L. R. Landerman. "Modeling the Cross-Sectional Relationships between Religion, Physical Health, Social Support, and Depressive Symptoms." *American Journal of Geriatric Psychiatry* 5, no. 2 (1997): 131-44.

Koenig, H. G., and D. B. Larson. "Use of Hospital Services, Religious Attendance, and Religious Affiliation." *Southern Medical Journal* 91, no. 10 (1998): 925-32.

Koenig, H. G., L. K. George, and B. L. Peterson. "Religiosity and Remission of Depression in Medically Ill Older Patients." *American Journal of Psychiatry* 155, no. 4 (1998): 536-42.

Koenig, H. G., J. C. Hays, D. B. Larson, L. K. George, H. J. Cohen, M. E. McCullough, K. G. Meador, and D. G. Blazer. "Does Religious Attendance Prolong Survival? A Six-Year Follow-up Study of 3,968 Older Adults." *Journal of Gerontology* 54A, no. 7 (1999): M370-M376.

Landis, J. T. "Length of Time Required to Achieve Adjustment in Marriage." *American Sociological Review* 11 (1946): 666-77.

Larson, D. B., H. G. Koenig, B. H. Kaplan, R. S. Greenberg, E. Logue, and H. A. Tyroler. "The Impact of Religion on Men's Blood Pressure." *Journal of Religion and Health* 28 (1989): 265-78.

Larson, D. B., J. P. Swyers, and S. Larson. *The Costly Consequences of Divorce.* Rockville, Md.: National Institute for Healthcare Research, 1995.

Larson, D. B., J. P. Swyers, and M. E. McCullough. *Scientific Research on Spiritu-*

ality and Health. Rockville, Md.: National Institute for Healthcare Research, 1997.

Larson, L. E., and J. W. Goltz. "Religious Participation and Marital Commitment." *Review of Religious Research* 30 (1999): 387-400.

Levin, J. S. "Religion and Health: Is There an Association, Is It Valid, and Is It Causal?" *Social Science and Medicine* 38, no. 11 (1994): 1475-82.

Mahoney, A., K. I. Pargament, T. Jewell, A. B. Swank, E. Scott, E. Emery, and M. Rye. "Marriage and the Spiritual Realm: The Role of Proximal and Distal Religious Constructs in Marital Functioning." *Journal of Family and Psychology* 13, no. 3 (1999): 321-38.

Maugins, T. A., and W. C. Wadland. "Religion and Family Medicine: A Survey of Physicians and Patients." *Journal of Family Practice* 32 (1991): 210-13.

McCarthy, J. "Religious Commitment, Affiliation, and Marriage Dissolution." In *The Religious Dimension: New Directions in Quantitative Research*, edited by R. Wuthnow, pp. 179-97. New York: Academic Press, 1979.

McCullough, M. E., D. B. Larson, W. T. Hoyt, H. G. Koenig, and C. Thorensen. "Religious Involvement and Mortality: A Meta-analytic Review." *Health Psychology* 19, no. 3 (2000): 1-12.

McSherry, E., M. Ciulla, S. Salisbury, and D. Tsuang. "Spiritual Resources in Older Hospitalized Men." *Social Compass* 35, no. 4 (1987): 515-37.

Merikangas, K. R., B. A. Prusoff, D. J. Kupfer, and E. Frank. "Marital Adjustment and Major Depression." *Journal of Affective Disorders* 9, no. 1 (1985): 5-11.

Oman, D., and D. Reed. "Religion and Mortality among the Community-Dwelling Elderly." *American Journal of Public Health* 88, no. 10 (1998): 1469-75.

Ornish, D., S. E. Brown, L. W. Scherwitz, J. H. Billings, W. T. Armstrong, T. A. Ports, S. M. McLanahan, R. L. Kirkeeide, R. J. Brand, and K. L. Gould. "Can Lifestyle Changes Reverse Coronary Heart Disease?" *Lancet* 336 (1990): 129-33.

Post, S., C. M. Puchalski, and D. B. Larson. "Physicians and Patient Spirituality: Professional Boundaries, Competency, and Ethics." *Annals of Internal Medicine* 132, no. 7 (2000): 578-83.

Robinson, L. C. "Religious Orientation in Enduring Marriages: An Exploratory Study." *Review of Religious Research* 35, no. 3 (1994): 207-18.

Robinson, L. C., and P. W. Blanton. "Marital Strengths in Enduring Marriages." *Family Relations* 42 (1993): 38-45.

Roth, P. D. "Spiritual Well-Being and Marital Adjustment." *Journal of Psychology and Theology* 16, no. 2 (1988): 153-58.

Schumm, W. R., S. R. Bollman, and A. P. Jurich. "The 'Marital Conventionalization' Argument: Implications for the Study of Religiosity and Marital Satisfaction." *Journal of Psychology and Theology* 10 (1982): 236-41.

Shrum, W. "Religion and Marital Instability: Change in the 1970's?" *Review of Religious Research* 21 (1980): 135-47.

Sloan, R. P., E. Bagiella, L. VandeCreek, M. Hover, C. Casalone, T. J. Hirsch, Y. Hasan, R. Kreger, and P. Poulos. "Should Physicians Prescribe Religious Activities?" *New England Journal of Medicine* 342, no. 25 (2000): 1913-18.

Spiegel, D. "Health Caring: Psychosocial Support for Patients with Cancer." *Cancer* 74, no. 4 supp. (1994): 1453-57.

Sporakowski, M. J., and G. A. Hughston. "Prescriptions for Happy Marriage: Adjustments and Satisfactions of Couples Married for Fifty or More Years." *Family Coordinator* 5 (1978): 321-27.

Strawbridge, W. J., R. D. Cohen, S. J. Shema, and G. A. Kaplan. "Frequent Attendance at Religious Services and Mortality over Twenty-eight Years." *American Journal of Public Health* 87, no. 6 (1997): 957-61.

Strawbridge, W. J., S. J. Shema, R. D. Cohen, R. E. Roberts, and G. A. Kaplan. "Religiosity Buffers Effects of Some Stressors on Depression but Exacerbates Others." *Journal of Gerontology, Psychological Science and Social Science* 53, no. 3 (1998): S118-26.

Vaughn, R. A., and T. B. Heaton. "Religious Influence on Marital Stability." *Journal for the Scientific Study of Religion* 36, no. 3 (1997): 382-92.

Weaver, A. J., H. G. Koenig, and D. B. Larson. "Marriage and Family Therapists and the Clergy: The Need for Clinical Collaboration, Training, and Research." *Journal of Marital and Family Therapy* 23, no. 1 (1997): 13-25.

Wilson, M. R., and E. E. Filsinger. "Religiosity and Marital Adjustment: Multidimensional Relationships." *Journal of Marriage and the Family* 48, no. 1 (1986): 147-51.

Wineberg, H. "Marital Reconciliation in the United States: Which Couples Are Successful?" *Journal of Marriage and the Family* 56 (1994): 80-88.

CHAPTER 14

Marriage, Family, and Health in Selected World Religions: Different Perspectives in an Increasingly Pluralist America

Paul D. Numrich

Introduction

Most accounts of the current state of distress in the American family mark its onset in the 1960s. With regard to divorce, for instance, Barbara Dafoe Whitehead observes that the U.S. rate during the 1950s and early 1960s "held steady at fewer than ten divorces a year per 1,000 married couples," but "beginning in about 1965, the rate increased sharply, peaking at twenty-three divorces per 1,000 marriages by 1979."[1] Between 1960 and 1998 the number of unmarried cohabiting couples increased by nearly 1,000 percent while the percentage of children living in single-parent families increased from 9 to 28 percent.[2] Bearing children outside of wedlock, a "highly stigmatized" behavior in 1950s America generally, became more accepted by virtue of the "sexual revolution" of the early 1960s.[3] Between 1960 and 1992, although the total number of juveniles in America remained fairly constant, the number of violent

---

1. Barbara Dafoe Whitehead, "Dan Quayle Was Right," *Atlantic Monthly,* April 1993, p. 50.

2. *The State of Our Unions, 2000: The Social Health of Marriage in America* (New Brunswick, N.J.: Rutgers University, the National Marriage Project, June 2000), pp. 26, 31.

3. Sara McLanahan and Gary Sandefur, *Growing Up with a Single Parent: What Hurts, What Helps* (Cambridge: Harvard University Press, 1994), p. 54.

crimes committed by them jumped sixfold.[4] In short, generally speaking, the American family has suffered ill health for four decades.

But the 1960s marked another important watershed in American history, setting in motion a parallel trend that deserves consideration here. Coincident with increasing family distress among the general population, American society has become more ethnically and religiously diverse by virtue of significant immigration and conversion trends in the last four decades. In 1960 none of the top ten source countries for American immigration was in Asia. The 1965 Immigration Act lifted previous restrictions on Asian immigration, so that by 1985 six of the top ten source countries were in Asia and the percentage of Asian immigrants in the 1970s and 1980s jumped to more than one-third of the total.[5] Moreover, many indigenous "spiritual seekers," especially in the so-called baby boomer generation, have adopted alternative religious affiliations since the 1960s. As a result, Buddhism, Hinduism, and Islam, the largest of the "new" religions,[6] boast a growing presence in contemporary American society. In each case the religion comprises two branches — an ethnic/immigrant branch which practices a religio-cultural heritage transplanted from the respective home countries, and a convert branch for whom the religion signifies a worldview shift from an upbringing in Judaism or Christianity. For Buddhism and Hinduism, ethnic/immigrant adherents come primarily from Asia while convert adherents are predominantly white. For Islam, ethnic/immigrant adherents come primarily from Asia, the Middle East, Africa, and Europe while convert adherents are predominantly African American.

These new religions bring new perspectives to the national discussion about marriage and family. At times they vocalize (or at least imply) pointed criticisms of American cultural norms and values, at other times they simply present alternatives to the Judeo-Christian heritage that has informed American culture to date. Their experience has largely been ignored, due mostly to oversight, but nonetheless to the impoverishment of the discussion. What cultural and religious resources do these groups bring to the national conversation about marriage, family, and health? What might these groups be doing that "works," and what insights might they offer about what is not "working" in the

---

4. David Popenoe, *Life without Father* (New York: Martin Kessler Books, 1996), pp. 52-53.

5. James T. Fawcett and Benjamin V. Carino, eds., *Pacific Bridges: The New Immigration from Asia and the Pacific Islands* (New York: Center for Migration Studies, 1987); Richard T. Schaefer, *Racial and Ethnic Groups,* 7th ed. (New York: Longman, 1998), p. 105.

6. Technically, none of these religions is completely "new" to America; what is new is their significant growth since the 1960s due to immigration and conversion trends.

larger society? Will such new groups be overwhelmed by America's social problems, or can they help to stem the tide of family distress in this country?

Professionals may find the following overviews of beliefs and practices in Buddhism, Hinduism, and Islam helpful as they interact with members of these growing American religions. Indeed, given recent immigration and conversion trends, many professionals reading this chapter may themselves be Buddhists, Hindus, or Muslims. In addition to practical benefits, I hope this chapter will contribute a fruitful, at times critical, pluralist perspective to current and future dialogue about the state of the American family, as the collective identity of that "family" becomes ever more religiously diverse. In particular, this chapter will challenge some fundamental and largely unexamined American values, including individualism and the optimal configuration of the family unit.

Buddhist Beliefs and Practices[7]

Buddhism contains an inherent tension regarding marriage and family. Despite being practiced by the vast majority of Buddhists, the so-called householder's lifestyle is seen as involving many hindrances to the pursuit of the ideal spiritual path. The Buddha admitted the possibility of laypeople attaining the goal of a liberating, enlightened consciousness (nirvana), but he nevertheless founded a monastic community of celibate followers to pursue that goal without family encumbrances. His ancient words set the tone for Buddhism:

> The household life is full of hindrances, a path for the dust of passion. How difficult it is for the man who dwells at home to live the higher life in all its fullness, purity, and perfection. Free as the air is the life of him who has renounced all worldly things.[8]

> Monks, there are two kinds of happiness. Which are they? The happiness of domestic life and that of monastic life. Of the two, the happiness of monastic life is superior.[9]

---

7. As a matter of convenience, I have deleted most of the diacritical marks in foreign terms in this chapter.
8. Cited in Geoffrey Parrinder, *Sexual Morality in the World's Religions* (Oxford: Oneworld Publications, 1996), p. 43.
9. Cited in Mohan Wijayaratna, *Buddhist Monastic Life: According to the Texts of the Theravada Tradition*, trans. Claude Grangier and Steven Collins (New York: Cambridge University Press, 1990), p. 173.

This ancient privileging of monasticism continues today, especially in south and southeast Asia, and has contributed to renunciatory practices among Buddhist laity even in areas where the monastic ideal does not prevail (in Japan, for instance, Buddhist priests may marry). Many devout lay Buddhists take renunciatory vows during religious holidays, and in countries with a tradition of temporary monkhood, men and boys regularly enter temples for short-term religious instruction and practice — in fact, young men are not considered marriageable until experiencing this monastic ideal. Married converts in America struggle with the renunciatory ideal of Buddhism. *Tricycle,* a periodical aimed at American converts, recently carried a feature on Buddhism and marriage in which the problematic notion of attachment stood out: How can one avoid spiritually unconducive attachments while participating in the worldly institutions of marriage and family? The feature included a report, oxymoronically entitled "A Marriage of Monks," describing a "spiritual union" ceremony for members of the Mountains and Rivers Order at Zen Mountain Monastery in New York State.[10] This brought a scathing rejoinder from a Buddhist reader who lamented that "the value and importance of a non-familial lifestyle has apparently become very confused."[11]

Buddhism's fundamental goal of liberation from worldly existence rendered the kind of systematic doctrinal understandings of marriage and family found in Western religions superfluous. Buddhism developed no injunction to marry and multiply. Indeed, in his discussion entitled "Buddhism and Marriage," one authority on Buddhist ethics feels obliged to borrow concepts from traditional Christianity in order to construct a consistent Buddhist perspective on sex within marriage.[12] Since it did not privilege marital status, Buddhism granted more respect to single laywomen, whether never married, divorced, or widowed.[13] At the same time, it found motherhood ambiguous, the obvious sexuality involved in it stigmatizing mothers as attached to worldly encumbrances.[14]

Moreover, Buddhist doctrine did not invest marriage or the wedding ceremony with spiritual significance. Marriage is a civil and contractual

---

10. "Tying the Knot," *Tricycle: The Buddhist Review* (spring 1998): 26-39.

11. Sally George, "Unholy Matrimony?" *Tricycle: The Buddhist Review* (summer 1998): 10.

12. Damien Keown, *Buddhism and Bioethics* (New York: St. Martin's Press, 1995), pp. 127-28.

13. Peter Harvey, *An Introduction to Buddhism: Teachings, History, and Practices* (Cambridge: Cambridge University Press, 1990), p. 215.

14. John Renard, *Responses to 101 Questions on Buddhism* (New York: Paulist Press, 1999), p. 140.

(read: "worldly") matter: "[F]or Christians marriage is a sacrament, whereas it does not have this status for Buddhists."[15] In traditional Buddhism monks play a minimal role in the marriage event — they bless the couple before the ceremony, for example — but they do not serve as clergy officiants. As the various cultural forms of Buddhism developed over time, marriage rituals were borrowed from surrounding religions — Hinduism in south Asia, Shinto in Japan, and so on. Attempts to "Buddhicize" weddings have occurred in the modern period, both in traditional Buddhist countries and in the West.[16] One Japanese American Buddhist priest speculates that the lack of Shinto temples in the United States contributes to the desire to consecrate one's marriage at a Buddhist temple.[17] Thai couples receive traditional blessings from monks, but much of the ceremony is strictly secular, and some Thai marriages have no ceremonies at all. The community may even consider cohabiting couples with a child as "de facto married."[18]

Much traditional Buddhist teaching about the roles, rights, and responsibilities of family members was adapted from cultural practices or generic ethical guidelines found in the religion's Asian homelands — the influence of Confucian ethics is prominent in many east and southeast Asian countries, for instance — which is another indication of the importance Buddhism placed on the ultimate goal of liberation from worldly hindrances.[19] Early Buddhism made monogamous marriage normative. One scriptural passage promises "that a husband and wife, if matched in trustful confidence, virtue, generosity and wisdom, will be reborn together [in the next lifetime] if they

---

15. Keown, p. 127. Keown's characterization of Christian marriage here invokes only one of several understandings, namely, that of marriage as "sacrament"; for a fuller treatment, see John Witte, Jr., *From Sacrament to Contract: Marriage, Religion, and Law in the Western Tradition* (Louisville: Westminster John Knox, 1997). Keown's larger point is well taken, however, in that Buddhist doctrine did not bestow spiritual significance on marriage in the way that Christian doctrine did.

16. Richard F. Gombrich, *Theravada Buddhism: A Social History from Ancient Benares to Modern Colombo* (London: Routledge, 1988), pp. 27-29; Paul David Numrich, *Old Wisdom in the New World: Americanization in Two Immigrant Theravada Buddhist Temples* (Knoxville: University of Tennessee Press, 1996), pp. 44, 142.

17. Shu Shu Costa, *Wild Geese and Tea: An Asian-American Wedding Planner* (New York: Riverhead Books, 1997), pp. 96-97.

18. Megan Ratner, "Thai Americans," in *Gale Encyclopedia of Multicultural America*, ed. Judy Galens, Anna Sheets, and Robyn V. Young (New York: Gale Research Inc., 1995), 2:1329-30.

19. Winston L. King, *In the Hope of Nibbana: Theravada Buddhist Ethics* (La Salle, Ill.: Open Court, 1964), pp. 201-4.

wish."[20] Asian Buddhist populations in the United States continue to favor the extended family type over the nuclear type and arranged over romantic marriages, though both preferences are becoming more difficult to maintain due to immigration restrictions and American cultural influences.[21]

Ethical guidance for family relationships derives from two main sources in ancient Buddhism — the Third Precept and miscellaneous scriptural texts. The precept is one of five basic ethical vows taken by all Buddhists, namely, to refrain from killing living beings, stealing, sexual misconduct, lying, and taking intoxicating drinks. For monastics the Third Precept is interpreted as prohibiting all intentional sexual activity, and breaking this vow results in summary dismissal from the monastic order. For laity the Third Precept prohibits sexual promiscuity generally, especially adulterous acts by married people. One ancient text likens the relationship between virtuous spouses to a marriage between god and goddess, but an adulterous spouse is likened to a corpse.[22]

The most important text for family ethics is the Sigalovada-sutta, or Discourse on the Advice to Sigala. The Buddha once encountered a householder named Sigala practicing a common ritual of worshiping the four cardinal compass points (east, south, west, north) plus the nadir and zenith. The Buddha advised Sigala to ethicize his ritual, showing true worship through proper behavior toward parents (east), teachers (south), wife and children (west), friends, relatives, and neighbors (north), servants, workers, and employees (nadir), and spiritual leaders (zenith). Elaborating, the Buddha explained that children should honor and support their parents, and that parents should raise their children well and arrange their marriages suitably. Moreover, the husband should respect his wife, remaining faithful to her and granting her authority over household affairs, while the wife should remain faithful to her husband, managing both their affairs wisely.[23]

Buddhism considers divorce, like marriage, primarily a civil matter. Social conventions rather than religious prescriptions tend to keep divorce rates low among Asian Buddhist populations. One respected contemporary monk comments on the effects of marital dissolution from a Buddhist perspective:

> There are also the sorrows of children in such broken marriages. The loss of one parent frequently leaves a deep scar upon young minds and may be

---

20. Harvey, p. 215; cf. Wijayaratna, pp. 169-70.
21. E.g., Ratner, p. 1329.
22. Wijayaratna, pp. 169-70.
23. Walpola Rahula, *What the Buddha Taught*, 2nd and enlarged ed. (New York: Grove Press, 1974), pp. 78-80, 119-25.

the cause of much trouble in their later lives. Then there are economic difficulties which may come about when marriages are broken in this way. A whole heap of dukkha [suffering and dissatisfaction] is caused just because men and women cannot keep in check their desire for sexual pleasures and do not have contentment, the positive counterpart of this [Third] Precept, with their marriage partner.[24]

Observers of the contemporary American family have amassed empirical verification of this whole heap of *dukkha*.

Hindu Beliefs and Practices

In Hinduism social responsibilities are determined by the principle of *varnashrama-dharma*, a Sanskrit term meaning "duty *(dharma)* according to class *(varna)* and stage of life *(ashrama)*." Of the four traditional life stages — student, householder, retirement, holy person *(sannyasin)* — that of householder holds special importance because during that stage a person marries and produces progeny, both considered normative human obligations. A study of life cycle rites of passage in Bengal points up the place of marriage in traditional Hindu society: the researcher noted "the very nearly universal unwillingness of Bengalis to neglect the [rite] of marriage, which gives it a place of particular importance in the cycle."[25] The duties *(dharma)* of marriage and family pervade Hindu society since not everyone will be fortunate enough to become a student, take retirement, or attain the status of holy person, while all will either marry or be part of a family. Nevertheless, as in Buddhism, Hindu doctrine sees family life as a worldly encumbrance to be transcended, ideally through spiritual reflection during the retirement stage of life and finally through liberation via holy person status. American converts to Hinduism, like their Buddhist convert counterparts, often seek a difficult balance of renunciatory spirituality and householder responsibilities in their everyday lives.

Over many centuries the traditional Hindu social system of four classes *(varna)* with numerous subclasses *(jati)*, often collectively called castes, developed a strict endogamy, and marriage within subclass is still strongly pre-

---

24. Bhikkhu Khantipalo, *Buddhism Explained: An Introduction to the Teachings of Lord Buddha* (Taipei, Taiwan: Corporate Body of the Buddha Educational Foundation, 1996), p. 97.

25. Ralph W. Nicholas, "The Effectiveness of the Hindu Sacrament *(Samskara)*: Caste, Marriage, and Divorce in Bengali Culture," in *From the Margins of Hindu Marriage: Essays on Gender, Religion, and Culture*, ed. Lindsey Harlan and Paul B. Courtright (New York: Oxford University Press, 1995), p. 140.

ferred. Classified advertisements in Indian newspapers and at Internet sites routinely list caste identity along with the socioeconomic status and physical attributes of prospective spouses. Traditional Hinduism favors arranged marriages over romantic or "love" marriages. As one writer explains, "Cautionary tales about love marriage hold that love is so intoxicating that it can never be the basis of marriage."[26] Far more reliable is the wisdom of one's extended family in procuring a suitable marriage partner: "Because a marriage affects the status of the entire family and its lineage, it is deemed too important a decision to leave to the persons actually getting married. Rather, the decision rests with the heads of extended family units. Consequently, arranged marriages are the norm; marriages undertaken by the marrying parties themselves, so-called love marriages, are considered deviant, even dangerous."[27] Many Indian immigrants bring with them an image of America as "a permissive, sex-crazed society," compounding their anxieties about potential sexual entanglements of their American-born children.[28] It is not hard to imagine the chagrin with which immigrant parents would react to the following description of their children's American peer generation: "The mating culture for today's twentysomethings is not oriented to marriage, as it has been in times past, nor is it dedicated to romantic love. Based on the reports of these noncollege singles [in the National Marriage Project study], it is perhaps best described as a culture of sex without strings and relationships without rings."[29]

A conventional Hindu marriage represents a contract between extended families primarily, not individuals; thus weddings are typically public ceremonies at which the two families gather to symbolize the familial dimensions of the relationship.[30] In Asian Indian communities in the United States, the issue of arranged marriages has become a source of some tension between American-born young people and their Indian-born extended families, some of whom still live in India, others of whom have recently joined earlier immigrant cohorts. It still seems to be the case that "in India most brides and grooms are complete strangers to each other,"[31] but in America

---

26. Steve Derne, *Culture in Action: Family Life, Emotion, and Male Dominance in Banaras, India* (Albany: SUNY Press, 1995), p. 78.

27. Lindsey Harlan and Paul B. Courtright, "Introduction: On Hindu Marriage and Its Margins," in *From the Margins of Hindu Marriage*, p. 5.

28. Padma Rangaswamy, *Namaste America: Indian Immigrants in an American Metropolis* (University Park: Pennsylvania State University Press, 2000), p. 121.

29. *State of Our Unions*, p. 9.

30. Derne, pp. 127-28.

31. Prakash N. Desai, *Health and Medicine in the Hindu Tradition: Continuity and Cohesion* (New York: Crossroad, 1989), p. 61.

compromises between the generations are becoming more common.[32] Outmarriage among second-generation Asian Indians in the United States has been a concern to their immigrant parents who fear the dilution of ethnic identity and also feel deprived of acquiring a new extended Indian family through marriage ties.[33]

Typical Hindu weddings extend over several days but are usually truncated in the American context. As one writer summarizes, "Ritual purification, the sacred fire, the joining of hands, the symbolic mixing of bodies and lineages, and the act of walking around the fire are the most common features of a wedding ceremony."[34] Another writer connects the religious connotations of the wedding with the Hindu understanding of the larger marriage relationship: "The sacred nature of the ceremony implies that the relationship between the married couple is not a contractual one but of a sacred nature," that is, a "holy or sacramental union."[35] Brides typically bring a dowry to the marriage, and tragic "dowry deaths" sometimes occur in India in cases where the husband's family considers the dowry insufficient.[36]

Joint-family living arrangements are common in India; for instance, a "nuclear family" of husband/wife/children may share a home with the husband's parents, siblings, and uncles and their families.[37] Such arrangements are less typical in America, although extended family members often live in close proximity to each other here, and groups of Indian families gather regularly for both formal and informal fellowship occasions.[38] Those with the means often visit extended family in India, sometimes in order to facilitate arranged marriages for their American-born children. The importance of family over individual identity finds expression in the practice of addressing family members by kinship titles ("father," "wife," "mother-in-law," etc.) rather than personal names.[39] The relative valuations are nicely summed up in an article of practical advice about providing nursing care to immigrant Hindu patients: "It is important for the nurse to appreciate that the tradi-

---

32. Rangaswamy, p. 182.
33. Rangaswamy, p. 180.
34. Desai, p. 29.
35. Ranjana Kumari, *Female Sexuality in Hinduism* (Delhi: ISPCK, 1988), p. 20. This is comparable to one view of marriage within Christianity.
36. Desai, p. 71; Paul Mandelbaum, "Dowry Deaths in India," *Commonweal*, 8 October 1999, pp. 18-20.
37. Derne, pp. 40-45.
38. Charles Leroux and Ron Grossman, "Fast-Forwarding the Dream," *Chicago Tribune*, 10 September 1998, sec. 5 (Tempo), p. 1.
39. Harlan and Courtright, "Introduction," p. 8.

tional East Indian Hindu family is the basic unit wherein values, manners, and morals are learned as part of its social structure. The pursuit of individualism, which is so predominant in Western culture, is not the accepted norm."[40]

Traditional Hindu ideals about the marriage relationship derive from certain classical scriptures, particularly the legal texts known as Dharma Shastras and the epic story of the Ramayana. In the latter, an extremely popular tale, the divine hero's wife, Sita, models the virtues of the ideal Hindu wife — fidelity and obedience to her husband. Although some sources within traditional Hinduism portray male/female relationships in complementary or even egalitarian terms, the weight of the cultural and religious heritage tends toward female subservience, or perhaps "honourable subordination," as one author puts it.[41] Modern conceptions of spousal roles now challenge such traditional Hindu views.

Classical Hindu law allowed for a polygynous family configuration (i.e., one husband with more than one wife), but Indian civil law now forbids it. In principle the marriage bond is considered indissoluble, thus Hindu law makes no provision for divorce. Those divorces that do occur are often explained as casualties of the debased moral era in which we live (called the *Kali Yuga*, or "Dark Age") and treated like annulments of a marriage that was never properly constituted.[42] Upon the death of a spouse, only the man may remarry according to Hindu custom. A widow is expected to remain unmarried for the rest of her days, a marginal status in a culture that expects females to be under the supervision of a male (as daughter or wife, for instance). This perspective led to the historical practice of *sati*, or self-inflicted widow immolation on the husband's funeral pyre, outlawed in India since the early 1800s but still widely admired as the ultimate fulfillment of a wife's devotion.

From a Hindu perspective, the individual is incomplete or unfulfilled alone. Spouses are mutually transformed by their marriage, the husband made complete by his wife, the wife transferred from her birth family into her husband's.[43] Their marriage finds its significance not in itself, but in the context of the now-related extended families. The most fearful prospect befalls the married couple abandoned by family and society because they married

---

40. Scott Wilson Miller and Jill Nerala Goodin, "East Indian Hindu Americans," in *Transcultural Nursing: Assessment and Intervention,* ed. Joyce Newman Giger and Ruth Elaine Davidhizar, 2nd ed. (St. Louis: Mosby, 1995), p. 487.
41. Kumari, p. 23 and passim.
42. See Nicholas, "The Effectiveness of the Hindu Sacrament *(Samskara)."*
43. Nicholas, p. 140.

merely "for love." As one observer puts it, such people are considered "abandoned to themselves," "facing the most horrible fate of all — the fate of losing social support."[44]

Muslim Beliefs and Practices

Writing in the late 1970s, a Muslim author concluded his book with the following admonition for those troubled by the contemporary crisis of the family: "If the true structure of the family in Islam is successfully brought to their attention, they may well discover how the classic solutions of Islam can help to solve their modern problems."[45] With lower divorce rates in the Muslim world than in the United States, the author makes a case worth considering.[46]

In Islam family parameters are defined by either blood or marriage ties. Islamic law does not stipulate a normative family configuration, but in practice Muslims favor the extended over the nuclear type. Through chain migration of relatives, many extended Muslim families have been reconstituted in the United States, and some households may include three generations — the initial immigrant couple, their American-born children, and the children's grandparents. "I would never dream of putting an elderly relative in a nursing home," vows one Muslim immigrant, barring medical necessity, we presume.[47]

Islamic allowance of a polygynous family configuration deserves special comment due to its inordinate place in the public perception of this religion. The Qur'an permits men as many as four wives, provided all receive equitable treatment. The impracticality of this provision, plus (according to some legal authorities) the first wife's option of divorce at the taking of a second wife if so stipulated in a premarital agreement,[48] has made monogamy the norm in the Muslim world. Cases of Muslim polygyny in America are rare, certainly minuscule compared to Mormon examples (both historically among Latter-day Saints and in today's heterodox offshoots) or to what Muslim social critics call the "serial polygyny" of many American males through the marriage/

---

44. Derne, p. 47.
45. Hammudah 'Abd al 'Ati, *The Family Structure in Islam* (Indianapolis: American Trust Publications, 1977), p. 283.
46. Yvonne Yazbeck Haddad and Adair T. Lummis, *Islamic Values in the United States: A Comparative Study* (New York: Oxford University Press, 1987), p. 152; Jane I. Smith, *Islam in America* (New York: Columbia University Press, 1999), p. 118.
47. Smith, p. 124.
48. 'Abd al 'Ati, p. 173.

divorce/remarriage cycle.[49] Muslim women surveyed on the matter show a distinct preference for monogamy over polygyny.[50]

Islamic law does not require adherence to Islam as a necessary constitutive element of a family or even the marital bond. Legal rights and privileges apply to relationships between Muslim parents and non-Muslim children, and vice versa, as long as Muslim family members are not hindered in their religious practice and non-Muslim family members do not actively seek the detriment of the religion. Islamic law restricts interfaith marriages in two ways, however: (1) only the man may marry a non-Muslim, and (2) only Jewish and Christian wives are eligible. The rationale for the first restriction is that a Muslim husband would theoretically allow his wife to practice her own religion under Islam's principle eschewing force in religion, whereas a non-Muslim husband might require his Muslim wife to convert from Islam. Also, with the presumed leadership of the family vested in the husband/father (see below), raising the children according to Islamic principles might be jeopardized by a non-Muslim in that position. The second restriction limits interfaith marriages to the three historically related religions having scriptures revealed through prophets, namely, Jews, Christians, and Muslims, the designated "People of the Book."[51] Observers report that interfaith marriages, even those sanctioned by Islamic law, are controversial among American Muslims primarily due to the perceived inegalitarian restriction on women's freedom to intermarry and the threat of identity dilution through marriage outside of the minority Muslim community here.[52]

Arranged marriages are common in Islamic cultures and represent the junction of two families rather than merely the spouses; in the case of first cousin pairings, the marriage joins two branches of the same extended family. Traditional aspects of arranged marriages remain strong even in modernized Islamic countries and in the West where young people take a more active role in the process.[53] Muslim apologists are quick to point out the dubious record

---

49. On Muslim polygyny in the United States, see Smith, p. 116; Kambiz GhaneaBassiri, *Competing Visions of Islam in the United States: A Study of Los Angeles* (Westport, Conn.: Greenwood Press, 1997), pp. 125-26.

50. John Renard, *Responses to 101 Questions on Islam* (New York: Paulist Press, 1998), p. 128.

51. 'Abd al 'Ati, pp. 33-38, 137-45.

52. Smith, pp. 112-14; GhaneaBassiri, pp. 122-23; Haddad and Lummis, pp. 144-49.

53. Eleanor Abdella Doumato, "Marriage and Divorce: Modern Practice," in *Oxford Encyclopedia of the Modern Islamic World,* ed. John L. Esposito (New York: Oxford University Press, 1995), 3:51; W. Murray Hogben, "Marriage and Divorce among Muslims in Canada," in *Muslim Families in North America,* ed. Earle H. Waugh, Sharon McIrvin Abu-Laban, and Regula

of the romantic marriage model that holds sway in Western societies. Marital candidates may be solicited through classified advertisements in Muslim or ethnic periodicals and over the Internet, and preferences for matching the ethnicity and social standing of the two families remain strong. Premarital sexual behavior is censured and socializing activities of unmarried youth are closely monitored. Dating has become a contentious issue between many immigrant Muslim parents and their more Americanized children.

Muslim writers tend to reject sacramental notions of marriage, preferring to point up the contractual emphases of the Islamic institution. As one scholar summarizes, "Marriage is a legal arrangement in Islam, not a sacrament as in the Christian sense, and is secured with a written contract."[54] In some contexts signing a marriage contract initiates an engagement period during which the couple can evaluate the prospects of their impending relationship.[55] The wedding ceremony is not primarily a religious rite and typically is not performed in mosques in Muslim countries, though this practice has increased in the United States.[56] Even so, marriage has a spiritual foundation within Islam as a religious duty enjoined by scripture and tradition on all who can undertake its responsibilities, and so marriage can be described as "a solemn covenant between Allah and the human parties as well as between these parties themselves."[57] Other purposes and benefits of marriage from a Muslim point of view include containment of sexual drives within legitimate social bounds, procreation, companionship, and a loving and joyful personal relationship.[58]

The Shiite branch of Islam preserves a pre-Islamic form of temporary marriage *(mutʻah)* that was eventually rejected by the larger Sunni branch. It is tempting to draw an analogy here to the widespread American practice of cohabitation as a kind of trial marriage. However, one Sunni writer, presumably representing the general view of that branch of Islam, castigates the attempt to connect the notion of *mutʻah* to recent social trends that deride and

---

Burckhardt Qureshi (Edmonton: University of Alberta Press, 1991), pp. 157-59; Haddad and Lummis, pp. 150-51.

54. Smith, p. 118. Again, this does not distinguish nonsacramental understandings of Christian marriage.

55. Nabeel Abraham, "Arab Americans," in *Gale Encyclopedia of Multicultural America*, 1:91.

56. Haddad and Lummis, p. 53.

57. ʻAbd al ʻAti, pp. 52, 60. Such a "covenantal" view of marriage is emphasized in certain branches of Protestant Christianity.

58. Shahid Athar, "Sex Education, Teenage Pregnancy, Sex in Islam and Marriage," in *Sex Education: An Islamic Perspective*, ed. Shahid Athar (South Elgin, Ill.: Library of Islam, 1995), p. 13; ʻAbd al ʻAti, p. 169.

weaken "institutional marriage," creating "chaos in contemporary sexual behavior [that] almost defies description."[59] One Shiite *mullah* (clergy authority) recently responded to a query about the acceptable boundaries of friendship and dating by recommending a variation on the *mut'ah* relationship, "excluding, if the parties so wish, any carnal physical contact."[60]

Islam spells out the roles, rights, and responsibilities of family members in detail. The husband/father clearly heads the household in traditional Islamic understanding, though the contours of his leadership have shifted somewhat in modern times. Islam greatly enhanced the wife's status over pre-Muslim standards in the religion's Middle Eastern homeland, and Islamic law grants her more rights and privileges than non-Muslims typically realize. For example, the wife is entitled to her own dowry gift, may hold property in her own name, and may initiate divorce proceedings in cases of desertion, maltreatment, impotence, or financial insufficiency by her husband.[61]

Parents are enjoined to nurture the well-being of their offspring, the latter in turn to obey, honor, and care for their parents in old age. Islam places special emphasis on the father's relationship with his children. Every Muslim child has the right to paternity, that is, to know the identity of his/her biological father. Islam thus institutionalized legitimacy. Stressing paternal duty in this regard, one Muslim author writes that "a father who obscures his child's legitimacy by denying his responsibility for its conception has offended God and inflicted upon himself universal disgrace."[62] Such teachings have recently energized African American Muslim groups like Imam Warith Deen Mohammed's Muslim American Society and Minister Louis Farrakhan's Nation of Islam. The latter group, although heterodox in some of its Islamic teachings, was instrumental in organizing the 1995 Million Man March that called African American males to fulfill their God-given family responsibilities. Children conceived out of wedlock or through adulterous liaisons are denied paternity rights from the biological father, however, and are assigned descent through the mother by Islamic law. Interestingly, given its emphasis on biological paternity, Islamic law does not recognize adoption. The entire Muslim community takes responsibility for the welfare of orphaned children.[63]

---

59. 'Abd al 'Ati, pp. 290-91 n. 45; cf. pp. 40, 103-9 for a full discussion of *mut'ah* marriage.

60. "Platonic Dating," 'Aalim Network QR: at http://www.al-islam.org/organizations/aalimnetwork/msg00157.html, 2 May 1996. The wording here seems to open the possibility of contracting a *mut'ah* arrangement that includes carnal physical contact.

61. 'Abd al 'Ati, pp. 148-68, 243-44.

62. 'Abd al 'Ati, p. 190.

63. 'Abd al 'Ati, pp. 188-98.

Should divorce occur, Islam follows the general principle of safeguarding the welfare of the children. Case law decisions differ but typically favor placement of younger children with the mother, though older children "usually stay with the father on the assumption that he will be better able to provide for their increasing financial needs."[64]

Islam advocates the permanency of marriage but allows for the realities of divorce. The Prophet Muhammad reportedly called divorce the most hated legal act in God's eyes, so Islam treats it as a last resort in cases of marital discord and provides incentives to keep marriages intact. For instance, if after exhausting numerous steps toward reconciliation a couple still intends to divorce, the families on both sides will intervene in an attempt to arbitrate the conflict. Moreover, a standard waiting period of about three months following the divorce allows time for reconsideration and possible reconstitution of the marriage.[65] In predominantly Muslim Syria, civil law requires the husband to support an ex-wife for at least one year as a curb on frivolous male-initiated divorces.[66] Islamic law grants certain rights to both parties in a divorce.

Observers note the social and legal challenges faced by Muslim American families today. Socially Muslims perceive serious threats to their traditional religious and cultural norms, perhaps most pointedly with regard to temptations facing American-born Muslim generations. In sum, "The pervasiveness of alcohol in America and the cultural acceptance of sexual permissiveness and immodesty (in clothing and comportment) are seen as negative influences on the faith community, particularly on its young people."[67] One Muslim writer shares some "candid talk" about American Muslim youth that will certainly concern parents: "There are many more Muslim children than our community would like to admit who are sexually active, some unapologetically. . . . They seem content with living dual lives, one for the mosque and one for themselves."[68]

Legally, although American society offers the benefits of religious freedom, it is not a Muslim society, and so American law and Muslim law sometimes conflict, or at least offer alternative courses of action. Muslim legal and religious leaders counsel that God's law supersedes civil law, but it is up to Muslim individuals, families, and communities to make their choices. As Is-

64. Renard, *101 Questions on Islam*, p. 125; also, 'Abd al 'Ati, pp. 202-3.
65. 'Abd al 'Ati, pp. 230-31, 245-46.
66. Renard, *101 Questions on Islam*, p. 126.
67. Gisela Webb, "Expressions of Islam in America," in *America's Alternative Religions*, ed. Timothy Miller (Albany: SUNY Press, 1995), p. 237.
68. Farhad Khan, "Candid Talk," in *Sex Education*, p. 78.

lam in America comes of age, perhaps we will see "a blend of Muslim and American institutions," as a recent report in the popular press suggests.[69] If so, what will this mean for the family, both Muslim and American?

New Perspectives in the Dialogue on Marriage, Family, and Health in America

Buddhism, Hinduism, and Islam illustrate the increasing religious diversity of American society, which also includes growing numbers of immigrant Christians from Asia and Latin America, Sikhs and Jains from India, and adherents of traditional religions from around the globe.[70] In addition to introducing professionals and other interested readers to selected non-Christian religious understandings of marriage and the family — a notable practical achievement in and of itself — this chapter seeks to widen the current dialogue on the social health of the American family beyond its heretofore predominantly Western Christian parameters. These new religions certainly join the chorus decrying the breakdown of the American family, but their critique cuts deeper than expected. This chapter teases out important challenges of beliefs and practices that have contributed to the current state of distress in the American family, specifically exposing a fundamental blind spot of the recent dialogue.

Several observers agree that certain cherished American values have perversely contributed to the recent instability of the American family, most notably individualism and its concomitant notions of free choice and self-fulfillment. We live in a hyper-individualistic culture, as William Doherty puts it elsewhere in this volume.[71] Yet, at the same time, proposals for restoring the stability of the American family also typically adopt the language of individualism, as, for instance, in Linda Waite's examination of the costs and benefits of marriage.[72] Barbara Dafoe Whitehead notes that "one of the central features of a strong civil society is the freedom of individuals to arrange private domestic time according to their own inclinations and preferences,"[73]

---

69. Carla Power, "The New Islam," *Newsweek,* 16 March 1998, p. 35.

70. See, e.g., *On Common Ground: World Religions in America* (New York: Columbia University Press, 1997).

71. Also, see Popenoe, *Life without Father;* Whitehead, "Dan Quayle Was Right"; Barbara Dafoe Whitehead, *The Divorce Culture* (New York: Alfred A. Knopf, 1997).

72. Linda J. Waite, "Does Marriage Matter?" *Demography* 32, no. 4 (November 1995): 483-507.

73. Whitehead, *The Divorce Culture,* p. 167.

even though the cumulative weight of her argument is that this very freedom undermines the family that undergirds a strong civil society.

The religions featured in this chapter call for a Copernican shift of perspective with regard to the place of the individual in the family. These religions begin with consideration of the extended family, fitting the individual's orbit into that system. Hence their consensus in preferring arranged over romantic marriages, and the common practice of joint-family or close-proximity extended family living. Ideally a combination of factors in arranged marriage customs supports stable families, including efforts to match spouses according to compatible demographic variables (ethnicity, class, religion, etc.) and encouragement (sometimes pressure) from extended family members to maintain the marriage. Contrast such joint, deliberate efforts to the solitary serendipity of the romantic marriage model. It is true that couples in either the romantic or arranged marriage model may not know each other very well upon entering their marriage, but the arranged model has the advantage of surrounding the couple with an established, supportive social matrix.

It is also true that arranged marriages can go wrong and traditional, extended families can be dysfunctional. This chapter does not intend undue idealization of non-Western and/or non-Christian religions and religious groups, nor to draw specious arguments in their favor and over against America's conventional religions (Judaism and Christianity, and their predominantly Eurocentric expressions). All religions have their faults, and we certainly can find them with regard to marriage and the family if we look hard enough. For instance, complaints of patriarchal dominance come from immigrant Muslim communities,[74] and we have reports of domestic violence and family breakdown in certain Asian American populations.[75] We must beware touting a facile "model minority" ideal here, as some do when noting the general stability of the Asian American family.[76] But I find it telling that discussions of cases of family breakdown within new immigrant populations often identify absence of a traditional social network, including extended family members, as a contributing factor. As one researcher writes, "What might have remained minor problems given extended family support and the

---

74. GhaneaBassiri, pp. 126-31.

75. Rangaswamy, pp. 311-15; Young I. Song-Kim, "Battered Korean Women in Urban United States," in *Social Work Practice with Asian Americans*, ed. Sharlene Maeda Furuto et al. (Newbury Park, Calif.: Sage Publications, 1992), p. 224.

76. See the critique by Jung Ha Kim, "A Voice from 'the Borderlands': Asian-American Women and Their Families," in *Religion, Feminism, and the Family*, ed. Anne Carr and Mary Stewart Van Leeuwen (Louisville: Westminster John Knox, 1996), pp. 344-57.

familiar environment in India turn into major crises in Chicago given the economic and cultural pressures, the adaptation demands, and the increased vulnerability of the immigrant."[77]

Unfortunately, demographic data on new religious populations in America are more provocative than conclusive at this time. The divorce rate and percentage of female-headed households among Asian Americans as a group are significantly lower than that of the general population, which is all the more remarkable given the presence of refugees and other traumatized individuals and families in that pool.[78] Since the category "Asian Americans" includes many Christian as well as Buddhist, Hindu, and Muslim families, it is likely that traditional cultural perspectives held in common across religious identities contribute to the statistical social health of families in this group.[79] The few studies that provide data on the religions profiled in this chapter point to greater family stability than in the general population, e.g., a low divorce rate among immigrant Muslim groups (though it appears to be on the rise)[80] and a low incidence of female-headed households among immigrant Laotian Buddhists.[81] But much more research is needed here to isolate the re-

---

77. Rangaswamy, pp. 314-15; also see Kim, pp. 350, 352; Song-Kim, p. 221.

78. Rangaswamy, p. 58; Timothy P. Fong, *The Contemporary Asian American Experience: Beyond the Model Minority* (Upper Saddle River, N.J.: Prentice-Hall, 1998), pp. 204-10; Ruben G. Rumbaut, "Vietnamese, Laotian, and Cambodian Americans," in *Contemporary Asian America: A Multidisciplinary Reader,* ed. Min Zhou and James V. Gatewood (New York: New York University Press, 2000), pp. 186-87. Cross-ethnic or cross-racial comparisons in the marriage literature are typically limited to whites, blacks, and Hispanics; see, e.g., *The State of Our Unions, 2000;* McLanahan and Sandefur, *Growing Up with a Single Parent;* Waite, "Does Marriage Matter?"

79. Chinese American Christians, for instance, share a common foundation of Confucian ethics with Asian Americans of other religious identities due to the influence of Chinese culture over large parts of Asia; on Chinese American Christians, see Fenggang Yang, *Chinese Christians in America: Conversion, Assimilation, and Adhesive Identities* (University Park: Pennsylvania State University Press, 1999).

80. Abraham, p. 92; Hogben, pp. 168-72; Barbara C. Aswad, "Yemeni and Lebanese Muslim Immigrant Women in Southeast Dearborn, Michigan," in *Muslim Families in North America,* p. 266; John R. Weeks, "The Muslim Population of San Diego County: An Assessment of Pilot Project Methods and Results: A Final Report Submitted to the American Muslim Council and Dar al Islam," International Population Center, San Diego State University, July 1996, pp. 11, 18; Mohamed Nimer, "Muslims and the 1996 Elections: Survey of American Muslim Political Attitudes: Selected Questions on Domestic Issues," American-Muslim Research Center, Washington, D.C., 16 August 1996, p. 3.

81. Carl L. Bankston III and Min Zhou, "De Facto Congregationalism and Socioeconomic Mobility in Laotian and Vietnamese Immigrant Communities: A Study of Religious Institutions and Economic Change," *Review of Religious Research* 41, no. 4 (June 2000): 462-66.

ligious factor from the myriad other variables affecting the social health of immigrant families.

The recent dialogue on the declining social health of the American family does not seriously consider the option of the arranged marriage/extended family model preferred by Buddhism, Hinduism, Islam, and other traditional religions of the world. As Whitehead correctly notes, "the arranged marriage has never figured significantly in American family life."[82] Mention even of the contribution of grandparents to the health of the typical American family is rare.[83] The discussion is usually framed as a shift from the healthy nuclear to dysfunctional post–nuclear family models, the latter including single-parent families and a type of surrogate extended family comprising step-relatives and unrelated significant others.[84] The claim that the nuclear family unit of American tradition is the most satisfying arrangement possible,[85] which thus should be granted renewed social privileging, deserves testing vis-à-vis the alternative arrangement of an extended family in which the nuclear family is embedded. In such an arrangement, ideally, excessive individualism encounters significant checks by relatives.

Ironically the extended family model may not get an American hearing in time. As noted throughout the sections on Buddhism, Hinduism, and Islam above, traditional religio-cultural beliefs and practices encounter the threat of erosion in an American context. Social scientists, for instance, tend to predict the gradual breakdown of traditional immigrant values through the Americanization process.[86] The words of one Indian immigrant may be sadly predictive: "We are able to give our children about 50 percent of Indian culture. They will give their children one half of that. And so, eventually, it will die out.... It's the price of migrating to this country."[87] With regard to the social health of the American family, the dynamics — and dysfunctions — at work since the 1960s may prove too powerful in the long run.

---

82. Whitehead, *The Divorce Culture*, p. 165. I think Rangaswamy, p. 181, overstates the public interest generated by a 1994 *Oprah Winfrey Show* on the merits of arranged marriages.

83. E.g., *State of Our Unions*, p. 20.

84. E.g., Whitehead, *The Divorce Culture*, chap. 7.

85. See, e.g., Whitehead's statement in "Dan Quayle Was Right," p. 48: "The social arrangement that has proved most successful in ensuring the physical survival and promoting the social development of the child is the family unit of the biological mother and father."

86. See, e.g., Schaefer, p. 339, regarding Japanese Americans.

87. Leroux and Grossman, "Fast-Forwarding the Dream."

List of Contributors

Don S. Browning is the Emeritus Alexander Campbell Professor of Religious Ethics and the Social Sciences at the Divinity School of the University of Chicago, Director there of the Religion, Culture, and Family Project, and the Woodruff Visiting Professor of the Interdisciplinary Study of Religion in the School of Law, Emory University. He is most recently co-author with Gloria Rodriguez of *Reweaving the Social Tapestry: Toward a Public Philosophy and Policy for Families* (2001), senior advisor for the national PBS documentary called "Marriage — Just a Piece of Paper?" and co-editor of the book by the same title published by Eerdmans.

Jason S. Carroll is an Assistant Professor in the Marriage, Family, and Human Development Program in the School of Family Life at Brigham Young University. He is an executive member of the Marriage Study Consortium and co-author of *Premarital Prediction of Marital Quality or Breakup: Research, Theory, and Practice* (2001).

Muller Davis graduated from Yale University and Harvard Divinity School and has been practicing family law for 35 years. His most recent publication (with Jodi Meyer Yazici) is the fourth edition of *The Illinois Practice of Family Law* (2000).

William J. Doherty is Professor and Director of the Marriage and Family Therapy Program in the Department of Family Social Science at the University of Minnesota. He is past president of the National Council on Family Relations and author of a recent book for married people, *Take Back Your Marriage: Sticking Together in a World That Pulls Us Apart* (2001).

List of Contributors

Christine Firer Hinze is Associate Professor of Christian Ethics at Marquette University, where her current research focuses on economic justice for workers and families. Recent essays include "Identity in Feminist Theology," *Concilium* 2001/2; "Dirt and Economic Inequality," *Annual for the Society of Christian Ethics* 21 (2001).

Richard A. Hunt is Senior Professor of Psychology at Fuller Theological Seminary and an ordained United Methodist minister. He is first author of *Marriage Enrichment: Preparation, Mentoring, and Outreach* (1998) and six editions of the United Methodist *Candidacy Guidebook* (2000), as well as author with his wife Joan of *Growing Love in Christian Marriage* (2001).

David B. Larson is the president and founder of the International Center for the Integration of Health & Spirituality (ICIHS) and adjunct professor of psychiatry and the behavioral sciences at both Duke University Medical Center and Northwestern University Medical School. He recently co-authored *The Handbook of Religion and Health* (2001).

Bonnie Miller-McLemore is Professor of Pastoral Theology at Vanderbilt University, author of *Also a Mother: Work and Family as Theological Dilemma* (Abingdon, 1994), co-author of *From Culture Wars to Common Ground: Religion and the American Family Debate* (1997, 2000), and recipient of the Henry Luce III Fellowship in Theology for work on a book, *Let the Children Come: Care of Children as a Religious Practice* (2003).

Paul D. Numrich is a Research Associate with The Park Ridge Center for the Study of Health, Faith, and Ethics, Chicago, and writes about Baha'i, Islam, Pentecostal Christianity, and Eastern religions in the United States. He is author of *Old Wisdom in the New World* (1996) and co-author of *Buddhists, Hindus, and Sikhs in America* (2001).

Edmund D. Pellegrino, M.D., is Professor Emeritus of Medicine and Medical Ethics and a Senior Research Scholar of the Kennedy Institute of Ethics at Georgetown University. He is the former Director of the Center for the Advanced Study of Ethics and founder of the Center for Clinical Bioethics at Georgetown University, and author of over 500 published items, including 24 books, in medical science, philosophy, and ethics.

David Popenoe is Professor of Sociology and Co-Director of the National Marriage Project at Rutgers University. He is author of *Life Without Father: Compelling New Evidence That Fatherhood and Marriage Are Indispensable for the Good of Children and Society* (1996) and co-editor of *Promises to Keep: Decline and Renewal of Marriage in America* (1996).

List of Contributors

Stephen G. Post is a professor in the Center for Biomedical Ethics, School of Medicine, Case Western Reserve University, and Editor-in-Chief of the *Encyclopedia of Bioethics* (5 vols., 3rd edition, in preparation). He is most recently the author of *More Lasting Unions: Christianity, the Family, and Society* (2000), *The Moral Challenge of Alzheimer Disease* (2000), and *Homo Religiosus* (2002).

Shirley J. Roels taught business and management courses at Calvin College and is currently Dean of Academic Administration there. She is the author of *Organization Man, Organization Woman* (1997), "Dealing with Vulnerability," in *Faith in Leadership* (2000), and "The Business Ethics of Evangelicals," in *Spiritual Goods: Faith Traditions and the Practice of Business* (2001).

Max L. Stackhouse is the Stephen Calwell Professor of Christian Ethics and Director of the Kuyper Center for Public Theology at Princeton Theological Seminary. His recent publications include *Covenant and Commitments: Faith, Family, and Economic Life* (1997) and *God and Globalization: Theological Ethics and the Spheres of Life* (3 vols.) (2000-).

James P. Swyers is senior research consultant to the International Center for the Integration of Spirituality and Health and past consultant to the National Science Foundation, the National Institutes of Health, and the White House. He co-authored a report, *The Costly Consequences of Divorce* (1995).

Mary Stewart Van Leeuwen is Professor of Psychology and Philosophy and Resident Scholar at the Center for Christian Women in Leadership at Eastern University. Her most recent book is *My Brother's Keeper: What the Social Sciences Do (and Don't) Tell Us about Masculinity* (2002).

John Wall is Assistant Professor of Religion and an Associate at the Center for Children and Childhood Studies at Rutgers University. He is recently author of "The Marriage Education Movement: A Theological Analysis," *International Journal of Practical Theology* (2002) and "Animals and Innocents: Theological Reflections on the Meaning and Purpose of Child-Rearing," *Theology Today* (2003).

Linda Waite is Professor of Sociology and Co-Director of the Alfred P. Sloan Center on Parents, Children and Work at the University of Chicago, where she also directs the Center on Aging. She is author, with Maggie Gallagher, of *The Case for Marriage: Why Married People Are Happier, Healthier, and Better Off Financially* (2000), which won the 2000 book award from the Coalition for Marriage, Family, and Couples Education.

List of Contributors

Barbara Dafoe Whitehead is the co-director of the National Marriage Project at Rutgers University. She is author of *The Divorce Culture: Rethinking Our Commitments to Marriage and Family* (1996, 1998).

John Witte, Jr., is Jonas Robitscher Professor of Law and Ethics and Director of the Law and Religion Program at Emory University, and has published 100 articles and 12 books, including most recently *Law and Protestantism: The Legal Teachings of the Lutheran Reformation* (2002).